THE HARPER RECORD

Edited by Teresa Healy

CCPA
CANADIAN CENTRE
for POLICY ALTERNATIVES
CENTRE CANADIEN
de POLITIQUES ALTERNATIVES

Copies of this book may be purchased through the CCPA
online bookstore at www.policyalternatives.ca.

Library and Archives Canada Cataloguing in Publication

The Harper record / edited by Teresa Healy.
Includes bibliographical references.

ISBN 978-1-897569-06-1

1. Canada—Politics and government—2006–. 2. Canada—Economic policy—1991–. 3. Canada—Social policy. 4. National security—Canada—History—21st century. 5. Environmental policy—Canada—History—21st century. I. Healy, Teresa II. Canadian Centre for Policy Alternatives

FC640.H37 2008 971.07'3 C2008-906097-0

Printed and bound in Canada.
Cover photo: Tom Hanson/THE CANADIAN PRESS

CCPA
CANADIAN CENTRE
for POLICY ALTERNATIVES
CENTRE CANADIEN
de POLITIQUES ALTERNATIVES

Canadian Centre for Policy Alternatives
Suite 410, 75 Albert Street, Ottawa, ON K1P 5E7
Tel 613 563-1341 Fax 613 233-1453
ccpa@policyalternatives.ca
http://www.policyalternatives.ca

CAW 567
OTTAWA

Energy and Environment

(*In*)Equality and Public Services

Culture and Communications

Federal-Provincial Relations

Acknowledgements

I WOULD LIKE to acknowledge the solidarity of the Canadian Labour Congress which permitted me to devote an extended period of time to this project. I would like to thank Lauren Halonen for her tireless work in the preliminary formatting of the chapters. I benefited immensely, as I always do, from Andrew Jackson's insightful analysis of the federal political and economic context. I thank Bruce Campbell not only for seeing this project through with determination, but for his ongoing commitment to opening alternative spaces for critical thinking in a time of such intellectual and political closure. I am enormously grateful to the editorial production team at the CCPA: Kerri-Anne Finn, Ed Finn, Tim Scarth, Erika Shaker, Roy LaBerge and Jason Moores for their commitment to the project. The speed and competence with which they transformed the manuscript into a book was nothing short of miraculous. Most of all, I would like to acknowledge the commitment of the contributors who, with such clarity, put aside other responsibilities through the late spring and summer to produce these chapters. Their efforts are, in each and every case, a testament to the creativity and depth of the democratic movements we serve. It was an honour to work with them in this collective project. I thank

Tom Juravich for always encouraging the individual, collective and written voice as it rings out for democracy.

Teresa Healy, Ottawa

Preface

THE CCPA HAS previously published assessments of the Martin, Chrétien and Mulroney governments. *The Harper Record,* however, is the most ambitious effort to date, thanks to the vision and energy of its editor Teresa Healy. Her accomplishment in bringing together the policy expertise of some 47 contributors from across civil society is truly remarkable. My thanks to the Canadian Labour Congress for endorsing this project and for freeing up her time during these last four months to devote to it.

The CCPA is non-partisan in that we are not connected with any political party. Where we have a partisan bias, however, is for *progressive* policies. We research, develop and promote policies that advance the values of a just, sustainable and democratic society. These values are consistent with those embedded in the *UN Universal Declaration of Human Rights* and its related covenants and declarations.

Progressive policies require a leading role for the federal government in managing the economy; in providing public infrastructure and vital services; in educating our children and youth; protecting our health and our environment; protecting our citizens in times of unemployment, infirmity, disability and old age. Policies that address the great challenges of our time — climate change, inequality and poverty, and peace — are at the heart of what should define a progressive government.

We critique policies that move us away from these values and priorities. The essential question the authors address in this volume is: do Conservative government policies meet the progressive test outlined above? The short answer is No. The Harper government's policies are moving our country backwards toward a vision of society, the role of government, and the nature of the federation reminiscent of the 1920s. To gain a deeper understanding of the Harper government's record and why this is so, I encourage you to read on....

Bruce Campbell
Executive Director, Canadian Centre for Policy Alternatives

Introduction

Teresa Healy

AS THE "NEW" Conservative government of Stephen Harper prepared to go to the polls in the autumn of 2008, it was evident that a broad accounting of his current minority government's record was needed. The months since the previous election had slipped by quickly and, as the government engaged in reshaping both the form and substance of Canadian political life, many of these changes were undersold in the media and underplayed in public discussion.

The Harper government tried to avoid public scrutiny. This government will indeed go down in history, not only as a highly centralized administration run out of the Prime Minister's Office, but as an activist government that did everything in its power to avoid public debate about its activities. Meanwhile, the Harper government was engaged in consultation with the Canadian corporate élite, as well as corporate and political officials from the United States and, to a lesser extent, Mexico. These are the consultations that identified the government's key priorities, and these are the fora through which the government measured its progress.

After the election of the Conservative party to a minority government in 2006, it was expected that the Harper government would quickly show its radical conservative colours. Indeed it did so, but, since the previous government was already extremely *laissez-faire*, Harper often appeared to be travelling along the same neoliberal path he had helped to clear as leader of the opposition. Harper's strategic pragmatism continued to lead him to compromise on conservative policies only with the aim of building a coalition which could ensure a majority government (*Patten*). The most alarming development under Harper's leadership, however, was the deafeningly quiet weakening of democracy.

Redefining centre-periphery relations

Since the Conservatives came to power, the country has experienced a prolonged crisis in the manufacturing sector, together with an overheated expansion of the tar sands in Alberta and a boom in mining and minerals production. The result has not been simply a relocation of economic activity to Western Canada. Indeed, by abandoning manufacturing, the Harper government has overseen serious structural changes in the economy. On the horizon is the prospect of a very difficult period of economic downturn. Since Harper became Prime Minister, the government has done nothing to respond to the thousands of jobs lost in manufacturing (*Stanford*). Instead, it worked to increase the state's role in expanding the private sphere and to reduce the state's capacity to intervene in defence of communities. In this respect, the dramatic Conservative tax-cutting policy represents a continuation of the Liberal agenda (*Jackson and Weir*).

On immigration questions, the Harper government has created a harmful "us-them" dynamic. He is on record as linking the refugee determination system with a threat to national security. The government fails to grasp the most significant demographic changes in Canada and has weakened Canada's international commitment to fight racism in Canada. Furthermore, the government has reneged on its commitment to assess and recognize international credentials, creating instead a poorly funded "referral office" for newcomers (*Flecker*). Meanwhile, the program which brings racialized workers to Canada only as temporary workers is booming. Under the Conservatives, the redesigned Temporary Foreign Worker Program gives employers almost absolute discretion in determining the living and working conditions of migrant workers. There is virtually no mechanism which would enforce labour rights in the program, despite the number of workers affected under its rapid expansion. This dynamic has created what some consider a highly privatized immigration system (*Encalada, Del Carmen Fuchs and Paz*).

The tar sands development has had devastating results for indigenous communities downstream from the Athabasca tar sands, yet the Conservative government has done everything it can to expand the production of bitumen (*Kalman*). It has done so through changing the regulatory regime covering oil and gas pipeline production, for example. Regulatory reform is a wide-ranging policy direction which not only deregulates economic sectors. It also is meant to impose a new layer of regulations on workers, with specific impacts on racialized communities, including energy, construction, and transportation workers.[1]

Because the oil is extracted from the sand using vast amounts of water, as well as natural gas, it is a highly costly industry as far as the environment is concerned. As one observer remarked on the rapid depletion of natural gas resources, "it is like using caviar to make fish-sticks."[2] Canada's needs a legislative framework to protect freshwater resources, but the Conservatives have responded with a patchwork of funding proposals and privatization strategies (*Barlow and Karunananthan*).

The Harper government has been able to fashion an agenda which appears to take into account the aspirations of Quebec by giving all provinces the same powers (*Cameron*). Harper's commitment to the rights of provinces has not fared well in Newfoundland and Labrador, however (*Payne*). Also of significance to the Atlantic provinces was the Conservatives' failure to follow through on their own commitment to a national Pharmacare program. They have, moreover, undermined the future ability of the federal government to establish such a program by creating an unnecessary legislative conflict between the provinces and federal government (*White and McBane*). This neoliberal strategy conveniently confirms the weakening of the federal role in social policy (*Cameron*). In less than three years, the Harper government has systematically cancelled or wound-down almost all federal commitments for shared programs with the provinces (*Mackenzie*).

Building consensus among the executives

Under the Harper government, there has been virtually no distinction between international and domestic issues. All of the government's main issues have been established as priorities by consensus of North American business, military and government executives. Shortly after the Conservatives came to power, for example, the Prime Minister's National Security Advisor, William Elliot, participated in the planning of a highly secretive gathering of military, government, and corporate leaders from across North America.[3] The North American Forum (NAF) documents state the goal of the annual meeting was not to make public pronouncements:

> Rather, the outputs of the NAF will be ideas and approaches that are quietly explored and privately conveyed to policymakers, or are individually pursued by participants, at their own initiative and in their own name.[4]

As Thomas d'Aquino, long-time President of the Canadian Council of Chief Executives, is reported to have said at the meeting, the assembled leaders would need to engage in "aggressive incrementalism" and "evolution by stealth" to see their ambitious plan for North American integration realized.

Perhaps it is only one of a score of such meetings that have happened since Harper came to power, but the influence of the North American Forum indicates how corporate forces have successfully shaped political consensus around their interests. Under Harper, Canada is working over-time to create strategic alliances on trade, investment *and* security that exclude popular participation and democratic alternatives.[5]

As an official policy framework, these priorities have been outlined in the Security and Prosperity Partnership of North America (SPP), which was first established while Paul Martin's Liberals were in power. Under Harper, the "leaders" of North America introduced a formal structure for receiving policy direction from the CEOs of 30 of the largest companies in North America, thereby institutionalizing the historically privileged relationship between business and government. The

North American Competitiveness Council (NACC) has a formal place in the SPP process, while the legislatures do not.[6]

The SPP is a framework for dealing with "security" and "prosperity" issues as defined by the executive-level of governments in consultation with corporate executives. One of their main goals from the outset has been to see how much cooperation could be achieved without changing a single law. The SPP was meant to avoid further "bruising battles" like the ones they faced during the NAFTA debate. There are currently three key groups of issues dealt with under the SPP: 1) border issues (cross-border policing and emergency management); 2) regulatory reform as defined by private industry; and 3) energy issues (securing U.S. energy supply, developing new resources in the North, and working to privatize Mexico's public energy resources).[7]

While the North American Competitiveness Council (NACC) focused on three key issues in the short term, the NACC was designed to build consensus for a more ambitious plan for the ongoing restructuring of North America. These include calls to build a common security perimeter; agree to a unified border action plan, including a North American pass with biometric identifiers; expand customs facilities; establish a common tariff; develop a common energy strategy and a regional alternative to Kyoto; revisit NAFTA to include excluded sectors; develop a common regulatory plan; expand the Temporary Foreign Worker program; increase foreign investment in Mexico's energy sector; and convene an annual North American summit of leaders.

Now, almost three years later, these initiatives are well under way. As well, efforts are being made to secure the supply chain or, in other words, to permit the seamless movement of goods throughout North America by imposing more security on workers and in the production process. Full labour mobility and efforts to create a North American investment fund are less advanced.[8]

Weakening democracy

As the creation of the NACC indicates, Harper does have a "new" agenda. He has endeavoured to legitimize his authoritarian mode of leadership by waging a battle against "dithering" and broad consultation. The

Harper government's first act was to cancel the child care agreements that had been negotiated with the provinces. Instead of respecting the process by which a Canada-wide child care program had been established, he abandoned all consultation and coherent policy-making for a taxable monthly allowance and transfers to private businesses and groups for child care infrastructure — an initiative doomed to failure (*Ballantyne*). Harper furthermore undermined all attempts to develop a rational child benefits system in favour of returning to an incoherent child tax benefit which helps the poorest families the least (*Battle*).

In a bizarre twist of logic, the government argued that it was no longer necessary to fund advocacy work for women's equality, even though by all measures women's economic inequality persists. Conservative government policies reinforced this inequality in policies such as income-splitting which direct tax benefits directly to higher-earning men. Nor was it necessary, the Conservatives decided, for the Status of Women Canada to include the word "equality" in its mandate, since the word already exists in the Charter (*Ad Hoc Coalition on Women's Equality and Human Rights*).

The government's disdain for democratic politics was also evident in its opposition to the public sector and collective rights. Harper maintained a clear commitment to usher the private sector into areas previously reserved for government and the public economy. As a result, the government's commitment to privatization is evident in big policy moves such as the setting-up of PPP Canada Inc. This is the institution which is intended to compel municipalities to chose public-private partnerships (P-3s) when beginning infrastructure projects (*Sanger and Crawley*). The government's privatization agenda also meant turning public resources over to the private sector in a myriad of ways, including program reviews; contracting-out; selling public assets; leasing-back institutions from the private sector; private financing of public projects; creating markets for public services; and permitting the private delivery of health care without enforcing the Canada Health Act (*Sanger and Crawley, West*).

The impatience with which the Harper minority government treated democratic opposition became quickly evident. As the government tried to liberalize markets in grains, the Wheat Board CEO was fired and the government worked to prevent Board members from speaking out in support of the marketing board. Board members were replaced through dubious election practices. Harper tried to remove barley from the Wheat Board's jurisdiction and, although stopped by a court order, has vowed to try again, in all likelihood through Orders-in-Council which evade the need for Parliamentary approval (*Forsey, Campbell*).

The government overrode court decisions in order to avoid environmental assessments of the tar sands development (*Frampton and Redlin*). It severely weakened the access-to-information system (*Hennessy*). It reneged on Canada's international obligations on climate change issues (*Sanger*), and it was clearly frustrated with court decisions impeding its plans to allow grains to trade on the free market (*Forsey, Campbell*). Harper announced a trade deal with Colombia before the Parliamentary committee studying the matter had reported (*Katz*). The government made significant changes to immigration policy and gave arbitrary powers to the Immigration minister without debate by bundling it in the 2008 Budget implementation bill (*Flecker*). Harper cancelled the Court Challenges Program which funded equality-seeking groups, such as disability activists, to bring legal interventions of national importance into the courts. The program was internationally recognized for its role in helping define the meaning of the Canadian Charter (*Rae*).

The government cut the position of national science advisor and appointed Preston Manning to advise the government on scientific issues (*Sanger and Crawley*). The government faced serious opposition because on many occasions it objected to scientific opinion when it suited its purposes. The government continuously rejected all scientific evidence defending the harm-reduction benefits of the Vancouver safe injection site, for example (*Moore and Donohue*), and proposed untested policy options on underground carbon capture (*Frampton and Redlin*), as well as second generation biofuel technologies (*Mooney*). Perhaps most shocking was its disregard for the scientific evidence concerning climate change and its confused and contradictory policies on the environment (*Sanger and Saul*). This included a focus on pollutants and moved Canada away from international norms on the reduction of absolute levels of greenhouse gas emissions.

The Conservative "tough-on-crime" approach was similarly directed to a problem which social science research indicates is not growing. Instead of community-based correction programs, the federal government moved toward a more punitive and individualistic approach. For example, the new "anti-drug" strategy was shifted to the Justice Department away from Health Canada (*Moore and Donohue*). A similar perspective was elaborated as the Harper government continued to reject the literature on the social determinants of health. Instead, it focused on individual responsibility for health outcomes and took money away from programs supporting community-based responses to ill-health. (*Edwards*).

When the Canadian Nuclear Safety Commission ordered the shutdown of a nuclear reactor in Ontario, the president was fired and the reactor remained operational (*Moll*). The case is a good example of what the government did on regulations more generally. Under the Security and Prosperity Partnership, the Harper government moved from the "precautionary principle" to an industry-led model of regulation focusing on "risk-management," with implications for food as well as drug safety. In pharmaceuticals, the Conservatives were in the process of changing the way in which regulations apply to drug-testing. The net result is meant to bring drugs to market more quickly, shift testing responsibilities to the pharmaceutical companies, reduce the role of government in ensuring drug safety, and enshrine secrecy and commercial confidentiality in legislation (*White and McBane*).

Canada-U.S. relations

As Prime Minister, Stephen Harper took very dangerous positions on Canada-U.S. relations. Very soon after taking office, the government gave in to U.S demands on softwood lumber and signed a poor deal for Canada with the United States. Even as NAFTA tribunals, U.S. trade courts and the WTO did not accept the Bush administration's contention that Canada was subsidizing softwood lumber production (*Caron*), the Harper government undermined the position of Canadian producers and negated all court decisions which had been decided in Canada's favour since the latest round in the softwood lumber conflict began in

2001 (*Campbell*). Similarly, the Conservative position at the WTO has acted only grudgingly in favour of Canadian producers on the issue of supply-management. In fact, Harper's attack on the Wheat Board and the Grain Commission has severely undermined Canada's own defence of marketing boards in international negotiations.

Moreover, Harper has on more than one occasion campaigned in the United States in favour of Bush's trade deal with Colombia and the further extension of the U.S. security perimeter in the Americas (*Katz*). On intellectual property rights, Canada under the Conservatives bowed to U.S pressure to increase patent protection for pharmaceuticals, thus further restricting the provision of cheaper generic drugs to the Canadian population (*Campbell, White and McBane*). The government appointed an industry panel to seek recommendations for new legislation in telecommunications, and the panel recommended increases in foreign ownership (*Watkins, Moll and Regan Shade*).

In some respects, this Conservative government acted not so much like a minority government, but more like a war-time "union government" demanding loyalty from the opposition in times of national crisis. Since September 11, 2001, both Liberal and Conservative governments have been unwavering in their adherence to the U.S-led "war against terror," but it was the Conservatives who restructured Canadian border and security forces to mirror the U.S. Department of Homeland Security. These security forces were given access to the police records of Canadian citizens. In these police records is information which has not been tested by the courts, yet accusations and tossed-out charges are being used against travellers, with serious repercussions.

In 2006, the government was compelled to call an inquiry to find out whether the detention of Abdullah Almalki, Ahmad Abou-Elmaati and Muayyed Nureddin in Syria or Egypt resulted, directly or indirectly, from actions of Canadian officials during 2001 to 2004. The report of the Iacobucci Commission was originally meant to be submitted the week before the 2008 election was called, but was delayed until the week after the election.[9] Both the Liberals who were in power during the events in question and the Conservatives, who are in favour of the anti-terrorist agenda, were thus spared public scrutiny on these issues during the election campaign.

The Conservatives did not only continue with the Liberal anti-terrorist legislation, but they also expanded it. For example, they instituted the No-Fly list which identifies "suspicious" people without charging them or relying on convictions. With no hearing or independent review, the lists are then used to curtail mobility rights. They further rob people of their privacy and security as persons on the lists are shared with other governments and airlines (*Campbell*). Canada's security agencies have intensified their activities since the Conservatives came to power. A shocking example is to be found in the continued use of "security certificates" and secret trials. Although the Supreme Court of Canada found Canada's secret trials process to be unconstitutional, the Conservatives' subsequent tinkering with the legislation continued to undermine Canadians' fundamental democratic rights. One aspect of the security certificate legislation ensures that the accused may not see the evidence for the case against them. They are permitted to know the allegations only (*Behrens*).

Unlike that period of history in which Canada granted asylum to 50,000 U.S. war resisters during the Viet Nam war, the Conservatives have begun deporting U.S. soldiers who refuse to fight in Iraq (*Harden*). Meanwhile, in Afghanistan, Harper increased the "interoperability" and cooperation of the Canadian armed forces with those of the U.S. and virtually gave up on peacekeeping (*Warnock, Staples*). Under the Conservatives, Canada is the only developed democracy to leave one of its citizens and a child soldier to face an illegal military commission in Guantanamo (*Foster*). Under Harper, the increase in military spending in support of the war in Afghanistan did not enhance international security, but remade Canadian conservatism in the image of the United States (*Staples*).

Under Harper, Canada reneged on previous commitments to developing countries in multilateral trade negotiations and pursued an aggressive bilateral trade policy, especially in the Americas (*Sreenivasan*). The previous Liberal government was also very committed to the liberalization of trade, finance and investment across borders, but in maintaining its commitment to neoliberal internationalism and multilateral institutions, it promoted neoliberalism at the WTO within a set of norms acceptable to élites in the global South. The Harper government has been anything but diplomatic on the international stage and, in line with the Bush administration, pushed unreasonable demands for market-access in industrial products and for the rapid liberalization of services. This strategy was echoed in the UN Climate Change negotiations in Bali, where Canada almost derailed consensus by pushing developing countries to reduce emissions at the same rate as developed countries (*Sanger and Saul*). Canada weakened the international human rights framework, most notably by voting against the UN Declaration on the Rights of Indigenous peoples (*Foster*).

Conclusion

In the 32 months that the Conservative minority government was in power between 2006 and 2008, the people of Canada faced significant challenges because of the substance of what the Harper government achieved and because of the anti-democratic way in which he went about it. What becomes clear from the Harper Record is that the Conservatives are as committed to a market-driven world economy as the Liberals were, but that Harper is not committed to national democratic or multilateral institutions in the same way. For Harper, the only international relationship that matters is the one between Canada and the United States. He does not criticize the Bush administration for its ineptitude in living up to its own conservative commitments. Nor does Harper shine a bright light on a tattered U.S. hegemony. Rather, he reflects to the world an enhanced image of conservative unity in North America and a resolute commitment to market forces that is undeterred by the noisy democratic rabble. Indeed, his calling of the election so close in advance of the U.S. election might well be timed to offer support to the Republicans as they go about trying to elect a McCain administration. It certainly does Harper no harm to be running a campaign while Barak Obama is not the president of the United States.

Civil society organizations must become quite the opposite of what Harper has offered up as the model of leadership in a "turbulent" time. In these times we need a strategic sense of how to affirm a broad and diverse range of possibilities. It is through openness and not closure that our own deeply felt convictions that another world is possible can be articulated. It is this collective capacity we must seek to strengthen as we face the political power of CEOs as embodied in ruling parties, whether in the majority or minority. Indeed, before the next government takes shape, we will need to remember what happened during the last and reassert what it is we are prepared to commit to from now on.

ONE

GOVERNANCE

Understanding Stephen Harper

The long view

Steve Patten

CANADIANS NEED TO understand the political and ideological temperament of politicians like Stephen Harper — men and women who aspire to political leadership.

While we can gain important insights by reviewing the Harper government's policies and record since the 2006 election, it is also essential that we step back and take a longer view, considering Stephen Harper's two decades of political involvement prior to winning the country's highest political office. What does Harper's long record of engagement in conservative politics tell us about his political character?

This chapter is organized around a series of questions about Stephen Harper's political and ideological character. Is he really, as his supporters claim, "the smartest guy in the room"? To what extent is he a conservative ideologue versus being a political pragmatist? What type of conservatism does he embrace? What does the company he keeps tell us about his political character? I will argue that Stephen Harper is an economic conservative whose early political motivations were deeply ideological. While his keen sense of strategic pragmatism has allowed him to make peace with both conservative populism and the traditionalism of social conservatism, he continues to marginalize red toryism within the Canadian conservative family. He surrounds himself with like-minded conservatives and retains a long-held desire to transform Canada in his conservative image.

The smartest guy in the room, or the most strategic?

When Stephen Harper first came to the attention of political observers, it was as one of the leading "thinkers" behind the fledgling Reform Party of Canada. His speech on regionalism and fairness in the Canadian federation was hailed as a highlight of the Reform party's founding convention.[1] As delegates to the convention treated Harper to a standing ovation, Preston Manning claims he "knew the party had found a potential policy chief."[2] Over the next four years, Harper and Manning worked closely as co-architects of the Reform party's policy agenda.

Following the party's breakthrough 1993 federal election, Harper assumed a prominent role in the Reform caucus, and the parliamentary press gallery quickly learned that the young MP was one of the most likely Reform party sources of intelligent and perceptive comment. Reflecting on those early days, Manning has described Stephen Harper as the party's "best mind" in terms of policy analysis and strategy development.[3]

It is certainly true that Harper is a smart man. He is well read and holds an MA in economics from the University of Calgary. All the same, his partisan supporters and the conservative journalists who have penned the most widely read Harper biographies tend to exaggerate the uniqueness of his intellect. When it comes to public policy, Harper is not a particularly insightful or original thinker, and he is certainly not the first Canadian political leader to demonstrate a capacity to remain well-informed, focused, and to think quickly on his feet.

Few political associates or friends understand Stephen Harper better than Tom Flanagan, the well-known University of Calgary political scientist. When the two met back in the early days of the Reform party, Flanagan was impressed by the extent to which Harper "combined a remarkably wide knowledge of politics with a keen strategic mind."[4] This observation goes to the heart of Stephen Harper's smarts. While merely one among many well-informed policy wonks to engage in active politics, he displays a unique astuteness when it comes to the strategic dimensions of partisan politics. He is able to look beyond the moment and engage in long-term strategic thinking about his political goals and the tactics and immediate actions required to attain his desired outcomes.

Interestingly, Harper's strategic mind and attention to tactics may underpin what some political journalists have identified as his "autocratic tendencies" — his desire to keep cabinet ministers on a short leash and maintain an "exhaustive system of information control."[5] It seems that his personal sense of ideological and strategic certainty makes it difficult for him to devolve control or trust others who might not share his political agenda or insights.

Of course, the centralization of control is not unusual in the context of Canada's notoriously undemocratic political parties, but Stephen Harper's strategic character does explain his somewhat autocratic nature and desire for hands-on control of the policy-making and political messages that define the public face of his party.

Harper has a sharp mind, but it is a bit of myth-making that has created the impression he is the smartest guy in the room. All the same, those who wish to understand Harper should remember that his every political move is, almost without fail, guided by astute strategic calculations. Stephen Harper understands Canadian politics and the challenges associated with building a coalition in support of his conservative agenda. He should not, in other words, ever be underestimated.

Ideologue or pragmatist?

During the lead-up to Stephen Harper's campaign to replace Stockwell Day as leader of the Canadian Alliance, *Globe and Mail* columnist Jeffrey Simpson publicly counselled Harper to take a pass on his run for the leadership. According to Simpson, Harper was "too ideological to succeed in Canadian politics."[6] Harper's Liberal and New Democratic competitors have worked hard to perpetuate the image of Harper as a conservative ideologue with a hidden agenda to impose policies that would be unpalatable to moderate, middle-of-the-road Canadians. Interestingly, however, committed conservative pundits like Gerry Nicholls, a former colleague of Harper's at the National Citizens Coalition and an active supporter of Harper's bid for the Alliance leadership, now criticize Harper for abandoning principled conservatism in favour of a "deliberate strategy of diluting conservative principles and moving the [Conservative] party to the left."[7] To what extent, then, is Stephen Harper a conservative ideologue? Is there any validity to the characterization of Harper as more pragmatic than ideological?

There is no shortage of evidence in support of the characterization of Stephen Harper as an uncompromising conservative ideologue. In the early 1980s, Harper studied economics at the University of Calgary. His early connection to conservative politics was shaped by Calgary's political culture in the heyday of the National Energy Program. Harper soaked up the political analysis that motivated conservative Alberta's frustration with the Liberal government in Ottawa. As his biographer, William Johnson, explains, the youthful Stephen Harper "felt there should be clear-cut answers to problems. You should implement the best economic decisions, and then it would work over time."[8]

Harper was a Progressive Conservative, but when Brian Mulroney's PC government was slow to deliver the "fundamental conservative transformation" for which Harper had "high hopes," he became disillusioned.[9] Convinced that Mulroney was unwilling to make tough decisions and that his party lacked the "conservative philosophical grounding" necessary to differentiate the PCs from the Liberals, Harper and his close friend, John Weissenberger, committed themselves to building a "Blue Tory network" of party members interested in the purer form of conservatism that was then transforming the U.K. and U.S. under Margaret Thatcher and Ronald Reagan.[10]

Some would dismiss this initiative as an example of the youthful dogmatism many young activists display. But even Harper enthusiasts who balk at labelling him an ideologue, like *Maclean's* columnist Paul Wells, will admit that Harper has always wanted to champion stronger conservative ideological commitments in Canadian politics: he "would never lose sight of the long game, which was to transform Canada, if it would let him, into a profoundly different place."[11]

During his years of active involvement in the Reform party, and despite their close working relationship, Harper often challenged what he considered to be the ideologically vague and deceptive populism of

Preston Manning. Contrary to Manning, Harper argued in favour of positioning Reform as a "party of the Right."[12] While temporarily out of formal partisan politics from 1997 to 2001, Harper opted for a stint as President of the ideologically uncompromising National Citizens Coalition. This is an organization founded by anti-Medicare crusader Colin Brown, which now promises to defend free enterprise, free speech and accountability to taxpayers under the slogan "More freedom through less government."[13]

Not unsurprisingly, when Harper decided to run for the leadership of the Canadian Alliance, he called on the party "to be a clear voice for conservatism" that rejected any flirtation with the Red Tory orientation of Joe Clark and the Progressive Conservative party.[14]

To that point in time, Harper had always put principles ahead of political victories. Indeed, he and Tom Flanagan were convinced that the Reform party had had considerable success at getting new issues on the Canadian political agenda, while also laying the foundations for a generalized cultural shift toward the ideological right.[15] None of this, he believed, would have been accomplished without ideological conviction on the part of conservatives within the Reform party. By the time he assumed the helm of the Canadian Alliance, however, Harper seems to have become increasingly convinced that the time had come to do all that was necessary to form a government. To the extent that Harper has a pragmatic side, this has been revealed in his efforts to form and lead a majority government.

The term pragmatic is used in more than one way in Canadian politics. At its simplest, pragmatism involves worrying more about immediate and tangible occurrences than grand ideas, theories, or ideologies. In other words, a pragmatic approach to public policy-making is rooted in our observable reality and sense of what is both necessary and practical. Pragmatism, however, is also often associated with avoiding the political commitments of the ideological left and right in favour of centrist policies that will be politically popular with mainstream voters — that is, voters who avoid extremes in favour of either centre left or centre right policy prescriptions.

For many pragmatists, hugging the centre is more than a mere political calculation; they believe there is political virtue in the supposedly non-ideological "centre." Former Ontario premier Bill Davis was often described as this sort of pragmatist, a fact that frustrated the more conservative members of his cabinets.

Stephen Harper has never shunned clear and strong ideological commitments. Still, he is keenly aware of the importance of doing what is necessary to win. Contrary to what some conservative pundits, such as Gerry Nicholls, have argued, he may not be willing to sell his principles to win, but he is willing to engage in a form of "strategic pragmatism" that involves making concessions designed to ensure political victory in the long term. Moreover, since aspiring to positions of political leadership, Harper has regularly demonstrated a pragmatic willingness to position himself in the middle of the diverse conservative coalition to which his party aims to appeal.[16]

Harper recognizes that a winning conservative coalition will include a very diverse group of Canadians. In a 1989 memo to Preston Manning, he argued that the core political cleavage in contemporary Western democracies pits taxpayers and private sector-oriented citizens (the ideological right) against the public sector-oriented political class and "tax recipients of the Welfare State" (the ideological left).[17] The conservative coalition of the right would include the corporate sector and the private sector urban middle class, but also aspects of the urban working class and rural classes that have an interest in lower taxes and are resistant to the social values and "liberal intellectualism of the Welfare State class."[18]

In more traditional political terms, Harper told the group of partisan activists and conservative journalists assembled at the 1996 Winds of Change conference in Calgary — a group brought together by author and journalist David Frum to discuss uniting the partisan right — that to be successful a Canadian Conservative party would need to bring together traditional Blue Tories, grassroots populists, and French-Canadian nationalists.[19] At its heart, then, Stephen Harper's strategic pragmatism is most evident in his dogged pursuit of strategies to build this coalition, to reach out to Québécois nationalists, old Tories, populists, and private sector-oriented urban sophisticates, as well as that significant demographic that Conservative operatives now call "the Tim Hortons and Canadian Tire crowd."

To hold this coalition together, Harper has had to position himself in the middle of the party.[20] This has meant a unique range of initiatives such as delivering on cuts to the GST and recognizing Québec as a nation, while stressing that this apparent departure from his Reform roots is not inconsistent with his long-term goal of a more decentralized federalism, appealing to his party's Reform wing with a free vote on gay marriage and tough-on-crime legislation, while working to silence those Reform voices that once embarrassed the party in urban Canada.

In the end, then, Stephen Harper practises strategic pragmatism. For both strategic reasons and in the interests of party unity, Harper is now more pragmatic than one would expect of a politician who was initially written off as "too ideological." He is a politician who knows what he wants to accomplish. His record suggests that he is enough of an ideologue that he would rather win one majority and introduce significant policy changes than win three and not leave a clear legacy in terms of the structure and character of governance in Canada. To appreciate the possible consequences of a Harper majority, we must consider the nature of the conservatism to which he personally subscribes.

What type of conservative?

One of the realities of party politics in Canada is that each of our parties tends to represent a range of ideological perspectives. Of course, this range of perspectives is most obvious when a party is out of power; ideological differences are often submerged by the discipline of power. On the partisan right, conflict over which variant of conservatism would be predominant has been central to everything from leadership politics to the rise of splinter parties (Reform) and the efforts to "unite the right" under one party banner between 1998 and 2003.[21] Over the past quarter century, there have been at least four conservatisms competing for dominance on the partisan right.

- *Economic conservatism* is the free enterprise ideology of small government and low taxes that is advocated by ideological libertarians, neo-liberal free traders and the "Blue Tories" who have always wanted enterprise and economic logic to trump politics.

- *Social conservatism* entails a commitment to traditional social structures and morality. While often associated with evangelical Christian politics, social conservatism is also rooted in the traditionalism of classical conservatives and Blue Tories who are predisposed against the embrace of rapid social change.

- *Conservative populism* takes at least two forms. For some libertarian-minded conservatives, populism is about democratic processes that stress the importance of finding ways to hear the unmediated voices of individual citizens. For others, populism is about standing up against the élite in defence of the common people. What is unique about conservative populism is its definition of the élite as the entrenched welfare state bureaucracy and special interests that speak for privilege-seeking minorities, and the common people as hard-working taxpayers.[22]

- *Red Toryism* is the more progressive conservatism that has transformed the old Tory notion of *noblesse oblige* into conservative support for the welfare state, and a willingness to tame the free market by allowing social concerns and politics to trump economic logic. Red Tories tend to be more comfortable than economic conservatives with state programs to assist those in need.

Stephen Harper's core ideological commitments are rooted firmly in the traditions of *economic conservatism*, and they have been for some time. As a youthful supporter of the Progressive Conservative party, Harper hoped Mulroney's landslide 1984 electoral victory would bring the politics of Thatcher and Reagan to Canada.[23] After the election, he went to Ottawa to work for his local PC Member of Parliament, Jim Hawks. It was not long, however, before he was disillusioned by the lack of change Mulroney brought to the character and policies of the federal government.

Unhappy in Ottawa, Harper returned to the University of Calgary, where he met John Weissenberger, an equally disgruntled Progressive

Conservative who would become one of Harper's closest friends. The two students began reading the works of influential neoconservative thinkers and talking about what it would take to build a network of true conservatives committed to transforming the PC party of Canada.[24] Their ambition was to be involved in building a right-wing movement capable of challenging the governing ideology of Liberal Canada.

Among the authors Weissenberger and Harper read was Friedrich Hayek who, at the time, was a leading voice within the free market-oriented Austrian school of economics. Echoing the Thatcherite claim that "there is no such thing as society," Hayek argued that what we call society is a "spontaneous order" that emerges out of social and economic interactions between individuals. This deeply libertarian perspective runs counter to both socialist and classical conservative ideas. It is also the perspective that would come to underpin Harper's growing commitment to the importance of protecting individual social and economic freedoms, restricting the size and reach of government, lowering taxes, and providing constitutional protection of property rights.

By the time Harper abandoned the PCs to join Preston Manning in the founding of the Reform party, he clearly identified with the libertarianism of economic conservatism.[25] Prior to the March 1987 convention at which the decision was taken to found the new party — the Western Assembly on Canada's Economic and Political Future in Vancouver — Harper and Weissenberger prepared an eleven-point manifesto titled a "Taxpayers Reform Agenda." It focused on changing the character of Canadian politics (ending patronage, regional inequalities, etc.) and committing to strong conservative principles and a "new economy" of smaller government. It championed political reform and economic conservatism and, according to Harper's biographer, "offered not the slightest hint of social or moral conservatism."[26]

It is a mistake, however, to ignore Harper's relationship to *social conservatism*. It is true that the Conservative party's deeply committed social conservatives "know Harper is not one of them." He has demonstrated that "[l]egislating right moral conduct isn't his game."[27] Still, there is an under-appreciated place for "moral traditionalism" in Hayekian conservative thought. Libertarian commitments to individual freedom can be read as hostile to any impediment to change (even when proposed by social traditionalists); all the same, many followers of conservatives like Hayek view moral and social traditions as the collected wisdom of the past, a wisdom that justifies nothing more than incremental and gradual social change.

Lloyd Mackey is one of the few Harper observers to explore his relationship to evangelical Christianity. Mackey describes the "United-Presbyterian-raised" Harper as a one-time "religious skeptic" who only "came to his faith" well into adulthood.[28] He does not portray Harper as a committed social conservative, but as an economic conservative who believes that faith, compassion, and ethical judgment are central to a well-functioning market economy.

Politically, Harper has worked to discredit portrayals of social conservatives as bigots, while people close to him have done the work associated with encouraging these moral traditionalists to "let things happen incrementally when the times are right."[29] Harper's faith, his approach to the Christian gospel, and his chosen place of worship now link him to evangelical communities in a way that was not the case when he first got involved in politics in the 1980s. He remains, however, far more of an economic than a social conservative.

A lot is made of Stephen Harper's disdain for the democratic tools and trappings of *conservative populism*. Preston Manning wrote that Harper has long-held reservations about the wisdom and value of grassroots consultation.[30] But this populist critique of Harper misses the point. Conservative populism is about much more than providing ordinary people with a voice in politics. Underlying any form of populism is an ideological construction of a political cleavage that pits the common people against the powerful entrenched interests. In this respect, Stephen Harper is at one with conservative populists.[31]

In the mid-1980s, Harper and Weissenberger read Peter Brimelow's *The Patriot Game: National Dreams and Political Realities*. This book, which so inspired the pair that they purchased 10 copies to share with friends, laid the foundations for Harper's embrace of conservative populist ideas.[32] Brimelow wrote of Canada's under-performance as an economy and as a nation. He painted the Liberal party of Canada as the villain behind Canada's decline. Brimelow, like Harper at the time, singled out the special treatment accorded the province of Québec as an important source of unfairness and under-performance in Canada. In addition, however, Brimelow borrowed from American neoconservatives such as Irving Kristol, to paint a portrait of a "new class" of civil servants, academics, journalists, and cultural industry workers who thrived on public sector interventionism and benefited from the very pathologies that were undermining the Canadian nation.

Stephen Harper embraced much of Brimelow's analysis in developing his critique of the welfare state. When he made his public political debut in a speech at the Reform party's founding convention in 1987, Harper articulated his populist critique of the welfare state:

> The welfare state has placed unprecedented power in the centralizing hands of the federal bureaucracy, both in terms of its new reaches into Canadian life and its insistence on standardizing all policies and practices on a national scale. The welfare state has witnessed the phenomenon of greedy pressure-group politics reaching unprecedented depths. The vested interests of the welfare state operate in the guts of government decision-making machinery. Thus, their networks have been highly successful in achieving constant growth for their programs and bureaucracies.[33]

The one group within Canada's conservative family with whom Harper has been unwilling to associate are those who continue to embrace *Red Toryism*. From his early days as a disgruntled Progressive Conservative, Stephen Harper has often characterized the Red Tory conservative establishment as his immediate enemy. In the 1980s, he believed it was Mulroney's embrace of the left-leaning Red Tory tradition that prevented a full-fledged neoconservative revolution in Canada. When he ran for the leadership of the Canadian Alliance, Harper rejected any suggestion of unifying Canada's two conservative parties so long as Joe Clark remained Progressive Conservative leader.

In sum, then, Stephen Harper is, first and foremost, an economic conservative. But he is an economic conservative who has made peace with social conservatism. He is comfortable with an alliance of economic and social conservatism for two reasons. In part, it is because he is a man of Christian faith with the associated moral values and an underlying streak of traditionalism. But also it is because many social and economic conservatives share a populist analysis of how a self-interested progressive liberal élite has for many years undermined the social, economic, and political interests of ordinary hard-working, tax-paying citizens. They share, as Tom Flanagan argues, "a common enemy" in the public sector-oriented political class of liberal intellectual and cultural workers who "wish to re-make society according to its own rationalistic vision."[34]

The company he keeps

For over two decades, Stephen Harper has chosen to associate with people who are politically ambitious and deeply ideological. When he first met Preston Manning in 1986, Harper was quick to jump on board the project to launch the Reform Party of Canada. While working for Manning and Reform, Harper met Tom Flanagan, the deeply conservative academic who remains one of his closest political associates. Flanagan has taken a leadership role in several of Harper's major political campaigns and served for a time in Ottawa as his Chief of Staff.

Harper's subsequent Chiefs of Staff have been Ian Brodie and Guy Giorno. Brodie received his PhD in Political Science in Flanagan's department at the University of Calgary. His dissertation supervisor was Ted Morton, now one of the more right-wing members of Alberta Premier Ed Stelmach's cabinet. Giorno was a senior staff member in the office of the premier of Ontario during the Mike Harris years and was known for his capacity to provide central oversight to the Harris team's policy agenda (the Common Sense Revolution) as it worked its way through the provincial bureaucracy.

Harper is known for his association with the "Calgary school" of conservative academics. While the ongoing importance of his ties to the university are sometimes exaggerated, it was members of the Calgary school, including Flanagan, Morton, and Rainer Knopff, who joined Harper and conservative policy analyst Ken Boessenkool in the writing of the infamous 2001 Alberta Agenda that encouraged Premier Ralph Klein to embrace policies that would build a political "firewall" capable of stopping an "aggressive and hostile federal [Liberal] government" from imposing big spending and interventionist policies that don't reflect true Canadian values.[35]

In recent years, Harper has put considerable trust in the advice and work of less ideologically-driven conservatives like Brian Mulroney and cabinet ministers David Emerson and Jim Prentice. Harper is aware of the strategic advantages associated with welcoming some non-Red Tory elements of the old PC party into his inner circle. But, time and again, he has placed most of his trust in individuals who were among the neoconservative warriors of the 1980s and 1990s, including numerous members of the Mike Harris team that designed and implemented Ontario's Common Sense Revolution.

For example, during the first Canadian Alliance leadership race, Harper supported Tom Long. Like Harper, Long had done battle with Red Tories in the 1980s. As a keynote speaker at the January 2000 convention to launch the Canadian Alliance, Long lashed out at PC leader Joe Clark, saying he is not a true conservative and has "no meaningful record of accomplishments on promoting the things conservatives really care about."[36] Members of the Harris team who now work closely with Harper include federal ministers Tony Clement and Jim Flaherty (both former members of Harris cabinets), Conservative House Leader Peter Van Loan (former President of the Ontario PC party), and Harper's new Chief of Staff, Guy Giorno.

This picture of the company Stephen Harper keeps is decidedly incomplete. But it reveals the extent to which Harper has chosen to associate with many of the more ideological and deeply conservative members of Canada's conservative family. He has done battle with the more progressive Red Tories, while simultaneously creating productive working relationships with influential economic and social conservatives.

Conclusion

Stephen Harper is an astute political strategist with a sharp mind and a solid understanding of Canadian politics. He is far too strategically pragmatic to be blindly ideological, but he is deeply committed to economic conservative principles and unwilling to turn from his goal of re-making Canada in his conservative image. While not known as a social conservative, Harper needs the support of this influential wing of Canadian conservatism, and he knows that political victory requires social and economic conservatives to work together in political contests against more progressive voices. Entrenched as he now is within the Canadian political elite, Harper seldom articulates the views or analyses of Reform-style conservative populism, but this world-view remains a part of his ideological DNA.

Like many strategically minded political leaders, Harper is goal-oriented, and he maintains control of his government's policies and political messages to ensure they align with achieving his goals. He hasn't wandered far from the ideological beliefs that first motivated him to engage in politics. He surrounds himself with conservatives who share his strong ideological beliefs and, when he compromises on policy or the membership of his team, it is typically a strategic move designed to bring him closer to winning a majority government.

To know what Harper would do with his majority, Canadians need to understand his political and ideological character. This chapter has examined Harper's long record of engagement in conservative politics in the hope that it will contribute to developing such an understanding.

Chill Effect

Stephen Harper's cold war on freedom of speech

Trish Hennessy

THERE IS THIS quintessential Stephen Harper moment, mercilessly frozen in time by virtue of film, where early in his mandate as Prime Minister of Canada he takes the advice of his communications staff and allows television cameras to follow him to his son's first day of school.

This is the day Canadians are going to see the human side of the man who has just squeaked into minority government.

Harper's son looks understandably nervous, stiff with the pressure of outside eyes. It is one of those pained childhood moments where you look to your parents and think: *Make it go away or make it better.* He looks up at his dad, who is now bending toward him, hand outstretched to deliver his son a brief, formal, cool...um...handshake.

Now, there are many options for fathers who send their children off to school in this age of involved parenting. They could have held hands the rest of the way. Or dad could have said goodbye with a reassuring hug and a kiss. But Stephen Harper, ever the consummate professional, chose the classic business handshake.

Stephen Harper's public persona is not that of a warm and affable man. He is considered a cool-headed strategist willing to do what it takes to hang onto the reins of power and, while Canadians don't expect their Prime Minister to go around bear-hugging, there is such a thing as the

Harper chill effect and it runs deeper than whether he is warm and fuzzy with his own children in public photo opportunities.

The Harper chill effect has been evident from the very beginning, and it has been consistent throughout his first two years in office. During this brief period, Harper has used the court system to help silence foes, critics, and generally anyone with whom the Prime Minister might have a disagreement. It turns out this includes Elections Canada and Canadians seeking equality justice, as well as his political opposition, the Liberal party.

He has picked public fights with dissenting bureaucrats and shut down normal bureaucratic flows of public information. He treats the national press corps like a special interest group that has to be managed, controlled, and contained. He has muzzled his own cabinet, elevating this practice to new heights, and he swiftly implemented funding cuts to groups which ensure ordinary Canadians have a public voice and access to legal representation within the court system.

All this has been enacted with only minority government power at Harper's disposal. Left unchecked, the Harper chill effect threatens to profoundly undermine the core institutions that ensure the health of Canada's democracy. It also gives a glimpse into changes Canadians might expect should Harper secure a majority government.

As this chapter will demonstrate, the chill effect is rooted in two unshakable realities: 1) The Prime Minister holds a deep, personal distrust of traditional Canadian institutions, not the least of which is the mainstream media; and 2) Harper's personal style is more authoritarian than it is democratic — a style that runs against the grain of modern Canadian political leadership but is intertwined with what it means to be an extreme Conservative in this day and age.

As an extreme conservative, Harper is often described as a hard-right ideologue, but, tellingly, cognitive scientist George Lakoff says that underneath the ideologue lies a set of hard core values. Lakoff says extreme conservatives (in the United States, at least) ascribe to a moral worldview that is akin to "father knows best"[1] where authority, discipline and merit are cherished values that play themselves out in the day-to-day of extreme conservative politics.

Lakoff devotes an entire book relating his theory to the political style of U.S. President George W. Bush, who frequently adopts the strict father model, applying tough love or meting out justice. This chapter illustrates how the theory applies to Stephen Harper as well, and is evident in the Harper chill effect.

Loosening the promise of equality

Early into its mandate, in September 2006, the Harper government announced cuts to 66 federal programs totalling $1 billion[2] — cuts reminiscent of the mid-1990s, when federal Finance Minister Paul Martin claimed he had to pull out all the stops to keep Canada from hitting the "debt wall."[3] But these were no ordinary cost-cutting measures, and in September 2006 Canada could not pretend to be facing a debt wall. In fact, the coffers were flush with cash and Canada was boasting one of the lowest debt-to-GDP ratios in the industrialized world. There was a $13.2 billion fiscal surplus and no clear and present danger to public programs.

What was significant about these cuts was not so much the amounts, but "what" got cut: groups that give voice to Canadians. Some of the core cuts were delivered to the Court Challenges Program and to the Status of Women Canada, which were both originally established explicitly as part of the federal government's role to protect minority rights and to ensure all Canadians have access to fundamental justice. In fact, the government of Canada's own website[4] describes the Court Challenges program as a non-profit organization "which was set up in 1994 to provide financial assistance for important court cases that advance language and equality rights guaranteed under Canada's Constitution." It has been a key tool for women and historically disadvantaged groups to seek redress.

According to lawyer Alison Brewin, court challenges under this program led to the recognition of pregnancy discrimination, ended the practice of using what a woman wears as an argument for implied consent in sexual assault trials, and banned discrimination based on sexual orientation. "The Court Challenges Program is there to provide an important piece of democracy in our system," Brewin said. "Access to our courts is essential for historically disadvantaged minorities to address the sometimes discriminatory impact of majority rule."[5]

Given the nature of the cuts, there was push-back from Canadians. The Harper government responded by restoring the money it had taken from the Status of Women Canada, adding a bit more, but, tellingly, it removed the term "advocacy" from Status of Women's mandate, refusing to fund equality-seeking research and analysis.

Why the drastic cuts to programs designed to ensure equal voice and fairness to all Canadians — rights embedded within our own constitution? At heart, Harper hates the kind of government Canadians have grown up with. He would prefer to dismantle Canada's modern Keynesian welfare state and he eschews the notion that government has a supportive, nurturing, social role to play on behalf of its citizens. In the extreme conservative world, people earn what they get on merit, and they are individually responsible for making (or breaking) it. Harper's vision of government, the extreme conservative vision, is one of retribution, order, and civil obedience. It is more authoritarian in nature, less democratic and more divisive: The kind that says you're either with me or you're against me.

Harper also isn't keen on open political debate. His government finds public debate a threat to its goal of majority government. Canadians have seen this kind of ideological fervour at the provincial level under the Ontario Mike Harris government, the Alberta Ralph Klein government, but never before on the national stage. On this stage, the Harper government kneels at the altar of small government, a euphemistic term that implies fewer public programs and far greater reliance on the private sector to determine the Canadian agenda. It evokes a more American way of running government. Funding cuts that limit the services government provides — services that might help Canadians challenge the limits of an extreme conservative government — are fundamental to Harper as he diligently builds a foundation for majority rule.

According to the *Georgia Straight*, independent MP Garth Turner, who began his term as a Conservative member of Harper's caucus, alleges the Prime Minister "threatened" MPs to remain silent and not oppose him on the funding cuts. Turner recalls a meeting where Harper, in "strict father" mode, briefed his caucus on the budget cuts to the

Court Challenges Programs and to Status of Women Canada. "He said, 'We have determined a series of cuts, expenditure cuts, which will be announced. They have been determined. They are our position. And... anyone [who] has got any problem with that — who says anything about it — is going to have a short political career.' He said that in caucus," Turner told the *Straight*. "It was a threat."[6] Muzzling his caucus and cabinet members is but one of many strategies Harper has employed in his mission to centralize communications and maintain firm control over his government's plan to change government as we know it.

In caucus, Harper controls backbenchers with what is widely perceived as a gag order to maintain the appearance of a unified political party — despite well-known fissures. Major announcements come out of the PMO's office, generally, and not out of cabinet ministers' offices. Cabinet ministers who wish to speak to the media require "message event proposal" approval by the PMO's office.[7] When a cabinet minister gets unleashed, it's so unusual it becomes part of the news.

To date, all have stood loyally in line, backbenchers and cabinet ministers alike, with the exception of defector Belinda Stronach, one who is not easily intimidated, and maverick Garth Turner. Some contend this is characteristic of all ruling governments: that keeping disenchanted backbenchers in line has always been a leadership challenge. But consider the internal fortitude required to hold together a party with two radically different visions of the political right wing: the traditional blue Conservative brand which sees a social role for government in public society that is counterbalanced by the extreme conservative element of the party — Stephen Harper's wing — which detests the notion of an active government promoting progressive ideas such as equality and minority rights.

Within this harder core, Harper's challenge has been to keep at bay some who would like to turn back the clock on gay marriage, legal abortions, women's rights, and support for the poor. Keeping the extreme conservatives quiet as a requisite to maintaining minority government status has been one of Harper's most significant chill effect operations; his caucus has been obedient.

Chill effects only work if they're supported by language and rationale that make authoritarian actions appear reasonable. It is telling that the

Harper government framed its first round of funding cuts as reducing government "waste"—as if programs ensuring public voice and access to justice could be dismissed in a media soundbite as wasteful. In fact, many of the funding cuts were aimed at advocacy groups with no history of "waste," organizations big and small across the nation who operate on lean budgets, rely on the *pro bono* work of lawyers, and whose *raison d'etre* is to give voice to vulnerable, powerless Canadians. Groups, for instance, that provide legal services to poor people or that promote programs to support women who are abused or struggling financially. As a result of the funding cutbacks, a number of Canadian organizations have been forced to shift their mandates away from public advocacy, a core element of a vibrant democracy, toward something the federal government might find worthy of funding.

Lining up the enemies

The funding cuts were one of several arrows slung by a government intent on silencing its critics and maintaining complete and absolute control over its public service. It has led to some ugly and unprecedented public battles between public servants and their Prime Minister. For instance, in 2008, the Harper government unceremoniously fired Linda Keen, president of the Canadian Nuclear Safety Commission, after she imposed the closing of the Chalk River nuclear reactor. The closure resulted in a temporary domestic shortage of life-saving medical isotopes for cancer and cardiac diagnosis and other treatment, but there was more to the firing than the brief shortage in nuclear capacity.

On the Hill, where politicians enjoy revelling in such controversies, the story wasn't so much about Keen's firing as it was about the ham-fisted treatment of public servants who happen to cross Stephen Harper. "I have to tell you, it's quite a story," said Liberal environment critic David McGuinty. "Anybody who seems to try to do their job in this town these days...seems to lose it. These are the kinds of Republican tactics this town has never seen before." McGuinty suggested that it was part of a pattern that reminded him of the U.S. government's witch hunt for Communists following the Second World War.[8]

Speculation sprouted ears, but, incredibly, it was the Conservative booster paper, *The National Post*, which wrote:

> Mr. Harper was unable to resist blaming the impasse...on Ms. Keen, who he suggested was a Liberal partisan. Why he did this is open to conjecture, but as the *Post* reported this week, Ms. Keen has made enemies in the nuclear industry because she has imposed tough new international standards on any new reactor built in Canada, in doing so hurting AECL's ability to sell new reactors to the government of Ontario. She has also ended "pre-reviews" of new reactors, a process that warns operators if there are fundamental barriers to them being granted operating licences. Both measures have made AECL less attractive to potential investors at a time when the government is mulling whether to sell off all or part of the nuclear operator.[9]

"If there is a single Canadian public agency with an outstanding international reputation, it is Elections Canada."[10] And yet, in its harshest assault on a public agency to date, the Harper government has launched a law-suit against Elections Canada for supporting a search warrant to raid Conservative party headquarters to make sure the party's advertising financing is on the level. In moments like this, it is often wise for the sitting government of the day to welcome the transparency of open scrutiny as an essential element of ensuring accountability. Not so in Stephen Harper's government.

The Harper Conservatives are not only suing Elections Canada, but they also voted against a symbolic motion that would have expressed all-party confidence in Elections Canada. "It means that they don't have any respect for what they are, a government, and that Mr. Harper doesn't feel at ease with civil servants, with independent organisms, organizations or offices, with journalists, with oppositions, in a word with democracy," said Bloc Leader Gilles Duceppe of the Conservatives' vote.[11]

National Post political editor Kelly McParland wrote this about the Harper government: "The thing is, if you expect to find enemies everywhere, you'll probably succeed."[12] *Globe and Mail* columnist Lawrence Martin wrote: "Hardly a week goes by without the Conservative government, with the subtlety of a dump truck, adding a delightful example to its control-freak highlight reel."[13]

But this isn't the story of a control-freak out of control. This is the story of someone who is diligently trying to choke the sources of communication that do not reflect the Harper agenda. At times, it expresses itself in foolhardy attempts: Trying to force the impenetrable, immovable Auditor General Sheila Fraser to allow central control over her press releases was an act of pure folly. The Auditor General brought down the seemingly teflon Liberal government under Jean Chrétien; she is no shrinking violet.

Choking the information flow

Choking the information flow by quietly killing Canada's Coordination of Access to Information Requests System (CAIRS) has been one of the more authoritarian attempts to stifle freedom of speech in Canada. Access to Information is the way most Canadians can learn about the hidden dealings of their government, and the requests system is a way of channelling such requests. It is a bureaucratic, formalized way of asking questions and getting answers. It is essential to open, accountable government — something Harper himself promised during the election campaign. But it is yet another casualty of the Harper chill effect. Before the Harper government decided to scrap CAIRS, it had been publicly criticized for taking too long to respond to requests and for heavily censoring documents that revealed information the government didn't want made public.

> The number of complaints received by the information commissioner in 2007–08, for example, soared to 2,387 — more than 1,000 higher than the previous year. The level is the second-highest on record, next to the 2,821 received in 1983 — 2,242 of those from a single complainant.[14]

The Canadian Association of Journalists, which isn't prone to political intervention, has expressed concern over the decision to shut down the information registry. In a May 2008 news release, it wrote: "The CAJ believes the elimination of the CAIRS database is part of a disturbing trend by Ottawa toward less openness toward government information, a trend that could ultimately result in the public only getting the information government wants it to know."[15]

With the scrapping of CAIRS, the Harper government has revealed the core of its playbook: Make sure your central staff has the power to say yes or no to information. Make your core "leak-proof," so the fortress of government is hard to shake, rock, or topple. It is anti-democratic, authoritarian in its approach. In an earlier era, we would have decried it as fascism or communism, take your pick. Either version hurts the free flow of an open democracy. But governments can only get away with drastic measures if they use words that make their extreme actions feel reasonable. The Harper government's explanation for rendering access to information ineffectual: They said it's no longer useful. Not useful for whom?

The media as "special interest"

Every centrally controlled, authoritarian government in the world has successfully choked the free flow of public information and clamped down on a right that is seen as fundamental to Canada: Freedom of the press. Stunningly, Harper has waged an unprecedented war on the national media, raising all manner of warning flags in the process. First, a primer on Canadian journalism: In Canada, it is among the highest journalistic honour to be given the right to report on the dealings of our federal government. The profession's cream tends to rise to the top on Parliament Hill, creating an unwieldy group of smart, driven journalists who are not easily intimidated and who are skilled at squeezing answers from the very best.

Communications experts have long advised their Prime Ministers: Fight with the national press corps at your peril. But to understand Stephen Harper is to understand that he holds a deep and long-abiding distrust of the media. He treats the nation's press corps as though it were a special interest group whose dissenting voice must be silenced. Since its inception, the Harper government has tried, overtly and probably in vain, to control, contain, and manage the news in ways not previously seen in Canada. Anaskis and Heer argue that Harper has tried everything he knows to de-legitimize the media's "role in holding his government to account."[16]

It began almost as an inside joke, where in the early days of the Harper mandate the most precarious job on the Hill appeared to be that of Communications Director. Harper went through three directors before he finally landed on staunch Conservative communications advisor Sandra Buckler, who was widely seen as one of his most trusted advisors before she stepped down in the summer of 2008. Buckler has been described as keeping "an iron grip" on the parliamentary press gallery, which is how Harper likes it. Buckler's treatment of the national press gallery has been the subject of great debate — often by national reporters who are disgruntled by obvious attempts to muzzle.

Early into Buckler's job, the press gallery found itself fighting her attempts to restrict journalists' access to cabinet ministers, to withhold basic statements by heads of state and premiers, to issue stock photos for closed meetings instead of allowing photographers in, and to stop holding the Prime Minister's news conference in the national press theatre, favouring instead the freedom of the Commons foyer. CanWest reporter Meagen Fitzpatrick wrote:

> Harper's resistance to holding formal seated press conferences has been one of many ongoing irritants between his office and the national press gallery. The spats have escalated at times to the point where Harper has said he will bypass the national media completely and only speak to local media.[17]

According to the reporters themselves, it quickly became commonplace that journalists who report stories the Harper government doesn't like would find themselves frozen out of the Prime Minister's media loop. During an April 2006 news conference, Harper decided to overlook the practice of media lined up to take their turn to ask questions, ignoring a question by CBC reporter Julie Van Dusen and picking another reporter in the audience instead. "Van Dusen was shocked. After a stunned pause, she interrupted the Prime Minister, 'Why are you ignoring the lineup? We're in a lineup, and I'm next.' Harper continued to ignore her until the other reporter chose not to ask his question. Van Dusen then asked her question, but Harper gave a very short answer and left."[18]

After that incident, full-fledged press conferences in Ottawa became a rarity. Veteran Hill reporter Hugh Windsor says something is different under Harper: "Other Prime Ministers have always accepted the press, but Harper's essentially said, 'Fuck you,'" he explains.[19] *Maclean's* magazine reporter Paul Wells says Sandra Buckler is the first Prime Minister's Communications Director who won't return most routine phone calls from reporters looking for information.[20] Even bureaucrats who normally help to answer media questions have been forbidden to do so under Harper.

A wave of fury over the Harper government's treatment of the media erupted in early 2006, when Harper imposed a media ban on covering the return of the bodies of soldiers killed in the line of duty in Afghanistan — a widely accepted American practice that is considered greatly out of step in Canada.[21] Some speculated the media ban was imposed for political reasons, to minimize Canadians' negative view of our nation's participation in Afghanistan, which moves Canada out of the role of peacekeeper and into active combat.[22]

Scott Reid, former spokesperson for Paul Martin, said, "It's not so much the decision they took...but the motivation... It was that they are concerned that permitting these pictures to be published will lead to deterioration in public support for the mission in Afghanistan." Reid argued that the Conservative government has "torn a page from the Bush White House."[23] In an emotional eulogy for his daughter, the father of slain Canadian soldier Captain Nichola Goddard issued a stern rebuke to the Prime Minister for barring the media from his deceased child's homecoming. Tim Goddard said he could "see no reason" why the media should be kept away from ramp ceremonies at Canadian Forces Base Trenton. "I find it troubling that the privacy decision means that we are keeping the press outside the wire, where the bad guys are," he said during his daughter's funeral.[24] *The Toronto Sun*, a media outlet that should naturally be in sync with a Conservative federal government, warned in an editorial: "This is about democratic freedom — the very thing we are asking our soldiers to fight and die for overseas. Lest we forget."[25]

A naughty or nice list

In March 2006, *Embassy* writer Sean Durkan reported on the press gallery's complaints that Buckler and Harper were trying too hard to control the press rather than let the press do its job.[26] Durkan wrote: "...Ms. Buckler made it clear she didn't care about any of the gallery's concerns, and indicated that even more plans were in the works to control the flow of information to reporters and limit their access to government." In its efforts to control the media, the Harper government began the practice of a central list where reporters were forced to sign up in order to have a chance of covering a PMO story.

During an announcement on the controversial settlement to the softwood lumber dispute, the PMO's office decided to have Harper appear in the foyer of the Commons for brief remarks. He made his statement, then left the foyer without answering questions.

> Later that evening, Harper called four parliamentary reporters from three different news organizations and granted them interviews about the softwood deal. All four had earlier told the PMO that they were prepared to put their names on its list, though they had neglected to tell press gallery officials of their decision. Two of the reporters were employed by CanWest Global, the country's largest media chain, which has now instructed all its correspondents to sign the PMO list.[27]

Toronto Star Parliament Hill reporter Richard Brennan, known in political circles as "The Badger" because he is tenacious, says that, when it comes to controlling the media, Harper is simply taking a page out of the Republican handbook in the U.S. In October 2007, Brennan said:

> Nothing Mr. Harper does surprises me. He is all about control—controlling the message and his own caucus. Do I find it threatening? I most certainly do. Any time a politician attempts to subvert freedom of expression, it is a matter that should be of concern to every Canadian... Reporters are appalled, but again not surprised. The reporters on the Hill are used to the PM's bully tactics by now.[28]

The *Toronto Star*'s editorial writers refer to Harper's "obsession with controlling the message, and his penchant for secrecy"[29] as though it's simply how Canada's Prime Minister does business. Control and secrecy are the waters Harper swims in. The *Vancouver Province*'s Alan Ferguson refers to it as Harper's "ill-concealed contempt for the media."[30]

At one point, in May 2006, about two dozen national reporters walked out of a Harper press conference to protest his muzzling tactics.[31] For his part, Harper blames the national media, accusing them of being biased against him. He prefers local media, where he feels he has greater control over the message. "Unfortunately, the press gallery has taken the view they are going to be the opposition to the government," Harper told London's A-Channel TV. "They don't ask questions at my press conferences now. We'll just take the message out on the road. There's lots of media who do want to ask questions and hear what the government is doing for Canadians, or to Canadians. So we'll get our message out however we can."[32]

In a CBC online article entitled *Spin Class, Part 2: How Stephen Harper Beat the Press Gallery*,[33] Ira Basen unpacks the government spin behind the media debacle. The government has framed the issue as trying to bring "order" to a practice that is "chaotic" and an institution that is outdated. Claiming the national media are dominated by "left-wing ideologues," Harper asserted that breaking up media control over what is determined as news on the Hill would be "helpful for democracy." He said: "I've got more control now... I'm free to pick my interviews when and where I want to have them."[34] In reality, Harper has blatantly put into motion a strategy to bypass the media filter and instead secure media coverage that favours his agenda, rather than questions it.

> He has turned to sympathetic newspapers and radio talk shows, direct emails, websites, friendly blogs and podcasts... According to one survey in an online magazine, Harper's podcast is the fifth most downloaded podcast in the country. Check out the official Prime Minister of Canada website at www.pm.gc.ca and the Conservative party website at www.conservative.ca and see if you can tell which is funded by taxpayers and which is a party organ.[35]

His distrust of media — of a free and unrestricted press — isn't the only example of Harper's chill effect. Media pundits talk openly of the Prime Minister's dislike of the culture in Ottawa: "[He] seems to distrust many of Canada's national institutions."[36] But when it comes to Canada's military, the Harper government is frequently orchestrating American-style photo-ops with soldiers in the background. In a discussion dissecting whether the Harper government was taking the military photo-op too far, CBC television's Peter Mansbridge's *At Issue* panel on May 15, 2008, seized upon Harper's systematic attempts to control the media and attack anyone who might present an opposing viewpoint.

Toronto Star columnist Chantal Hébert explained the Harper method by pointing out his party's oppositional roots: "We have a government currently that is having a really hard time getting rid of its opposition mentality...even in power after two years, the Harper Conservatives still act like an opposition, but with a lot more power."[37] Pollster Allan Gregg agreed, calling Harper's controlling, manipulative actions "unique behaviour" for a federal government. He noted the populist roots of this particular Conservative government, saying, "if you are a populist you have an anti-establishment" mentality, and "the best way to deal with them is to attack before they attack us." *National Post* columnist Andrew Coyne defended the Conservatives, saying they merely want to oust the Liberal machinery within the public service and replace it with their own.

Canadian Press Ottawa Bureau Chief Rob Russo said the government is so wary of its public servants that it views the public service as part of its opposition, rather than as potential architects for future policy-making. The result, Russo said, is an atmosphere of fear and tight lips within the federal public service. "I think they're terrified," he said, "and those that aren't terrified are leaving."

Conclusion: What this really means

The Harper chill effect is a by-product of an extreme Conservative running a democratic country in which freedom of expression, as well as belief in a welfare state that ensures government exists for the greater public good over individual benefit, are still strongly held social values. The chill effect is a reflection of Harper the man: authoritarian, controlling in style, distrusting of public institutions, and ideological to the bone. As Prime Minister, Harper has taken a few pages out of the American

Republican playbook, where the leader of the country behaves like "father knows best" and does what it takes to bring dissenters in line.

The Harper chill effect has crept into how his government frames important public policies that are quietly changing the nature of Canada — changes that aren't publicly debated and considered. Above all, the iceberg beneath the Harper chill effect masks a profoundly radical political agenda, but also an authoritarian implementation of that agenda.

Why risk the most stable minority government status in history and the opportunity to act as though you have majority rule? Upon review, there is a surprisingly long list of examples illustrating not only the Prime Minister's fundamental "contempt for Canadian institutions"[38] but also a list of aggressive, authoritarian actions which threaten the vibrancy of Canadian democracy. It reveals Harper's deep-seated desire to change Canada as we know it.

As political scientist David Taras suggests, every prime minister tries to set his own agenda and control spin, but Harper has taken the practice to new heights. "What we're seeing here is a degree of control within the government, within the caucus...that we haven't seen for a very long time," Taras said.[39] This attitude comes with a price tag. In terms of the Harper government's popularity, Taras predicts Harper's "zeal for message control" will take a political toll on the party:

> You can only control events for so long, you can only manipulate for so long, and ultimately I think this has harmed the Harper government to the extent that Harper's image has become 'Mr. Partisan, Mr. Mean, Mr. Control Freak.' It's just got to a point where control is the image of what his government is. That's damaging... You wonder what they're running from and what they're afraid of.

The question is: Have Canadians been paying close enough attention to Stephen Harper and his strong-arming tactics — or will the stern father figure get a free pass for displaying something that looks like leadership but threatens the health of our democracy? Only time will tell.

TWO

ECONOMY, TRADE AND INVESTMENT

The Conservative Tax Record

More of the same, or a turn for the worse?

Andrew Jackson and Erin Weir

A PROGRESSIVE TAX system and strong public fiscal capacity are needed to secure a more equal and inclusive society. In Canada, wages and market income are very unequally distributed, but the tax and transfer system redistributes income from the more to the less affluent. Taxes also finance public services — such as health care and education — that benefit all Canadians regardless of income. Countries with relatively high taxes as a share of national income also have higher levels of public social spending and, as a result, have much narrower income and opportunity gaps between rich and poor.

In recent years, Canada's rising corporate profits and worsening personal-income inequality have been amplified by lower, less progressive taxes and reduced social spending.[1] As a share of Gross Domestic Product (GDP), pre-tax corporate profits rose from 8% in the 1990s to above 13% since 2004. After-tax corporate profits doubled from 5% in the 1990s to 10% since 2004. The richest 1% of taxpayers increased their share of total pre-tax income from 8.6% to 12.2% between 1992 and 2004.[2] An important Statistics Canada report that carefully documents the rise of after-tax family income inequality finds that, between 1996 and 2004, the main driver was changes to the tax/transfer system.[3]

This chapter examines the federal corporate and personal tax cuts implemented since 2000, evaluates recent Conservative restructuring of the personal tax system, and compares the Liberal and Conservative records on taxation.

Corporate tax cuts

Budget 2000 cut the general corporate income tax rate from 28% to 21%. Budget 2003 extended this cut to resource companies and began phasing-out the corporate capital tax. Budget 2005 proposed to eliminate the corporate surtax by 2008 and to further cut the general rate from 21% to 19% by 2010. The NDP, which then held the balance of power in Parliament, re-negotiated the Budget to delete these corporate tax cuts and to invest the revenues retained in public programs. Notwithstanding its arrangement with the NDP, the Liberal government used the 2005 Economic and Fiscal Update to reinstate the corporate tax cuts originally proposed in the Budget and to eliminate the federal capital tax in 2006, two years ahead of schedule.

In Budget 2006, the Conservative government confirmed the corporate income tax cuts from the 2005 Update, reduced the small business rate to 11% by 2009, and made more profits eligible for this preferential rate. The October 2006 Tax Fairness Plan pledged a general rate of 18.5% by 2011. However, the relentless campaign for more corporate tax cuts ignored these sharp reductions. In June 2007, for example, *The Globe and Mail's* Report on Business ran the following headline: "Taxes are Falling, but Not Here."

In September 2007, Jack Mintz moved the goalposts again by calling for a combined federal/provincial corporate tax rate of "roughly 20%".[4] The following month's federal Economic Statement proposed a combined rate of 25%. The Government of Canada pledged to cut its own rate to 15% by 2012 and is asking provincial governments to cut their rates to 10%. The federal small-business rate dropped to 11% in 2008, a year ahead of schedule.

Lower corporate taxes are supposedly needed to make Canada internationally competitive. However, when the Conservatives took power in 2006, combined federal/provincial corporate tax rates were already well below the U.S. average, among the lower half of G-7 countries, and only two percentage points above the world average.[5] Nevertheless, the

Conservatives decided to cut federal corporate tax rates by seven percentage points.

KPMG's 2008 *Competitive Alternatives* report constructed an index of corporate income taxes, other business taxes and employer payroll taxes for 10 countries. Based on tax rates announced for the coming decade, KPMG concluded that Canada will be tied with the Netherlands for the second-lowest business taxes. Only Mexico will have (slightly) lower business taxes. The other G-7 countries and Australia will have significantly higher business taxes than Canada.[6]

These huge corporate tax cuts have not stimulated additional investment. As a Statistics Canada paper observes, "Over much of the last decade, corporations as a whole have been posting record profits. Meanwhile, business fixed capital investment has been relatively sluggish in recent years."[7] Similarly, TD Bank notes that the ratio of business investment to profits has fallen to an all-time low.[8]

Gross investment by private corporations currently equals about 10% of GDP, only slightly above the level that it has consistently averaged since the 1960s. In other words, gross investment (which includes depreciation) approximately equals after-tax profits (which exclude depreciation). Historically, non-financial corporations took out loans and sold stock to fund investment in excess of internally-generated funds. Corporate tax cuts have contributed to a reversal of this pattern. Today, non-financial corporations lend surplus funds to households and "issuance of common stock by Canadian companies has turned negative for the first time since the 1960s."[9] The C.D. Howe Institute, an organization committed to tax cuts, argues that Canada has comparatively high marginal effective tax rates (METRs) on capital. In calculating this measure, the Institute excludes local business taxes, which are particularly low in Canada, and research and development tax incentives, which are particularly generous here. It includes inventories, which Canadian tax-accounting rules subject to a particularly high METR. However, fixed capital such as machinery and equipment is what matters most for productivity and economic growth.

Marginal tax rates are not the appropriate measure of international competitiveness. An investor deciding where to locate a facility is concerned about the investment's total tax liability (i.e., the average tax rate), not the tax on the last dollar invested (i.e., the marginal rate).

Even if METRS were the appropriate measure, across-the-board CIT cuts are not a cost-effective way of reducing METRS. Finance Canada's Budget Plan 2007 indicated that its permanent Capital Cost Allowance (CCA) changes, which are projected to cost $145 million in 2008, will reduce Canada's METR almost as much as the Budget 2006 CIT cuts, which are projected to cost $3 billion in 2008.

Budget 2007 also introduced a temporary accelerated CCA for manufacturers at a cost of $1.3 billion over three years. The C.D. Howe Institute recently revealed that this measure, along with similarly targeted provincial incentives, dramatically reduced Canada's overall METR on capital from 37% in 2006 to 31% in 2007.[10] Not surprisingly, measures tied to new investment have relatively more effect at the margin.

The U.S. government taxes American corporations on a worldwide basis. Profits from the Canadian subsidiaries of American corporations repatriated to the U.S. are subject to American tax minus credits for Canadian tax paid. Therefore, if effective tax rates are lower in Canada than in the U.S., American-controlled corporations pay the difference back to the U.S. government. Japan and the United Kingdom also tax their corporations on a worldwide basis. Further CIT rate reductions and/or targeted tax incentives could simply transfer revenues from the Canadian treasury to foreign treasuries.

Canadian rates are well below American rates, but only the U.S. federal rate applies to profits repatriated from Canada. Clearly, the U.S. federal rate already exceeds the overall Canadian rate in lower-tax provinces. Any further CIT cuts could cause most Canadian subsidiaries of American corporations to pay U.S. tax.

Personal tax cuts

The 2000 Budget and Economic Statement cut personal tax rates from 29% to 26% on income from $61,000 to $100,000, from 24% to 22% on income from $30,000 to $61,000, and from 17% to 16% on income under $30,000. Then Finance Minister Paul Martin also eliminated the 5% high-income surtax and reduced the proportion of capital gains subject to tax from 75% to 50%. Taxable capital gains (outside of tax-exempt pension plans and RRSPs) are overwhelmingly concentrated in the hands of the very affluent. Mackenzie calculates that about one-third of the value of the 2000 income tax cuts went to the richest 5% of taxpayers.[11]

By enabling provincial governments to set their own rates and brackets instead of setting provincial taxes as a percentage of federal taxes, Martin also facilitated inequitable provincial tax changes. For example, Alberta implemented a flat tax and New Brunswick has proposed one.[12] Murphy, Roberts and Wolfson calculate that the federal-provincial effective tax rate for the richest 0.01% of taxpayers (with average incomes of $5.9 million in 2004) fell from 42% to 31% between 1992 and 2004.[13]

The 2005 Economic and Fiscal Update proposed to cut the bottom income tax rate to 15% immediately, as well as to cut the middle two rates by 1% and raise the threshold for the highest rate to $200,000 by 2010. The Liberals also promised to raise the basic personal credit to $10,000 and to institute a modest employment tax credit.

In the 2005–06 federal election, the Conservatives campaigned on cutting the GST from 7% to 6% immediately, and to 5% within five years. Their other major personal-tax promise was to exempt "reinvested" capital gains from taxation *(Stand Up for Canada, January 2006).* The first Conservative budget cut the GST to 6%, raised the basic personal credit to $10,000, and cut the lowest income tax rate to 15.5% in 2006 and 15% in 2007. Budget 2006 also introduced several new non-refundable tax credits, including an employment tax credit similar to the one promised by the Liberals and a child tax credit worth up to $300 per child under 18 at an annual cost of $1.5 billion. Most progressives believe the money would have been better spent on improving the targeted refundable child tax credit.

In November 2006, the Conservative government unveiled an economic strategy (*Advantage Canada: Building a Strong Economy for Canadians, November 2006)* that unsurprisingly gave pride of place to establishing "Canada's Tax Advantage" and called for "lower taxes for all Canadians and the lowest tax rate on new investment in the G-7." Even Conservative politicians are usually somewhat coy about cutting taxes for the very affluent, but *Advantage Canada* went beyond the populist promise of tax cuts for all Canadians embodied in the headline-grabbing pledge to cut the GST. It clearly called for lower marginal and effective tax rates on the "highly skilled" — described as those making more than $120,000 per year. It is worth noting that the text and chart in the paper on the need for lower taxes for "highly skilled workers" were almost identical to those found in the Liberals' 2005 *Economic and Fiscal Update*.

Advantage Canada also called for reduced savings on savings and investment income, including capital gains. High taxes on high earners and investors were seen as disincentives to work and savings. These claims have been routinely made in recent federal Budgets introduced by Liberals and Conservatives alike, even though the consensus of the academic literature is that high tax rates on the rich have very little impact on their work effort or savings.[14]

Budget 2007 promised to devote all future interest savings from debt repayment to reducing personal income taxes. Budget 2008 cut the GST to 5%, well ahead of schedule. Lowering the GST by two percentage points will cost over $12 billion per year of foregone revenues, eliminating much of the underlying federal government surplus. As a result, the 2008–09 Budget is now widely believed to be barely in balance.

While derided by right-wing economists as an inefficient tax cut in terms of increasing those all-important incentives to work and invest, the GST cut has resulted in tax savings across the income spectrum, with the largest proportional impacts among middle income groups. (The poor usually pay a bit less than average in GST since they spend more than average on tax-exempt essentials such as food and shelter, and receive the GST credit, while the very affluent tend to save rather than spend a significant proportion of income.) Most progressives believe that the small tax savings dispersed across the tax-paying public would have been better directed to child care, urban and environmental infrastructure, or other programs. However, no major opposition party has endorsed the idea of restoring one or two points to the GST to rebuild the lost fiscal capacity.

New directions in personal taxation

The Conservatives have also undertaken three initiatives which, while not having major fiscal implications to date, could gradually change the overall personal tax system moving forward. There has been at least tentative movement to shifting to a family-based income tax system; and to further exempting investment income from tax through Tax Free Savings Accounts. The Conservatives also introduced a Working Income Tax Benefit, as promised by the Liberals, which could grow to significance over time.

Finance Minister Jim Flaherty has made pension income divisible between spouses for tax purposes. As documented by the Caledon Institute, this initiative "will provide windfall benefits to some of the wealthiest seniors, only modest benefits to middle-income seniors, and nothing at all to the poorest of Canada's elderly."[15]

Flaherty has also mused about making all income divisible for tax purposes. This proposal would cost about $5 billion and would be similarly inequitable. By definition, single parents, unattached individuals, and families without income would not be eligible.

Because the spousal tax credit already equals the basic personal credit, couples could take advantage of income-splitting only if one spouse is in a higher tax bracket than the other. In other words, at least one spouse would have to be making more than $37,000 annually. If both spouses make less than this amount, they could not benefit from income-splitting.

By far the greatest gains would accrue to rich people whose spouses stay home. For example, a single-earner family with an income of $240,000 or more would retain an extra $9,000 in unpaid federal tax.[16]

In 2004, taxpayers making more than $250,000 declared $11 billion in capital gains, or 43% of the total amount of taxable capital gains income, and $6 billion or 36% of all dividend income. Most of the rest is declared by those with much higher than average incomes of more than $100,000 per year. Other investment income such as interest income is a bit more widely distributed, especially among seniors, but the essential reality is that very few middle- and lower-income individuals and families have significant savings and investments outside of tax-sheltered pension plans and RRSPs. (In fact, only about one in four private sector workers now has an employer pension plan, and most ordinary Canadians have only contributed a small amount of their allowable savings to an RRSP.) Lighter taxation of investment income — like the Liberal government's cut in the inclusion rate for capital gains and increases in the contribution limits for tax-sheltered RRSPs — thus overwhelmingly benefit very-high-income individuals and families, and reduce the progressivity of the personal income tax (itself the only progressive element of our tax system).

The 2006 Conservative election campaign promised to eliminate capital gains tax on the sale of assets when the proceeds are reinvested was likely dropped (or perhaps just deferred) due to the cost and complexities of implementation. Instead, the 2008 Budget introduced Tax Free Savings Accounts (TFSAs) which will likely prove a Trojan Horse, initially innocuous, but dangerous in the long-term as the hidden reality emerges.

From age 18, anyone will be able to save up to $5,000 per year (roughly indexed to inflation) in a TFSA. Any money removed can be re-contributed as savings room accumulates, so the total limit in 10 years will be $50,000 plus any inflation adjustment. All income earned in TFSAs, as in RRSPs, will be exempt from taxes. While contributions will not be tax-deductible, there will be no taxes on withdrawals.

A modest tax exemption for some savings income makes some sense. Anti-poverty activists have long noted and deplored the fact that saving by many older lower-income workers approaching retirement is punished, since income from savings is clawed back from the income-tested Guaranteed Income Supplement to Old Age Security after they turn 65. This could be remedied by exempting modest savings from social program clawbacks.

At the other end of the income spectrum, however, the very affluent can and do accumulate investments above and beyond their pension and RRSP savings, and would be in a position to invest $5,000 each and every year in a TFSA. Over 20 years, a couple who maximized contributions and earned income at a 5% rate within this vehicle could accumulate a non-taxable fund of well over $300,000, and earn untaxed investment income in excess of $7,500 a year. If the scheme becomes a permanent feature of our tax system, more and more investment income will be stored in TFSAs, and the loss of revenue for Ottawa in a "mature" system will likely be far more than the $3 billion per year estimated in the Budget. And the financial industry will have a new vehicle to sell and on which to collect fees.

It is worth noting that Jack Mintz, former president of the C.D. Howe Institute and a huge fan of Tax-Free Savings Accounts, suggests essentially the same thing in the April 4, 2008 issue of *Canadian Business Magazine*:

> Flaherty was able to bring in a substantial tax reform at little fiscal cost to the government for the next few years. The real cost will be down the road, when many seniors will have untaxed investment income sheltered in the TFSA. Of course, someone else will be in power by then, and Flaherty's new account will make life a lot tougher for tax-and-spend governments in the future.

The Conservatives introduced a small Working Income Tax Benefit (WITB) in the 2007 Budget, worth a maximum of $500 for single persons earning between $5,500 and $9,500, with lesser amounts for those just below and just above these limits. The maximum rises to $1,000 for couples and single parents. Such a measure, almost identical in design, had been put forward for discussion purposes in the 2005 (Liberal) Economic and Fiscal Update. The hopes of some social advocates that the WITB would be ramped up over time, on the model of the Canada Child Tax Benefit, were dashed when the 2008 Budget failed to implement any increase.

While income supplementation of very low wages can indeed help people leave social assistance for paid work and raise the incomes of the working poor, such schemes, according to the OECD, have the potential to function as a subsidy to low-wage employers unless they are twinned with a decent minimum wage floor.[17] Yet the Conservatives have failed to act on the recent recommendation of the Federal Labour Standards Review that the federal minimum wage should be reinstated at $10 per hour.

Conclusion

Has the Conservative tax record been more of the same or a turn for the worse? On corporate taxes, it has clearly been more of the same. Indeed, the first round of Conservative corporate tax cuts were taken directly from the previous Liberal government's 2005 Budget and Fiscal Update. The new Liberal leader, Stéphane Dion, has committed to slash corporate taxes "deeper than the Conservatives."[18] His Green Shift proposal includes cutting the federal corporate tax rate to 14% from the Conservative government's proposed rate of 15%.

On personal taxes, the Conservatives have pursued a different approach than their Liberal predecessors. However, it is debatable whether this approach constitutes a turn for the worse. The Conservative focus on cutting the GST has distributed tax savings more equitably than proposed Liberal income tax cuts. On the eve of electoral defeat, the previous Liberal government promised to reduce the 22% rate to 21%, reduce the 26% rate to 25%, and raise the threshold for the 29% top income tax rate from $116,000 to $200,000 in 2010, at an annual cost of $2.7 billion in lost revenue. Dion's Green Shift revives the first two of these proposals. To date at least, the Conservative approach has been to direct modest income tax savings to a broad spectrum of "ordinary working Canadians" rather than to higher-income earners.

The Conservatives have also pursued some new directions in personal income taxation. While the Working Income Tax Benefit is a modestly progressive initiative, income-splitting and TFSAs are definitely turns for the worse. However, the leading parliamentary advocate of expanded income-splitting, MP Garth Turner, is now a member of the Liberal caucus. There is some continuity between Liberal initiatives to shelter investment income from tax, such as higher ceilings on RRSP contributions and lower inclusion rates for capital gains, and TFSAs.

Of course, a critical test of tax policy is how much revenue it generates to finance important public priorities. Table 1 shows federal revenues overall and by source as a share of the economy (GDP). This is a more useful measure of major changes than dollar amounts, since seemingly large tax changes measured in terms of dollars often turn out to trivial as a share of the economy. Revenue changes, of course, reflect

TABLE 1 *Federal expenditures and revenues (% of GDP)*

	Actual 1993–94	1997–98	2005–06	2006–07
	(Liberal Government)			(Conservative Government)
Program expenditures	16.8	13.0	12.7	13.0
Total revenues	17.0	13.0	16.2	16.3
of which				
Tax revenues	12.8	14.6	13.5	13.7
Personal Income Tax	7.6	8.5	7.5	7.6
Goods and Services Tax	2.2	2.2	2.4	2.2
Corporate Income Tax	1.3	2.4	2.3	2.6

		Forecast 2007–08	2008–09	2009–10	2010–11
Program expenditures	A	13.2	13.1	13.2	13.1
	B	12.0	12.0	12.0	11.9
Total revenues	A	16.0	15.3	15.3	15.2
of which	B	14.8	14.7	14.6	14.4
Tax revenues	A	13.4	12.8	12.8	
Personal Income Tax	A	7.4	7.5	7.6	
Goods and Services Tax	A	2.0	1.7	1.7	
Corporate Income Tax	A	2.8	2.3	2.2	

NOTES Forecast A is from the 2008 (Conservative) Budget. Forecast B is from the (Liberal) November 2005 Economic Statement.
SOURCES Budget Plan 2008. Table 5.4. p. 201, Table 5.5 p. 205; November 2005 Economic and Fiscal Update. Table 1.4. p. 15; Department of Finance Fiscal Reference Tables. September 2007. Tables 3 and 4.

the interaction of the tax structure and the state of the economy, but the period considered has been (until very recently) one of fairly steady economic expansion and buoyant federal revenues. Data are provided for 1993–94 when the Liberals took office; 1997–98, when the federal deficit was eliminated and surpluses began to emerge; 2005–06, the last year of the Liberal government; 2006–07, the first fiscal year of the Conservative government, and for 2007–08 through 2010–11. For these latter years, the Table provides the current fiscal forecast from the 2008 Budget and that of the November 2005 Economic Statement, reflecting the Liberal agenda forecast forward.

Looking first at the Liberal period, the federal revenue share of GDP fell, by a significant two percentage points of GDP from the high point in 1997–98, though by a more modest 0.7 percentage points of GDP over their entire term. In the Conservative period, the revenue share is forecast to fall by 1.1 percentage points of GDP from 2006–07 to 2010–11. Over this period, the Liberals had anticipated an even greater decline of federal revenues as a share of GDP, a total of 1.9 percentage points. Given that one percent of GDP today is equivalent to $15.6 billion, this amounts to a very large difference in fiscal capacity. While the two percentage-point cut to the GST has, in itself, clearly cut federal fiscal capacity moving forward, the fact remains that federal revenues in 2010–11 are now forecast to be significantly higher than was the case under the last Liberal fiscal plan.

It is also interesting to note that total program expenditures as a share of GDP have been and are forecast to remain almost constant as a share of GDP, while the Liberal period saw a very sharp cut of 4.1 percentage points in the deficit-cutting period to 1997–98 (by far the largest reduction of any OECD country in recent years), and a further modest decline of 0.3 percentage points thereafter. There have, of course, been shifts in spending under the Conservatives — notably to transfers to the provinces and security spending, and away from federal social programs — and their spending priorities have not matched progressive priorities as registered in the CCPA's Alternative Federal Budgets.

Much of the decline in revenues under the Liberals was accounted for by lower Employment Insurance premiums and lower excise taxes. The personal income tax share of GDP, however, was cut from a high of 8.5% in 1997–98 to just 7.5% in 2005–06 (at a cost of roughly $15 billion per year in annual revenues), and was expected to fall further due to the tax cut package in the 2005 Economic Statement.

The impact of the Martin personal income tax cuts of 2000 on revenues were considerable, even though they were offset in significant part by the fact that most of the income gains of the past decade went to high-income earners in correspondingly relatively high tax brackets.

While taxes on the affluent have fallen as a proportion of income, they still pay higher than average effective tax rates.

Conservative tax cuts have reduced the Canadian tax system's capacity to redistribute wealth and raise revenue for public purposes. On the whole, this approach represents a continuation of previous Liberal policy.

Backsliding

Manufacturing decline and resource dependency under Harper

Jim Stanford

THE STEPHEN HARPER government has presided over a dramatic restructuring of the sectoral make-up of Canada's economy. The national economy is becoming more dependent on the production and export of natural resources, especially petroleum. Meanwhile, the manufacturing sector — the industry which transforms natural resources into more useful, valuable products — has been in recession almost since the day Harper took office. Several dramatic changes related to this sectoral restructuring include a record-breaking inflow of foreign direct investment, mostly aimed at takeovers of Canadian-owned resource companies, the flight of the Canadian dollar to parity with the U.S. dollar, and the shift of all net new job-creation to service industries, mostly in the private sector.

This restructuring has both its "positive" sides and its "negative" sides. Some sectors of the economy, led by resources, are vibrant and expanding. Others are contracting and retrenching. The whole restructuring process is driven — unsurprisingly, since Canada's is a profit-driven, capitalist system — by the quest for maximum profits by private businesses and investors. In particular, absolutely phenomenal profit rates in resource industries (again, especially petroleum), the result of sky-high global commodity prices, are the driving force behind all the sea changes noted above.

Overall GDP growth and job-creation numbers seemed relatively positive at first, but have more recently turned negative: indeed, Canada's real GDP, adjusted for inflation, began to decline in the beginning of 2008, possibly heralding the arrival of recession.[1] And, apart from the near-term damage resulting from the loss of hundreds of thousands of manufacturing jobs and the potential for a broader recession, this powerful resource-led restructuring should spark intense concern among Canadians regarding our long-run economic stability and prosperity, our role in the world, including our geopolitical security as an energy exporter, our environment, and our federation.

This historic structural change in Canada's economic make-up was not directly "caused" by the Harper government. It reflects the impact of global changes in commodity prices, in energy markets, and in manufacturing trade on a national economy which has been organized, long before Harper came to office, around the operating principle that most major economic decisions will be made on the basis of maximizing corporate profits. But the Harper government's general ideological and policy orientation has clearly ratified this general worrisome direction in our national economic evolution.

The Harper team fully accepts an economic regime in which "free" business decisions, motivated by the hunt for more profit, shape what we produce, where we sell it, and what we buy. Free trade, corporate tax cuts, and a strictly limited role, both regulatory and fiscal, for government are the main pillars of the Harper economic vision. From this perspective, the main fault of the Harper government has been to do nothing to arrest or actively manage this sea-change in Canada's economic trajectory. Their main error has been to sit on their hands.

But there have been sins of commission, as well, not only sins of omission. A number of important actions of the Harper government, from its gigantic corporate tax cuts, which significantly reinforce the dominance of corporate profit over economic decision-making, to its rubber-stamping of foreign takeovers of Canadian resource companies, to its stated explicit preference for a very high dollar, have all clearly made things worse. Despite being constrained — nominally, at any rate — by its minority status, the Harper government's discretionary economic policy actions have all strongly reinforced the dominance of resource exports, with all its associated side-effects: skyrocketing currency, surging foreign takeovers, shrinking non-resource exports. Worse yet, the government has mapped out a vision for its future direction should it be re-elected (most frighteningly with majority status) that would undoubtedly cement Canada's emerging role as a highly profitable but structurally underdeveloped energy warehouse for other countries.

Manufacturing meltdown

Not surprisingly in light of our geography, our population, and our colonial heritage, Canada has always been uniquely dependent on natural resource industries. Indeed, Canadian political-economy traditionally emphasized the role of successive waves of resource-led development, or "staples," according to the economic historian Harold Innis, to our economic development, our global relationships, and our internal politics. However, even before Confederation, Canadian policy-makers recognized the inherent limits of dependence on unprocessed resources, and worked pro-actively in various ways to stimulate a more diversified, "value-added" economy.

Many different tools were used over the decades to foster other export industries, especially value-added manufacturing sectors, including high tariffs to stimulate domestic industry, targeted public procurement policies to capture industrial spin-offs from our own purchases, strategic trade policies (the Canada-U.S. Auto Pact was especially important), technology and investment supports, and others.

This pro-active approach bore fruit. By the mid-1990s, following decades of gradual progress, Canada had become a global manufacturing powerhouse. For the first time in our history, we had become, in aggregate, self-sufficient in the production of manufactured products. In other words, we exported as much as we imported, and then some. For a country which traditionally relied on the export of natural resources to pay for imports of value-added merchandise, this was a tremendous achievement.

One summary indicator conveniently describes this structural progress. Chart 1 indicates the proportion of Canadian exports — the

CHART 1 *Canada's growing resource reliance: Unprocessed or barely-processed resources as share total merchandise exports*

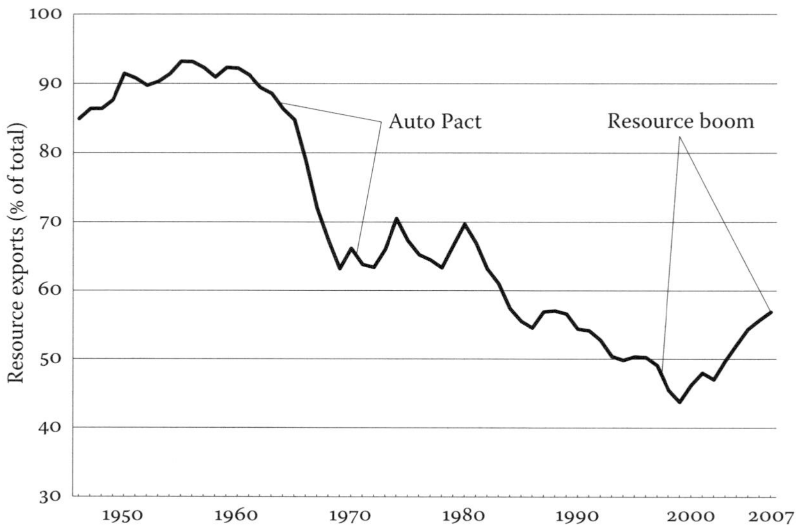

SOURCE CAW Research from Statistics Canada, *Canadian Economic Observer* and *Historical Statistics of Canada*.

things we sell to the world in order to "pay our way" in world trade and finance needed imports — that consist of unprocessed or barely-processed resource-based products, including agricultural goods, forestry products, minerals, and energy. At the end of World War II, Canada was still very much a "hewer of wood and drawer of water." But our reliance on raw resource exports steadily declined over the post-war era. By the early 1990s, Canada reached a turning point. For the first time in our history, a majority of our exports consisted of value-added, higher-technology products, including machinery, automotive products, and higher-value consumer goods.

Sadly, however, this achievement would not last. The importance of value-added exports peaked in 1999. Since then, the importance of resource exports, especially petroleum, has rebounded, and this trend has accelerated markedly since 2002, when global commodity prices began to rise dramatically. In 1999, resources accounted for just over

CHART 2 *Total employment in Canadian manufacturing*

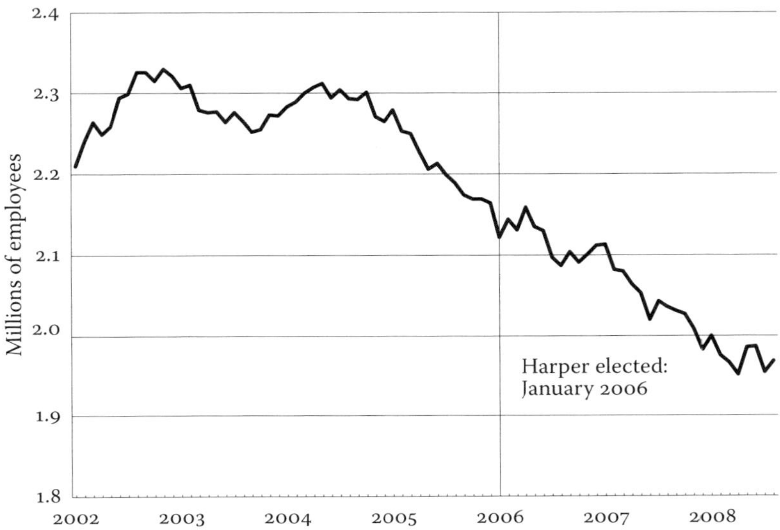

SOURCE CAW Research from Statistics Canada CANSIM Table 282-0094, seasonally adjusted labour force data.

40% of our exports. That has increased by almost half in just eight years: by 2007, resources accounted for almost 60% of our exports. In other words, fully one-third of the post-war progress attained by Canada in diversifying its role in the world economy has been undone in a few short years by the resource boom.

The most visible and painful symptom of this restructuring has been the unprecedented and continuing crisis in Canadian manufacturing. Canada's manufacturing sector has lost almost 400,000 jobs since employment in the sector peaked in 2002 (illustrated in Chart 2). That's a decline of over 15%, and the job loss has accelerated in 2008. Over half of the lost jobs have disappeared since the Harper government came to office in January 2006. Since they took power, Canada's manufacturing sector has lost an average of about 200 jobs a day — the equivalent of closing a medium-sized manufacturing plant each day.

CHART 3 *The manufacturing recession*

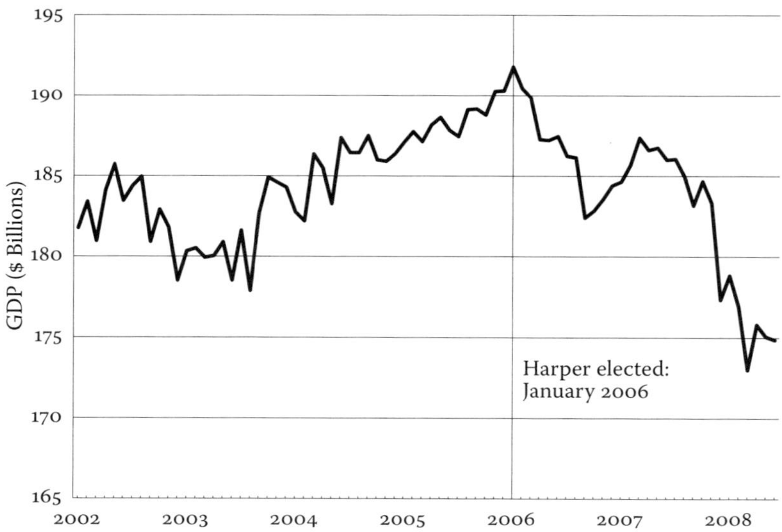

SOURCE CAW Research from Statistics Canada CANSIM Table 379-0027, at factor prices, $2002 constant.

In relative terms, measured as a share of total employment, the decline in manufacturing jobs began earlier: back in 1999, about the same time as Canada's export profile began to change so radically. The share of manufacturing in total employment has fallen by 4 percentage points, or over one-quarter, since 1999, to 11.5% by 2008, by far the lowest in our post-war history. Canada's manufacturing employment has fallen well behind those of several other developed economies, including Germany and Japan, although it is still proportionately larger than in the U.S., which has suffered an even worse and longer-lasting decline in manufacturing.

Initially, the job losses in manufacturing were associated with continuing growth in actual manufacturing output. Real GDP in Canadian manufacturing continued to grow, albeit slowly, through the first few years of the employment downturn; a situation of rising output with falling employment implies especially rapid productivity growth. But, beginning in early 2006, ironically just as the Harper government came

CHART 4 *Manufacturing trade collapse*

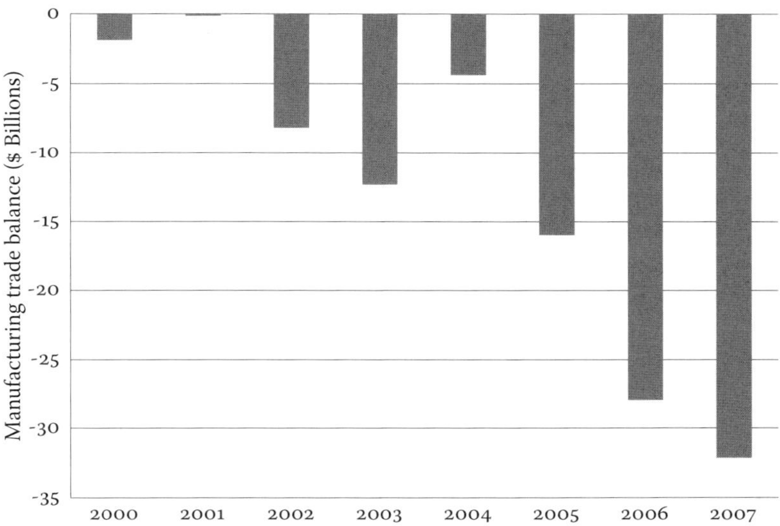

SOURCE CAW research from Industry Canada Strategis database, NAICS codes 31-33.

to power, the crisis in manufacturing intensified, and real output began to shrink (see Chart 3). By early 2008, real GDP in manufacturing was down 8% from the same period of 2006.

Manufacturing has thus been in more-or-less non-stop recession, with shrinking output, except for a temporary rebound in early 2007, since the Harper government came to power. And, by early 2008, a sharper decline in manufacturing output, focused on the crisis in Canadian automotive production, pulled Canada's total real GDP into negative territory. It is now clear that Ottawa can no longer simply ignore the painful shake-out occurring in Canadian manufacturing. The shake-out in manufacturing is on the verge of causing a nation-wide recession.

Another glaring perspective on the manufacturing crisis is obtained from international trade data. At the turn of the century, Canada was broadly self-sufficient in manufactured goods for the first time in its history, an important achievement given our resource-dependent past.

TABLE 1 *Hard-hit manufacturing sectors: Job losses since August 2002*

Sector	Job losses to November 2007
Textiles and clothing	70,000
Automotive	30,000
Food and beverage	28,000
Metal and steel	22,000
Paper	21,000
Wood products	16,000
Furniture	16,000
Electronics and appliances	12,500
Plastics and rubber	12,000

SOURCE CAW Research from Statistics Canada data, Table 282-0007.

That achievement has been wasted, however, by the resource boom and the associated squeezing-out of manufacturing exports by oil shipments and the soaring dollar. From a balanced position as recently as 2001, Canada's manufacturing trade has sunk deeply into deficit, which reached over $32 billion by 2007 (Chart 4). Over half of that turnaround represents the shocking deterioration of Canada's trade performance in automotive products. Manufactured imports are pouring into the country, while manufactured exports are shrinking due to an overvalued currency and global competition from new manufacturing leaders, especially China.

Particular sectors of manufacturing industry have experienced especially severe job losses, although the decline in manufacturing has been experienced very broadly, in almost every sector and in every region of Canada. Table 1 summarizes the job losses, to late 2007, in some of the hardest-hit sectors. The Canadian textile and clothing industry has been driven to near-extinction by import competition and the soaring loonie, losing over 70,000 jobs. The broad auto sector, considering both assembly and parts, has lost close to 30,000 positions. The paper and wood products industries have been hammered, in part by the dollar, and in part by the decline in sales to the U.S., including the crisis in the

TABLE 2 *Employment restructuring in Canada: Since August 2002 (Manufacturing employment peaked at 2.4 million jobs in August 2002)*

Sector	Change employment August 2002–June 2008
Manufacturing	-367,000
Construction	+329,000
Mining/oil and gas	+81,000
Sub-total: Goods producing	*+43,000*
Public services (incl. education, health)	+722,000
Retail/wholesale trade	+266,000
Finance, insurance, real estate	+161,000
Transportation	+103,000
Hospitality (food, hotels)	+71,000
Other services	+379,000
Sub-total: Services producing	*+1,702,000*
Total economy	**+1,745,000**

SOURCE CAW Research from Statistics Canada data, Table 282-0007.

American housing industry. The food and beverage, metal, electronics, and plastics industries have also lost thousands of positions.

The loss of manufacturing jobs far outstrips the new positions that have opened up in other sectors of Canada's economy. It is not remotely true that displaced manufacturing workers could easily find new work in the Alberta tar sands — as some commentators have crassly suggested. There has only been one new job created in the broader mining and energy sector for every 4.5 jobs lost in manufacturing since 2002 (see Table 2). Job growth in construction has been fairly strong, thanks mostly to the housing boom, although how long that persists through the U.S. mortgage crisis and broader economic weakness is anyone's guess. New jobs in construction and resources roughly offset the jobs lost in manufacturing, and so the overall goods-producing sector has seen no net job creation at all in the last half-decade.

All net new jobs, therefore, have been created in the services sector. That's not all bad news. For example, an impressive 40% of those new service jobs have been in public services, reflecting growing budgets for health care and education in most Canadian jurisdictions. But the bulk of new service positions are in private services, most of which constitute lower-income, lower-productivity jobs, in sectors such as retail trade, hospitality services, and general personal and business services.

The auto industry

Canada's post-war success in building a more diversified, productive, value-added industrial base reflected incremental progress across a range of different high-value industries, including aerospace, specialty vehicles, telecommunications equipment, and certain types of machinery. But no single sector was more important to our post-war industrial development than the automotive industry, which remains, despite recent tribulations, the most critical pillar in our industrial economy.

When Canada's automotive industry peaked in 1999, we ranked as the fourth largest assembler of motor vehicles in the world, an astonishing achievement for a country of our size. On a per capita basis, we were the largest automotive producer in the world. And we enjoyed a $15 billion trade surplus in automotive products. Canadian facilities benefited from strong investment throughout the 1990s, attracted by highly cost-competitive conditions, including a then undervalued currency, cost-efficient public health care which saved automakers as much as $10 per hour worked in total labour costs, and superior productivity performance. New investment in capital equipment enhanced productivity growth; Canada's auto industry became one of the rare manufacturing industries in which labour productivity is higher in Canada than in the U.S.

Since 1999, however, this key industrial success story has been abandoned by changing economic realities and inaction by policy-makers. By 2006, the large automotive trade surplus of 1999 had melted away into Canada's first automotive trade deficit in a generation; that deficit has ballooned and will exceed $10 billion in 2008. This large automotive trade deficit results from the fact that Canada's automotive trade surplus with our major customer, the U.S., no longer offsets our large and growing trade deficit with other producers. This non-U.S. auto trade deficit reached nearly $18 billion last year. The imbalance is particularly acute with Japan, from whom Canada imports 120 times as much automotive products as we export there, and Korea, from whom we import 185 times as much automotive products as we export.

The auto trade debacle has been even further worsened by the U.S. economic downturn (the U.S. being the market where over 85% of Canadian-made vehicles are sold), and by record fuel prices which have shifted consumer demand further toward the smaller vehicle segments which are especially dominated by imports.

The shocking decline of Canada's once vaunted automotive sector has been a major source of the decline in our overall value added industrial capacities during this decade. By the same token, arresting and reversing the auto crisis will need to be a central component of a broader strategy to nurture Canadian manufacturing. By all means, a successful auto strategy for Canada must involve measures aimed at improving the fuel efficiency and environmental performance of vehicles. But it must also involve measures to require automakers to maintain Canadian production content, in both assembly and auto parts, broadly proportionate to their sales in Canada. That sensible principle, as enshrined in the Canada-U.S. Auto Pact — which was unfortunately overturned by the World Trade Organization in 2001, just as Canada's manufacturing industry went into decline — will be required to preserve Canada's past automotive success in light of the challenges posed by globalization, energy prices, and environmental concerns.

Why manufacturing matters

The argument is often made that manufacturing must inevitably decline as a result of the transformation toward a "service economy," and that the loss of manufacturing jobs is being experienced broadly across all developed economies. Governments shouldn't attempt to interfere with this historical trend, but rather should embrace the creation of new jobs in whatever sectors are favoured by free-market business decisions.

It is certainly true that services are becoming more important as a share of total employment and GDP, although addressing the fundamental weakness in quality and productivity of many service jobs should also be a central focus of government economic policy. But it would be very wrong to write off the whole manufacturing sector as "yesterday's" industry. Since the turn of this century, Canadian manufacturing has declined far more rapidly as a share of total employment, by over a quarter, than in comparable OECD economies. By the late 1990s, Canada was a relatively successful manufacturing jurisdiction; but today we are an underperformer. We produce less manufacturing value-added than we consume.

And within the context of the broad structural evolution of our economy, policy-makers should make strong efforts to preserve as much manufacturing activity as possible. For several important reasons, manufacturing makes a disproportionate contribution to our overall productivity and well-being.

- Manufactured goods are essential to successful participation in global trade. Manufactured products account for 75 % of total merchandise trade. A country must be able to participate successfully and competitively in global markets for manufactured goods, to support overall engagement with the global economy and avoid chronic balance of payments difficulties.

- Manufacturing industries demonstrate both higher productivity levels and higher rates of productivity growth. On one hand, this implies ongoing negative pressure on manufacturing employment, unless demand for manufactured output is growing fast enough to absorb higher-productivity labour without job losses, which does not consistently occur. On the other hand, it implies that manufacturing is especially important to national productivity performance. Economists have recognized for decades that a smaller manufacturing sector implies both lower average productivity and lower productivity growth in the broader economy. The sharp decline in Canadian manufacturing is a crucial factor behind Canada's poor productivity performance this decade.

- Higher productivity allows manufacturing employers to pay incomes that are, on average, some 25% higher than in the rest of the economy. Manufacturing jobs are a crucial source of decently-paid, higher-quality work for working-class Canadians. They are important to maintaining decent income and employment opportunities in key communities, including among newcomer Canadians.

- Manufacturing firms demonstrate much higher levels of commitment to R&D and other forms of innovation. Manufacturing accounts for well over half of all private-sector R&D spending in Canada, paid from a much smaller share, just 15%, of national GDP. Hence manufacturers devote a much higher share of GDP to R&D than resource or service producers. Again, the decline of Canadian manufacturing during this decade is a key factor behind the continuing poor R&D performance of the overall Canadian business community. The rapid decline of Canadian manufacturing implies that Canada's record in this regard will get worse, not better, in the years to come. Minerals and energy firms enjoyed rapid growth in revenues and profits in this decade, yet re-invest very little back into innovation.

In short, there are unique, strategic reasons why a country should work deliberately to retain a viable, competitive manufacturing sector, with special emphasis on high-productivity, technology-intensive sectors, such as automotive products, aerospace, advanced electronics, life science products, and other high-value industries. The broader spin-off benefits of industrial success in those key sectors on national trade performance, productivity growth, and incomes justify the special policy attention that should be paid to manufacturing.

Putting the pieces together

The boom in exports of non-renewable resources, especially petroleum, and the corresponding decline of Canadian manufacturing, are two sides of the same coin. Understanding the links between these trends requires an analysis of the broader economic and financial trajectory of the national economy. Here, in summary, is how the rapid, unsustainable expansion of resource exports, focused mostly in Western Canada, has sparked the broader sectoral adjustments that pose such signifi-

CHART 5 *Foreign direct investment coming into Canada: Total FDI, and takeovers of Canadian companies*

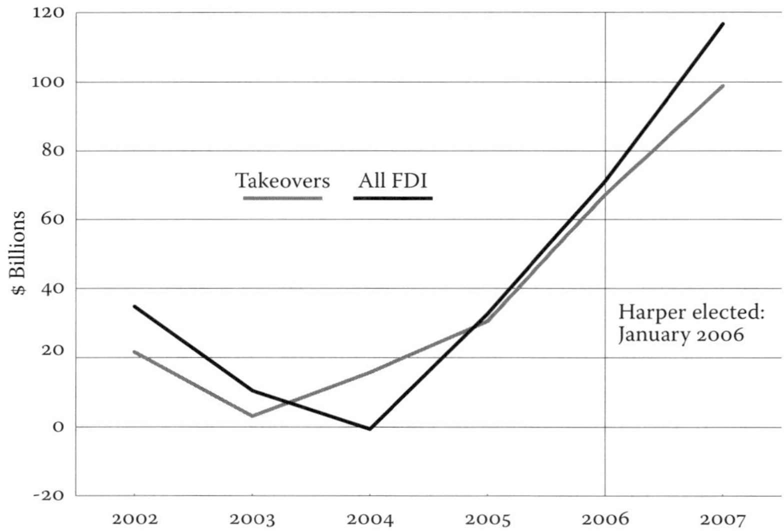

cant risks, both today in the form of 400,000 lost manufacturing jobs, and long into the future, to the rest of the national economy. Moreover, understanding those links will help to inform policy responses aimed at slowing and managing this restructuring process.

- *Super-high resource prices lead to super-high resource profits.* Canadian resource producers, again, especially in the oil and gas business, have enjoyed spectacular profits in recent years, thanks to record global prices for oil and other resource commodities.

- *Record profits have made Canadian companies very valuable.* Canada's economy is now more profitable, measured by corporate profits as a share of GDP, than the supposedly more business-friendly U.S. Canada's stock market has continued rising despite the current economic downturn, mostly because resource profits are so high. Indeed, resource companies alone account for half the market value of the Canadian stock market — and Canada's

CHART 6 *The skyrocketing loonie*

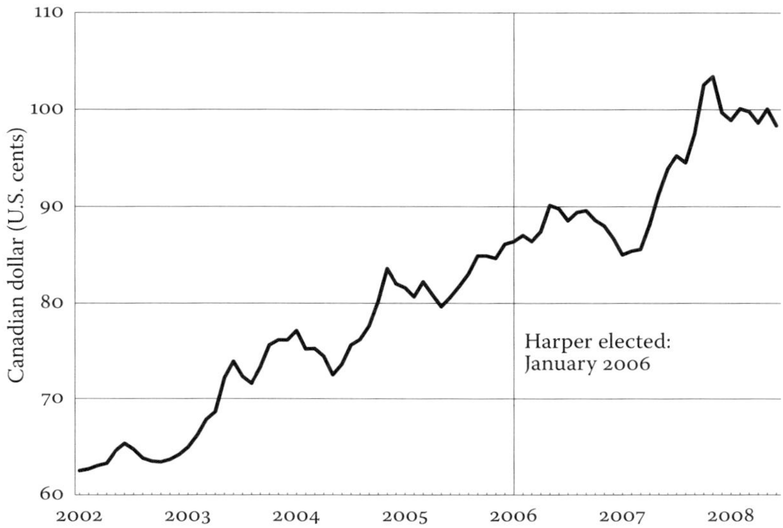

SOURCE CAW Research from Bank of Canada data.

perpetually-profitable financial industry accounts for another quarter.

- *Foreign investors want Canadian companies.* Foreign purchases of Canadian equities have contributed to the record highs reached by Canadian stock markets, even as Canada's economic and trade performance has been crumbling. More dramatically, many Canadian companies, especially in the resource sector, have been snapped up entirely by foreign investors. Canada attracted over $200 billion worth of incoming foreign investment in 2006 and 2007, by far the largest surge of foreign investment in our national history (see Chart 5). This inflow was not aimed at building new facilities and creating new jobs; it was aimed overwhelmingly at taking over existing super-profitable Canadian companies. Indeed, 94% of all incoming foreign investment in the last five years consisted of takeovers of existing firms.

- *Financial inflows drive up the Canadian dollar.* Both types of financial inflow — to purchase shares in Canadian companies or to buy out Canadian companies entirely — drive up the value of the Canadian dollar. The dollar's value is determined on financial markets by the inflows and outflows of financial capital. It does not directly depend on trade performance, productivity, or other "real" economic factors, all of which, perversely, have deteriorated in recent years. The Canadian dollar has been rising against its U.S. counterpart since late 2002, when world commodity prices first started to rise. But the dollar's rise got completely out of control with the wave of foreign takeovers in 2006 and 2007 (see Chart 6). It appreciated by 20% in 2007 alone, reaching and then exceeding par with the U.S. dollar. The dollar has soared by over 60% since 2002 — meaning that Canadian-made products are now 60% more expensive than they were six years ago. International economists, such as those with the Organization for Economic Cooperation and Development (OECD), estimate that a "fair" value for the Canadian dollar, reflecting relative prices for consumer goods and other products, is about 80–82 cents U.S. Thus, with the Canadian dollar at par, the currency is overvalued by as much as 25%.

- *Non-resource exports are squeezed out.* The dollar's rise reflects the powerful impact of resource prices and resource profits on Canadian corporate valuations, and hence on financial flows. It reflects intense international demand for Canadian *companies*, not international demand for Canadian *products*. But many other Canadian industries also aim to sell their products to international markets, especially manufacturing, but also tourism, which has suffered even worse business and employment changes than manufacturing, and other tradeable services, like finance, transportation, consulting, etc. International sales of those products have fallen because the dollar has made them 60% more expensive, too.[2] Record energy and resource prices are in effect "subsidizing" Canada's international trade balance despite the loss of non-resource exports, although not completely: the overall national balance of payments has deteriorated rapidly during the resource boom. How long this "subsidy" can continue, and what Canada will be left with once the bubble inevitably bursts, is very much in question.

- *Employment and production is shifting to non-tradeables.* This is perhaps the least understood, but most damaging, consequence of the resource boom. The overvalued currency makes it very difficult for Canadians to sell anything other than resources into international markets. But resource industries don't create nearly enough new jobs to absorb the loss of employment in manufacturing, tourism, and other export-oriented, tradeable industries. As a result, most new work and most new production occurs in non-tradeable sectors of the economy: that is, in sectors which produce and sell their output to nearby Canadians, rather than into larger regional and international markets. It seems bizarre in this era of omnipresent globalization, but the proportion of Canada's GDP which is exported has plunged dramatically during the resource boom — from a historical record of 45% of GDP in 1999 to less than 35% today. Non-tradeable sectors include construction, public services, and most private services. In particular, our growing reliance on low-wage, low-productivity private service industries, which is an indirect but clear consequence of the resource boom, may be the most damaging long-run side-effect of the current trajectory.

The overall picture that we paint, therefore, is much more complicated than suggesting that Canada's economic centre of gravity is shifting from manufacturing to resources. That is partly true. But the real growth in resource production, employment and exports is far from adequate to offset the erosion of manufacturing. The whole restructuring process has been intermediated by financial flows, in particular the intense interest of foreign investors in capturing a piece of Canada's uniquely lucrative resource industry. The most important real economic shift that we observe is not from manufacturing to resources; rather, the largest shift is occurring from all non-resource export industries — manufacturing most importantly among them — into non-tradeable services, most of which demonstrate low productivity and low incomes.

Harper's attack on manufacturing

As discussed above, the forces ultimately causing this broad restructuring of the Canadian economy are largely global in nature, and were exerting their influence well before the Harper government's ascension to power. The Harper government's general endorsement of free trade, deregulation, and business-led economic development has clearly reinforced the growing resource dependence and corresponding deindustrialization, which have become so evident during his tenure. The government's failure to respond to the new and worrisome economic challenges resulting from sky-high global commodity prices, a soaring currency, and the other side-effects of the resource boom, gives plenty of reason to strongly reject the far-fetched claim that Conservatives are the best economic "managers."

But more than this, there are several key ways in which the pro-active policy direction of the Harper regime has incrementally contributed to the resource-led restructuring of our economy. Some of the specific ways in which the Harper government has aided and abetted Canada's resource-led deindustrialization include:

- *Massive corporate tax cuts.* Finance Minister Jim Flaherty promised in his 2007 fiscal update to enact a historic schedule of corporate tax reductions, taking the general federal corporate tax rate down to 15% by 2012, from just over 22% when his government came to office. This one-third reduction in corporate taxes, far outstripping the smaller reductions Flaherty also engineered in personal income and sales taxes, will cut federal revenues by 6%, a very substantial reduction in the national government's total revenue base. Flaherty justified this expensive move, in part, by saying that Canadian businesses, including manufacturers, needed help to adjust to the challenges posed by the high dollar and other economic changes. For manufacturers, whose taxable profits currently range from small to non-existent, a corporate tax rate reduction offers little if any benefit.[3] More importantly, considering the broader economic and financial linkages mapped out above, these tax cuts will make matters *worse* for Canadian non-resource exporters. It is their already-superior profitability performance, centred in resources, that explains both the surge in foreign purchases of Canadian firms and the resulting take-off of the Canadian currency. Tax reductions to make these companies even more profitable and appealing will only accelerate foreign takeovers and further boost the Canadian dollar. Notably, Flaherty's tax reductions overwhelm the very limited increase in provincial royalty rates which the Alberta government recently imposed on super-profitable petroleum companies, as a half-hearted attempt to capture a slightly larger share of petroleum super-profits for Albertans. Thus, perversely, new investments in Alberta's already overheated tar sands sector appear more profitable today than they did before the Alberta royalty changes.

- *Explicitly endorsing an overvalued currency.* Unfortunately, the Bank of Canada has officially ratified the appreciation of Canada's currency as a welcome sign of "adjustment to change." Unlike other countries, most of which have attempted to contain the economic damage caused by rapid, undue currency fluctuations,[4] Canadian authorities have steered clear of attempting to slow down the loonie's flight. Quite the contrary, Canadian officials have actually and explicitly *endorsed* that rise. In unusual testimony to the Senate in December 2007, former Bank of Canada Governor David Dodge seemed to endorse a Canadian dollar at near-par with its U.S. counterpart. Then, early in 2008, Finance Minister Jim Flaherty seconded that opinion, indicating that he explicitly favoured a trading range for the Canadian dollar of 95–98 cents U.S. It may be coincidence that this is in fact where the Canadian dollar has mostly hovered since that time; it wouldn't be unusual for currency traders, in the absence of overarching pressures to the contrary, to use remarks like Flaherty's as broad "guideposts" for their own trading activity and expectation. At any rate, for Flaherty to wade so forcefully and explicitly into the fray of currency markets, contrary to his official view that the exchange rate should be determined by "market forces," let alone to endorse an exchange rate that is so clearly destructive to the clear majority of Canadian industries, surely damages his already crumbling reputation as a rational and effective economic steward.[5]

- *Rubber-stamping foreign takeovers.* Not surprisingly, the Harper government has continued the recent federal tradition of rubber-stamping foreign takeovers of Canadian firms. After all, it was the previous Conservative government, headed by Brian Mulroney, that dismantled restrictions on foreign takeovers as one of its first acts in 1984. Since then, the largely toothless Investment Canada process has approved over 1,600 takeovers and rejected only one: the proposed takeover of Canadian space company MD&A, which was turned down by Industry Minister Jim Prentice in 2008, thanks solely to a firestorm of political pressure. Worse yet, in July 2008, the Harper-appointed "Competition Policy Review Panel," headed by business magnate Red Wilson, issued a shockingly pro-business manifesto, proposing the elimination of whatever remaining control the federal government holds over foreign investment.[6] Signals from the Harper government indicate its full agreement with the direction proposed by Wilson. Like corporate tax cuts, making it still easier for foreign investors to buy out Canadian resource companies will exacerbate the chain of economic linkages, resource profits, foreign takeovers, rising currency, and declining non-resource industries, which has already critically damaged our manufacturing sector.

- *Derailing an auto strategy.* The decline of Canada's once outstanding auto industry was well in motion before Harper's election, the result of globalization, the World Trade Organization, and the competitive failures of the U.S.-based auto-makers. But cautious, uneven steps were being taken to address the problem. In particular, the previous minority Liberal government had established a new multi-stakeholder body the Canadian Automotive Partnership Council (CAPC), to address the industry's problems and make policy recommendations, and the federal government had invested in several initiatives, including participation in several key auto restructuring investments and support for new infrastructure and training initiatives, which were helpful to the industry's attempts to re-invent itself. These initiatives were completely at odds, however, with the Harper government's *laissez faire* ideology, and this hesitant progress toward an industrial strategy for Canada's most important value-added export industry has ground to a dead halt since his election. CAPC has hardly met since Harper's election; there seems little point, given the deafening indifference emanating from Ottawa. And Ottawa has indicated its opposition to playing a hands-on role in the industry — for example, rejecting appeals to participate in potential new "green" power-train investments in Windsor and St. Catharines, or to support threatened assembly plants in Oshawa, St. Thomas, and elsewhere. Finance Minister Jim Flaherty, who hails from Whitby, an auto riding, can barely contain his disdain for the industry that employs so many of his constituents, telling laid-off auto-workers in Oshawa to get new jobs in the financial industry, and trying fruitlessly to pin all the blame for the auto industry's tribulations on the Ontario provincial government's refusal to copy his own counterproductive corporate tax cuts. If the Harper government cannot be pushed into action on the auto industry, given its immense economic and political importance in vote-rich Ontario, then there seems little hope of expecting any reversal of its hands-off approach to the overall manufacturing meltdown.

- *More free trade*. The Harper government has enthusiastically endorsed the general free trade orientation of Canada's economy, and worked actively to strengthen and deepen the free-trade relationships that have been a key factor behind Canada's emergence as North America's energy warehouse. Harper has given full support to the Security and Prosperity Partnership, which is exposed and critiqued elsewhere in this volume, and his government has pushed aggressively to negotiate new bilateral free trade agreements, under the leadership of the turncoat Trade Minister David Emerson. The government's first priority in this regard was a bilateral deal with South Korea, a successful manufacturing powerhouse. Canada's bilateral trade with Korea already perfectly indicates the dangers of our emerging resource pigeon-hole: most of our exports to Korea are resources, most of our imports are high-value technology-intensive manufactured goods, led by $2 billion worth of automotive imports. And the "balance" of these two flows (surprise, surprise) is a large and growing trade deficit.[7] The push to sign an FTA with Korea was derailed by strong political opposition, led by the CAW, but the government is nevertheless committed to proceeding whenever political conditions allow. And the Harper government has forged ahead with other deals, most notoriously including the agreement with Colombia, signed in spite of horrendous human and labour rights violations in that country. If Harper is re-elected, expect an all-out push to implement free trade deals with Korea, followed by Japan and China, that would devastate what's left of Canadian manufacturing.

For all these reasons and more, a re-elected Harper government will only reinforce the dramatic decline in Canadian manufacturing. Supported so powerfully by Western resource élites, who have reaped unimaginable profits from the oil boom, the Harper regime actively celebrates Canada's regression into an energy-producing superpower.

Nothing is inevitable

Supporters of the *laissez-faire* approach of the Harper government claim that it's impossible to do anything about these broad, globally-motivated shifts in Canada's economic make-up. This isn't remotely believable. There are several links in the causal story outlined above, where a determined and pro-active government could successfully engineer a role for Canada in the world economy that reaches beyond simply extracting and exporting natural resources. Instead, we could aim to maximize the spin-offs from those resources, by maximizing the employment and technology benefits resulting from resource development, stimulate desirable non-resource industries, and regulate and improve the quality of work in non-tradeable industries, like private services.

The notion that Canada's resource dependence is an inevitable result of global market forces is mere camouflage for the underlying issue that really explains why our economy is evolving in that direction. Powerful vested interests, led by the Western petroleum industry, prefer that course of development, because of the immense profits generated by the resource bandwagon. Government policies aimed at enhancing the broader interests of Canadians and building a more diversified, stable, and sustainable economy, in both the economic and the environmental senses of that word, could interfere with the resource boom at several different points:

- *Capture resource profits.* The one-time profits resulting from the extraction of non-renewable resources, especially petroleum, in conditions of record global prices, have flowed mostly to private companies rather than to the people of Canada who, nominally, own those resources. By increasing royalties at the provincial level and corporate taxes at both the provincial and federal levels, governments could capture a fairer share of those resource profits — money which could then be used to support a range of public priorities, including support for industrial strategies in other sectors of the economy.[8] More importantly for the present discussion, higher taxes on resource profits would reduce the appeal of Canadian resource companies in the eyes of foreign purchasers.

- *Slow down new resource developments.* The uncontrolled pace of resource development, especially in Alberta's tar sands, has created numerous negative side-effects for Canada's economy and environment, including regionally concentrated inflation, escalating greenhouse gas emissions, and dramatic shifts in fiscal federalism, since only the three oil-producing provinces now qualify as "have" provinces for purposes of federal equalization transfers. The pace of new tar sands and other mining developments should be deliberately restricted through development and environmental planning measures.

- *Restrict foreign takeovers.* Foreign investment aimed at genuinely enhancing Canada's economic capabilities, with new investment, technology, and jobs, should be welcomed. But straight-out foreign takeovers of existing Canadian firms serve no positive economic purpose and should be prohibited or restricted under a much more forceful foreign investment review process. This is especially true in the resource sector. Canada is the only major oil-exporting country in the world which imposes no domestic ownership restrictions on this vital industry. The uniquely deregulated status of Canada's oil wealth is a major factor behind the intense global interest in purchasing Canadian resource companies and hence behind the run-up of our currency.

- *Reorient Canadian monetary policy.* The resource boom is the major structural force behind Canada's soaring currency, and the preceding recommended measures — to limit the super-profits of the resource sector and control foreign takeovers of Canadian firms — would automatically release much of the steam from the Canadian dollar. Nevertheless, the hands-off policy of the Bank of Canada has played an important role, too, in the dollar's unsustainable flight and the resulting manufacturing crisis. The Bank can and should be instructed to explicitly take account of the exchange rate and the broader competitiveness and stability of the Canadian economy in its interest rate and other policy interventions, rather than focusing solely on its inflation targets, as is its current policy. These instructions are fully compatible with the language of the existing *Bank of Canada Act*, which instructs the Bank to regulate the overall stability and well-being of the Canadian economy, not just inflation.

- *Actively support non-resource export industries.* Canada's past manufacturing success stories had nothing to do with "comparative advantage," free trade, or the natural workings of markets. They had everything to do with pro-active, effective industrial strategy. Our successes in automotive products, aerospace, telecommunications equipment, transit equipment, and a few other high-value sectors were the result of flexible, pragmatic efforts to nurture high-value sectors and diversify and enhance Canada's role in global markets. Unfortunately, that activist tradition was largely abandoned in the 1980s, as free trade became, by default, the only "industrial policy" market-oriented governments were willing to consider. Other countries, however, have continued to utilize and refine techniques of active industrial strategizing, using a range of tools — capital market tools, exchange rate policies, technology transfer, active trade promotion, and more — to foster the domestic presence of desired high-value industries. Unless and until Canada learns from those lessons, and begins to actively target and support high-value industries, including tourism and higher-value service sectors, not just manufacturing, our structural degeneration will surely continue.

These policies are all there for the using. Other countries, including most of our trading partners, rely on them every day. Canada's federal government has chosen to remain passive in the face of a historic restructuring that will limit our national economic prospects for generations to come, even if it generates quick bucks for a concentrated group of resource interests today. This passivity reflects its deliberate and biased *choice* — not any inevitable economic reality. It's a choice that Canadians, especially those whose prosperity is not tied solely to resource extraction and export, should remember well.

Lost Jobs

Erosion of a caring culture

Eileen Corbet

WHEN YOU SAY you're born and bred in Oshawa, Ontario, people tend to look at you in amused disbelief, since it seems everyone who calls Oshawa home is invariably from somewhere else. I'm one of the ones seen as an oddity, having been here all of my 52 years.

Although it has long been known as "the City That Moto-Vates Canada," there has been a slight smoothing of my city's blue-collar exterior over the past 20 years or so, largely due to the influence of Torontonians looking for a cheaper, safer place to raise their families. The "factory" jobs and the people who toiled at them are still here, but our city council has undergone a radical shift in personnel and attitude. We became "Oshawa, Prepare to Be Amazed" (sounding more like a De Beers diamond commercial). A huge debt load was taken on for really gorgeous, sparkly new recreational facilities and the highly controversial General Motors Centre in the beleaguered downtown core. Our elected officials hadn't noticed that the Auto Pact was murdered in 2001.

I do admit I didn't realize what the WTO decision entailed at the time, even though I'm an employee of Canadian Auto Workers Local 222. Hired in 1994 because I knew computers, had a newspaper background and could type 100 wpm, my work largely involved producing the Local's monthly newsletter for its 23,000 members, active and retired, getting newfangled things like email and the Internet installed in our Union Hall. Single with two kids, I was trying to learn to balance a household budget now that I was making good money. A right-wing carte blanche shift to a global economy wasn't something that worried me.

Seven years later, I've rocketed past worry to agonizing in abject terror about what the future holds for my children, their friends and many peers, now beautiful young adults full of intelligence and potential. They confess to me the prospect of holding two or more jobs at once seems inevitable; I can tell they long for their own financial independence and despair they'll ever achieve it. Even if they score a "good" job, it will be on contract with no benefits.

Essentially self-employed, they face the fact their own families (if they're brave enough to have children) won't benefit from the dental, vision and health care I receive through my employer. They know they must rent with no hope of ever buying a home. If they have the opportunity to live in a house, it's usually from a parent who still has to charge them rent because their own financial future is unstable. Even after graduating college, they work full-time at Canadian Tire to put a roof over their head and food in their tummies, yet they need to sling beer part-time at Shoeless Joe's so they can pay their car insurance.

With the job losses, people are getting mean, petty, and desperate. Thefts at the gas station where my daughter works are an everyday occurrence, not just drive-offs from the pumps but the taking of anything that isn't tied down, even in the middle of the day. People wait until an employee's back is turned, literally, and off they go. Counterfeit money is the currency of the day.

The stories I hear from many depressed men and women coming from my city's shrinking and disappearing workplaces are the same. Honest individuals are afraid of a world where it's more lucrative to be sneaky, and if you don't have enough money for what you want, steal it. There's no pride in working at a coffee shop where the owners jet off to the Caribbean regularly and leave an 18-year-old in charge, with no extra pay for all the additional responsibility.

Stealing a person's livelihood is an absolutely despicable form of disrespect. This is what Canada's manufacturing job loss all comes down to, for me. Beginning in 2002, I watched manufacturing job loss start as a trickle: 12 jobs here, 28 jobs there, another 120, a few hundred more, an entire company or two goes out of business, then a complete shift's worth of 1,200 people, and now we learn that in 2009 a source of great pride, our GM Truck Plant, will no longer be available as sources of income for fine individuals anyone would enjoy having as friends.

In June I saw one of those quicky TV news headlines, "Study shows Canadian manufacturing saved if jobs outsourced overseas," and had to uncover whatever ridiculous rationale was behind this. According to the Canadian Press, manufacturing executives and the TD Bank see another 250,000 jobs in Ontario leaving the province in the coming year. They're actually optimistic the sector will be healthy by the time all this "restructuring" is done. Who's worried about the health of the displaced employees, their families, and the communities they live in?

It's obvious the federal Conservatives aren't worried, but, with General Motors' callous closure of the award-winning truck plant, we will lose an additional 2,600 jobs. With spin-off employment, that's 19,500 individuals minimum who are going to suffer thanks to a bloated Canadian dollar, the lack of fair foreign trade, and inexplicable gasoline prices. What good is "restructuring" if we end up with jobs that will never pay more than $12 an hour? All I can see is a government that is insensitive to laid off workers and families who worry that they can't pay their mortgage or send their kids to university.

My 20-somethings are far more politically aware than the 50-somethings who are losing their jobs. They are my hope for the future.

Foreign Ownership

Mel Watkins

A MIRACLE OCCURRED on May 9, 2008, right here in Canada. For the first time in 23 years, that routinely spineless entity known as the Government of Canada said "No" to a foreign takeover of a Canadian company.

Literally thousands of foreign acquisitions had been approved since 1984 when then Prime Minister Brian Mulroney declared Canada "open for business." Among the fallen were such Canadian icons as Falconbridge, Inco, Domtar, Algoma Steel, Hudson's Bay Company, Stelco, Fairmont Hotels, Four Seasons Hotels, Molson's, Labatt's, and the Montreal Canadians. Indeed, the *Investment Canada Act*, which formally took effect in 1985, mandated Investment Canada to shill for *more* foreign investment, so much so that some of us imagined that somewhere, perhaps not even in Canada, there was a giant machine for approving or rejecting foreign takeovers that automatically stamped "Yes" to every request for approval made to it. Was it possible that, finally, the machine itself had rebelled in boredom?

Regardless, there was that rarest of moments; the ground moved in Ottawa. I know. I felt the tremor, albeit the slightest, where I live, on the outer skirts of the capital. How could this have happened? Would there be aftershocks?

Messrs. Mulroney, Chrétien and Martin had never seen fit to "interfere" with the operations of external, frequently imperial, capital. How was it possible that Harper, the first truly neoliberal Prime Minister, had done such an amazing thing, causing the right-wing press, the *National Post* and *Maclean's*, to go ballistic and allege that Canada had become, I kid you not, North Korea.

The case in point was the sale of the space division of MacDonald Dettweiler & Associates (MDA) to Minneapolis-based Alliant Techsystems for $13 billion. MDA had the famed Canadarm to its credit and, more recently, the satellite Radarsat 2, largely financed by the Canada Space Agency and used for Arctic surveillance and the maintenance of Canadian sovereignty. Alliance Techsystems is a weapons company, a bomb manufacturer. To their everlasting credit, at least two MDA employees quit over objections to working for it, and retired MDA co-founder Vern Detweller said he supported them.

It's doubtful that the Harper government cared much about any of that. It can be presumed to have taken the unusual step of turning this takeover down for reasons of national security, not wanting Radarsat 2 under foreign control.

Steven Staples, social entrepreneur *par excellence* and the head of the Rideau Institute which led the successful campaign to block the takeover, thinks most Canadian prime ministers can be seen as appendages of the American president managing Canada as a subsidiary of the United States, but that Harper is a clone of George W. Bush and, being like him, gives the highest priority to national security.

If so, it's best not to expect any aftershocks. MDA looks like one of a kind, an example of that weird hybrid, neoliberal nationalism. This country is as "open for business" as ever. If there's not as much happening at the moment as there was, it's not because Canadian companies are suddenly playing hard to get, or because foreign buyers are deterred by the MDA case. It's because the chaos in global financial markets has made it harder to raise the funds to finance mergers and acquisitions.

There was the hope, albeit the slightest, that a Competition Policy Review Panel appointed by Harper in the immediate aftermath of the spate of takeovers in 2007 and mandated to look at both the *Competition Act* and the *Investment Canada Act*, would be compelled to do something positive. True, in a truly shameless act, all five panelists were business people, but it was possible to imagine that they would realize, now that they were on the public payroll, that they ought to make the effort to think like citizens. But they didn't. Their report at the end of June 2008, with the sporty title *Compete to Win* and full of the clichéd boosterism of Don Cherry, called for the Government of Canada to make it even easier for Canadian companies to be taken over.

It was the kind of recommendation that was reported only as business news because otherwise it risked being read by the unwashed and laughed out of court. It was so mindless, bordering on the embarrassing, that even the Harper government let the report be issued at the end of a week when Parliament was not sitting. The Minister of Industry received it without comment, and the likelihood of a minority Harper government taking it seriously — it also advocated that Canadian banks be allowed to merge and be available for takeover by foreign banks — is slight.

The press did, however, quote an anonymous source within the government as saying it would be a blueprint in the event Harper got a majority, which is a way of reminding us that a majority Conservative government would quickly rediscover the fullness and foulness of the ideological roots that it has been compelled to hide as a minority government.

It seems improbable that Canada, decent country though it is thought to be, should, late in the dying days of neoliberalism, with its poster boys George W. Bush, Tony Blair and John Howard thoroughly discredited, have a neoliberal leader. Likewise, it seems odd and badly behind the times to have an official panel, funded by taxpayers, advocate an intensification of globalization, foreign ownership as practised by the multinational corporation being at its very core, at a time of global financial chaos and global warming that have come in the wake of existing globalization.

The panelists are honest enough to say that Canadian business is insufficiently innovative. As business representatives, they share that deficiency. We have good reason in this country to know that foreign ownership is not without its costs. Historically, it created an inefficient branch-plant economy protected by the tariff. We went the free trade route — under the last Conservative government, it might be noted — and eliminated the tariff, our leaders confident that our firms would become efficient. They haven't, which raises the distinct possibility that foreign ownership is itself the problem.

Today, that problem takes the form of the hollowing-out of corporate Canada, its head offices, and the myriad of jobs associated therewith. A Conference Board of Canada study released in early 2008, timed to be useful to the panel, was duly reported in the media as showing there was no problem. In fact, the conclusions of its study are much more nuanced than that and show that real costs inhere in foreign ownership.

Let me cite the Executive Summary, with my translation in the square brackets: "Overall, CTES [Corporate Takeover Effects] on acquired companies are positive for shareholders [a.k.a. as windfall gains], mildly positive or neutral for operations, capital, people and community involvement [little or no benefit on a long list of things that matter and it is "benefit" that the *Investment Canada Act* is supposedly looking for], and negative for governance [which means for decision-making, power and control, which are the guts of the matter]." Furthermore, at the conference at which these results were released, on a panel on "Insights from the Boardroom," of five panelists two said unambiguously from their experience at the top of the pyramid that in foreign-owned companies in Canada the real action was in the head-office outside Canada and that letting our companies be taken over was sending the bad message to young people interested in business careers in Canada that they should settle for the second-rate.

The Competition Policy Review Panel shrugged the whole matter off with the facile comment, already worn out by frequent use by Harper, that whatever hollowing-out was done to us we get back by our foreign investment abroad. In fact, Canadian investment abroad has risen significantly in the decades since the foreign ownership debate began in the 1950s and '60s of the last century, but there is no automatic offset. Between the centre of an empire and its margins there is no symmetry, and none should be expected.

When a Canadian company successfully penetrates the much larger American market, there will be a tendency for head-office functions, like marketing and advertising and record keeping, to be pulled to that larger market. So it is that Thomson enterprises, which is often cited as an example of a Canadian-based company that has gone abroad successfully, has most of its head office functions in Stamford, Connecticut. *Globe and Mail* columnist Margaret Wente, whom I rarely have reason to cite, describes Thomson as "Canadian in name only." In its heyday, Nortel had its head-office in Brampton, Ontario, but its executive office was in Dallas, Texas. Its retreat back to Canada was a sign of its failure.

On the matter of foreign ownership, as well as the overall rules of Investment Canada, which can be carved in large letters on the head of a pin with space left over, there are restrictions on foreign ownership in certain designated sectors, like banking, telecommunications, transportation, culture, uranium. The ideologues at home and abroad gnaw away at these, but governments tend to know, unless hopelessly neoliberal (which Harper is at heart), that these are sectors designated in the first place because of public interest and therefore must be meddled with cautiously. Canadians distrust banks too much to let them be merged, but like them too much to let them fall into foreign hands. Telecommunications co-exists with culture and the latter is already beleaguered.

The Canadian need is not to deregulate these sectors, but to add to them — like resources in general, oil and gas in particular, and specially the tar sands. The world is in the midst of a great commodities boom that, albeit with ups and downs, may go on indefinitely. Most commodity-rich countries have state-owned enterprises, which automatically excludes being bought out by foreign companies, to assure that gains stay inside its borders. The issue is not national vs. foreign ownership, but public ownership vs. private, but in Canada, in spite of a historic tradition of public enterprise which has served us well, we are unable to come to terms even with the first.

There is something just plain bizarre about every other oil-rich country having a state-owned petroleum company while we spend our time worried about whether their state-owned companies can be counted on to develop our resources in our interest. If that isn't bad enough, there's the overriding matter of the global interest in producing energy with minimal impact on global warming. Oil-rich countries, it might be thought, have a special obligation of stewardship.

We must be frank and recognize that it is rare for a provincial government to "interfere" with the exploitation of its resources for export, or for the federal government to assert its rights and duties. The likelihood of a Harper government with its head office in Alberta coming to terms with these issues is nil. We may find ourselves in the odd position with respect to oil from the tar sands of being compelled by the Americans to clean up our act environmentally.

Once Bush is gone and, let us pray, Obama takes his place, Harper will have no one to appeal to, or imitate. President Obama will hardly be opposed to globalization, but his administration may want to "manage" the American connection more in the public interest of Americans. To so manage the Canadian connection is utterly alien to Harper.

Should McCain triumph, bet on continuing catastrophe and lament for Canada, America, and the world.

Continuity and Change[1]

Canadian Trade and Investment Policy, 2006–08

Gauri Sreenivasan

WHEN THE CONSERVATIVE party came to power in February 2006, the multilateral trade system was in trouble. A series of high-profile collapses in global negotiations had signalled the beginning of an era of significant dysfunction and stalemate. The December 2005 World Trade Organization (WTO) Ministerial in Hong Kong had breathed new life into global trade talks, but it was to be short-lived. The much touted Doha Development Agenda was headed for its rockiest years yet. Indeed, the Conservative government has helmed Canada's trade agenda in the most serious years of crisis in the multilateral trade system. But this system, whose health is vital to Canada's interests, has not been the government's top priority.

The Conservative government has shifted Canadian attention to the pursuit of bilateral trade deals as part of a controversial trend forged by many other industrial powers. In addition to significant updating of the NAFTA framework, Canada has put particular emphasis for its bilateral strategy on the Americas as part of a new "neighbourhood" focus in foreign policy announced by Prime Minister Stephen Harper.

This chapter provides some critical reflection of Canadian trade and investment policies in 2006–08 from the perspective of Canada's development efforts to reduce poverty and protect human rights. What is the Canadian government's orientation to the WTO's ill-fated

Development Round? What can be gleaned from the pursuit of new bilateral agreements?[2] While much of this trade and investment agenda has been a constant in Canadian policy, there are new characteristics in the Harper era that should be examined. Given the reception of this agenda from civil society and Parliament, it is clear that trade and investment issues remain highly contested terrain and a likely flash-point for years to come on the Canadian public agenda.

Sidelined and subverting: Canada at the WTO

The Doha Development Agenda — What context for Canada?

Launched in November 2001, in the context of global "togetherness" pressure after September 11, the Doha Development Agenda committed WTO members to put the needs of developing countries at the heart of global trade rules. This commitment came barely a year after the Millennium Summit at which the world's governments pledged to reduce by half the proportion of people living in poverty by 2015. Developing countries, though not monolithic in their interests, were united in the need for significant reform in global trade rules to enable the achievement of development goals.

There was strong and widespread criticism of the net impact for developing countries of the previous Uruguay Round of WTO talks. Promised market access to Northern markets was illusory or delayed in agriculture and textiles, while the costs and development implications of new rules, for example to raise intellectual property standards and liberalize trade in services, were severe. The poorest countries had experienced declining shares of global trade, the haemorrhaging of prices for their exports, an onslaught of subsidized goods from wealthy countries that swamped local producers, and rising levels of poverty and inequity. As a result, business as usual was not on the menu for the South in the Doha Round.

In rough, Southern countries have expected not only a major re-balancing of global rules, but the creation of new arrangements to address the special constraints of developing economies. Developing countries have also been adamant that the WTO not expand its scope to create new trade disciplines in areas such as government procurement, investment and competition.

The geo-political distribution of power in the global economy has also made for a new ball game. Brazil, India, South Africa, and other industrializing developing countries have significant clout and are no longer "policy takers." Indeed the famous walkout of the Africa Group and others from WTO talks in Seattle in 1999 proved to be an early foreshadowing of the rocky ride ahead for the Doha talks. Though many developing countries clearly wield little negotiating power on their own, a plethora of new negotiating groupings that have developed over the course of the Doha talks have built creative and surprisingly resilient solidarity among Southern blocks.[3]

For its part, the Canadian government has seen its negotiating position marginalized in this new round, as bigger economies have commanded the front row seats. Canada went from being an actor in the heart of "the Quad" in the Uruguay Round to a spectator on the sidelines of the so-called Five Interested Parties (FIP) process, (India, Brazil, the E.U., U.S., and Australia). The "FIP" emerged as the power-brokering hub of the WTO after the Cancun Ministerial collapse of 2003. The FIP eventually accepted Japan into the fold, becoming the G-6, which continues its power hub role today.

Demise of the Development Agenda

Any cautious expectations that existed at the launch of the Doha round that Northern countries would make space for a new pro-equity agenda in global trade rules have been woefully un-met. Significant Southern proposals to address development issues in trade rules been dismissed or attacked. And, with a few exceptions, the direction of negotiations across the three "pillars" of agriculture, industrial tariffs and services is distinctly *anti*-developmental.

There has been an excessive focus on generating new market access for Northern corporations into large developing country economies, unabashedly often described as the price to be paid for any minor scaling-back in unfair Northern trade practices. Pressures to open developing country borders would force weaker but vital developing industries to "compete" with global corporate giants, while marginalized sectors of society would be exposed to increased price volatility.

Instructively, many Southern governments have also oriented their demands towards market access concessions for their products in the North. Limited political energy has gone to consideration of a trade framework that would enable all governments to meet their obligations to ensure decent work, address food insecurity and climate change, and reduce poverty. In short, the Doha "Development Round" has become a business-as-usual WTO trade round.

Most independent analyses have either drastically scaled back projections of poverty reduction gains from the Doha round or predict that the lion's share of gains will flow to the developed world, while the majority in Africa and low-income countries will actually be made worse off.[4] So much for the development agenda.

Canada's approach to the Doha Agenda, set under the previous Liberal government, has not changed much in recent years. "Development" has been rather narrowly cast as a question of time and money. That is, longer time frames for developing countries to hurry up and liberalize, and a rather disingenuous use of aid and technical assistance as a "development measure" to help developing countries adapt to trade rules not of their making.[5] Indeed, despite our successful experience as a mixed economy — partly open, partly closed, with a healthy role for government and public regulation to address market inadequacies — successive Canadian governments have advocated a more dogmatically open-border, market-based approach to development in trade rules.

Old wine and old bottles: Canada's WTO agenda since 2006

As the Conservative party took power in 2006, trade negotiators were still basking in the success — from their view — of rescuing the WTO Hong Kong Ministerial from collapse. The celebration was short-lived. Within six months, WTO Director General Pascal Lamy would announce the suspension of the Doha talks, given the complete standoff in the negotiating positions of the G-6. Although negotiations would officially resume the following year, the period since Hong Kong has been marked more by stop than by go. Two years of any-minute-now progress and breakthroughs have left a wake of missed deadlines, protracted negotiating stalemates, and failed Mini-Ministerials, including most recently in July of 2008. The lack of a full WTO Ministerial in December 2007 was the first missed biennial Ministerial since the WTO was created in 1995.[6]

In effect, the Doha Development Agenda is dead. Whatever deal may eventually come out of these protracted negotiations (and it is not a sure thing that one will), it will not have the scope that any party originally intended. Developing countries in their new strength and sophistication have been able to prevent many of the agendas to which they are opposed, without, however, being able to achieve very much of their own.

Although Canada has reduced political clout at the WTO, the Canadian government (with little distinction in the transition from Liberal to Conservative stewardship) has been an active participant in corroding the developmental prospects for the Round. In agriculture, Canada has joined a handful of countries aiming to weaken tools for developing countries to safeguard food security and shield millions of small farmers from being undercut by cheap or dumped products.

In the NAMA (Non-Agricultural Market Access) negotiations on industrial tariffs, Canada has sought an aggressive formula for market access that would hit developing countries disproportionately hard. As the chair of the NAMA negotiations from 2006 thru 2008, Canada came under fire from developing countries and southern analysts, who charged that draft texts were poorly crafted and biased, disregarding previously negotiated commitments to the South.[7] In the services negotiations, Canada has pushed for an aggressive liberalization approach, while not defending the right of all governments to pursue regulation of services in the public interest.

Canadian civil society and producer groups have also voiced strong concerns that Canada is not effectively containing threats in WTO rules to our own domestic public interest. For example, aspects of the services negotiations threaten the ability to maintain effective and well-regulated public services, while key tenets of the Canadian agricultural system, notably supply management, are directly targeted by the liberalization drive of WTO talks. Ironically, after years of successful defences of the Canadian Wheat Board (CWB) before WTO panels, the Conservative government has now distinguished itself through its election commitment to undo the Board's monopoly powers. If implemented, this would sound the death knell on a vital institution that increases farmers' power in highly concentrated corporate markets.[8]

Importantly, the past few years have seen a growing debate and challenge to the WTO's agenda — both within developing country government caucuses and among citizen movements around the world. Clear messages have been sent, to capitals and Geneva-based ambassadors, of the political costs at home for bad performance abroad. Citizens have mobilized nationally and globally, given the profound impacts of binding neoliberal trade and investment rules on lives, livelihoods, and the environment. Demands have grown for more consideration and debate of the public interest as it relates to the trade and investment regime, and for more accountability in policy agendas linked to States' binding obligations to human rights and the environment. There is a growing push for multilateral trade rules to provide more policy space for governments to discuss and decide appropriate development strategies with their own citizens as a matter of democratic practice.

How did the Harper government approach this era of heightened citizen expectations and profound illness at the WTO? Canada remains rhetorically committed to the multilateral trade system and still uses its institutions to defend Canadian interests. Indeed, the WTO has been a pillar of Canadian trade strategy as a middle power that is highly dependent on trade but with limited scope for direct influence on our largest trading partner. Canada's 2007 WTO challenge of U.S. corn subsidies was cheered and then joined by Brazil, Argentina, and many other countries. But, while lamenting the WTO stalemate, Canada has displayed no interest in any significant re-think of our approach to multilateral trade policy.

Canada has essentially fiddled while the WTO burns. No consideration has been given to the possibilities of new allies and shared interests with the South's development agenda.[9] There has been no push for fundamental institutional reform of the WTO, let alone creative thinking about multilateral trade policy that might better meet our legal obligations to human rights standards and citizens expectations for an international agenda that promotes equity and safeguards health and the environment.

Keeping familiar wine in familiar bottles, the Harper government even asked David Emerson, the previous Liberal Trade Minister, to cross the floor and join the Conservative cabinet to continue leading Canada's trade agenda. Canadian voters, not least of all in Vancouver Kingsway who thought they voted Liberal, were shocked at this sacrifice of democratic principle. But it displayed a kind of pragmatism in Canadian trade policy that would be echoed by the Conservative government in the ensuing years, including in the bilateral agenda.

Canada and the pursuit of bilateral trade deals

Adding to the global spaghetti bowl

As the multilateral system founders, large trading powers have accelerated the pursuit of bilateral trade agreements and partnerships — quite outside a development agenda. Canada has participated vigorously in this trend to sew up bilateral trade deals while whipping the proverbial Doha Round horse, which continues its loop of stagger and collapse.

Previous Canadian governments have pursued bilateral trade deals: NAFTA 1994, Israel 1997, Chile 1997, and Costa Rica 2002. Lower on the radar, talks with India and China for bilateral investment agreements have been pursued by Canada for some time. But the Harper government era has been marked by a much more aggressive pursuit and closure of bilateral trade and investment agreements, completing three deals in its short tenure, including the European Free Trade Association (EFTA) group of countries (Liechtenstein, Iceland, Norway, and Switzerland in 2007), Peru (2008), and Colombia (concluded 2008 but not yet signed or ratified at time of printing).

Several others have been launched though are not yet concluded, including with South Korea, Jordan, the Dominican Republic, Panama, and exploratory talks with CARICOM countries of the Caribbean. The recent Canadian push for bilateral trade agreements reflects the new prioritization of the Americas as a focus for Canadian foreign policy. There has also been a wave of bilateral investment agreement negotiations launched.[10]

Placed in the larger global context, these bilateral agreements have contributed to what has been termed a "spaghetti bowl" of bilateral trade and investment obligations around the planet, undermining attempts to build meaningful global rules.[11] The power dynamics of bilateral negotiations (typically between a Northern and a Southern country or sub-region) are much more uneven than in multilateral negotiations, in which small countries can band together with larger to form more powerful negotiating blocks. Bilateral negotiations in the modern era have produced highly controversial agreements. Concessions made in bilateral negotiations then erode both incentives and prospects at the global level for any substantive re-working of trade arrangements to favour global equity and international development goals.[12]

Something old...

Many features of Canadian bilateral trade deals pursued by the Harper government reflect a continuing commitment to the now long-standing NAFTA model. In the first instance, the bilateral deals maintain an essential orientation to further open borders for key goods and services exports. Moreover, while there may be cooperation agreements, financing, and phased-in implementation timing for the developing partners, there are none of the more substantive and innovative developmental elements that developing countries are fighting for at the WTO. For example, in agriculture there are no provisions for a "special safeguard mechanism" that would enable the developing country partner to raise duties in response to a sudden import surge, or a "special product" designation that would exempt crops key to food security from further tariff lowering.

While government procurement, competition and e-commerce are issues expressly resisted by the South as an area for new disciplines in multilateral negotiations, they are present in many Canadian bilateral FTAs. Canadian agreements also always contain an investment chapter. These chapters are based on the NAFTA Chapter 11 and offer protections and rights for foreign investors unparallelled in any other multilateral agreement. Provisions include investor rights to sue governments in closed commercial hearings over alleged public policy measures that interfere with profit-making.[13]

Importantly, since 2005 there has been significant evolution in public policy debate in Canada regarding investors' social responsibilities overseas. There is growing consensus on the inadequacy of voluntary measures to ensure good performance in environmental or human rights terms, particularly in the extractive sector — one of the main areas of Canadian investment in the Americas. Recommendations from a June 2008 report from Canada's Standing Committee on International Trade (CIIT) called for legislative measures to ensure corporate accountability to the implementation of human rights standards in any future Canada-Colombia trade deal. But these preoccupations are not reflected in any recent Canadian FTA or investment agreement. Rather, ineffectual exhortations to encourage corporations to respect social responsibility standards can be found in the preamble to the recent Peru and, likely, Colombia deals.

Many of the recently-launched bilateral deals also continue the NAFTA tradition of side-deals on labour and environment, despite the overall criticism of these as ineffectual tools to address the labour rights and environmental issues generated from liberalized trade.[14] The 2008 Peru Agreement was hailed by the government as carving new ground for labour protection. It mirrors the labour chapters of the recent deals signed by Peru and Colombia with the U.S. It includes the possibility of fines paid to a special jointly managed labour assistance fund by an offending government in cases of protracted violations. Since the same government is likely to be the main recipient of the funds, the mechanism has come under attack by opposition and labour voices as a means to "pay a fine" to oneself for labour rights violations.[15]

The essential point of the weakness of side-deals and labour chapters as a means to address the labour rights issues raised by trade liberalization has been stated well by the Canadian Association of Labour Lawyers, who point out that trade agreements are not written to improve labour standards, and their general effect has been to bring downward pressure on labour rights.[16]

Finally, a continued hallmark of Canadian bilateral trade deals remains the closed and non-transparent process for their negotiation. Input may be formally solicited from the public through internet-based consultation processes. However, these provide little if any information to organizations seeking to understand and influence the government's agenda and have no feedback loop, rendering them pointless. In the summer of 2007, an internet-based consultation to help develop Canada's agenda for intellectual property issues was launched even as negotiators were already pursuing an IP agenda in bilateral trade talks with Peru and Colombia. Officials would provide no information on what Canada was seeking, and no response was ever received from letters of concern that were sent by civil society organizations.

Draft texts or even basic negotiating goals and positions are not disclosed or debated publicly on bilateral deals. Even for WTO processes there is more publicly available information on proposals and counter-proposals made by governments. It is important to note that, in contrast, industry groups have considerable access and substantive consultation roles on texts and positions.

...Something new

Apart from its breadth and pace, what else differentiates Canada's bilateral trade agenda in this period? There has been a decided Americas slant to the recent pursuit of bilaterals. Trade agreements seem to be the primary implementation feature of Canada's otherwise not well-defined new "Americas Strategy."[17] This strategy was launched in July of 2007 by the prime minister with ambitious talk of a higher profile for Canada in our own hemisphere to promote prosperity, security, and "the fundamental values of freedom, democracy, human rights, and the rule of law."[18] Understanding this wider foreign policy context provides important insight into some of the new features of the recent bilateral trade agenda.

In launching the Americas Strategy with a major speech in Chile, Prime Minister Harper raised concerns regarding the wave of governments choosing populist, authoritarian, and socialist paths in the region. With little reflection on the substantive differences among Latin America's new "left" economic experimentation, let alone the importance for countries to set their own development path, Harper warned against this trend. Canada was identified as offering a different, more balanced model to be emulated over the more extreme capitalism of the

U.S. At the same time, "free trade" was positioned explicitly as a means to set countries on the right path.[19]

While heralding human rights as core Canadian values and trying to differentiate Canada from the U.S., the prime minister courted U.S. allies in the region for trade partners, including Peru and, most controversially, Colombia, the government with arguably the worst human rights record in the region. Incredibly, Harper even lobbied for the U.S.-Colombia trade deal, urging Democrats who were withholding support for the deal on principled human rights grounds to support the deal to save democracy in Colombia. (See Katz elsewhere in this volume.)

The point to note is that previous Canadian governments often took pains to downplay the political implications of trade agreements, pointing to basic market efficiency theories as the rationale. With the Americas Strategy, the Harper government has identified bilateral trade deals as an explicit component of a new U.S.-style strategic approach for Canada's role in the region to help keep governments on the "right" political path. Other analysts have also noted the growing links under the Harper government between the trade and security agendas in the Americas, as profiled in the Security and Prosperity Partnership Initiative with the U.S. and Mexico.[20] The link to a more U.S.-influenced trade agenda can also be seen in the details of the bilateral trade deals in the Americas. Perhaps the most significant policy departure is in intellectual property rights (IPRs).

At the multilateral level, there is a heated debate on the developmental impacts of high intellectual property standards. At the World Intellectual Property Organization (WIPO) and the WTO TRIPS Council, developing countries are working for a developmentally-friendly policy environment for technology issues, from protection of biodiversity and addressing bio-piracy, to technology transfers, to generic competition for medicines.

This development agenda for IPRs has been met with resistance and backlash from pharmaceutical companies, among others. Industry groups have mounted a number of initiatives to lock-in market protections and monopoly control.[21] Pursuing IPR commitments beyond WTO requirements has been a hallmark strategy for U.S. bilateral trade agreements. Canada has not historically been a promoter of this agenda. Yet, as a part of the new focus on bilateral trade deals in the Americas, the Canadian government pursued intellectual property demands in the negotiations with Peru, Colombia, and the Dominican Republic. While the goals and agenda for Canada were never made public, one can assume Canada was not seeking to lower IP standards.

More generally, signals from the Harper government on intellectual property have been troubling. In 2006, Canada unilaterally changed its policies to increase data exclusivity protection for patented drugs from five to eight years.[22] This move surprised analysts, since it was a "concession" made outside the context of a trade negotiation and beyond what Canada's WTO commitments require. It also had significant cost implications for Canadian health care.[23] The move to add IP to bilateral trade negotiations fits this trend of a growing pro-IPR orientation in Canadian policy.

Finally, it is worth noting a pragmatist trend on the bilateral agenda, perhaps one which is part of the commitment to rapid acquisition of new trade deals. While there is a new political framework clearly at play in the Americas and in the trade agenda generally, the government has also been adaptable to circumstance. When negotiations on the Andean pact for a joint agreement with Peru and Colombia began to falter, because the Colombia negotiations were more difficult, the Canadian government severed them and moved to close the Peru deal separately and in record time. When talks on intellectual property were proving difficult with these same Andean partners, Canada dropped its insistence on an IP chapter.

Parliament and civil society respond

The context of minority government

What has been the public and political reaction to the Canadian agenda on trade and investment since 2006? A defining part of the Canadian political context in the last five years has been minority governments. In the parliamentary system, a minority government still holds executive power and wields control over policy. But there is a sharp public and political sensibility that the mandate is limited, the threat of confidence motions is potent, and the legislative agenda requires careful manoeuvring. The role of Parliament in shaping the public agenda, in addition to controlling legislative outcomes, becomes more pronounced. This has been no less true with respect to the trade agenda.

As a result, Parliament has become an important entry point for civil society and for the concerned public on trade issues. Where constituencies raised concerns, notably with the South Korea deal and Colombia, the role of parliamentarians and parliamentary committees has been important. Parliament has been able to question deals, prolong debate, and shape the media reporting on the negotiations, ultimately influencing the negotiating context. Other deals, such as with EFTA and the Dominican Republic, have received less public attention and correspondingly there has been less parliamentary involvement.

The power of constituency and citizen action: Korea and Colombia

Canadian labour, notably the auto-workers' union, mobilized in significant numbers against the Korea deal, based on the likely adverse consequences for Canada in terms of manufacturing exports and jobs.[24] Opposition parties, through the Standing Committee on International Trade (CIIT), devoted significant resources and time to hearings, questioning officials and ministers repeatedly on the terms of the deal. The Canada-Korea deal remains not concluded, due not only to public critique but also significant challenges in the negotiations themselves and domestic political uncertainties in South Korea.

The Canada-Colombia deal was intended to be a quick process. Negotiators of the deal, launched in July 2007 alongside Peru, aimed to wrap up the talks by the end of that year. The executive power of Canadian government meant that nothing, in principle, stood in the way of a signing, save the negotiations themselves. Achieving a quick deal with Canada was important to the political agendas of both President Alvaro Uribe, who needed a good housekeeping seal of approval from the international community, and of Prime Minister Harper. For the latter, the deal was the flagship initiative of his new Americas Strategy and a nice deliverable for President George Bush, who could use Canada's approval as motivation to move the U.S. agreement through Congress.

But neither civil society nor Parliament would let the Colombia deal go by without a fight. Human rights, labour, and development organizations mobilized significant media attention at Canada's choice of Colombia as a trade partner. For its part, while the CIIT was slow to take up Colombia, being preoccupied with the larger South Korea deal, it eventually forced Minister Emerson to appear to answer questions. The CIIT also undertook a major study on the human rights and environmental impacts of the deal.

The visit to Canada of U.S. Congressman Michel Michaud, a leader in the Democratic caucus against the U.S.-Colombia deal, played an important role in alerting Opposition parties and the Canadian government to the wider geopolitical implications for Canada in forging ahead to sign with Uribe, especially in the context of the impending U.S. elections. Colombia sent senior officials and the Vice-President to Ottawa, and Ottawa sent ministers to Bogotá in an obvious effort to regain moral ground and set the public record straight regarding the "commitment" of the Colombian government to human rights and democracy. This, notwithstanding the continued serious human rights violations in Colombia and a growing political scandal that was engulfing the Uribe administration, linking it to paramilitary death squads.

The Canadian government concluded negotiations with Colombia in June 2008, and with incredibly audacity announced that the deal was done just days before the CIIT was to wrap up hearings and produce its recommendations regarding the agreement. But with the negotiations closed, the CIIT report was superfluous. Parliament was not amused. This final act of arrogance united all three Opposition parties. The recommendations in the CIIT report include that no agreement with Colombia should proceed without a human rights impact assessment and without legislative provisions for ensuring corporate accountability of Canadian companies to human rights standards for their operations in Colombia. Shortly after the report's release, the Conservative party disassociated itself from the recommendations.

Power and vulnerability for the Harper trade agenda

On the whole, the Harper trade and investment agenda has obvious momentum. On the multilateral front, it is so similar to previous Canadian agendas that it generates little controversy. But on bilateral issues (and on NAFTA), which are more infused with signature new foreign policy directions, the agenda is more vulnerable. Parliament has the power to demonstrate that the new directions are a minority agenda and may not reflect the majority political will of the country. Could this ever have substantive policy effect? Not easily, but maybe.

The power of executive government, including the power to negotiate and ratify new treaties, remains intact. But the Conservative government, as part of its new "accountability" agenda, has brought in policy that requires all new international treaties to go before Parliament before ratification.[25] The new policy affords the possibility that Parliament can discuss, debate, or even vote on a treaty (even if not binding). If parliamentary opposition were united in the majority against a particular treaty, a vote could display that the will of Parliament opposes a deal. The jury is out on whether the government would exercise its legal authority to continue with the deal, or bow to Parliament's wish not to ratify. This would pit the government's commitment to parliamentary accountability against its commitment to free trade agreements. The government's recent dismissal of the CIIT report on Colombia bodes ill for the "accountability" side.

One thing is certain: recent public debate over the direction of trade and investment policy is unlikely to diminish. The world's current triple crises — finance, food and climate — are all linked to an overly dogmatic commitment to the liberalization of capital, trade, and investment flows. These predilections are compounded by inadequate public oversight and regulation to safeguard the interests of ordinary people and the environment. The debate — in Canada and globally — will continue.

Harper and NAFTA-Plus

Deep integration by stealth

Bruce Campbell

THE NORTH AMERICAN Free Trade Agreement (NAFTA), along with its predecessor, the Canada-U.S. Free Trade Agreement (FTA), has been the primary legislative edifice shaping Canada-U.S. integration since 1989. However, NAFTA was never the end-game for business élites. Rather, it was a vehicle for advancing the broader goal of deepening integration. Rarely articulated, the end-game is a unified continental market with harmonized institutions, policies and regulations, and with the border as an economic impediment fading into insignificance.

Given the huge power imbalance among the three countries, "adjustment" by the smaller partners to the more privatized, deregulated U.S. model — a kind of informal political integration — is the desired ultimate outcome.

Especially after September 11, 2001, it became obvious to big business and the policy establishment that NAFTA by itself was no longer adequate. Moreover, at the same time as incremental measures to extend and deepen NAFTA were being implemented, the U.S. preoccupation with homeland security was forcing the project into a defensive mode. Instead of the border fading into insignificance, it was actually thickening, thanks to intensified U.S. security measures and Canadian efforts to comply with them.

At the urging of big business, North American leaders convened the Security and Prosperity Partnership accord (SPP) in March 2005. Political leaders knew that a highly visible, comprehensive NAFTA-plus negotiation would be politically risky, given the level of public controversy it was sure to provoke. The SPP (now in its fourth year) is their Plan B — an executive-level process, out of the eye of the public and parliamentarians, through which they are advancing their deep integration priorities incrementally. NAFTA Leaders and key Ministers meet regularly with business representatives through an SPP advisory body called the North American Competitiveness Council (NACC). Business outlines its priorities, the politicians respond, consensus is reached, and civil servants implement.

The Harper government's initiatives to deepen NAFTA-style integration with the United States appear more like a continuation than a radical departure from the Martin Liberals. This is not surprising since big business (to which both parties have close ties) has been driving the agenda and since the policy establishment is on board with the general direction, if the not the precise shape and speed, of integration.

Modest differences, however, can have large consequences. For the Liberal government, deep integration was more a practical necessity — inevitable if not desirable. The Harper Conservatives are more enthusiastic about deep integration, which they see as part of their long-term goal to remould Canada into a conservative society more in the image of the United States.

Minority status has thus far limited the Harper government's ability to implement its agenda through legislation. But it has made significant progress at the executive/administrative and regulatory levels, largely out of public view. Since the dominant political culture in Canada is progressive, Conservative strategists know they must move carefully, maintaining a moderate image if they are to avoid electoral defeat and eventually achieve a majority government.

This chapter examines several NAFTA-plus initiatives that illustrate the Harper government's efforts to cement even further its alliance with big business, ingratiate itself with the U.S. administration, and use NAFTA to advance its own political agenda. Security and military initiatives — also part of the deep integration agenda — are not covered here. Finally, it addresses the issue of NAFTA renegotiation in light of a possible U.S. Obama presidency and makes some preliminary suggestions for a progressive response to the renegotiation challenge.

The Softwood Lumber Agreement

In April 2006, several months after the Harper government took office, it signed a preliminary settlement to the long-standing softwood lumber dispute, the latest round of which had dragged on since 2001.

The deal, ratified in the fall of 2006, was a major capitulation to U.S. demands. The Canadian industry had won virtually all of its appeals under NAFTA and the WTO against U.S. countervailing and anti-dumping duties on Canadian exporters. Yet the U.S. government continued to ignore the rulings, using every trick in the book to delay and obstruct. More recently, Canada had taken its case to the U.S. trade court, where it was also winning.

The previous government had balked at the American demands — even as the major exporting provinces (notably British Columbia) unilaterally changed their forest policies to comply with U.S. demands — choosing to let the legal proceedings run their course. But the Harper government was eager to demonstrate that it was better able to "normalize" relations with the U.S., which had become strained in the wake of Canada's opposition to the Iraq war and Missile Defence, and get the softwood issue off the front pages in order to pursue its own deep integration agenda. Moreover, American demands were more in line with the kinds of "free market" changes that the Conservatives favoured.

In July 2006, as the deal, which imposed a combination of quotas and a 15% export tax on Canadian producers, was being finalized, a U.S. court issued a preliminary ruling in favour of the Canadian exporters. Also on October 13, 2006, one day after the Softwood Lumber Agreement entered into force, the U.S. Court issued its final ruling: there was no subsidy to Canadian exporters and no injury or threat of injury to U.S. producers.

With the exception of a small group of multinationals, most producers were unhappy with the Softwood Agreement. But most were experiencing severe financial stress, and the Harper government bullied them into accepting the settlement by threatening to withhold future finance or support.

The deal gave back 80% of the $5.2 billion in duties that the U.S. authorities had collected from the Canadian industry. Contrary to U.S. and international law, the U.S. government kept a 20% cut, half of which it distributed to the U.S. lumber lobby, also contrary to both U.S. and international law. The deal also implicitly accepted the U.S. argument that Canadian governments were in fact subsidizing producers, when in fact all legal rulings found otherwise. Finally, it gave the U.S. government the right to oversee any future changes in Canadian forest policies.

The deal set up a new dispute resolution mechanism, replacing international and national court processes: the London Court of International Arbitration. With the Agreement barely in effect, the U.S. government was back knocking at the Court's door, alleging Canadian breaches of the agreement on the tax and quotas levels and government assistance to producers in Québec and Ontario.

In June 2008, the U.S. Congress, contrary to the Agreement, passed legislation authorizing U.S. border officials to monitor the Agreement and verify that Canadian exporters were complying with the Agreement, and empowering them to conduct audits and issue fines for non-compliance. Thus continues — despite the "settlement" and the loss of sovereignty over forest policy — another round of U.S. harassment and obstruction.

The combined effect of export tax, the dramatic rise of the Canadian dollar, record fuel prices, and the slump in the U.S. housing market have all been catastrophic for Canadian softwood producers. Mills, often in single-industry communities, have shut down, businesses have gone bankrupt, and thousands of workers have been thrown out of work.

Canadian Wheat Board

The U.S. government has long pressured Canada to dismantle the Canadian Wheat Board (CWB), the government farmer-run agency that is the sole marketer of prairie grain. Unsuccessful in the FTA and NAFTA negotiations, the U.S. government brought numerous complaints against the CWB before NAFTA and WTO tribunals, all of them unsuccessful.

At last the U.S. had a powerful ally within Canada to achieve a goal that had so long eluded it. The Conservatives themselves (as well as the Alliance and Reform parties from which they had sprung) have long wanted to get rid of the Wheat Board, and they see NAFTA as a lever to help achieve their goal.

The legality of the Wheat Board under NAFTA and the WTO stems from the fact that it is a monopoly. Once the Harper government succeeds in breaking down its monopoly from within, and once private companies are allowed to compete alongside the Board, then American WTO and NAFTA challenges to the legality of the CWB become much more likely to succeed.

Shortly after the Conservatives assumed power, the Minister of Agriculture convened a task force on the Wheat Board, which the Board itself boycotted. The task force's October 2006 report recommended ending the Wheat Board monopoly in two years. U.S. trade officials publicly praised the Canadian announcement.

The government wasted little time in setting in motion its strategy, as a cabinet document recently released under court order has revealed. Following this blueprint, the government imposed a gag order on the Board to prevent it from defending itself, fired its CEO, Adrian Meisner, held a rigged plebiscite on whether to remove single-desk CWB authority for marketing barley, and announced that, as of August 1, 2007, barley would no longer be under the exclusive marketing control of the CWB, but would have to compete with private companies.

However, a federal court judge ordered the government to halt the removal of barley from the CWB's control, determining that its action was illegal because, among other things, it did not hold the required parliamentary vote. Then, in June 2008, another judge ruled that the government acted illegally in imposing the gag order on the Board.

These setbacks have not weakened Harper's resolve. In the wake of the barley ruling, he said the government would succeed "one way or another." Clearly frustrated after the court's lifting of the gag order on the Board, Harper responded with his own heavy-handed view of democracy: "The bottom line is this, mark my words… Western Canadian farmers want this freedom and they are going to get it, and anybody who stands in their way is going to get walked over."[1]

Several bills currently before Parliament would do just that. Bill C-39 would take away the Canadian Grain Commission's mandate to inspect and regulate grain. Bill C-46 would take away the right of barley producers to a vote on the CWB's role, and Bill C-57 would revamp the voters' list for Director elections taking place in the fall, disenfranchising even more farmers.

If Harper were to achieve his coveted goal of majority government, the major stumbling block to the Conservatives' efforts would be removed. The impact on farmers, grain handlers, and grain-dependent communities would be devastating. (See Forsey elsewhere in this volume.)

Intellectual property

At about the same time as the Harper government was caving in on softwood, it was amending Canada's drug patent regulations on data exclusivity, effectively extending the period during which the drug multinationals have exclusive monopoly rights — something the U.S. had been demanding for years. Generic drug companies now have to wait six years after a brand name drug has entered the market to *apply* for approval to market a generic equivalent, and another two years to actually obtain market approval. Until then, the government could *approve* a generic drug during the first five years after the brand name drug received market approval, using the brand name company's test data.

This change makes it even more difficult to bring cheaper generic drugs to market, and hence tilts the balance even further toward protecting patent holders and away from the law's mandate to balance patent protection with affordably priced medicines.

The other issue, currently before Parliament, is Canadian copyright law. The U.S. has been pushing hard for Canada to adopt its copyright infringement laws. USTR officials have for several years put Canada on its annual intellectual property Priority Watch list.[2]

U.S. Ambassador David Wilkins has made it a priority, publicly calling on Canada to toughen its copyright law and alleging that Canada's copyright law was "the weakest in the G-7," then following it up with a letter to Stephen Harper urging greater enforcement.[3]

The U.S. administration also made intellectual property a top priority at the SPP table, as did the big business council's (NACC) February 2007 report to SPP ministers. One of the four priority deliverables announced at the Montebello summit was an Intellectual Property Action Plan to combat piracy and counterfeiting. Though not reported, sources told University of Ottawa Internet expert Michael Geist that U.S. officials told their counterparts that any progress on Canadian concerns such as "the thickening border" would be contingent on "progress" on Canadian copyright changes.[4]

The government introduced its amendments to the copyright act in June 2008 (Bill C-61). According to Geist, priority No. 1 for the Harper government was to meet U.S. demands, and Bill C-61 delivered. The bill has been dubbed by its critics the *Canadian Digital Millennium Copyright Act* because of its close resemblance to the U.S. legislation of the same name. Geist said the bill skews the balance between creator and user rights, eviscerating the latter, erects new barriers for teachers and students, and makes it impossible to protect privacy against invasion by digital media companies.

Regulatory harmonization: Food, drugs and chemicals

Continental regulatory harmonization is central to the deep integration, or NAFTA-plus, agenda. Many of the SPP initiatives are regulatory in nature. One of the few announced "deliverables" of the Montebello Summit was a regulatory harmonization framework agreement and a sub-agreement on chemicals regulation, and one of the five action priorities identified by the leaders coming out of the 2007 Montebello summit was "safe food and products." This was reinforced by the 2008 leaders' joint statement at the New Orleans summit, which directed officials to "collaborate to promote the compatibility of our related regulatory and inspection regimes" in the area of food and product safety.

It is extremely difficult, given the lack of transparency, to trace the line from the SPP to Canadian policy outcomes, but from the fragmentary information that has leaked out, the direction is toward relaxing rather than tightening existing regulations. For example, we've learned the following:

- An SPP working group has been negotiating the raising of limits of pesticide residues for produce entering Canada.
- The Montebello agreement on chemicals has shifted the Canadian chemicals regulation regime, which was till then positioned somewhere between the more stringent safety-first regime of the European Union's REACH program and the business-friendly American approach, into the U.S. regulatory camp.
- The American chemicals industry is using the SPP agreement in its global lobbying campaign to dilute and diminish the global impact of the European program, which they say puts too great a burden on the industry. The three NAFTA governments are pushing the Montebello accord as a counterweight to REACH in international forums.[5]
- In December 2007, the government announced its new policy on food and product safety. While giving the government new powers of product recall and enforcement, it also allowed the government to put new drugs on the market faster without the current level of safety testing. This business demand for relaxing drug-testing requirements was made by the NACC in its report to SPP Ministers.
- A leaked November 2007 Treasury Board memo revealed that the government was mandating the Canadian Food Inspection Agency to move toward the U.S. model of handing over key parts of food inspection to the industry, and downgrading the agency to performing an oversight role. According to an "anonymous leading Canadian academic expert on food risk management" interviewed by CanWest News, there is almost unanimous agreement among public health experts that the greatest risks of new infectious disease are related to animal products and food, and that "reducing food safety controls could be disastrous if there is an outbreak of a new food-borne disease..."[6] Moreover, these changes, along with the elimination of the payments to producers to test cattle for BSE, will increase the risk of another outbreak and U.S. closure of the border. (As this book goes to press, in the

wake of a deadly listeria outbreak at a Toronto meat processing plant, media reports reveal that the CFIA had already begun implementing [in March 2008] these food inspection deregulation measures outlined in the Treasury Board document.)

Foreign investment

The heart of NAFTA was the extensive deregulation of foreign investment controls, new limitations on the activities of public corporations, and new powers and freedoms for multinational corporations.

The NAFTA investor-state dispute mechanism is one of the most insidious provisions in NAFTA. It allows corporations to challenge (before an arbitration panel of judges) governments whom they claim have implemented laws or regulations that impede their profit opportunities. It has led to some 50 claims (18 against Canada), almost half of which involve challenges to policies or laws on environmental protection or resource management.[7]

Successful complaints have led to the reversal of some measures, but, more significantly, it has created an atmosphere of regulatory chill, discouraging governments from bringing in measures to protect the public. Moreover, because of its almost unlimited scope, it has extended NAFTA's reach into areas that were supposedly excluded from the Agreement, including water exports, log export controls, public postal services, agricultural supply management systems, cultural policy, etc.

The investor-state dispute provision allows corporate interests to trump the public good. Even FTA negotiator Gordon Ritchie called it "an ill-conceived construct." It should be scrapped. The Harper government has not called for changes to investor-state. Rather, it has stated emphatically that NAFTA should not be reopened. Given the Harper government's track record, it is almost certainly supportive of NAFTA's investor-state clause.

Foreign ownership limits in key sectors such as banking and telecommunications were maintained. Government could still screen foreign investment, but its scope and enforcement capacity were weakened. Until May 2008, when Industry Minister Jim Prentice denied the takeover of Canadian space company MacDonald Dettwiler by U.S. armsmaker Alliant Techsystems, Investment Canada had a "perfect" record of approving all 1,500 foreign takeovers since its inception in 1985. (See Watkins elsewhere in this volume.)

The MDA decision went against the Conservative image of opposing interference in corporate decision-making. This case was unique, however, and is unlikely to be repeated. On the contrary, it is more likely that the Conservative government will deregulate foreign investment beyond NAFTA.

Following a massive wave of foreign takeovers, Harper's handpicked panel of businessmen on foreign investment and competition policy, like the Manley panel before it, delivered the desired result. The June 2008 Panel report's recommendations included: tripling of the threshold that would trigger a review; shifting of the onus of proof from companies having to show "net benefit to Canada," to the government having to show that a proposed takeover is not in the "national interest;" and lifting of restrictions on foreign investment in banking, telecommunications and broadcast, airlines, uranium and cultural sectors.[8]

Deep integration extremists have been advocating these NAFTA-plus measures for years. They could well be part of a Harper majority government agenda.

Oil and gas

Arguably the biggest single concession Canadian negotiators made in NAFTA was to surrender control over our energy resources. With the U.S. share of Canadian production now guaranteed, soaring demand has boosted its share of Canadian gas to over 60%, and its share of oil to two-thirds and growing quickly. U.S. and Canadian corporations — with the blessing of the Alberta and federal governments — have been investing massively in the vast (and now commercially viable) Athabasca tar sands.

The main purpose of the SPP energy working group is to help reduce environmental and other regulatory barriers that stand in the way of tar sands development and construction of the pipeline infrastructure necessary to transport oil to U.S. markets. Bilateral pipeline agreements have been signed; and understandings have been reached on regulatory approvals, environmental assessments, etc. Little is known about these accords. However, the National Energy Board has recently approved several massive pipelines to carry raw bitumen from the tar sands to U.S. refineries. The capacity of the two most recent approvals exceeds the total volume of Alberta's 2006 oil exports.[9]

NAFTA renegotiation

The issue of NAFTA renegotiation came to the fore during the U.S. Democratic party primaries in the winter of 2008. Front runners Barack Obama and Hillary Clinton both pledged to reopen NAFTA, and, if Canada and Mexico refused, to scrap it altogether. Obama said NAFTA was a mistake and told *Meet the Press*: "I will make sure that we renegotiate NAFTA." He said he would use the threat of opting-out as the hammer to get improvements in NAFTA.[10]

Obama's stated renegotiation priorities are three-fold:

> We must add binding obligations to the NAFTA agreement to protect the right to collective bargaining and other core labour standards recognized by the International Labour Organization. Similarly, we must add binding environmental standards so that companies from one country cannot gain economic advantage by destroying the environment. And we should amend NAFTA to make clear that fair laws and regulations written to protect citizens in any of the three countries cannot be overridden simply at the request of foreign investors.[11]

Obama also said he would continue having annual meetings with the other NAFTA leaders, but that they would, unlike the SPP, be transparent and that big business would no longer have exclusive access. He would seek "active and open involvement of citizens, labour, the private sector and non-governmental organizations in setting the agenda and making progress."[12]

In March 2008, Obama's senior economic advisor, Austin Goolsbee, told Canadian consular officials not to worry about NAFTA renegotiation, that it was merely campaign posturing. Their notes from the meeting that were leaked to the press provoked a mini-incident in the Democratic campaign; and a louder scandal in Canada over the source of the leak (ostensibly from the Prime Minister's Office) and whether Stephen Harper was trying to influence the American presidential race.

Canadian politicians, business leaders, media pundits and peddlers of free trade conventional wisdom responded with predictable bluster. Then Trade Minister David Emerson warned: "If you open it [NAFTA] for one or two issues, you cannot avoid reopening it across a range of issues." He added that Americans' privileged access to Canada's massive oil and gas reserves could be disrupted.[13]

NAFTA leaders and business representatives assembled for the fourth SPP summit in New Orleans also warned against reopening the agreement. At the leaders' press conference, Harper stated that "we" need to "deepen NAFTA even more." He then repeated the oil threat: "Canada is the United States' No. 1 supplier of energy. We are a secure, stable supplier. That is of critical importance to the future of the United States... If we had to look at this kind of an option, I'd say quite frankly we'd be in a stronger position now than we were 20 years ago, and we'll be in a stronger position in the future."[14]

Obama, now confirmed as the Democratic presidential candidate, has softened his tone. In a June 2008 interview with *Fortune* magazine, he conceded that the campaign rhetoric got a little overheated. Obama said he believed in "opening up a dialogue" with trading partners Canada and Mexico, "and figuring out how we can make this work for all people." His opponents have characterized this as a flip-flop, dismissing the likelihood of a real NAFTA renegotiation. However, this "don't worry" approach may be premature. Though his tone may have changed, there is no indication at this point that his original intent with regard to labour and environmental standards and foreign investor rights has altered.

What the people think...

In the U.S., a May 1, 2008 Pew Research Centre poll found that 48% of Americans think free trade agreements such as NAFTA are bad, compared to 35% who think they are good; 61% think that they have destroyed jobs, 9% think they have created jobs, and 56% think they depress wages. A June 20, 2008 Rasmussen Reports national poll found that 56% of Americans want NAFTA renegotiated, including 49% of Republican voters.

In Canada, a March 10, 2008 Angus Reid poll found that 45% of Canadians think the federal government should "do whatever is necessary" to renegotiate NAFTA; 24% think NAFTA should continue under its current terms, and 8% think Canada should do what it can to leave NAFTA altogether.

Finally, a June 2008 Strategic Council Globe-CTV poll comparing Canadian and American opinions found that 44% of Canadians think free trade has been bad for Canada; 43% think it has been good. This compares with 36% of Americans who think it's been bad for the U.S. and 46% who think it's been good for their country.

The Strategic Counsel expressed surprise at the Canadian results:

> Given the prominence of the issue in the U.S. in recent years, and especially in the presidential primaries, it's not surprising that opposition is high in that country. In Canada, with broad cross-party support for free trade and the almost universal buy-in from our media, government and business élites, the high level of opposition will surprise many. This is a sleeper issue among Canadians.[15]

The degree of Canadian public discontent with NAFTA, despite the relentless pounding of the NAFTA propaganda machine for the last 20 years, is truly remarkable. Imagine how much more widespread the discontent would be if inconvenient truths about NAFTA impacts or the actual contents of the Agreement were given a fair voice in the mainstream media.

Conclusion

Clearly, the Harper government and the Canadian business community do not want to renegotiate NAFTA. They especially don't want environment, labour, or investor issues on the table since it could mean a serious recasting of the NAFTA model. They want to advance their NAFTA-plus agenda defensively to reverse the thickening of the border, and offensively to push ahead with military and security integration, harmonized regulations, laws and policies, a customs union, a North American dispute tribunal, etc.

A majority of Canadians, on the other hand, want to renegotiate or scrap NAFTA. As with many other public policy issues, the gap between élite opinion and that of the general public is wide, indeed.

Although not currently high on the list of Canadians' priorities, it could become a proxy for discontent, for example, around economic issues such as the loss of manufacturing jobs. The NDP is the only major national party calling for renegotiation. The Liberals might, if this occurs, jump on the renegotiation bandwagon, but the Chrétien flip-flop over NAFTA during the 1993 election could present credibility problems.

The items Obama put on the table — environmental and labour protections and investor rights — could benefit people in all three countries if they succeed in rebalancing power relations between corporations and citizens, between private interests and the public good.

However, they will meet with powerful resistance from entrenched corporate interests in all three countries. Obama may not have the will or determination to follow through and make a truly significant reform. In the face of other more pressing issues, NAFTA may take a back seat and changes may be disappointing. Nevertheless, progressive forces in Canada should embrace the renegotiation challenge.

Integral to building the case for renegotiation, as the 15th anniversary of NAFTA and the 20th anniversary of the FTA approaches, progressives should step up their efforts to educate Canadians about the failure of NAFTA within the broader frame of the failed neoliberal experiment: how it depresses wages, displaces jobs, exacerbates patterns of inequality, heightens insecurity, constrains the ability of governments to act in the public interest, and limits the scope of public services.

Progressives in all three countries should outline what a set of labour and environmental provisions should look like in a revised NAFTA. (Perhaps it should be renamed the North American Trade and Development Accord to signal a change in the model.) They should jointly call for the scrapping of the investor-state dispute mechanism, and they should call for the replacement of the SPP initiative with a different mandate: transparent, and with full participation of parliaments and civil society.

They should explore other common proposals for reshaping the terms of North American integration to curb the power of the corporations. These could include joint or complementary industrial policy initiatives to curb corporate offshoring of production and jobs, and measures to limit tax avoidance by corporations and the wealthy. They could include provisions that place a floor, preventing downward harmonization of environmental, labour, and social standards and social dumping, while providing incentives to jurisdictions to implement higher standards and protections.

Progressives in each country will also want put forward issues specific to their national reality. For Canada, the priority list would include:

- an end to proportional sharing of energy;
- exclusion of water from NAFTA;
- restoration of active industrial policy measures; and
- strengthening of government powers to protect and enhance public programs and services.

Progressives in all three countries should pursue, wherever possible, common or complementary strategies and policies. However, processes of continental integration (benign or otherwise) very quickly spill over into to the political realm, raising questions of nationalism, diversity, democracy, culture and values, especially for the smaller partners. How to achieve the right balance between national policy flexibility, autonomy consistent with democracy and international cooperation, and the strategic pooling of sovereignty is an ongoing challenge of our time. In the case of North America, the concept of pooling sovereignty, where one partner vastly outstrips the others in size and power and is congenitally averse to the idea, is challenging in the extreme.

The Softwood Lumber Agreement

Snatching defeat from the jaws of victory

Guy Caron

IT WOULD BE difficult to deny that Canadian politics have been increasingly polarized since January 2006. The handling of most public policy issues by the minority Conservative government has usually led to a great deal of acrimony and confrontation among political parties and stakeholders.

The 2006 Softwood Lumber Agreement is the exception to the rule. Inheriting the trade dispute which predated the Canada-U.S. Free Trade Agreement (CUFTA), the Conservatives managed to unite usually disparate voices against them, such as the *National Post*, the NDP, a major Fraser Institute spokesperson, and almost all players in the crucial forestry industry.

How did they enrage so many, so quickly? In recent years, the dispute had cost Canadian producers US$5 billion as Canadian softwood lumber was exported to the United States. The U.S. producers maintained that Canada was engaged in unfair trading practices and imposed an extra duty, which was then collected into a fund. Although trade panels continued to rule in Canada's favour, the U.S. lobby was relentless. A few weeks after coming to power, the neophyte Conservatives announced they had come to a deal with the Americans.

Conservative broken election promises

The public flogging the Conservatives received was well deserved. A few months earlier, at the Conservative party's Halifax convention, Stephen Harper, then leader of the Official Opposition, stated that any Canadian Prime Minister should ensure that the U.S. respect the rule of trade law:

> It is at least now established that the Prime Minister and President will speak about the softwood issue in the hopefully not too distant future. If I were Prime Minister at that time, what would a Conservative Prime Minister say in that conversation?
>
> First and foremost, I would seek a clear commitment of the United States to comply with the NAFTA ruling. If the Canada-U.S. trade relationship is to remain a fair, stable, rules-based system, then the United States has a moral obligation to return those duties to Canadian lumber companies.
>
> There can be no question of Canada returning to a conventional bargaining table, as the U.S. ambassador has suggested.
>
> You don't negotiate after you've won.
>
> The issue is compliance. And achieving full compliance should be the objective of the Prime Minister.[1]

It is now clear that Stephen Harper did not follow his own advice before signing the Softwood Lumber Agreement. Worse, the Conservatives were so desperate to get an agreement — any agreement — that they broke no less than three 2006 electoral campaign promises to get it.[2]

First, in line with Harper's Halifax speech, the Conservatives promised to "demand that the U.S. government play by the rules on softwood lumber" and "that the U.S. abide by the NAFTA ruling and return more than US$5 billion in illegal softwood lumber tariffs." This did not happen.

Secondly, the Conservatives reneged on the promise to "provide real help for Canadian workers and businesses coping with illegal American trade actions" by guaranteeing the repayment of the illegal tariffs through

Export Development Canada. The forest companies were thus promised a win-win situation: they were getting back what they paid in tariffs from the U.S. (provided they won in court), or from the Canadian government (if they lost). In either case, they would get the much-needed security necessary to ensure sound investment decisions.

Once in power, the Conservatives refused to provide direct help or guarantee any loan to help the industry stay afloat. There were dire consequences, as the president of the Québec Forest Industry Council (QFIC), Guy Chevrette, attested to the House of Commons Standing Committee on International Trade[3]:

> On August 18, the Québec industry considered whether it would be better to accept a somewhat imperfect agreement or not have an agreement at all. The consensus was that we should accept the imperfect agreement, for a whole host of reasons...
>
> Would the result of vote [of the members of the QFIC] have been the same? Well, I can tell you that there would not have been as broad a consensus if there had been real loan guarantees in place...
>
> A whole host of reasons prompted people to vote the way they did. Some were just completely fed up and disgusted with the whole dispute. In other cases, their financial position is extremely weak. And as you know full well, others still have just asked for protection under the Bankruptcy and Insolvency Act. For them, these deposits will be a shot in the arm.

The third broken promise? The Conservative electoral platform vowed to "make all votes in Parliament, except the budget and main estimates, free votes" for ordinary Members of Parliament. But Stephen Harper declared the ratification of the Agreement by the House of Commons to be a motion of confidence in the government, in spite of this electoral commitment.

The root of the problem

The 2006 Softwood Lumber Agreement didn't put an end to the crisis which, it should be remembered, dates back over 25 years, not to 2001, as is commonly assumed.[4]

TABLE 1 *History of the Softwood Lumber Agreement*

Countervailing duty investigations	Outcome
Softwood Lumber I: 1982	U.S. authorities decided there was no Canadian subsidy
Softwood Lumber II: 1986	15% U.S. Import tax; Replaced by 15% Canadian export tax in MOU
Softwood Lumber III: 1991	After CUFTA, Canada unilaterally terminates the MOU; Countervailing case filed by U.S.; Canada wins appeal against countervailing duty in CUFTA (1993 and 1994); U.S. revokes duties against Canadian lumber (Aug. 1994); Bilateral consultation ends with a five-year Softwood Lumber Agreement (1996 SLA)
Softwood Lumber IV: 2001	In 2001, the U.S. imposes countervailing and anti-dumping duties amounting to 27.2% (Apr. 2002); Canada wins a series of WTO, U.S. International Trade Tribunal and NAFTA decisions; One day prior to the final appeal of the NAFTA panel decision ruling, the 2006 Softwood Lumber Agreement is signed.

SOURCE Gulati, Sumeet and Malhotra, Nisha, Estimating Export Response in Canadian Provinces to the Canada-US Softwood Lumber Agreement, Canadian Public Policy, Vol. XXXII, No. 2, 2006 (updated by author)

Act I

In 1982, the U.S. lumber industry was in bad shape. Interest rates had peaked at 20.5% the previous year and were in double-digit country in the four previous years, slowing down the housing industry. The Canadian lumber industry, boosted by a simultaneous 25% depreciation of the Canadian dollar, suddenly found itself in position to take over the North American market.

The U.S. industry cried foul and called for the Reagan administration to slap an import tax on Canadian lumber, claiming that the fees charged by some provincial governments for harvesting softwood on Crown lands were too low. The U.S. government was unwilling to follow up on these charges, and the first act of the softwood lumber dispute died down.

Act II

In 1986, the situation had barely improved, and the U.S. industry once again complained that the stumpage fee on Crown lands (as opposed to their auctioning) constituted an unfair trade practice. The industry's arguments may have been more convincing this time around, or it might have been that the Reagan government wanted a trump card for their ongoing trade agreement negotiations with Canada. In any case, the U.S. government slapped a 15% countervailing duty on Canadian lumber.

The Mulroney government felt the pressure and caved in by agreeing to set a 15% export tax that replaced the U.S. import tax through a Memorandum of Understanding (MOU). This MOU was eventually included as a side agreement to the Canada-U.S. Free Trade Agreement (CUFTA). In buying the peace in this manner (or more accurately, by using the industry's money to buy the peace), Canada closed the second act in the softwood lumber drama.

Act III

In 1991, feeling that CUFTA (the Canada-U.S. Free Trade Agreement, which came into effect in 1989) provided sufficiently adequate provisions to regulate the lumber trade, Canada terminated the export tax. The U.S. replied by re-establishing the countervailing duty. The U.S. was compelled to revoke this action after Canada won its case through CUFTA's dispute settlement mechanism appeal process. Bilateral negotiations were then undertaken, and a five-year Softwood Lumber Agreement was signed on April 1, 1996. That is how the curtain fell on the third act.

Act IV

The Agreement ran its course and expired in March 2001. The U.S. response was swift: A mere month later, the U.S. Department of Commerce initiated yet another investigation, and the following March applied countervailing duties of up to 35%. The curtain was lifted, and the fourth act included ongoing litigation in trade courts at all levels of governance. In a short while, the U.S. had collected over $5 billion in duties from Canadian producers exporting to the U.S.

In the spring of 2006, the Conservative government was swift to declare victory, claiming the Softwood Lumber Agreement ended the fourth instalment of this drama, which Canadian lumber companies would surely call a tragedy. But most industry experts and players quickly predicted that the terms of this Agreement all but ensured there will be an Act V to the softwood lumber dispute in the near future.

Privatized forests vs. socialized Crown lands?

Why is the Canadian lumber industry consistently in the cross-hairs of the U.S. Department of Trade? Are the companies and provincial government really guilty of unfair trade practices? Are they illegally pricing the U.S. lumber industry out of their own markets?

The core of the dispute lies in the ownership of North American forests and the way access to the resource is distributed.

In the United States, most forestland is private and, in large part, belongs to lumber companies. Constitutionally protected property rights provide full freedom for these owners to dispose of these forests as they see fit, and, because of their importance, the companies largely set market prices.

Canada's forests belong mostly to the Crown. Logging rights are attributed at a set price, and, unlike the U.S. public forests, the industry here pays for most of the costs attached to roads, replanting, and protection against forest fires and other disasters. Other conditions are regularly set, depending on the provinces, such as "appurtenance," or the obligation for a company to cut and transform the lumber where it is picked up, thus ensuring livelihood for communities living near the resource.

Living in a privatized world, the U.S. lumber industry perceives Canada's largely public forests to be an example of creeping socialism, contrary to the principles of free enterprise, and concludes that, because it exists in a "socialized" system, the Canadian industry must be living off subsidies and thus unfairly competes with the U.S. market system.

This explains why the U.S. has repeatedly tried to impose its system in Canada, albeit with limited success so far. British Columbia has agreed to implement some form of auction, but no province is seriously considering privatizing its forests in the American way. At least, not yet.

The terms of the Agreement

For two countries that are consistently praying at the altar of freer trade and unfettered markets, the 2006 Softwood Lumber Agreement is deeply interventionist and protectionist — even though the protectionist aspect is one-sided in favour of the southern industry.

There are three main aspects of the Agreement:

- Canada received US$4 billion back from the total of US$5 billion in duties illegally collected by the U.S.
- Canadian producers were compelled to choose between two options involving export taxes and quotas.
- Canada had to forfeit $1 billion of the disputed funds, which were then distributed to U.S. lobby and industry groups.

1. Canada gets back some of the money illegally collected

At the heart of the matter was the US$5 billion paid over the previous five years by Canadian lumber producers in duties. Trade courts from NAFTA and the WTO repeatedly ruled that such duties were illegally collected, but, in signing the Agreement, Canada agreed to forfeit a portion of these duties, collecting only US$4 billion.

To add insult to injury, the Canadian forest industry paid $5 billion in countervailing duties with a strong U.S. dollar, but got $4 billion back of a much weaker currency. This means that the industry didn't get back 80 cents on the dollar, but more around 60 cents on the dollar. In other words, if Canadian lumber companies were to get back these duties with a constant U.S. dollar, they would have obtained close to $6.5 billion.

TABLE 2 *2006 Softwood Lumber Agreement export tax and quota formulas*

Prevailing Monthly Price	Option A: Export Tax (as a % of Export Price)	Option B: Export Tax (as % of Export Price) AND Quota
Over US$355	No Export Tax	No Export Tax and No Quota
US$336–355	5.00%	2.5% Export Tax and 34% U.S. Market Share
US$316–335	10.00%	3% Export Tax and 32% of U.S. Market Share
US$315 or under	15.00%	5% Export Tax and 30% of U.S. Market Share

2. Canadian producers must choose between two options

As Table 2 shows, should the price of lumber fall below US$355 per thousand board feet, the main regions of Canada will either pay an export tax that increases as the price decreases or will be subject to a quota and an export tax, both varying according to the price of lumber.

Alberta and British Columbia chose Option A while Québec, Ontario, Saskatchewan, and Manitoba chose Option B. (The Maritimes were excluded from the Agreement, arguably because most of the softwood exploited in Atlantic Canada grows in private forests.)

At the time of the signing, the lumber price was US$290 per thousand board feet. Since then, it reached a peak of US$309 in August 2007. As these lines are written, in June 2008, the last month for which data were available, prices stood at US$281.[5] This means that Canadian producers have paid the highest export tax possible and were subjected to the lowest quota amounts during every single month that elapsed since the signing of the Agreement, and will continue to do so for the foreseeable future.

Over and above option A's export taxes is also a "surge mechanism," a surcharge that kicks in if a region exceeds a given maximum volume in exports. If this volume is exceeded by more than 10%, the applicable export tax increases by half.

CHART 1 *Prevailing monthly lumber price (US$)*

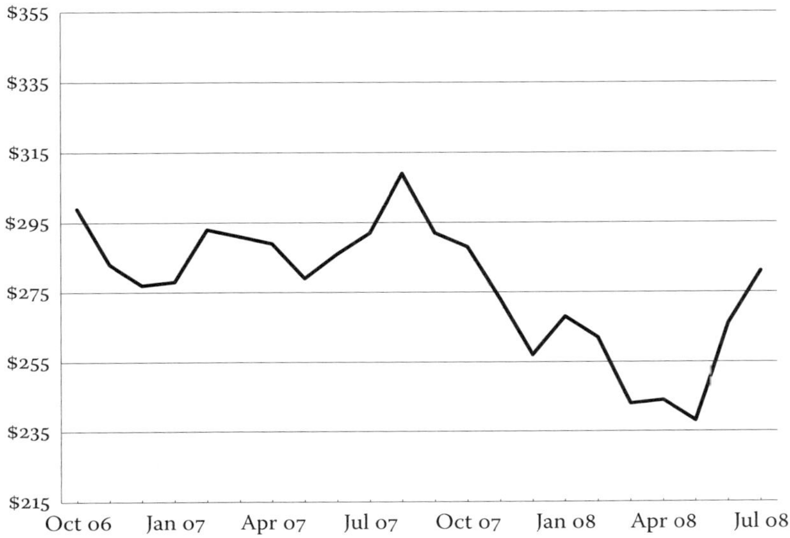

3. Canada must return US$1 billion to U.S.

The Harper government also agreed to give away US$1 billion of the collected duties that legitimately belonged to the Canadian softwood industry players. Half of this money found its way toward the coffers of the U.S. Coalition for Fair Lumber Imports, the same group that is behind all the trade challenges.

The Conservatives thus yielded lunch money to the school bully and undoubtedly endowed him with a war chest for future trade challenges.

The U.S. government announced that the remaining US$500 million would be distributed as follow:

- US$200 million to the U.S. Endowment for Forestry and Communities to support educational and charitable causes of public interest in American timber-reliant communities (Canada's timber-reliant communities receive nothing);

- US$150 million to the American Forest Foundation, an organization representing the interests of private forestland landowners;
- US$100 million to Habitat for Humanity, which announced the funds will be allocated through 4,000 grants of US$25,000 each — the cost of lumber for the typical U.S. Habitat home.
- US$50 million to the Bi-national Council, a mysterious organization whose officers are the executives of large timber companies and one of whose co-chairpersons is the chairman of the U.S. Coalition for Fair Lumber Imports, Steve Swanson.

When the deal was announced to Parliament on April 26, Stephen Harper said: "I am pleased to announce today that the United States has accepted Canada's key conditions for the resolution of the softwood lumber dispute. Canada's bargaining position was strong, our position was clear, and this agreement delivers."[6]

The Agreement did deliver...lots of moneybags to the U.S. lumber industry.

Canada comes to the rescue of the U.S....twice

Harper was at least right about Canada's bargaining position, which was strengthened by numerous decisions from international and American trade courts that consistently ruled in favour of Canada in this dispute. The last such decision prior to Harper's April 2006 announcement was rendered unanimously. A month before the Harper-Bush Softwood Lumber Agreement, a NAFTA panel ruled that Canada's subsidies to its lumber industry amounted to less than 1%[7]. Thus, the U.S. was not entitled to collect countervailing duties.

The panel itself was composed of three Americans (including a judge who had specifically been appointed by the U.S. to ensure the panel would respect the standard of review) and two Canadians. There was no impropriety noted during the decision, but the U.S. was entitled to a last kick at the can by filing an extraordinary appeal. It had until April 27 to do so, and a final decision would have been announced seven months later. That decision would have meant the end of the dispute. All the trump cards were in Canada's hand.

But Canada folded this winning hand. By announcing this Agreement on April 26 — the day before the extraordinary (and final) appeal-filing deadline, the Conservative government prevented this major case for jurisprudence from getting in the books. The announcement of the Agreement effectively suspended the NAFTA panel decision.

It gets worse. As long as a final Agreement was not signed — and negotiations were ongoing in regard to the last details of the deal — trade courts continue to study and rule on the cases that were presented to them. The World Trade Organization continued to assess the dispute. Canada's bargaining position was strengthened yet again with the August 15, 2006 WTO ruling in favour of Canada in the calculation of anti-dumping duties.[8]

Refusing to be swayed by this ruling in Canada's favour, the Conservative government reacted by announcing it would introduce the Softwood Lumber Agreement to Parliament and it would raise the stakes by making the vote a question of confidence. This meant Harper was threatening an election over the matter. The Agreement was signed on September 12 and, with the support of the Bloc Québécois, it was adopted on September 19 to come into force on October 12.

Fool me once, shame on you; fool me twice, shame on me

The announcement of the Softwood Lumber Agreement occurred the day before the deadline for the filing of a last appeal, while the signing occurred one day before a ruling of the U.S. International Court of Trade. The Court ordered the Bush administration to fully refund the US$5.3 billion in duties to the Canadian lumber industry.[9] By signing the Agreement, the Conservative government threw away a full victory, through a U.S. trade tribunal, in a decision that could not be appealed. It was, however, rendered moot since Canada abandoned its claims when Stephen Harper signed the deal. Thus, Canada bailed out the U.S. softwood lumber industry not once, but twice in six months.

By doing so, they all but ensured that there will be a fifth lumber dispute where both countries will start from square one again.

That October 13 decision isn't the only thing that was rendered moot. In fact, the Softwood Lumber Agreement nullified all of Canada's previous legal wins. As Carl Grenier, vice-president of the Free Trade Lumber Council, said after the April announcement: "Every victory obtained over the past three years under NAFTA has just been erased with the single stroke of a pen."

What Mr. Grenier means is that, if litigation starts again, for whatever reason, the Agreement leaves the United States entirely free to re-assert all its former positions, even those that were rejected as illegitimate by the NAFTA and WTO panels, as well as the U.S. courts.

Softwood lumber industry: Take it or leave it

Why would the Canadian softwood lumber industry agree to such a bad deal? By and large, it did not. In fact, most Canadian companies initially denounced the deal as a cop-out and accused the Conservative government of caving in. However, the industry was in such a dire financial situation that it was in no position to fight against the U.S. lobby and the Conservative government at the same time. It was a bad agreement, but, as these testimonies to the House of Commons Standing Committee on International Trade demonstrate, the deal was seen by the stakeholders as a better alternative than no deal at all:

> We've been told that this is the deal, take it or leave it, and if you leave it, don't expect support. Under these circumstances, given the state of the industry after four or five years of being bled to death, I doubt the industry would use its so-called veto, because it's a party to these litigations. It has to agree to drop these legal suits. I doubt, as we speak now, it would re-exercise that veto. It's just too badly off. That's unfortunate, in my view, but that's the situation we're in now.[10]

> When you don't have a financial quagmire over your head, it allows you to think more long term. I think right now, as everyone around this table has recognized, getting the deposits back is obviously a huge plus. It's a huge lure. It's short-term gain, and everyone needs that right now. But then, as Mr. Wakelin said, you have that short-term gain, but where are you going to be seven years from now? So you get this de-

> posit in year one — we won't get it back in a year, but maybe 18 months from now — and what happens after that? What happens for the next five and a half years?[11]

> If the only question were, do you want this deal, and if you don't we'll go back to Washington, carry on litigation, and try to get you a better deal, that's where we'd be today: at the second choice. But we haven't been given that choice. We've been told by the government, take it, or we're walking away and leaving you an orphan. That's the problem.[12]

> My conclusion is that this deal is not a good deal. It's very difficult, but it can be made acceptable to those who find it important to leave the uncertainty and the costs of the past several years and to go to a land where there will be greater certainty and greater ways to plan. There are things that can be done.[13]

Despite the federal government's arm-twisting of the industry, not all companies were coerced. The Agreement required Canadian companies holding a balance of 95% of the US$5 billion duties returned to Canada to promise the collective surrender of US$1 billion to the U.S., and it soon became obvious that the numbers wouldn't be there.

Resorting to the old divide-and-conquer strategy, the Conservative government bullied the resisters by promising, on the one hand, a tax amnesty on the returned duties if a company returned 20% of it to a fund that would be handed to the U.S. government and, on the other hand, by threatening to slap a special 19% charge on the returned funds for those companies who refused to pay their share of the US$1 billion. The Conservatives then added these fines to the same Washington-bound fund.

Behind the madness

A neutral observer could be excused for being unable to make sense of the situation. During the electoral campaign, the Conservatives promised to "stand up for Canada." Why would they sign a deal which:

- refunds the legal fees of their opponents and competitors five times over;

- gives an additional US$500 million to various industry groups;
- sets export taxes and a quota system that are certain to limit the growth and development of the industry; and
- arm-wrestled the industry to force them to accept a deal nullifying all the previous legal victories?

Gordon Gibson, former B.C. politician and a Senior Fellow at the Fraser Institute, provides an answer:

> The inexperienced Harper administration seized the chance to brag that in only a couple of months it had been able to fix an issue the Libs couldn't solve for five years. And it would validate Emerson's sleazy jump to the Tories. As a result, they bought a deal so loaded in favour of the Americans it was arguably worse than the one the Martin government had turned down earlier.[14]

Gibson will avoid any suspicion as to his beliefs in matters of trade. After all, he has written extensively in the past on the need for closer economic links with the U.S. But Gibson simply couldn't swallow this deal. In the same scathing opinion piece published in the *Globe and Mail,* he wrote:

> Bad deal? Never mind. On April 27, Mr. Harper told an astonished House of Commons the issue had been settled. At that very hour, American lawyers were filing papers to restart the legal process. The U.S. lied, and we said nothing. Without that betrayal, the very next day the final NAFTA decision would have kicked in and countervail duties would have ended at once.

Gibson's foresight was certainly confirmed by a leaked copy of a letter written by the U.S. Department of Commerce to the U.S. Coalition for Fair Lumber Imports. This letter stated the U.S. government viewed the Accord's purpose was to "mitigate to the greatest extent possible Canadian practices found by the Department of Commerce to constitute unfair trade practices... This will be a guiding consideration in the U.S. government's monitoring and enforcement of the 2006 Softwood Lumber Agreement."[15]

So intent were the Conservatives to claim victory at all costs that International Trade Minister David Emerson simply dismissed any allegation that his U.S. counterpart could be negotiating in bad faith.

A war to end all wars?

Canadian companies have paid a steep price for peace in the softwood lumber dispute. The industry is betting that the Agreement will bring peace and will allow them to concentrate on getting back on track. Should we then believe that stability is guaranteed?

Stephen Harper wanted us to do so when he said of the Agreement that "this Agreement will end years of costly legal wrangling, and allow us to move on to build a stronger, more prosperous Canada."[16] B.C. Premier Gordon Campbell celebrated the Agreement by saying, "It's time for the costly litigation and instability experienced over the last decade to end and for a new chapter in British Columbia's ongoing forestry revitalization to begin."[17]

In theory, the Softwood Lumber Agreement is a seven-year deal, with a possible two-year extension. But when the Agreement reached the 18-month mark in April 2008, a provision was activated giving either country the right to abrogate the accord with a mere six-month notice, by simply contending that the other signatory hasn't respected its terms. No proof needed.

It is thus very possible that (accounting for the effect of the U.S. dollar depreciation), the Canadian lumber industry was forced to fork out about 40 cents on the dollar — 40 cents that all trade courts stated rightfully belonged to these Canadian companies — for the privilege of having a Softwood Lumber Agreement over which is suspended Damocles' sword.

Recent events demonstrate that the sword is dangling dangerously.

In August 2007, merely nine months after the signing of the Agreement, U.S. trade representative Susan Schwab announced the U.S. was launching arbitration proceedings, claiming that Canada was violating the terms of the treaty. First, they claimed that the full export tax should have been imposed from October to December 2006 for the regions that chose Option B (Canada only collected a 5% export tax, while the U.S. contended it should have been 15%); and second, they claimed Canada hadn't properly collected the funds that should have been imposed through the surge mechanism.[18]

In a Solomon-like ruling, the London Court of International Arbitration rendered a split decision by agreeing with the U.S. on the first case, and with Canada on the second.[19]

It doesn't end there. In January 2008, the U.S. tabled a second complaint, arguing that the Conservative government's proposed creation of a $1 billion Community Development Trust was in violation of the Agreement. The Trust is aimed at helping communities that are dependent on a single industry (such as forestry, mining or automobile) to get through the manufacturing crisis, but the U.S. contends that the funds are used to subsidize the industry.[20]

In May 2008, the U.S. Congress passed a farm bill that will have serious repercussions on the Canadian lumber industry. The farming provisions won't affect softwood lumber, but a rider has been attached to the bill by some Congressmen sympathetic to the U.S. lumber lobby, which would mandate U.S. importers to certify that all taxes on the imported lumber have been properly paid.[21]

In the face of this evidence, it is hard to argue that the era of costly litigation is over.

Consequences for NAFTA

So far, we have seen that Canadian forest companies paid US$1 billion (of which US$500 million went to their direct competitors) for an Agreement that can be cancelled at any time, and which did not end litigation.

Is it getting any worse? It depends on what you think of the North American Free Trade Agreement (NAFTA).

Elliot J. Feldman, head of International Trade Practice at Baker Hostetler LLP, and a director of the Canadian-American Business Council, believes that the Agreement weakens NAFTA, to the point of making it irrelevant:

> It means that those countries that previously have agreed to settle their international trade disputes by the rule of law have succumbed to making deals instead. When deal-making replaces the rule of law, the process always favours the strong over the weak and rarely resembles anything like justice.[22]

In an editorial shortly after the April announcement, the *National Post* agreed with Dr. Feldman's assessment:

> The deal is too generous to American lumber producers. Even though they have been on the losing end of numerous World Trade Organization (WTO) and NAFTA hearings, the framework allows the United States to keep about US$1 billion of the penalty dues they have unfairly collected from Canadian softwood companies over the years.
>
> This is a terrible precedent to set. The message is that flouting trade rulings is not only acceptable behaviour, but will be rewarded. Acceptance of such a deal is a de facto admission by Canada that what we have with the United States is not free trade, as such, but trade on its protectionist terms.[23]

The Agreement doesn't ring NAFTA's death knell. However, it clearly shows that the dispute-resolution mechanisms that Canada fought for in CUFTA and NAFTA have no teeth and that, as was the case before these trade agreements were signed, Canadians will likely have to rely on U.S. trade law and U.S. administrative tribunals to right a wrong.

Conclusion

The Softwood Lumber Agreement is a victory of form over content. The Conservative government is possibly alone in believing that the Agreement settles the dispute, and represents a victory for Canada and its forestry industry.

In the end, the industry went along because it had no choice. Call it a survival instinct or merely resignation over things it can't change. Furthermore, the Conservatives can be expected to boast about their "win" during the next election.

TABLE 3 *Trade decisions from April 2001 to October 2006*

Date	Body	Decision
May 2002	US-ITC	Lumber imports from Canada threaten material injury to the U.S. Industry (but hasn't caused this injury yet)
July 2002	WTO	(1) Preliminary ruling that the U.S. should scrap or change the Byrd Amendment (which gives back the collected duties to U.S. industry); (2) Interim report that states Canadian stumpage fees can be a subsidy, but the U.S. cannot use cross-border comparisons to determine the level of subsidy.
May 2003	WTO	Final report is released confidentially. Canada claims it declared its lumber industry is not subsidized; The U.S. claims it declares it subsidized, but calls the U.S. method to determine the subsidy level improper.
July 2003	NAFTA	Anti-dumping duty on softwood lumber can stay in place, but needs to be lowered from its 8.4% level.
August 2003	NAFTA	The U.S. has been unable to properly demonstrate that Canada's "subsidies" provided a benefit to its lumber industry. It is given 60 days to restate the case that Canadian stumpage rates conferred a benefit to its forest companies.
September 2003	NAFTA	Remanded the 2002 U.S. International Trade Commission decision, citing "extensive lack of analysis"
April 2004	NAFTA	Remanded the 2002 U.S. International Trade Commission decision for a second time (after the U.S. modified their calculations), saying the U.S. International Trade Commission has not provided enough evidence to prove its case.
May 2004	USITC	Demanded that the NAFTA panel reconsider its position, saying it has "manifestly and repeatedly overstepped its authority".
June 2004	NAFTA	The NAFTA panel rejects the USITC request.
August 2004	NAFTA	Orders the USITC to rule that lumber imports from Canada don't pose a threat of injury to the U.S. industry.

The main question at this point is: will they still be at the country's helm to pick up the pieces for the inevitable Fifth Act?

TABLE 3 (CONT.) *Trade decisions from April 2001 to October 2006*

Date	Body	Decision
September 2004	USITC	Complies with the NAFTA panel's ruling and declares that lumber imports from Canada don't pose a threat of injury to the U.S. industry.
November 2004	NAFTA	U.S. government requests an Extraordinary Challenge Committee (ECC) to contest the NAFTA panel injury ruling.
May 2005	US-CIT	Canada files a lawsuit challenging the Byrd Amendment
August 2005	NAFTA	The ECC confirms the NAFTA panel's decision, ruling that lumber imports from Canada don't pose a threat of injury to the U.S. industry; The U.S. continues to collect duties, invoking the confidential WTO report declaring the threat of injury from subsidies existed.
August 2005	US-CIT	Following the previous ECC decision, Canada files another lawsuit with the U.S. Court of International Trade seeking the refund of duties collected.
October 2005	NAFTA	A NAFTA panel found once again that the countervailing duties were too high and orders the U.S. to lower them again. The U.S. tries to delay by asking for clarification of the ruling, but the NAFTA panel rejects the request. The U.S. appeals that decision.
March 2006	NAFTA	Denies a challenge filed by the Coalition for Fair Lumber Imports that the countervailing duty should have stayed above 1%. The U.S. government has until April 27 to request an Extraordinary Challenge Committee. On April 26, the Softwood Lumber Agreement is announced.
July 2006	US-CIT	Ruled that the U.S. can't legally collect duties on lumber shipped from Canada.
October 2006	US-CIT	The day after the implementation of the Agreement, the US-CIT ruled that Canada should be refunded the full amount of the duties.

ACRONYMS US-ITC: U.S. International Trade Commission (An independent federal agency determining import injury to U.S. industries in antidumping, countervailing duty, and global investigations); WTO: World Trade Organization; NAFTA: North American Free Trade Agreement; US-CIT: U.S. Court of International Trade (Customs panel with exclusive jurisdictional authority to decide any civil action against the United States, its officers, or its agencies arising out of any law pertaining to international trade).
SOURCE U.S.-Canada Trade Dispute Timeline — 1982 to present, Random Lengths Publication, http://www.randomlengths.com/pdf/Timeline.pdf.

The Harper-Bush Alliance On Colombia

Sheila Katz

> Why, Canada, why?... What is at stake is Canada's reputation as a highly-minted symbol for public rectitude and the politicians' projections of a principled government known for its integrity.[1]

IN MID-2007, THE Bush administration knew that it would lose a vote on the Colombia Trade Promotion Agreement if it were submitted to Congress, because of concern about ongoing violence, impunity, lack of investigations and prosecutions, the role of the paramilitary, and especially the murders of over 2,600 trade unionists in Colombia since 1986. Just then, the government of Prime Minster Stephen Harper suddenly turned its attention to the Americas and a trade deal with Colombia.

In part, Harper's Conservative government was stepping up the agenda of Canadian economic expansion in the Americas which had been a priority of political and business leaders since the 1990s. By 2006, Canada was the third largest foreign investor in Latin America and the Caribbean, the biggest investor in mining, and with a strong presence in financial services, telecommunications, and oil and gas, among other industries.[2] But Harper had another motive: to help George W. Bush, whose last visit to Latin America had sparked widespread protests, and to lend encouragement to free-market governments in the face of Venezuelan President Hugo Chavez's push for a new leftist, anti-capitalist consensus in the region.

"Mr. Harper has essentially acted as a messenger boy for Bush," said Ujjal Dosanjh, the Liberal party's critic on foreign affairs.[3]

In May 2007, speaking at the G-8 meeting in Germany, Harper signalled a major shift in Canadian aid policy, saying that Canada's primary focus would move away from Africa and toward the Western Hemisphere, "where we also have countries that have developmental challenges." Harper went on to say that Canada's new strategy for the Americas was to be based on Canadian defence of human rights, democracy, rule-of-law, and good governance, and would involve countries that are compatible "in terms of our fundamental values and our approach to democracy."[4]

On September 25, 2007, Harper began to lobby, actively, for President Bush's position within the United States itself, delivering the following message to the Council on Foreign Relations in New York:

> In my view, Colombia needs its democratic friends to lean forward and give them the chance at partnership and trade with North America. I am very concerned that some in the United States seem unwilling to do that. What message does that send to those who want to share in freedom and prosperity? There is a lot of worry in this country about the ideology of populism, nationalism and protectionism in the Americas and the governments that promote it. But frankly, my friends, there is nowhere in the hemisphere that those forces can do more real damage than those forces (sic) in the United States itself. And if the U.S. turns its back on its friends in Colombia, this will set back our cause far more than any Latin American dictator could ever hope to achieve.[5]

On October 12, in a speech to the Greater Miami Chamber of Commerce, George W. Bush referred back to Harper's speech:[6]

> As Prime Minister Stephen Harper of Canada put it, if the United States turns its back on its friends in Colombia, this will set back our cause far more than any Latin American dictator could hope to achieve.[7]

Again in March 2008, in a major speech addressing dock-workers in Jacksonville, Florida, President Bush urged the Democrats to heed the "wise words" of Prime Minister Harper.[8] President Bush again referred to the same quote when he signed controversial implementing legislation, in Congress, despite the opposition of the Democrats.[9]

Prime Minister Harper continued to work with Bush to weaken Democratic opposition to the deal in the United States, while the debate intensified in Canada. Indeed, the members of the Canadian International Trade Committee (CIIT), after having engaged in a two-month study of the humanitarian and environmental impacts of the Colombia negotiations, were furious when the government announced it had completed negotiations before receiving the committee's report.[10] The opposition parties concluded that the Canadian government undermined the democratic work of the Parliamentary committee and pushed ahead so quickly to further support the Bush administration's battle with Congress.[11] In Question Period on June 9, 2008, Liberal trade critic Navdeep Bains said:

> The Prime Minister and President Bush have been quoting each other for months to try to rush through these agreements with Colombia, ignoring serious concerns over human rights and the environment. The government's cozy ties and admiration for the Republican party are well documented... Could the minister explain why the Republicans continue to dictate our trade policy?[12]

The tactic was not lost on Colombian officials, who immediately met with their U.S. counterparts to discuss the stalled U.S.-Colombia deal. Colombia's Trade Minister, Luis Guillermo Plata, told reporters he hoped the Canadian deal would wake the Democrats up to the reality that there was a rival for the Colombian market.[13]

Despite Harper's circumvention of the democratic work of the CIIT, the Committee submitted its report, which recommended:

> an independent, impartial, and comprehensive human rights impact assessment should be carried out by a competent body...before Canada considers signing, ratifying and implementing an agreement with Colombia.[14]

and:

> any trade agreement with Colombia must be accompanied by legislated provisions on corporate social responsibility and reporting mechanisms to monitor the implementation of universal human rights standards by Canadian entities investing in Colombia.[15]

When the 39th Parliament adjourned on June 19, 2008, negotiations had been completed and a legal review of the negotiated texts had been announced. Despite the fractious political debate,[16] Parliament will not necessarily vote on the Colombia deal when it resumes. The government expects that ratification will take place in the fall of 2008, 21 days after the treaty is tabled in the House of Commons.[17] But, despite Harper's best efforts, the U.S.-Colombia deal is still stalled in the U.S. Congress because of serious doubts about the Colombian government's legitimacy, and the deal is increasingly unpopular in Canada for the same reasons.

THREE

RACIALIZATION AND (*IN*)SECURITY

Conservative Colours

The Harper Conservatives and the colour-coding of Canada

Karl Flecker

WHILE MAINSTREAM POLITICAL parties are unlikely to be consciously and overtly racist in the vein of white supremacist organizations, subtle and nuanced forms of racism do persist within Canadian institutions, including political parties. Some of the most insidious types of racism are the ones that are unconscious, unintended, or systemic in nature. This form of racism is often the result of individuals and/or organizations using their power and privilege in unconscious or unintended ways, but with negative impacts on racialized individuals and communities. The intention is not the issue, but the impact is. Indeed, the resurgence of colonialist discourse and public policy revives a debate about the true colour of the "new" Conservative government.

In the late 1980s, the Reform party was seen as being extremist and associated with white supremacists and the far-right after numerous Reform Members of Parliament and election candidates repeatedly made remarks that were considered xenophobic, homophobic, and sexist.[1] In addition, well-known racists such as Wolfgang Droege, Al Overfield, and others were found to play significant roles in the party as it attempted to gain ground in Ontario.[2]

When the *Toronto Sun* ran an article in late February 1992 reporting that the Reform party had been infiltrated by the Heritage Front, Reform party executive members scrambled to distance their party and leader

Preston Manning from these extremists.[3] Nonetheless, the image of intolerance continued to plague the party's fortunes, and was considered a major factor in its subsequent rebirth as the Canadian Alliance.

The contemporary Conservative party has made significant strides to shed its connections to the Reform party and some of its more unsavory right-wing characters, but the question of whether some of the less overt manifestations of racism still exist must be addressed.

The Lebanon evacuation

In summer 2006, the Middle East erupted into another violent conflict involving Israel and Lebanon. As many as 50,000 Canadian citizens, many with Lebanese ancestry or familial ties, were stranded in the midst of the battle. Others, including UN Observers (a.k.a. Canadian Peacekeepers) Major Hess-von Kruedener and Lieutenant Tom Farkash, were killed. Montrealer Hassan El Akhras lost 12 family members during an Israeli air strike in the south Lebanese village of Aitaroun.[4]

The Conservative government faced embarrassment and stinging criticism for its delay in mounting an evacuation of what eventually amounted to over 13,000 Canadians.[5]

The criticism softened somewhat when Harper, returning from a G-8 meeting in Paris, redirected his flight to land in Cyprus so that he could pick up about 100 Canadians evacuated from Lebanon. Even though thousands were struggling to get home at the time, Harper's stop-and-scoop action for just 100 stranded citizens garnered him front page news coverage [6]

Still, the conflict generated a national debate about the responsibility of the Canadian government for those with dual citizenship residing (temporarily or permanently) or vacationing abroad.

Immigration critics decried the costs of the evacuation, which by December 2006 was estimated to have cost $94 million.[7] Others raised questions about the "loyalty" to Canada of these "passport holders" (as the C.D. Howe Institute referred to them).[8] Monte Solberg, the Minister of Immigration, narrowed the issue to a particular group and stereotyped them when he singled out those who live abroad for many years and return to use health care and social benefits.[9] In November 2006, speaking to a House Committee on Immigration, Solberg said the Lebanon event raised questions about the rights of citizens who hold dual citizenship and don't live in the country. He went so far as to describe the situation this way, "Somebody's absent, isn't paying taxes, but is going to be using our social programs down the road; I think Canadians would feel that that is unfair."[10] It apparently mattered little to Solberg that dual citizens of Canada are *de facto* also Canadians.

The picture Solberg carelessly painted used a "them" and "us" dynamic, "them" being certain people who have little attachment to Canada, but all too eager to cash in on the benefits of the Canadian passport. But virtually no mention was made by Conservatives or other critics of our citizenship policy about Canadians like Wayne Gretzy, Celine Dion, Keifer Sutherland, or others who similarly live abroad for extended periods while maintaining their Canadian citizenship status. No criticism is aimed at celebrities like these who are living abroad, yet there is criticism aimed at "foreign born" Canadians. This is where unintentional but hurtful racism can be found.

One of Canada's 41 MPs born in other countries, Jim Karygiannis, responded to the blunt picture that Solberg was painting:

> This is a Conservative government trying to pit one Canadian against another Canadian in order to fulfill their Reform legacy of saying to the rednecks of this country that first and foremost we don't like the immigrants.[11]

It is noteworthy that, in other moments of crisis, the issue of rights and obligations of citizens, or questions about the costs borne by the Canadian government to repatriate citizens, generated no similar debate. For example, 500 Canadians were evacuated from Southeast Asia in the aftermath of the 2004 tsunami; 200 Canadians were evacuated from Cote d'Ivoire when a crisis erupted in West Africa in 2005; hundreds of Canadians were evacuated from the Cayman Islands and Haiti in 2004; and thousands of Canadians were flown out of China after the Tiananmen Square massacre in 1989. In none of those situations was there any hand-wringing or concern expressed about who is a truly loyal or deserving Canadian citizen and what obligations the government has for those living/touring abroad, much less a debate fuelled and framed by a governing political party in the way the Conservatives framed the Lebanon evacuation of Canadian citizens.[12]

Admittedly, this was the largest evacuation of Canadians abroad, but the colour-coded tenor and impact of the debate fomented by the Conservatives must be considered. The Conservative party point of departure for the post-Lebanon evacuation policy review was set against a discourse of who is a loyal or true Canadian and if Canada should maintain dual citizenship status. This focus was short-sighted and close to being misanthropic.

For a government so openly focused on the "bottom line," it is significant that neither Stephen Harper nor his ministers ever considered the economic, social, and cultural benefits of having a citizen-based unofficial ambassadorial pool residing in other countries.

On immigrants and photo-ops

During the election hustle of 2006, Stephen Harper took centre stage at a photo-op in Mississauga, Ontario, strategically flanked by a multicultured array of Conservative party candidates. Most striking about the picture was how colourful the candidates appeared. Given the high density of people of colour living in this major urban centre, such a photo should not have been a surprise. But it was striking simply because such photos are rarely seen, unfortunately, except when political parties are preparing fund-raising flyers or seeking to win seats in densely multicultural ridings.[13]

Harper specifically used the occasion and the backdrop to make an announcement significant to Canada's immigrant communities. "Immigrants and their families should be allowed to keep more of their own money in their pockets to start a new life in Canada," Harper said.[14] If elected, he promised his government would halve the $975 landing fee charged to new immigrants, and over time would work to reduce the fee "as the fiscal situation allows."[15]

But before this carefully staged and colourfully flanked photo was taken in Mississauga, Harper's views on immigration were a matter of public record.

Harper, it must be remembered, was a key architect of the Reform party's immigration policies that had the result of attracting members of the white rights Heritage Front to the Reform party.[16] Harper's record on immigration and race issues was summarized in a 2004 article published in *Now Magazine:*

- A Conservatives' interim policy document from 2004 refers to the need to attract immigrants who can best integrate into the "Canadian fabric"... read mostly white, mostly Europeans.
- Harper refused to revoke the nomination of Markham Unionville Conservative candidate Joe Li for referring to immigrants as "garbage."
- In Harper's own words: "West of Winnipeg, the ridings the Liberals hold are dominated by people who are either recent Asian immigrants or recent migrants from eastern Canada: people who live in ghettos, and who are not integrated into Western Canadian society."[17]

Earlier still, *Report News magazine* published the full transcript of a Q & A interview with Harper. Here are two excerpts exposing Harper's views on immigration, refugees, and Canadian culture.

> Q: "Is there such a thing as Canadian culture?"
>
> A: "Yes, in a very loose sense. But I think that Canadian culture is complex. It consists of regional cultures within Canada, regional cultures that cross borders with the U.S. We're part of a worldwide *Anglo-American culture and a worldwide Francophone culture* in the case of Québec. *We're part of a broader Western culture, Christian or post-Christian,* and there is a continental culture. There is a Canadian culture that is in some ways unique to Canada, but I don't think Canadian culture coincides neatly with borders."
>
> Q: "What's your view on immigration?"
>
> A: "I'm pro-immigration in principle. I think the biggest concern in the immigration system right now is the refugee determination process which has become such a boondoggle. It not only threatens the

> integrity of the immigration system, *it threatens national security.* I've been saying for years that the most important thing is that this country makes its own immigration selection and that this policy be consistent with Canadians' views. A refugee determination system that has effectively created a back door immigration stream that bypasses legal channels is unacceptable. And we need to tighten that system. But I want to make it very clear: I don't want it to be said that I'm anti-immigration. I'm very supportive of [a] significant [level of] immigration and always have been." [Emphasis added.][18]

Harper's use of language and reference to refugees and national security warrants further examination. Consider that a significant proportion of those admitted to Canada under our refugee determination processes had been, among francophones, Algerians, Moroccans and Haitians; and, among the larger anglo- or allophone group, Central Americans, Palestinians, South Asians (especially Sri Lankan Tamils), and Africans (among them a substantial number of Somalis).[19]

Harper's comments, in a post-9/11 context, suggest that these refugees are the people who could threaten "national security." Given that these source countries are largely non-white and non-Christian, it implies a profile of who, by virtue of colour and/or religion, is a security risk. Those Canadians with whose views Harper thinks refugee policy should be made consistent are presumably people of European origin, and Judeo/Christian faiths. The fact that growing numbers of Canadians don't fit this profile is perhaps the greater concern.

Changing demographics in Canada

Statistics Canada census reports have for at least two decades revealed dramatic changes in Canada's links to an Anglo-Franco/Christian history. In 1986, the census revealed that nearly 16 million Canadians had roots other than British or French. Not a surprise, really, given that since the 1970s our immigration policy focused on largely racialized immigrants from the global South. Back then, 70% of new Canadians hailed from Asia, Latin America, and the West Indies.[20]

From 1997 to 2006, Citizenship and Immigration Canada's (CIC) annual overview of immigration numbers, plus the 2001 and 2006 census data, showed clearly that increasingly Canada's citizens are of an ethnic origin *other* than British, French, or native-born Canadian. The 2006 Census showed that 83.9% of the immigrants who arrived between 2001–06 were born in regions other than Europe.

In March 2007, Statistics Canada reported that not only is immigration currently fuelling two-thirds of our population growth, but also that projections show immigrants are likely to be the primary source of population gains by 2030.[21] CIC's annual reports to Parliament also regularly point out that new Canadians increasingly originate from other than Anglo-Euro or Christian countries. The 2007 CIC report cited that 80% of immigrants today come from the *Middle East, Asia, and the Pacific regions.*

In short, the vast majority of immigrants who for the last two decades have been populating the country and defining its culture, are neither Anglo-Euro nor likely Christian in their traditional context. Yet Harper's public comments, cited above, demonstrate a profound failure — or perhaps a steadfast refusal — to grasp the cultural, religious, and immigration-related policy impacts of such a significant demographic shift — a change that has been in full swing since the 1970s.

Conservatives and their electoral base

For the last two decades, roughly half of the immigrant population has gravitated to three major urban centres: Toronto, Montreal and Vancouver. Today, nearly 80% of newcomers opt to settle in one of these cities.[22] Only recently is there evidence of Harper and the Conservatives beginning to understand the changing voting patterns of this portion of the immigrant electorate. Indeed, Conservatives won 123 seats in the 2006 federal election, but failed to win any in major urban centres such as Toronto, Vancouver, and Montreal.

In mid-October 2007, the *Globe and Mail* reported that the Conservative party had devised a strategy to secure votes from select ethnic and religious communities in multicultural ridings in the next federal election. The strategy was called *Building Bridges with Ethnic*

Communities, and pictured the Conservatives, rather than the Liberals, as the party of electoral choice in specific ridings. The document showed the Conservatives had ruled out gaining the favour of all ethnic groups, acknowledging that at least a fifth were not "accessible" to the party, but claimed that nearly 80% of "visible minorities" were "accessible to the Conservatives."

The strategy to turn some colour-coded ridings from red to blue involved "targeted mailings, one-to-one meetings at a major ethnic event involving key members of the Conservatives outreach team, and the creation of large databases of immigrants and newcomers."[23]

Identifying the voting patterns of ethno-cultural and racialized communities is only one part of the Conservatives' strategy. Party insiders concede they must also establish credibility with this crucial voting block if they are to garner the votes they need. A top Conservative insider spelled out why Conservatives are now targeting urban ethnic ridings in this election:

> Look at the traditional voting patterns. They [ethnic minorities] have been voting for the Liberals for years. So I don't know if they're going to change their vote right away. The problem with most of these minorities has been for the longest time that they all say that they like what the Conservatives are saying, they agree with what Conservatives are saying, but then, guess what, at election time, they still vote Liberal.[24]

Aside from the off-putting use of identifiers like "they" and citing minorities as "problematic," the party insider concedes that getting this community to actually vote for the Conservatives will take some serious work — work the Conservatives have been undertaking with diligence. They initiated the Air India Inquiry[25] and addressed the long-standing demand for redress of the infamous Chinese Head Tax.[26]

Canada's immigrant communities remain skeptical, however, because of the Conservative record. For example, the Conservative party's *Building Bridges* training materials used at the March 2008 "political training conference" took credit for spending over $50 million on *Canada's Action Plan Against Racism*, but ignored the fact that it was the Liberals who established the *Action Plan* and budget allocation in March 2005[27] as a direct outcome of the advocacy of anti-racist activists who were part of the *UN World Conference Against Racism, Racial discrimination, Xenophobia, and Related Intolerances* held in Durban in 2001.[28]

Furthermore, when Jason Kenny announced that Canada would withdraw from the upcoming UN Durban Review Conference, he undermined the Conservatives' credibility in many quarters. The Review Conference plans to assess the progress of member countries in fighting racism. Kenny made the announcement without public consultation. The withdrawal from the UN conference and credit-taking for the *Action Plan Against Racism* have seriously undermined the Conservative *Building Bridges* initiatives.

International education and credentials

On May 12, 2006, Harper announced his government would implement a number of initiatives to address concerns of immigrants in Canada. One of these announcements was a promise of more than $300 million of additional federal funding, to be allocated over two years to aid in the settlement of newcomers. In addition, the government's budget included allocations to improve the assessment and recognition of foreign credentials in order to help newcomers achieve their full potential in Canada.

Harper said at that time: "The goal for all of us will be to get those who are trained and ready to work in their fields of expertise into the workforce more quickly."

The Canadian Labour Congress wrote to Immigration Minister Monte Solberg on September 12, 2006, asking what the government's time-line was to meet the promises Harper had made.[29] These answers are still not forthcoming.

Instead, a number of other changes have contradicted the goal of getting immigrants into the workforce more quickly. Diane Finley, Minister for Human Resources and Social Development Canada (HRSDC), made a significant public announcement in March 2006 at the Public Policy Forum Conference addressing the theme of integrating immigrants into the workforce. Finley reminded the audience of the Conservative electoral platform's "commitment to create a *Canadian Agency for*

Assessment and Recognition of Credentials, to provide pre-assessment of international credentials and experience."[30] Finley went on to say:

> I am committed to working with my provincial and territorial colleagues and all of you to ensure foreign-trained professionals [*read as racialized individuals*] get properly trained and meet Canadian standards so they can start working here quickly.[31]

Finley gave voice to a dominant-culture assumption that internationally-trained individuals don't meet Canadian standards and that assurances must be in place for "proper training" — subtle racism on two fronts. First, the Minister's persistent use of the term "foreign-trained" rather than "internationally-trained" perpetuates notions of being alien, or "other," and certainly racialized. Secondly, like Harper, Finley failed to understand that, increasingly, newcomers to Canada bring with them a level of education that matches and often exceeds that of the general population.

Statistics Canada data show that, according to 2006 Census numbers, nearly one-third of immigrants are university graduates, compared with 23% of the general working-age population. Furthermore, there has been a huge jump in the qualifications of the newest arrivals; more than half of those who came between 2001 and 2006 hold university degrees. Immigrants now account for close to half of all those in Canada who hold a PhD, and 40% of those have Masters degrees.[32] And keep in mind that 80% of immigrants are coming from colourful countries.

Finley prefaced her comments by saying that the issue is complex and that the federal government's role was limited, given that the vast majority of professional regulated occupations fall under provincial/territorial jurisdictions. Her remarks suggested the Conservatives were stepping away from their earlier electoral commitments to create an agency that would facilitate the assessment and recognition of immigrants' credentials.

When the Conservatives did finally create an agency, its name — the Foreign Credentials Referral Office (FCRO) — reinforced the Conservatives' withdrawal from the issue. Although they had promised an $18 million investment in an agency that would assess and *recognize* international credentials,[33] Harper's 2007 budget offered only an annual contribution of $6.4 million to create the FCRO. Take note of the reduced dollar amount and the change in language of the agency. Highly credentialed newcomers are knocking on what they thought was an $18 million dollar rapid-entry door to the workforce, when in fact the FCRO simply refers them to one or more of the existing 400 professional regulatory doors that assess their credentials.

Canada's labour force is already hugely dependent on immigration, and this is expected to become the primary source of both net labour force and population growth in the very near future. The Harper government's failure to ensure that highly-credentialed newcomers are working at good jobs commensurate with their abilities is nothing short of colour-coded economic folly for the nation.

Two decades of data show that immigrants persistently earn less and are congregated in occupations that do not utilize their credentials and international work experience.[34] More recently, Statistics Canada has found that most immigrants aged 25–54 had unemployment rates higher than the 4.9% rate of their Canadian-born counterparts.[35] Another Statistics Canada study of economic gains over the 25-year period (1980 to 2005) showed that immigrants are twice as likely to earn significantly less than their Canadian-born age peers, despite being more credentialed. A recent male immigrant with a university degree earns 48% of what his Canadian-born counterpart gets.[36] Furthermore, it takes at least 10 years for this cohort to reach wage parity with their Canadian-born counterparts.[37]

As we near the point where immigrants will account for nearly all of Canada's population growth, their income levels are an important determinant for all Canadians. Apparently even the chief economist at the TD Financial Group recognizes the implications of this reality: "If we let immigrants fall behind, all of Canada will join them."

Despite this clarion call to change fundamentally Canada's immigration settlement and workforce integration patterns, Budget 2007 directed more than $84 million into Canada's infamous Temporary Foreign Worker Program (TFWP)—an amount that was 12 times the meagre $6.4 million he budgeted for a flaccid FCRO.[38]

Solving a labour shortage or creating a disposable workforce?

Canada's TFWP, historically, was a small program enabling employers (principally in the agricultural/horticultural sector) to import workers for seasonal employment in Canada. However, under Harper, this program has undergone massive changes, resulting in a huge increase in the numbers of guest workers. In 2003, the total number of guest workers in the country was just over 110,000, and by 2007 the number jumped to over 200,000.

After Harper's electoral win in 2006, then Immigration Minister Monte Solberg signalled the government's immigration priority by revealing that, while he had no "immediate plans to make significant changes to the overall annual target for immigration," he was committed to using "tools" like "work permits, to help meet some of the skill shortages that this country has in different sectors." Further:

> If we need workers for the oil rigs in Alberta or the East Coast, for example, then we need to put our energies into making sure we get them. The same goes for every part of the country, from Gander to Nunavut to Whitehorse, Whistler, Edmonton, and Québec City.[39]

In short order, Canada's TFWP underwent a series of "administrative changes,"[40] all benefiting employers and enabling them to fast-track access to import labour "for any legally recognized occupation from any country."[41] In equally short order, economic hot-house provinces like Alberta were soon importing more guest workers than newcomers destined to become permanent residents.[42] None of the administrative changes were directed at ensuring these workers would be entering the Canadian workforce with strong compliance, monitoring, or enforcement mechanisms to ensure their safety or protection from exploitation.

TABLE 1 *Stock of temporary foreign workers as of December 1*

	2003	2004	2005	2006	2007
Total	110,476	126,031	141,743	162,046	201,057

SOURCE CIC Immigration Overview

Many observers and advocates, including academics, the Alberta Federation of Labour, the B.C. Building and Construction Trades Council, the B.C. Government Employees Union, the Canadian Labour Congress, the United Food and Commercial Workers, faith groups, the Québec Human Rights Tribunal, and numerous advocacy groups supporting migrant workers have documented many cases of fraud, workplace abuse, labour brokers' and/or employers' exploitation. Serious injuries and fatalities on the job are also grim realities for these workers.[43]

Although racial status data are not collected for guest workers, clearly these workers are mostly people of colour. Employers claim they can't fill the jobs guest workers undertake by using the domestic labour force. Of the top 10 source countries for guest workers, half of them host racialized populations, and in 2006 nearly 35% of the 160,000-plus guest workers came from countries where the population is racialized.

The TFWP has been likened to a re-enactment of Canada's early racist history. Instead of importing Chinese labourers to build the national railway under horrific working and social conditions and inflicting on them the notorious head tax, the TFWP now imports workers largely from the global South to build urban transport infrastructure, pick our food, labour in the service or construction industries, or tend to the elderly and young. Guest workers now fill alleged gaps in all parts of the economy, including serving Canadians coffee.

Permanent residency for a few

In the face of growing criticism of the government's expanded and employer-friendly TFWP, and perhaps aware that strategically wooing parts of the colourful ethno-racial electoral block can help shift the Conservatives from a minority to a majority hold of Parliament, Harper has made other changes in immigration policy.

Acknowledging the country's need for some guest workers to remain in Canada as permanent residents, Harper's government introduced a special path to permanent residency called the Canadian Experience Class.[44] The CEC initiative, however, only gives highly-skilled guest workers and some international students the right to apply for permanent resident status. The initiative is further limited by the requirement that the applicants must demonstrate strong labour market integration. This means their employer has a key role to play in affirming or negating a guest worker's application for Canadian citizenship.

Critics of the initiative point out that not only is it unbalanced to have employers play such a prominent role in determining citizenship, it is also reminiscent of the excessive power employers held in determining the mobility rights and civil rights of workers of colour during the apartheid years in South Africa.[45]

The CEC initiative is consistent with what Harper described as his preference for an "immigration selection policy that is consistent with Canadian views,"[46] or at least his view of who should be eligible to remain in Canada.[47] By this program's definition, the vast majority of guest workers entering Canada under the Conservative regime are not highly skilled...but they are racialized.

A closer examination of the program's structure and funding reveals that, in addition to the skewed balance of power granted employers and the limited scope of coverage, the initiative is so inadequately funded that fewer than 10,000 applicants were expected to be processed within the first year, and no more than 25,000 by 2013. Meanwhile, nearly a million hopeful newcomers to Canada — most of them, not surprisingly, racialized — remain waiting in the queue, in the increasingly vain hope they and their family members will be able to become Canadian citizens.

Buried amendments to the *Immigration and Refugee Protection Act*

Federal Budget 2006 also levied a $20 million cut to a long-overdue review of the *Citizenship Act.* As the then Ministers of the Treasury Board and Finance put it, these cuts were about "trimming the fat and refocusing spending on the priorities of Canadians."[48] Which Canadians the Conservatives are prioritizing is increasingly a question equity advocates and the progressive movement at large must be prepared to define clearly.

The government quietly altered another critical Act of considerable concern to specific cultural, racialized and newcomer communities:

the *Immigration and Refugee Protection Act (IRPA)*. In Budget 2008, Harper's government introduced a series of amendments to the IRPA, but buried these changes in Bill C-50, part 6 of a 136-page "Budget implementation bill."

Rather than enable meaningful public and parliamentary debate on this Act, which plays a pivotal role in populating the country, growing the labour force and, not incidentally, building the citizenry, Harper opted to change things by legislative stealth. Without consultation or warning, the Conservatives introduced their bundled bill in mid-March. This legislation gives the Immigration Minister the power to decide who gets into Canada and who doesn't, regardless of Canada's admission criteria laid out in other legislation.

Against the very real backdrop of nearly a million people waiting for years in a growing backlog of applications for Canadian citizenship, Harper proposed to tackle the problem by changing the rules of selection and granting the Immigration Minister unprecedented powers to fast-track some classes of immigrants and discard others.

Visa officers would no longer use standardized rules to assess applicants. Instead, the Minister would determine who gets in and who does not.

"This sets a dangerous precedent for a healthy democratic system," said Naeem Noorani, publisher of *The Canadian Immigrant*.[49] Numerous immigrant settlement and refugee groups, labour and ethno-racial newcomer communities voiced strong criticism of the bill and the underhanded political process that used to muscle it through Parliament.[50] Their criticism included:

- concerns about embedding the reforms in a budget bill;
- failing to conduct meaningful and inclusive consultations prior to the development of the bill;
- granting arbitrary powers to the Immigration Minister that fail any reasonable test of transparency and accountability;
- disingenuously suggesting the changes will deal with the near million applicant backlog;

- giving priority to a process that will unfairly compete with other paths to permanent residency; and
- retaining the view of immigrants as economic units; and
- continuing to permit employers to play an unbalanced role in determining immigrants' citizenship.[51]

In the face of growing criticism of the bill, Harper's government allocated more than $3 million for an advertising campaign to sell the reforms, especially in ethnic newspapers. The print versions of the ads said they were public notices, the label given to advertising supposedly aimed at providing utilitarian information about a policy change. However, critics noted the ads contained little or no detail about the policy changes, and instead simply touted the bill's anticipated but unproven benefits.[52]

The parliamentary committee that hastily undertook to hold only a few hearings on Bill C-50 was chaired by Conservative MP Norman Doyle. The committee "concluded that part 6 of Bill C-50, the entire part on immigration, should be removed from the bill."[53] The government agreed to hold limited consultations on the bill, but the committee's recommendations had no substantive impact.[54] Consultations with stakeholders and interested citizens were limited to less than 30 days, and only a select number of national organizations with an interest in the issue were granted a mere two-hour consultation window scheduled for mid-August. The consultation agenda was predetermined and focused on "addressing specific labour market needs."

During the debate about the IRPA changes, immigrant and newcomer community members voiced their concern that changes could reduce the number of family class immigrants and further slow down the process for family reunifications. One critic put this way:

> It is clear that, if you are fast-tracking one group, you are slow-tracking another group, which is the family class. Essentially, you are putting more emphasis on newcomers as commodities, as workers rather than as people.[55]

The agenda for the summer consultations makes it clear that employers' interest in accessing short- and medium-term workers are the Conservatives' singular priority.[56] Minister Finley coyly responded to critics that the Conservative government does consider family reunifications to be a priority, with this telling quote: "And if, at a future point in time, we decide that is *the priority*, they could be fast-tracked just like any of the worker categories" [emphasis added].[57]

Ethno-racial communities have good reason to be skeptical about the Conservative party's pattern of stated priorities and real world outcomes.

Security and transportation workers

Harper's record on security measures that utilize racial and religious profiling practices goes beyond security certificates and rendition programs. For example, his Transportation Minister, Lawrence Cannon, has aggressively pursued the implementation of a security clearance program for marine industry workers. The Marine Transportation Security Clearance Program (MTSC) allows for an extreme invasion into an individual's privacy. Not only is the life of the individual seeking a security clearance in order to work on Canada docks exposed to the investigations of the RCMP and members of CSIS, but so also are the lives of their spouse, their parents, their spouse's parents, ex-spouses, and other family members.

The MTSC requires workers to consent to the release of their personal information to the governments of countries that the workers may have lived in or travelled to. If consent to disclose is not given, the MTSC will not be granted and the employee will not be able to work in designated areas.

The information on the MTSC form will also be disclosed to the RCMP, to law enforcement agencies generally, to CSIS, to other governments generally, and to virtually anyone or any other institution that Transport Canada may wish to contact to investigate the employees. Further, the MTSC form states that Transport Canada may disclose personal information collected to former employers, schools, and landlords of employees to verify such information.

In addition, the MTSC process creates a mechanism whereby, with "reasonable grounds to suspect" that one of the employees poses a threat to port security, they could be removed from their job by the Minister responsible for the legislation.

In short, the level of clearance required for a person driving a forklift on a dock is just short of the top security level required by those conducting the investigations into the workers' lives. Ironically, the Maxine Bernier-Julie Couillard controversy suggests that lesser security checks were done on Bernier's former significant other, who apparently had access to confidential foreign affairs documents, than the rigorous checks dock workers face on Canadian ports.

This example is relevant to racialized and newcomer communities because approximately 40% of B.C. unionized marine workers have dual citizenship.[58] Tom Dufresne, President of the International Longshore Warehouse Union, bluntly points out how the profiles are developed:

> [Marine workers] would have to give their hair colour, eye colour and complexion' information — that's code for "race." They would have to give permission for background searches into immigration, criminal, and Royal Canadian Mounted Police records. Simply put, they're trying to make a database to racially profile our members. They also want to politically and financially profile our members.[59]

Despite the ILWU efforts to resist the implementation of the MTSC program, using the grievance procedure and legal challenges arguing violations to the Canada Labour Code, the *Federal Privacy Act,* and Canadian Charter of Rights, Harper's government has been able to advance the program — which has been described as a "model for the marine world."[60]

Given the country's changing face, colour and ancestry, measures which increasingly rely on profiling individuals with information such as place of birth or travel history will likely result in differential and discriminatory colour-coded treatment, all under the rubric of security.

Conclusion

Racialized, religious, immigrant/newcomer and Aboriginal communities and allies of all stripes and colour will need to consider closely the Harper record, in terms of the equity impacts for them and for all Canadians. Our collective security rests on it.

Canada's Secret-Trial Detentions

The country's "intelligence" agencies set the agenda

Matthew Behrens

ON JANUARY 26, 2007, secret trial detainee Mahmoud Jaballah, then on day 52 of a punishing hunger strike at the "Guantanamo North" detention facility in Kingston, Ontario, called the office of the Campaign to Stop Secret Trials in Canada.

"I just saw Stockwell Day," Jaballah's weak voice reported, adding that the Minister of Public Safety and Emergency Preparedness had pulled aside a curtain to Jaballah's cell door, peeked in, and quickly bolted. The other detainees reported the same quick peek-a-boo.

Jaballah was being held on a "security certificate," a measure by which the Canadian government can indefinitely detain without charge refugees and permanent residents, all based on secret allegations neither they nor their lawyers are allowed to see.

It was the first time Day had come face to face with three of the five detainees who — though he had never met or spoken with them — he had condemned as "vicious individuals."[1] But rather than deal with the detainees' concerns, he instead insisted to the press that all was well, right down to the presence of chocolate sauce in the facility's refrigerator.[2]

Day's callous disregard for the safety of individuals on life-threatening hunger strikes reeked of an arrogant smugness that echoed his Liberal predecessor Anne McLellan. Indeed, both Liberals and Conservatives have long tried to reassure Canadians that indefinite detention without charge, based on the lowest standards of proof of any court in Canada, was a wholly legal and constitutional procedure.

Three weeks after Day's visit, however, the Supreme Court of Canada would unanimously find that the heart of the secret trial process was unconstitutional. "How can one meet a case one does not know?" the Court asked.[3]

This decision was far from perfect, since it failed to understand that being held for years with no charge and no end in sight constituted indefinite detention, nor that individuals' equality rights were denied by the two-tier justice that applied the low standards of a security certificate only against non-citizens. But it was nevertheless enough to send the issue back to Parliament.

Some commentators subsequently argued that security certificates required only a bit of tinkering to bring them in line with the Charter, but most opponents insisted that nothing short of abolition could serve the best ends of justice. They also argued that the certificates represent the thin edge of a wedge constituting a major assault on the human rights of targeted communities—"enemies *du jour*" who, for the past decade or so, have largely been Arab Muslims, First Nations activists, and anti-globalization organizers. All are named in reports by Canada's spy agency, the Canadian Security Intelligence Service (CSIS), as if they were the cesspools within which alleged national security threats germinated.

CSIS also dreams up the secret suspicions that underlie security certificates. The agency has a well-earned penchant for inaccuracy, exaggerated threat assessments, substitution of feelings for facts, racial profiling, and use of information gleaned from torture, all of which have been documented in revelations from the Arar Inquiry, the Air India Inquiry, and the annual reports of the agency's generally accommodating oversight body, the Security Intelligence Review Committee (SIRC).

The certificate process itself is terminally biased against a named individual. The government argues that detainees are allowed to see the case against them, yet the public "summaries" of allegations are just that: allegations. Inquiries into the sources of those allegations, requests for documentation, and attempts to cross-examine particular individuals are rejected on grounds of "national security confidentiality."

But how does one respond in 2008 to the following CSIS concern, recently released in one such summary: "In December, 1998, he looked over his shoulder on three (3) occasions for no apparent reason, after making a call from a public pay phone."[4]

It's a Kafkaesque nightmare with no end, as Jaballah learned when, cleared on a 1999 security certificate, he was re-arrested on a second certificate in August, 2001. That fall, CSIS explained that, although there were no new facts, they did have a "new interpretation" of what had already been found not credible by the Court. Despite this, the second certificate was upheld.

For Montrealer Adil Charkaoui, detained in May 2003 and under house arrest since February, 2005, the CSIS allegations against him have changed on three separate occasions, leading one to conclude that the spies in Ottawa are constantly nailing different types of Jello to the wall, hoping one will actually stay up.

Jaballah, Charkaoui, and the other three men subject to certificates — Mohammad Mahjoub, detained in June, 2000; Hassan Almrei, since October 2001, almost continuously in solitary confinement; and Mohamed Harkat, since December, 2002 — face an endless road ahead of detention, draconian house arrest, more hearings, and government efforts to deport them to torture.

CSIS and the "Super-Muslims"

Security certificates and related human rights violations occur as a result of official Ottawa's traditional deference to its scandal-plagued spy agencies. At the forefront of assuming the good-will and veracity of CSIS has been the Federal Court, which seems to overlook the annual findings of exaggerated threat assessments and Charter Rights violations by CSIS. Indeed, the *Globe and Mail* reported that, "between 1993 and 2003, CSIS filed warrant applications at a rate of between 200 and 300 a year, for a total of 2,544 applications. Only 18 of these requests were rejected by the Federal Court, the last denial occurring five years ago.[5]

Similarly, in security certificate cases, the Court continues to buy into the CSIS concept of Super-Muslims — individuals so thoroughly indoctrinated in the ways of evil and iniquity that they can never be released on bail. To take but one example, the denial of bail to Hassan Almrei, the last remaining detainee at Guantanamo North (aka Kingston Immigration Holding Centre), is based on the assumption, supported wholly by secret evidence, that Almrei "espouses the philosophy of Osama bin Laden which promotes violent acts of terrorism against civilian populations in Western countries, including Canada".[6]

Almrei has consistently denied such allegations. Nothing in the public record has ever shown him to pose a threat, and the Canadian government, in a document released during the Arar inquiry, admits that it does not have enough information on him to lay a criminal charge. But Almrei was still willing to wear a GPS monitoring bracelet, live under constant house arrest with video cameras at the only entrance to a basement apartment, have only limited supervised outings, have contact only with individuals approved by the state, have no computer or cell phone access, consent to a phone tap and mail opening, and consent to agents of the state entering his abode any time of day or night without notice or warrant. Despite these severe deprivations of liberty, however, the judge nonetheless was afraid that Almrei would spend considerable time alone in a basement and that "the risk of surreptitious communication by Mr. Almrei is too great."[7]

Unless Almrei has become telepathic during his more than seven years of confinement, it is unclear how, with phones tapped, video cameras at the entrance, agents likely monitoring the house from the outside, and no access to a cell phone or computer, he could engage in communications, surreptitious or otherwise. Smoke signals in an era of smoke alarms are out; halal carrier pigeons would be too obvious. It is only if one believes the concept of "Super-Muslim" that such a conclusion may seem plausible.

A nation run by fear

Regardless of who holds the reins of power in Ottawa, the environment in which survivors of torture seek answers and detainees under "security" laws seek disclosure has been marked by an Orwellian form of backlash: those attempting to use the tools of democracy to uphold things like the right not to be arbitrarily detained and tortured suddenly become accused of being the victimizers of the very spy agencies responsible for their suffering.

Indeed, the "intelligence community" treats efforts at disclosure, clarification, or accountability as a form of "judicial jihad,"[8] while a recently retired RCMP chief superintendent, Ben Soaves, calls it "judicial terrorism."[9]

The "CSIS agent as victim because he takes part in rendition to torture and then has to answer questions about it" syndrome is not just internal to the agency. The Inspector General of the Canadian Security Intelligence Service puts a caring arm around the shoulders of the beleaguered CSIS with her spring 2007 comment that, "Over the past two years I am sure that, at times, CSIS has felt 'overburdened' by review in their efforts to respond to various mandated reviews."[10]

Similarly, the former head of the Security Intelligence Review Committee, Paule Gauthier, declared in 2005:

> Canadians must decide if we have the stomach and the money for this kind of work... If we don't have the nerve for it now, we'd better develop it quickly... If we want to keep playing the national security game, we're going to have to play in the big leagues. It won't always be nice, it won't always be easy, and it won't always be pretty, but that's the world we live in. The sooner we get used to it, the better.[11]

It's small comfort to those for whom such practices as torture and indefinite detention are not nice or pretty, but there still remains an air of awe, or maybe fear, when it comes to challenging the basic assumptions and conclusions of CSIS and the RCMP. It's reminiscent of the way that J. Edgar Hoover and the FBI cowed an American public during the height of the manufactured "Red Scare."

A broader agenda of attacks

The cold-war-style imaginings of CSIS and the RCMP underlying these certificates would be comical were they not so devastating — not only to the men and their families, but also to the communities which, given the ripple effect of the certificates, hide away in fear, leaving those targeted ostracized and isolated.

The certificates are but one part of a much broader swath of damage to people and democratic structures in Canada, only a few among which would include:

- placement on no-fly lists with no right of appeal;[12]
- receiving an unplanned visit from CSIS while at work, creating an air of suspicion about oneself;[13]
- communities who cannot pray without fear they are being surveyed and recorded;[14]
- acts of extortion by CSIS, including threatening to jeopardize immigration for overseas loved ones if one does not spy on the community;[15]
- increasing use of secrecy in refugee hearings and greater government efforts to prevent disclosure in criminal court proceedings;[16]
- branding of charities as "terrorist" fronts without any due process;[17]
- increasing militarization of police actions in racialized communities, resulting in mass arrests that are designed as media stunts rather than crime-ending efforts;
- Islamophobic messages constantly generated in the media;[18]
- a free-wheeling racism that is defended as a justified response to "political correctness;"
- criminalization of refugees and immigrants, and vastly increased numbers of immigration detentions (which numbered 12,824 individuals in 2006-07); and
- deportations (12,636 for same reporting year).[19]

Another part of the equation is Canadian complicity in torture, whether through deportation or, in the case of citizens, working with overseas intelligence agencies to seize travelling Canadians, arrest and detain, interrogate and torture them. As was shown at the Arar Inquiry, there appears to be a disturbing pattern of such behaviour on the part of CSIS and the RCMP, which also led to the detention and torture of Muayyed Nureddin and Abdullah Almalki in Syria and Ahmad El Maati in both Syria and Egypt. These three men, though granted an inquiry into the role of Canadian officials in their torture, were not allowed to attend the entirely secret inquiry chaired by former Supreme Court justice Frank Iacobucci, nor were they allowed to see a single word of the 35,000 pages of government documents allegedly screened by the inquiry.

Keeping the lid on such an inquiry deflects attention from what is clearly a pattern of nefarious behaviour. Other cases of human rights violations continue to pop up. In April 2007, Stockwell Day promised to look into the case of Algerian refugee Benamar Benatta, whom Canada illegally transferred to the U.S. on September 12, 2001, with the dangerous proviso that he was a Muslim who knew about airplanes and might be connected to 9/11. Held for five years under conditions that the United Nations said constituted torture, Benatta, now back in Canada as a Convention refugee, is still waiting for answers from Day.

Then there is the case of Montrealer Abousfian Abdelrazik, who appears to have been detained at the request of CSIS and subsequently tortured in 2003 in Sudan, where he remains stranded five years later after his name was unjustifiably placed on a no-fly list.

Resisting new certificate legislation

It is against such a backdrop that the renewed battle against security certificates heated up in the fall of 2007. But despite the best efforts of people from across Canada to turn back the tide, the cards had already been stacked by the minority Conservative government, the duplicity of the Liberals, and the apparent bias of the Federal Court.

Indeed, while Stockwell Day promised immediate action following the February 2007 Supreme Court decision, not a word was heard from him for over eight months, nor were there any consultations with stakeholders. Stepping into the breach, quite helpfully, was the Federal Court, the same institution that had always upheld a process unanimously rejected by the Supreme Court, but which appeared unwilling to consider whether such affronts to justice were necessary in the first place.

Federal Court decisions following the finding of unconstitutionality still reflected a preferential option for the powerful, with one judge opining that "I do not believe that the Supreme Court intended the previous rulings are to be revisited or that current proceedings necessarily are to be altered as a result of its determination."[20]

In what worked extremely well as a vehicle to stamp out real debate and limit the terms of discussion to mere technicalities, the Court, in conjunction with the CSIS-friendly Canadian Centre of Intelligence and Security Studies (Carleton University), produced a study on the use of "special advocates," security-cleared lawyers who could look at what was secret, but who could never be properly instructed because detainees still did not know the case against them.

The report's publication in August 2007 was perfect timing to help shape the discussion when, six weeks later, Stockwell Day introduced a new bill that essentially mirrored the old legislation, save for a few bits of window-dressing (the much-criticized special advocate and an extremely limited "appeal").

Day praised his work as the best law of its kind in the world, and then pressured Parliament for rapid passage to prevent chaos.

When the House committee "studying" the bill planned hearings, it originally invited only seven witnesses, none of whom were involved in the day-to-day work surrounding secret trials in Canada. Pleas to hold real, democratic, accountable hearings were met with complaints by MPs that they wanted to go on Christmas vacation. "I haven't had a holiday since 2004," explained Liberal MP Ujjal Dosanjh, who ignored the warnings from leading law associations that the bill would not pass constitutional muster in a new court challenge.[21]

Meanwhile, the Department of Justice was already advertising for special advocates while Bill C-3 was still at the House committee, no doubt confident that legislation by steamroller would succeed. A Liberal party fixated with its own electoral dysfunction "held its nose" and supported the bill, and the Senate spent all of one day listening to some two dozen witnesses who, following Day's appearance, unanimously called for the "chamber of sober second thought" to exercise due diligence and stop the bill in its tracks.

Casting sobriety to the wind, the Liberal-dominated Senate passed the bill less than 24 hours later. A last-ditch campaign urging Governor-General Michaëlle Jean to refuse royal assent met a similar fate, and CSIS wasted no time in issuing "new" certificates that, like the bill that allowed for them, were slightly longer carbon copies of the old ones.

What was different this time, however, was the public availability of the inflammatory allegation summaries. They appeared not on the CSIS website, but, in an unprecedented move, on the website of the Federal Court itself. Critics were aghast, noting they had never seen a court post "evidence" until it had been properly tested in court.

Chief Justice Alan Lutfy was asked to remove the allegations and to post balancing material to undo the incalculable damage that had been done. But it was too late. For weeks the allegations remained, and newspaper stories incorrectly treated them as a sign that the government was finally revealing the cases against the detainees.

Since that time, the Federal Court has tried to rush these cases through, insisting, at all costs, that the cases move forward regardless of the wishes of those concerned. For the security certificate detainees, a new round of hearings is set to occur in the fall of 2008, with the ultimate aim of deporting them to countries where they will face torture, or worse.

This is all part of the $24 billion that has been spent on Canada's "national security" since 2001 — funding which never seemed to reach the women murdered by intimate male partners because the shelters were full, the homeless who froze on the streets because there is no national housing program, those who died awaiting medical treatment, First Nations reserves on boil water alerts, and millions of others for whom true national security has been denied.[22]

All this may seem overwhelming, yet it is significant to remind ourselves that grassroots action has made a difference. Between 1991 and 2001, CSIS issued on average two security certificates annually. Public efforts began in 2001 to abolish the process and, since the 2003 certificate issued against Charkaoui, only once has this mechanism since been enacted: a bizarre "Russian spy" case that appeared more a public relations exercise than a threat to national security.

Clearly, the security climate had not changed, but the political climate had. Demonstrations, public education, hunger strikes, civil disobedience, and legal challenges had all contributed to making security certificates an issue of national importance, and appear to have had a restraining effect on CSIS. The fact that four of the detainees are now home with their families, although under harshly restrictive bail conditions, does not mean this struggle has come to an end. The spies continue lurking in the shadows, waiting for their time to pounce, and the need for public vigilance remains incredibly high.

Migrant Workers Under Harper

"Guests," servants and criminals

Evelyn Encalada, Erika Del Carmen Fuchs and Adriana Paz

ON JUNE 23, 2008, eighty Mexican citizens (including women and children) were refused admission to Canada and were deported after being placed in detention centres for two days. Each of the men and women paid a fee of over $4,500 before leaving Mexico for the promise of a work visa to work in agriculture in British Columbia. A Canada Border Services Agency (CBSA) spokeswoman, Faith St. John, commented: "It's not unusual to refuse admission to someone, but it is unusual for a group in such large numbers to come on one flight."

Such an "unusual" incident showed only the tip of the iceberg of an immigration system that has steadily eroded under the Conservative federal government, to the point where it is difficult to make a distinction between immigration and market-driven economic policies. Indeed, profit seems to be the real determining factor dictating recent changes to the Canadian immigration system. Purported "Canadian" values of compassion and humanity have become irrelevant, even for public relations purposes. Conservatives are not shy in teaching us the hard lesson about who the real "bosses" are and who "deserves" to be exploited, under which circumstances, and under which immigration category: "guests," "temporary/seasonal," or "low-skilled" workers.

The "unusual" case of the 80 Mexicans who were deported was never reported or addressed by Canadian or Mexican government authorities.

There was a vague reference to unscrupulous labour brokers who had promised lucrative work in agriculture in B.C.: labour brokers whose activities were made possible by the current immigration and labour regimes implemented by the Harper government. These schemes are creating a new breed of "*coyotes*" promising opportunity in Canada.

During the last two years, we have seen the federal government's commitment to "efficiency," which has both created and massively expanded guest worker programs. The federal government has simplified the application processes for employers seeking to import labour to compensate for alleged labour shortages. Nandita Sharma, an activist academic, warns that "shortages do not always refer to a *quantitative* or actual lack of workers, but to the shortage of a particular *kind* of work force, that is, cheap, politically repressed, and so on."[1] Through guest-worker programs such as the CSWAP, and more recently the Temporary Foreign Workers Program (TFWP), employers are granted the power to secure a captive, cheap, flexible labour force that better meets the bottom line.

As a result, we have witnessed the arrival of thousands of indentured workers to work in agriculture and in many other sectors such as construction. Workers are recruited either through their own government officials or through private labour brokers. In either case, labour brokers or consular officials from sending countries do not seem to be responsible for or care about workers' labour or living conditions. Otherwise we would expect them to provide workers with basic information about their rights and social entitlements, such as health care or workers' compensation. As a migrant farm worker said, "These consular officials only care about the employer. If he is happy, everything is well. If we phone the Consulate, they don't ever bother returning our calls. We simply don't count."

The Canadian government, on the other hand, has not allocated any funding to service this growing population. There are currently no government services, programs or orientation for temporary migrants, rendering them all the more vulnerable and marginalized.

Even before the Harper government came to office, guest worker programs allowed employers to choose the sex, nationality, and race of their workforce. Through the new Temporary Foreign Worker' Program, employers have been granted further unrestrained power over their labour force. In effect, employers are functioning like *de facto* immigration officials in their own right, who can dictate the terms of life and work in Canada. Through these guest worker programs, employers have more of a say in "who gets in" and "who gets out." Those who "get out" are usually the ones who have not complied with employer demands or who simply have fallen out of favour with employers for trivial reasons. Many such dismissals have no legal grounding, but cannot be contested since losing work means being repatriated immediately and/or losing the legal right to work for another employer.

The practice of assigning migrant workers to only one designated employer goes beyond the usual labour contract by enabling a type of labour servitude. Workers have to abide by and acquiesce to objectionable and often detrimental conditions of life and work in Canada. It is ludicrous that, after more than 40 years of the SAWP and pressure among advocacy organizations to amend its most deficient facets, the Harper government responds by creating new guest worker programs with much worse terms of labour mobility and human rights.

The reality is that, during the two years the Harper Conservative government has been in power, the immigration system has been privatized, for all intents and purposes, according to purely economic criteria dictated by corporate greed. While permanent immigration has been discouraged, a "temporary-forever" migration policy has been aggressively expanded under the umbrella of free trade agreements such as NAFTA. The tragic part is that this trend is likely to continue under more pro-corporate agreements like the new Security and Prosperity Partnership (SPP) agreement between Mexico, Canada, and the United States.

Deep Integration: The case of Three Amigos and who they leave out

It is not new for the Canadian government to leave the most affected and most vulnerable out of important decision-making processes that have a deep impact on their lives. However, the current scenario in which Ministers and Prime Ministers meet "secretly" to discuss the Security and Prosperity Partnership (SPP) goes even further. The SPP is even more undemocratic than NAFTA and has effects that go beyond the three North American countries.

Considering how NAFTA has affected the agricultural population in all three countries, we can predict the SPP will have further negative impacts on rural communities throughout North America, and particularly on Mexican migrant workers. Mexico, for example, has already suffered massive losses, culturally and economically, due to the collapse of its staple corn production.

The Three Amigos, with their ever-changing faces, now with the disguises of Stephen Harper, George Bush and Felipe Calderón, decide our collective fate. With pressing issues like border security and business competitiveness, it isn't surprising that the loss of land, home, family, community, identity, and security of hundreds of thousands of Mexican migrant workers a year is not in the hearts and minds of those discussing how to make an even bigger buck.

Harper has continued and excelled at Canada's role of contributing to the displacement of peoples by taking a lead in promoting the weakening and dismantling of public services and institutions in all three countries, yet also at keeping a tight control on who comes into and especially who stays in this country. The flow of cheap migrant labour is as important as the flow of products, to ensure business competitiveness.

Under the rule of Felipe Calderón, desperate "out-migration" has continued steadily, aided and abetted by the privatization of land and resources, state-instigated and state-sanctioned violence, increasing poverty, insecurity, lack of decent and secure work, and displacement that compels Mexicans to leave home in order to support their families.

Calderón, like Harper in Canada, continues in the footsteps of his predecessors, but with more overt signs of a military police state, aided by the recent U.S. Congress's approval of a Mexican-style version of Plan Colombia, the Merida Initiative, a war against drugs, which is an unashamedly brutal counter-insurgency assault on the social movements struggling for what are legitimately the Mexican people's rights: to dignity, land, and the basic necessities of life.

Because it is necessary for Mexicans to seek alternatives to the desperate situation in their country, they are ripe for super-exploitation through guest worker programs such as the Seasonal Agricultural Workers' Program (SAWP).

Commodified peoples, disposable workers

Survival is becoming more difficult for working Mexicans living in the cities and the countryside. The price of basic staples like corn rise steadily, and the work that is available is often precarious and meagerly paid. As a result, Mexicans continue to look North for a way out of poverty. The intensification of security measures along the U.S.-Mexico border has not deterred border crossings, but has called for more resourcefulness among those seeking to leave. Nowadays, *coyotes* are not necessary and frankly too out of reach for many Mexicans who cannot afford to pay one to go to the United States. Many try their luck and risk their lives by attempting to cross the Rio Grande on their own. Some look further North.

Some see Canada as an alternative and more tangible possibility than the United States. Certainly, the economic integration of Canada and Mexico is becoming more discernible in rural communities such as Cuijingo, Guadalupe Zaragoza, and Atotonilco, where almost every house has someone working in Canada as a temporary worker, mostly in the SAWP. Their numbers and the importance of Canadian wages make Canada seem like a haven. Often the hardships faced by migrants in Canada are not communicated back to families in order to protect those left behind.

Not surprisingly, Canada is generally viewed in Mexico as a benevolent country that respects human rights more than the United States does. Those who cannot participate in the SAWP seek other ways to migrate to Canada to work and to possibly stay. Upon arrival, however, they come to know the Canada of the Harper government. Now, as soon as a plane lands from Mexico, border patrol officials are immediately lined up as passengers exit the plane in order to separate those who can from those who cannot enter. Many Mexicans finding themselves in dubious labour schemes realize that, through the Mexican consulate, their rights as Mexicans do not carry any weight. Even in moments of crisis, they have no leverage. They experience the shock of their lives when they learn that Canada, for them, is not much different from the United States.

Through these guest worker programs, poverty is being re-packaged and imported from the Third World into the First World, together with a slew of social and environmental consequences. NAFTA has meant the further "*maquiladorization*" of Mexico, including Mexicans, for the profit margins of U.S. and Canadian capital. Mexican families and communities find themselves paying the harshest price for economic restructuring in Canada and the United States. Impoverished peasants and workers have little bargaining power to demand better conditions and wages. When a full day of farm work in Mexico renders about $6, it is easy to be swayed by guest worker programs and the trek up North. Certainly, Canadian dollar earnings go a long way in Mexico, but it is precisely the non-economic issues that are often forgotten in the evaluation of these labour migration schemes.

In economic terms as well, these guest worker programs create dangerous dependencies on remittances. They undermine local labour market productivity and economic self-sufficiency. In a time of global food crises, farms in Mexico are idle due to lack of workers and infrastructure, and environmental degradation. Nowadays, children of migrants do not have the same ties to the land as their parents. They are provided for by remittances, and, when they reach a certain age, many see migration or leaving as a career choice.

The impact of separation between children and parents is immeasurable. Women who stay behind must contend with overwork and multiple roles in the family and in their communities. While their work facilitates the migration of others who provide their labour power in important sectors of the Canadian and U.S. economies, they themselves are made completely invisible.

Most importantly, through guest worker programs, certain people become commodified and disposable. Migrants are accepted into Canada as workers, not as citizens or human beings tied to families and communities. Once they fall ill or are unable to produce according to employer expectations, they are discarded. In Mexico, there are hundreds of forgotten families and untold stories of how migration to Canada has tragically changed the lives of people forever.

In the film *Migrants: Those Who Come from Within,* Alicia tells her own story of how her husband in the SAWP was discarded by Canada after being accidentally dosed with pesticides and chemicals. He was prevented by his employer from taking showers or missing work in order to seek medical attention. He was never the same and died a month later in Mexico, leaving Alicia and her son alone without any financial support.[2]

These stories repeat themselves across rural communities and cities in Mexico. These are among the liabilities of such labour *de-facto* immigration schemes that are conveniently hidden from the Canadian public. In an interdependent world and within increasingly regional economic integration, Canadian government policies affect millions of people, not only within our borders, but also in communities like Cuijingo, Guadalupe Zaragoza, and Atotonilco. Through Harper's immigration policies and new migrant labour schemes, Canada has regressed to a time reminiscent of the most blatant racist gatekeeping.

The incident of the 80 Mexicans workers who were jailed and then deported from the Vancouver International airport is a concrete example of how the Harper government's policies have caused the commodification as well as the criminalization of migrant workers. At first, they are turned into units of labour to be bought and sold and exploited by *coyotes* who seek to profit from free trade in workers. Then the workers run the further risk of the immigration system turning them into criminals, either when they try to enter to work in the country, or when they speak out against substandard working and living conditions. In both cases the results are similar: they are simply deported because, after all, they are seen as nothing more than "capital on two legs." This is what is really "unusual" and truly outrageous about the way Stephen Harper treats "guests" in Canada.

Conservatives' No-Fly List Violates Rights

Bruce Campbell

SINCE SEPTEMBER 11, 2001, both Liberal and Conservative governments have introduced a vast array of measures that they claim are needed to combat terrorism. Some are enacted through laws such as the *Public Safety Act* and the *Anti-Terrorism Act*. Many others have come into being through bilateral agreements with the United States, such as the Smart Border Declaration and Action Plan, and the Safe Third Country Agreement.

These measures, which dramatically expand state power at the expense of our deeply held rights and freedoms and the rule of law, were not needed to deal with a genuine security threat. They were introduced mainly in response to U.S. government intimidation to bring Canadian security measures into line with draconian U.S. practices, and from Canadian business wanting to "do what it takes" to keep trade flowing across the border. (This harmonization process continues under the Security and Prosperity Partnership of North America.)

Canada's No Fly-list, introduced by the Conservative government on June 18, 2007, is an example of the high price Canadians are paying in terms of state erosion of the rights and freedoms guaranteed under the Charter of Rights and Freedoms. The Charter is a cornerstone of our legal system and operates to protect citizens from unjustified intrusions by government. Charter rights include mobility rights (section 6 of the

Charter), due process rights (section 7), rights to be free from unreasonable search and seizure (section 8), and equality rights (section 15).

The No-Fly list is part of a federal initiative known as the Passenger Protect Program. It operates like a restraining order, preventing people on the list from boarding an aircraft. While restraining orders against individuals are normally issued by judges after a hearing, this is not the case with the No-Fly list. Instead, the Minister of Transport, on the recommendation of a committee of three bureaucrats from Transport Canada, CSIS and the RCMP (based on information provided by the RCMP and CSIS), decides who will be on the list. This decision is made behind closed doors, with affected individuals having no opportunity to challenge the decision adding them to the list.

Federal guidelines exist to help determine who should be listed, but they are vague and subjective. For example, according to the Transport Canada backgrounder, a person "who is or has been involved in a terrorist group and who, it can reasonably be suspected, will endanger the security of any aircraft or airport, or the safety of the public, passengers, or crew members" may be on the list.

At first glance, the guidelines may seem reasonable, but a closer look raises serious concerns, particularly since the list is secret and not subject to any independent scrutiny.

First, one need not be charged with, or convicted of, any offence to be put on the list. Mere "involvement" with a group defined in the Criminal Code as "terrorist" is sufficient. This definition of "terrorist group" has been widely criticized, including by the Canadian Bar Association, as being vague and broad enough to capture charitable organizations with no direct or indirect connection to terrorist activities.

Second, there is a risk that the information from the RCMP and CSIS used to list people may be unreliable, even misleading. We know from the Arar Commission of Inquiry, for example, that the RCMP passed on inaccurate information to U.S. authorities, information that wrongly portrayed Arar as a terrorist suspect. The U.S. later shipped him to Syria, where he was imprisoned and tortured.

Arar is not the only Canadian to have suffered this fate. The Iacobucci Commission is currently investigating the conduct of Canadian officials in the cases of three other Muslim men imprisoned and tortured in

Syria: Abdullah Almalki, Muayed Nureddin, and Ahmed El Maati. (Their stories are told in *Dark Days*, by Kerry Pither, Penguin Books, 2008.)

Third, the standard for deciding if someone will endanger aviation safety is disturbingly low: that of *suspicion*, instead of the higher standard of *reasonable belief*, which requires solid evidence.

The consequences of being on the No-Fly list could be serious, even deadly. What if, for example, the list is shared with other countries, including those who torture? Brion Brandt, Transport Canada's director of security policy, testified before the Air India inquiry that, once the names on the list are given to the private airlines, there is no way to prevent the airlines from passing them on to foreign governments.

A June, 2007 resolution adopted by Canada's Privacy Commissioners and Privacy Enforcement Officials reinforces this concern. The resolution states:

> It is alarming that Transport Canada has not provided assurances that the names of individuals identified on the No-Fly list will not be shared with other countries. We do not want to see, through the failure to take adequate safeguards, other tragic situations arise where the security of Canadian citizens may be affected or compromised by security forces at home or abroad.

The No-Fly list is the "trigger" that may prevent someone from flying. All airline passengers in Canada are automatically screened against the list before being issued a boarding pass. In the event of a possible match, airlines must contact Transport Canada for a decision on whether to issue an emergency direction barring the person on the list from flying. If barred from flying, the individual is grounded and the airport or local police notified. Detention could follow, and with it anxiety and stress. Unable to fly, the person's ability to earn a living may be jeopardized, not to mention the increased hardship in visiting family and friends.

The No-Fly list violates fundamental rights, such as due process rights under section 7 of the Charter. Section 7 guarantees the right to life, liberty and security of the person and the right not to be deprived thereof except in accordance with the principles of fundamental justice. If the state, through its officials, deprives us of our liberty by detaining us, or deprives us of our security by putting our names on secret lists and using secret information about us, then fundamental justice requires that we be told the basis for the allegations against us. It also requires that we have an opportunity for some type of hearing, by an impartial body, to challenge the actions of the state.

There is no fundamental justice in the case of the No-Fly list. Individuals are listed with no notice and no opportunity for a hearing. If names on the list are shared with other countries, individuals could face deportation and detention as a result, and never know why. Admittedly, individuals whose rights have been thus violated can seek a review of their inclusion on the No-Fly list through Transport Canada's Office of Reconsideration, but this is not an independent review. And the Office can only recommend. The ultimate decision-maker is the Minister of Transport, who had the person's name put on the list in the first place.

The No-Fly list impacts other Charter rights. Mobility rights, including the right to move anywhere in Canada, will be affected if those on the list are prevented from flying. Privacy rights may also be affected in violation of section 8 of the Charter if an individual's personal information is searched, seized, and possibly shared with other countries.

The list may also be a form of racial or religious profiling that would violate Charter equality rights; but this would be difficult to prove given that the list is secret.

The rule of law, a principle of fundamental justice central to our democracy, requires that any state action limiting rights must be authorized by law. This same principle is embodied in section 1 of the Charter. If a state measure is shown to violate a Charter right, the state then has the burden of showing that there is lawful authority for the measure.

Transport Canada argues that the *Aeronautics Act* and Identity Screening Regulations provide authority for the No-Fly list, but Canada's Privacy Commissioners disagree. They argue in their June 2007 resolution that there is no clear or adequate legislative framework to support the list. The Conservative government could have provided such a framework by proposing changes to the *Aeronautics Act* that would have to be debated in the House of Commons and subject to public scrutiny. Instead, like so many of the security initiatives introduced post-9/11, the No-Fly list came into effect through the back door, with no opportunity for the discussion and debate that are so essential in any democracy.

Other criteria must be met by governments wanting to defend rights violations under the Charter. First, they have to show some compelling justification for such rights infringements. Second, they have to show that the measures they have adopted are carefully tailored to minimize any Charter violations. These criteria cannot be met in the case of the No-Fly list. As the British Columbia Civil Liberties Association states in its position paper on the list: "There is no compelling justification presented for the use of No-Fly lists and no aspect of such lists is benign."

If the Conservative government was concerned about preventing terrorists and others from endangering aviation, they didn't need a No-Fly list to achieve this result. The *Aeronautics Act* already contained provisions to prevent persons believed to pose an immediate threat to airline security from boarding a plane.

There is no evidence that No-Fly lists make us safer. The U.S. list, originally intended to be narrowly focused, has ballooned, with estimates of the current number of names ranging from 30,000 to 120,000. Names on the list include prominent public figures such as Nelson Mandela and Bolivian President Evo Morales. Many people have also been stopped from flying simply for having names that were the same or similar to those on the list. For example, U.S. Senator Edward Kennedy has repeatedly had problems boarding flights because his name apparently corresponds to a "T. Kennedy" on the list.

To date, no terrorists have been apprehended through use of the U.S. list. The CBS show *Sixty Minutes* spent months with Joe Trento of the National Security News Service, going over names on the U.S. No-Fly list. Trento — asked about the quality of information that the U.S. Transportation Security Agency gets from the CIA and the FBI in order to compile the list — says:

> Well, you know about our intelligence before we went to war in Iraq. You know what that was like. Not too good... This is much worse. It's awful, it's bad. I mean, you've got people who are dead on the list. You've got people you know are 80 years old on the list. It makes no sense.

The Canadian No-Fly list (believed to be in the low thousands) is also fallible. Canadian Press reporter Jim Bronskill (April 19, 2008) was told by Transport Canada that it had received about 50 calls from passengers whose names turned up on the list, but all were false matches. A case in point is that of two Canadian boys, both named Alistair Butt. Shortly after No-Fly came into effect, a 10-year-old from Saskatchewan and a 15-year-old from Ontario were stopped while trying to board flights. It appears that their names matched a name on the No-Fly list. After long delays, the boys were allowed to board; but their families fear they will face the same problem every time they try to fly. Transport Canada would not confirm whether the boys were on the Canadian list, an airline No-Fly list, or the U.S. No-Fly list.

U.S. Homeland Security Secretary Michael Chertoff has called for the U.S. and Canadian No-Fly lists to be merged. (Even though the U.S. still refuses to remove Maher Arar's name from its list despite repeated requests from the Canadian government to do so.)

In the meantime, the U.S. is in the process of expanding its own No-Fly list with a new system called "Secure Flight." Under this program, the U.S. will not only vet passengers against watch-lists, but will also conduct routine background checks on all passengers. All airlines with international flights leaving from, flying to, or even flying over the U.S. (to Latin America), will have to hand over to Homeland Security passenger and crew manifest data, as well as the much more detailed and intrusive Passenger Name Recognition information (PNR). The Canadian government has requested a total exemption from the Secure Flight program, but it is not known whether this request has been granted.

How does the Conservative government defend intrusive measures such as the No-Fly list? It does so by trying to use the Charter of Rights and Freedoms as its shield. In a written reply to questions about the list from NDP MP Peter Julian, Minister of Transport Lawrence Cannon said the government, by preventing passengers who "may" be a threat from boarding aircraft, is fulfilling a duty under section 7 of the Charter to protect the right to life and personal security of the crew and other passengers.

According to human rights lawyers, however, Cannon has it wrong. *Section 7 exists to protect us from unwarranted government intrusions.*

Canada has laws such as the Criminal Code, as well as police and security agents, to protect our security. The government does have a legitimate role to play in aviation security, too, but the Charter does not authorize it to trample on our human rights in so doing. Intrusive and unreasonable state actions run directly contrary to the purpose of the Charter. Either the Minister of Transport is ignorant of the law or he is suggesting that the actions of the Conservative government are above the law. In either case, those concerned about these most deeply held Canadian values should be outraged.

Canada and International Human Rights

Opportunity abandoned

John W. Foster

> The United Nations Convention Against Torture is not a factor in deciding whether to send information to countries such as Syria and Egypt about Canadians detained there.
> —*Official, Department of Justice, Iacobucci Inquiry, January 2008.*

THE CAUSE OF human rights in the global community is threatened as never before. The assault on democratic rights and civil liberties undertaken by many governments following 9/11 and the passage of the *Patriot Act* in the United States continues, although the "moral panic" which led to extreme measures in the immediate wake may have faded. The persistent pressure to protect investor privilege and assert the claims of trade, investment, and intellectual property accords over established human rights treaties and environmental agreements continues apace. The indifference, sometimes ignorance, and posturing of many governments, often leave existing international human rights law without active advocates.

In this context, many eyes have focused on the Canadian government. Canadians, since the writing of the Universal Declaration on Human Rights after World War II, have often been in the vanguard of human rights advances, whether the rights of children, the struggle against violence against women, and the full recognition of equality itself.

Thus, particularly since the election of the Harper minority government, Canadians travelling outside the country can be caught short by the question, "What's happened to Canada?"

For reasons of economy of space and the patience of the reader, we have asked where has Canada had the opportunity to strengthen human rights internationally, to defend key elements which are threatened, and to advance the frontier of rights.

To this end, we have focused on three key and controversial recent instances:

- the resignation of Louise Arbour, UN High Commissioner for Human Rights;
- the government's response to the release of its orientation material on torture; and
- the government's about-turn in opposition to the UN Declaration on the Rights of Indigenous Peoples.

Louise Arbour as High Commissioner for Human Rights: Victim of "friendly fire"?

> The Conservative government essentially said goodbye to Louise Arbour by telling her: Good riddance. You were a disgrace and you won't be missed.[1]

There is a picture, taken in Valstica, Kosovo, in July 1999, showing the Chief Prosecutor for the International Criminal Tribunal for the Former Yugoslavia, visiting the site where several members of the Shabani family had been killed. Louise Arbour, the prosecutor, is holding the hands of two family members, the elderly Mihrije and younger Emin, as they recount the deadly event. The witness of violent and more subtle violation of fundamental rights has been part of the daily work of Louise Arbour in her work for international tribunals and since she left the

Supreme Court of Canada to serve as UN High Commissioner for Human Rights.

Arbour was a former prosecutor who could be not only persistent, but also tough. She had secured the indictment of the late Serbian leader Slobadan Milosevic. What is telling in the 1999 photo is that the visiting prosecutor does not hold back from what she is witnessing; unable to express overt solidarity, she is instead holding hands with two of the survivors as they bear witness together.

With the departure of Louise Frechette from her position as Deputy Secretary-General of the UN, Arbour, who is also Under-Secretary-General of the UN, was the highest placed Canadian international civil servant. Being High Commissioner for Human Rights means being a target for criticism from any state which feels its interests or reputation is under fire on human rights issues, as Arbour's predecessor, Mary Robinson of Ireland, well knew. Being the target of "friendly fire" from her own government was perhaps something Robinson avoided, but it characterized Arbour's final days at the Office of the High Commissioner.

In the Canadian Parliament, Treasury Board President and former Justice Minister Vic Toews yelled, "she's a disgrace" when Liberal Martha Hall Findlay called on the government to salute Arbour's work as High Commissioner. Later, Toews told the House that "the comments that Louise Arbour has made in respect of the state of Israel and the people of Israel are, in fact, a disgrace and I stand by those words."[2]

While newly appointed Foreign Affairs Minister David Emerson was quick to say the government "congratulate(s) the work of Louise Arbour," the Toews remark betrays an underlying attitude that has run long and deep within the government, and which, in denigrating the person, also denigrates the urgent work of international human rights bodies. The fact that the latest attack came from the mouth of a former justice minister, who should know much better, is particularly shocking, and, given his senior status in the tightly reined Harper government, brings his colleagues in Cabinet into question as well.

In a defence of Arbour, former Supreme Court justice Claire L'Heureux-Dubé noted the piquant coincidence of Toews attack with the release of a report from the Observatory for the Protection of Human

Rights Defenders, which notes that "human rights defenders around the world are facing increasing state efforts to stifle their actions and to clamp down on dissent."[3]

A detailed examination of Arbour's contribution came from former Canadian Ambassador to the E.U. (and formerly to Russia, the U.K., and various other highly rated capitals) Jeremy Kinsman.[4] Kinsman highlights some of the issues on which Arbour took position, first among them torture. As the U.S. prevaricated on such fundamentals as the definition of torture, Arbour denied that "waterboarding" was "enhanced interrogation," calling it torture. She also called for an absolute ban on the transfer of prisoners who could be tortured. Needless to say, her position was unwelcome in Washington. Arbour was also critical of the U.S. offshore prison at Guantanamo. She intervened at the U.S. Supreme Court with a "friend of the court" brief as it dealt with the status of Guantanamo detainees in August, 2007.[5]

Arbour's interventions in the Middle East seemed to particularly upset Minister Toews, and, according to some observers, was the key in motivating the Harper government's failure to support a further term for her as High Commissioner, as well as its belated and somewhat forced expressions of appreciation. When Israel went to war with Lebanon in 2006, Arbour, while aware of rights violations by Hezbollah, criticized the Olmert government's war as a disproportionate response to the kidnapping of Israeli soldiers by the Lebanese radicals. She also warned that "those in positions of command and control" might be subject to "personal criminal responsibility." As CBC News notes: "These words were seen by many as directed towards Israel, and were rejected by Israel's ambassador to Canada."[6] What may be forgotten is that Israeli bombs had killed, among others, UN peace-observation personnel, including one Canadian citizen.

Reactions to Arbour's assessment were strong, but, as Kinsman notes, a number of bodies, including commission investigations in Israel, have come to similar assessments. Nevertheless, attacks by some Canadian editorialists were nasty: "Was it necessary," Kinsman asks," to accuse her of bias and anti-Semitism, as several commentators did in the *National Post,* calling for her resignation?" The *Post's* nastiness continued through her resignation. Columnist Jonathan Kay could not forgive her for her assessment of Israel's role in civilian casualties in the 2006 war or for her criticism of the war on terror. "So long, you won't be missed," he snarled.[7]

Arbour was direct and outspoken on a wide variety of regional and thematic human rights challenges, including criticizing the Sri Lankan government for impunity in repressing the Tamils. She was equally critical of the Ugandan and Chinese authorities. She made a very positive yet realistic address to the International Conference on Lesbian, Gay, Bisexual and Transgender Human Rights in Montreal, July 2006, decrying the silence which often obscures violations of their rights and criticizing states who fail to recognize those rights and attack those who defend them.[8]

Arbour was also attacked for her more general but important assesment that the U.S.-defined "war on terror" had "inflicted a very serious setback for the international human rights agenda."

In 2005, as debate over U.S. practices was hot, Arbour declared that, "pursuing security objectives at all costs may create a world in which we are neither safe nor free. This will certainly be the case if the only choice is between the terrorists and the torturers." Then U.S. Ambassador at the UN, John R. Bolton, told Arbour she should concentrate on "real" abusers, not the U.S.[9] Nevertheless, Secretary of State Condoleezza Rice declared that the ban on torture applied to U.S. personnel overseas. Confusion over the U.S. position continued, however, not only because of Bolton's attack on Arbour, but also because Rice did not explicitly repudiate earlier positions taken by U.S. Attorney-General Alberto Gonzales.

U.S. attacks on Arbour were by no means the only pressures she had to deal with. Several assessments specify her disappointment with the behaviour of governments in the new UN Human Rights Council. The Council was created by the reforms instituted in 2005 in reaction to criticisms that the previous Human Rights Commission had become overly politicized. Countries like China, Belarus, Cuba and others resisted a more even-handed approach in the new Council, keeping the spotlight on Israel's policies alone. Given the power of state representatives in the UN system, Arbour found herself unable to bring the Council to more balanced behaviour.

A further instance of this kind of dispute has been brewing over the coming 2009 UN Conference reviewing the results of the 2001 Durban World Conference Against Racism, which had contributed to the political demise of Mary Robinson, who had presided as High Commissioner. Canada, the U.S. and Israel have all announced they will boycott the event.[10]

When Arbour announced that she would not seek a second term (her first and only term ended June, 2008)[11], she did not accuse any government of holding a knife. A government committed to human rights would presumably have campaigned for a second term. The sad drama of her resignation announcement in March testified to the grudging "support" which the Harper government was willing to offer. Reportedly, "the Canadian diplomat who was present barely acknowledged Mrs. Arbour's presence and issued a statement that other diplomats called remarkable for its blandness: 'Canada is and will continue to be a strong supporter of [the Human Rights Council] mandate and your office's work for the promotion and protection of human rights.'" A "back-handed rebuke."[12] It was reported that a direct order not to comment on her resignation originated in the Prime Minister's Office.

Amnesty International's Geneva representative and former Canadian diplomat Peter Splinter observed of the Canadian representative's statement: "I can't understand how any Canadian can behave like that, especially when she announced her intention to retire." He continued, "The criticism she receives is a tribute to the good work that she's been doing."[13] Reaction was sufficiently strong that Foreign Affairs Minister Maxime Bernier issued a later brief statement praising Arbour for "expanding the concepts of human rights and fundamental justice... She was steadfast in the pursuit of her vision of an independent High Commissioner who acts in new and energetic ways to increase the presence of her office around the world."

The views of many outside the Harper government were much more positive. As the Director of the Danish Human Rights Institute noted, "Despite [the "chill" following 9/11], she contributed a great deal to the creation of the new Human Rights Council at the UN, and she managed to enlarge the budget of the UN's human rights program. On the whole, human rights has been given a higher priority in the UN system, thanks to her efforts." Her departure is "sad and regrettable."[14] In an interview with CBC-TV, Arbour was asked if she had expected more from the Canadian government. She simply replied that a "thank you" would have been nice.

Kinsman concludes: "So a good woman steps down. Not a great day for the UN or for human rights. She will be missed."[15] Not a great day for Canada, either.

Torture: A national embarrassment

> An absolute ban on torture, a cornerstone of the international human rights edifice, is under attack. The principle once believed to be unassailable...is becoming a casualty of the so-called war on terror.
> —*High Commissioner for Human Rights, Louise Arbour, 2005.*

Canada signed the Convention Against Torture on August 23, 1985, one of the first countries to do so, and ratified the Convention on June 24, 1987. As the website of the Department of Canadian Heritage states succinctly: "When becoming party to a treaty, a State must execute, in good faith, the provisions of the treaty subject to the reservations it may have made."[16] But Canada's "good faith" has come under severe question as Canadians have suffered torture in jails abroad, as Afghan prisoners have been sent by Canadian forces to Afghan jails where torture is reported, and as Canada's collaboration in the U.S.-led "war on terror" involves our government and its agencies in complicity and collaboration in torture itself.

One of the positive results of the lengthy and tragic story of the treatment of Maher Arar was some attempt to ensure that the Canadian official personnel were better informed and prepared to deal with such threats to the welfare of Canadians abroad in future.[17] One of the modest but essential initiatives was the preparation of a manual and the introduction of training opportunities for Canadian diplomats, dealing with the issue of torture.

The 2007 document was given to Amnesty International (Canada) as part of a case it was pursuing regarding the treatment of Afghan detainees. It consists of an 89-page power point presentation[18] which provided legal definitions applied to torture, and informed officials of how to detect signs of abuse among detainees. It specified treatment at Guantanamo as well as a number of other country-specific examples, including Afghanistan, China, Egypt, Iran, Israel, Mexico, Saudi Arabia, and Syria. The manual included in its definition of torture such U.S. techniques as sleep deprivation and forced nudity. The news, injected into the midst of the continuing debate in the U.S. regarding "water-boarding" and other torture techniques, was headline material there and around the world. It also heated up the debate in Canada about the treatment of Afghan detainees in Afghan jails.[19]

The publicity regarding the manual was greeted positively by Amnesty in Canada, and by a number of foreign commentators. Jonathan Turley, Shapiro Professor of Public Interest Law at George Washington University in the U.S. capital, saluted the Canadian release, but stated with regret: "There was of course a time when the United States led the world in a campaign against torture."[20] Needless to say, the reaction from the ambassadors of countries named was less laudatory. Reuters reported: "U.S. ambassador David Wilkins said the listing was absurd, while the Israeli envoy said he wanted his country removed."[21] Canada's ill-fated Minister of Foreign Affairs, Maxime Bernier, on January 19, 2008, issued a disclaimer:

> I regret the embarrassment caused by the public disclosure of the manual used in the department's torture awareness training. It contains a list that wrongly includes some of our closest allies. I have directed that the manual be reviewed and rewritten. The manual is neither a policy document nor a statement of policy. As such, it does not convey the Government's views or positions.[22]

One of the shocking aspects of the torture imbroglio in early 2008 was the almost total absence, either in politician's commentary or in press coverage, of reference to the Torture Convention and Canada's obligations under it. Liberal foreign affairs critic Bob Rae aimed his shots at Foreign Affairs and the manual, rather than at the principles and legal obligations involved:

"It's incomprehensible to me that a document would establish an equivalency between the United States and Iran on the subject of the treatment of prisoners," said Rae. "It's too hard to understand how it (the document) could have gotten this far. There's a real issue now around the competency of the Conservative government on foreign affairs issues."[23]

Like Bernier, Rae's main concern seems to have been to avoid embarrassing the U.S., rather than reminding the government of its fundamental human rights obligations and legal commitments under the Torture Convention.

Too little discussion of Canada's involvement with torture ensued after the January foreign affairs imbroglio. However, the *Literary Review of Canada* published in May 2008 a useful essay by Calgary researcher Regan Boychuk on the ambiguous history of Canada's role in the development of torture techniques by the CIA.[24] This provoked responses from leading academics. University of Calgary's Barry Cooper argues that the United Nations definition of torture — i.e., inflicting severe pain or suffering — is "sentimental." He accuses Boychuk of being anti-American, but admits that torture is, in any case, ineffective.[25]

For his part, University of Toronto's Wesley Wark disputes Boychuk's emphasis on Canadian contributions to the CIA's buffet of torture techniques, and argues that *complicity* is not the issue. Rather, he suggests that Canadians lack strong moral bearings on the question of torture. "What is really difficult is to define our moral standards when upholding both national security and fundamental justice, and then stick to them."[26] Further, Erna Paris notes the phenomenon of "slippage" with regard to such standards, citing "the undermining effect on the rule of law in other countries when the most powerful democracy on Earth breaks long-established rules".[27] Wark's point is an appropriate evaluation of Canadian political leaders and their advisors. We can find illustrations under Martin as well as Harper of the kind of slippage that Paris specifies. These are allegedly justified by the diplomatic need to "improve" relations with our great ally to the south.

In response, Boychuk refuses to be drawn off course. He reiterates the *absolute* prohibition of torture under the international convention, and goes on to remind readers of Canada's dubious history in the development of "sophisticated" torture techniques. The techniques developed in Montreal several decades ago continue to be esteemed by the CIA. When the U.S. ratified the Convention Against Torture, it reserved for itself the possibility of permitting sensory deprivation. The more recent use of sensory deprivation in the treatment of Omar Khadr in Guantanamo sharpens the point. The conscious participation of the Canadian Security and Intelligence Service (CSIS) in its use and in attempting to benefit from it in their interrogation of Khadr brings it home.[28]

One might hope that the conclusions and recommendations of the inquiry into the case of Maher Arar would have closed the book on Canadian complicity with torture, but it didn't. Government officials testifying at its sequel, the Iacobucci Inquiry into the overseas detentions of Muayyed Nureddin, Ahmah Abou El Maati, and Abdullah Almalki, indicate little has been learned or applied. For example, Justice Department witness Michael Pierce, testifying at the latter inquiry, stated that the government was justified in sharing information with other governments that have a reputation for torture:

> Michael Pierce also told the internal inquiry yesterday that the United Nations Convention Against Torture is not a factor in deciding whether to send information to countries such as Syria and Egypt about Canadians detained there.[29]

Is the Canadian government truly opposed to torture? Does that opposition bind its agencies and security forces? Are the parliamentary and civilian review and accountability mechanisms adequately informed and vigilant in holding the government to account, given our international treaty obligations under the Convention?

Omar Khadr: Torture as public policy

The Khadr case is of urgent importance, not only because of torture, but because it brings into play (and into question) a number of other human rights concerns. The government has a fundamental obligation to protect the security and liberty of Canada's citizens. The contemporary world is replete with actual and potential challenges, given the multitude of legal and questionable activities of a highly mobile population.

In a recent joint article, former Rights and Democracy head Ed Broadbent and Amnesty International (Canada) Secretary-General Alex Neve summarize the issues involved:

- Khadr was a child soldier when the incidents from which charges of his alleged acts emerge. Child soldiers are due protection and rehabilitation under international law which views them as victims rather than criminals.
- Khadr's detention in Guantanamo violates Canadian and international human rights law, and Guantanamo detention has three times been ruled in violation of the U.S. Constitution.
- As indicated above, Khadr has been subjected to torture and other harsh treatment, with the collaboration of certain Canadian agencies.
- The legal processes instituted by the U.S. authorities are military and inappropriate.

Canada is the only developed democracy which has permitted one of its citizens to remain incarcerated in Guantanamo and in the U.S. procedures. He is being subjected to: "an illegal military commission, contrary to international law" as a joint release of the Canadian Arab Federation and the International Civil Liberties Monitoring Group stated on July 10, 2008.[30] The Canadian government has consistently refused to bring him home. On the other hand, the Harper government sent a private jet, at considerable public cost, to return another citizen, Brenda Martin, convicted under Mexican law, back to Canada. Bringing Khadr back to Canada would, of course, put in question U.S. practices — intelligence gathering and military legal — in Guantanamo, but no more question than either Canada's other Western allies or the U.S. courts have already raised.

Refusing to do so, as Broadbent and Neve point out, could create a nasty precedent. "The UN Special Representative for Children in Armed Conflict has warned against the precedent the Khadr case may set in prosecuting individuals as war criminals for acts they committed as children."[31] As the *Calgary Herald* put it recently: "They did it for Michael Kapoustin, and they did it for Brenda Martin. Now the federal government should do the right thing for Omar Khadr and bring him back to Canada. It's the only place where he can get due process."[32]

The Declaration on the Rights of Indigenous Peoples: Why does the government continue to do things it needs to apologize for?

> The Declaration provides a principled framework that promotes a vision of justice and reconciliation. In our considered opinion, it is consistent with the Canadian Constitution and Charter and is profoundly important for fulfilling their promise. Government claims to the contrary do a grave disservice to the cause of human rights and to the promotion of harmonious and cooperative relations.
>
> — *Open letter from over 100 legal experts and scholars.*[33]

On June 12, 2008, Prime Minister Harper made the first formal apology by a Canadian Prime Minister for the treatment of Aboriginal students in residential schools, terming the policy of assimilation on which it was based "wrong, has caused great harm, and has no place in our country."[34] While the indigenous apology by Prime Minister Harper was perhaps the most positive moment in his government's history, several responses to the apology urged that Canada reverse its opposition to the UN Declaration on the Rights of Indigenous Peoples. The apology represented a significant advance over the posture of the government on indigenous issues when it took office, but its role in active opposition to the UN Declaration stands to undermine the forward momentum that could emerge from the apology.

The United Nations General Assembly, on September 13, 2007, voted 143 to 4 (with 11 abstentions) in favour of adopting the Declaration on the Rights of Indigenous Peoples.[35] The four countries opposing the Declaration were Australia, Canada, New Zealand, and the United States. On September 12, 2007, Indian Affairs Minister Chuck Strahl announced that Canada would vote against the Declaration, because:

> it is fundamentally flawed and lacks clear, practical guidance for implementation, and contains provisions that are fundamentally incompatible with Canada's constitutional framework. It also does not recognize Canada's need to balance indigenous rights to land and resources with the rights of others.[36]

Reading these concerns, the priority interests of a government strongly committed to resource exploitation and the interests of the corporate sector engaged therein become clear. Strahl objects to "prior and informed consent when used as a veto," is concerned about "lands, territories and resources" and references to "self-government" related to them, intellectual property and the need to achieve appropriate balance between the rights and obligations of indigenous peoples, governments, and "third parties."[37]

The resource sector interests are just as strongly represented in examination of the concerns motivating Australia's objection to the Declaration. A joint risk briefing by the Centre for Australian Ethical Research and the Ethical Investment Research Services focused on seven companies (two — Barrick Gold and Suncor Energy — of Canadian origin) operating in countries with recognized indigenous peoples and engaged in activities that have the potential to infringe on indigenous peoples' land and/or sea rights. It examines issues and responses in such areas as litigations (by native peoples in New Guinea against BHP Billiton and other mine owners, for example), increased regulation provoked by inadequate consultation with indigenous peoples, injury to corporate public relations, etc.[38] Clearly the Declaration touched on many areas of considerable sensitivity and, while non-binding, could find its way into guiding the setting of standards and argument in litigation.

The Declaration, however, as its many advocates point out, is not a treaty; it is a statement of intention or aspiration. In fact, a number of native leaders considered it lacking. The spokesman for the Confederation of Indigenous Nationalities of Ecuador (CONAIE), Manuel Castro, concluded: "Twenty years of debate...and we end up with a non-binding Declaration that does not force governments to do anything; this is a disgrace." Others, like José del Val, former director of the Inter-American

Indigenous Institute, were more qualified in assessment: the Declaration should be taken "as an ethical and moral reference point for indigenous peoples, but nothing more than that."[39]

Nevertheless, the Declaration it is not without significance, as the minority opposition it engendered demonstrates. It recognizes the right of indigenous peoples to determine and develop priorities and strategies for the development and use of their lands, territories, and other resources, including the right to require that States obtain their free and informed consent prior to the approval of any project affecting their lands, territories or other resources (Art. 30).[40] As a joint statement by international NGOs, including several Canadian bodies, pointed out on passage: "Adoption of the Declaration sends a clear message to the international community that the rights of Indigenous peoples are not separate from or less than the rights of others, but are an integral and indispensable part of a human rights systems dedicated to the rights of all."[41]

The Declaration was the product of more than 20 years negotiation. Mary Simon, President of the Inuit Tapiriit Kanatami, one of the Canadians who participated in developing the Declaration, stated:

> The UN Declaration promotes minimum human rights standards necessary to the "survival, dignity and well-being of the Indigenous peoples of the world." These include the right of self-determination, protections from discrimination and genocide, and recognition of rights to lands, territories and resources that are essential to the identity, health and livelihood of Indigenous peoples.[42]

Canada, as Amnesty International (Canada) points out, after initial resistance, then became an active and positive ally, working with indigenous representatives and others in the UN Working Group on the Draft Declaration. However, with the Harper government setting policy, and Canada as a member of the new Human Rights Council, Canadian officials were "implacably and inexplicably opposed to the Declaration."[43] They forced a vote opposing consensus, and joined Russia in opposing the Declaration.

As Amnesty points out, Canadian officials had for years played a central role in drafting the Declaration. It was not only surprising but also unsubstantiated for the Indian Affairs Minister, Jim Prentice, to claim in the House of Commons that the Declaration was inconsistent with "the Charter of Rights...our Constitution...the National Defence Act... our treaties, and...with all of the policies under which we have negotiated land claims for 100 years."[44]

The current Canadian government spent the year following the Council's approval, actively worked to undermine the work which Simon, together with other international indigenous leaders and diplomats, had contributed. Assembly of First Nations National Chief Phil Fontaine pointed out that, while the Department of Indian and Northern Affairs promotes international rights on its website, at the UN Canadian government officials are actively lobbying other countries against the Declaration.

"I can't believe our own government would act this way," former Conservative cabinet minister David MacDonald said. "Our country should be setting a good example internationally."[45] High Commissioner for Human Rights Louise Arbour expressed her "astonishment" at the Canadian position and her "profound disappointment."[46]

While the Declaration was passed in mid-2006 by the UN's Human Rights Council, recommending speedy approval by the General Assembly, Canada was among those seeking further delay. When the document came to the General Assembly more than a year later, Canadian UN Ambassador John McNee stated that no "open, inclusive or transparent process" had occurred between the Council's approval and the General Assembly's consideration. He stated that Canada had urged such a process "with the effective involvement of indigenous peoples."[47]

Australia's Howard government collaborated with Canada in opposing the Declaration, but the chance that the Rudd government which replaced it may open a more positive path remains at time of writing. The new Australian government has announced its intention to consult with stakeholders on the possibility of reversing Howard's opposition. Two leading Australian human rights bodies, the Human Rights Law Resource Centre and the Indigenous Law Centre, have urged it to do so, supporting the "aspirational character" of the Declaration and arguing that the former government's opposition was based on "myths and misperceptions."[48]

The Canadian Parliament, on April 8, 2008, voted to endorse the Declaration, an action which has also been taken by the Government of the Northwest Territories. Here's how it was described:

> The declaration was endorsed by 148-113 in a vote divided exclusively along party lines, with the Conservative party providing all of the nay votes, said Craig Benjamin, campaigner for the Human Rights of Indigenous Peoples for Amnesty International Canada. "The three opposition parties — the Liberals, the New Democratic party and Bloc Québécois — brought forth the motion in direct response to requests made to them by national Aboriginal organizations," Benjamin said.[49]

The Harper Government appears to have felt the need to do some "damage control" at the UN, with Indian Affairs Minister Chuck Strahl hosting a luncheon at the Canadian Permanent Mission to the UN to "share...some of the novel approaches that my government has championed to increase the inclusion of Canada's Aboriginal peoples in the social and economic fabric of our country." Strahl admitted that the Declaration signalled "good intentions," but "fell short of our expectations in a number of areas — particularly the sections on lands and resources; the concept of free, prior and informed consent; and self-government."[50]

The government's position has continued to be negative since the General Assembly's overwhelming approval of the Declaration. The Human Rights Council renewed the mandate of the Special Rapporteur on the Situation of the Human Rights and Fundamental Freedoms of Indigenous People in the fall of 2007 and that person, S. James Anaya, a professor of human rights at the University of Arizona, began his mandate in March, 2008.[51] Canada insisted in inserting the words "where appropriate" in the mandate of the new rapporteur as it related to the Declaration. "Canada made it clear," Amnesty comments, "that the Special Rapporteur should not have jurisdiction to promote the Declaration in countries which had voted against its adoption." The U.S. later emphasized the point.

Amnesty International notes that this approach sets a very negative precedent. The Declaration is an aspirational document (in one sense like the UDHR) meant to guide and inspire governments and others. If some governments can opt out of such a statement of purpose when it has been overwhelmingly approved by their counterparts, this "dramatically undercuts the integrity of the international human rights system."[52]

With the Harper government's apology in June, responses from the New Democratic party and Bloc Québécois leaders stressed the importance of the government moving from opposition to support on the Declaration. The July meeting of the Council of the Federation was urged by AFN Chief Fontaine to join in pressure for Canadian endorsement of the Declaration.[53] Council host Québec Premier Jean Charest confirmed that the premiers had discussed the Declaration "and expressed the hope to see Canada eventually endorse the document." However, Charest indicated, "some premiers want clarifications on the Declaration" before acting. The AFN plans to continue its advocacy for the Declaration in provincial and territorial capitals.[54]

On May 1, 2008, in an open letter, 101 lawyers and academics across Canada stated that there is no legal barrier to Canada's endorsing the Declaration, ripping away the prevarications of the Harper team: "No credible legal rationale has been provided to substantiate these extraordinary and erroneous claims." The letter rejects the government's charge that the instrument is unbalanced. Further, the experts state, "The Declaration provides a principled framework that promotes a vision of justice and reconciliation. In our considered opinion, it is consistent with the Canadian Constitution and Charter and is profoundly important for fulfilling their promise. Government claims to the contrary do a grave disservice to the cause of human rights and to the promotion of harmonious and cooperative relations."

The letter goes on to express concern about the negative international consequences of the government's behaviour. "We are concerned that the misleading claims made by the Canadian government continue to be used to justify opposition, as well as impede international cooperation and implementation of this human rights instrument."[55]

The government's record: Opportunities missed or consciously denied

The three instances outlined above deal with only a few dimensions of Canada's role in the protection of human rights. It should be underlined that the failure in leadership in human rights goes far beyond rights-specific agencies, to the core of foreign policy and international relations. The Harper government, for example, has made much of a new "strategy" for the Americas. Secretary of State for Foreign Affairs Helena Guergis gave a major speech in Philadelphia on June 28, 2008, on the strategy. But many observers are skeptical, as a *Toronto Star* reporter commented: "A couple of trips, a couple of free trade agreements does not a foreign policy make."

Precisely. A foreign policy informed by human rights priorities would make developing strong links with indigenous-led Bolivia a priority, and would take the welfare of the indigenous people fighting mining exploitation in Ecuador much more seriously. Such a strategy would never forward a bilateral trade and investment agreement with Colombia as long as it is the worst human rights violator in South America. Such a strategy would prioritize the ratification, with appropriate gender-sensitive reservations, of the American Convention on Human Rights and the companion Protocol of San Salvador on Economic, Social and Cultural Rights. A human rights-infused strategy in the hemisphere would make the eradication of poverty and support of governments which share that value central. It would resist further U.S. militarization of the region.

When one adds the list of human rights implications, intermingling domestic and international, arising from the various border, immigration, military, intelligence and policy "harmonization" agreements made by Canada and the United States since 9/11, the challenges to human rights become even more daunting. Security analyst Maureen Webb says that: "In many ways, the era we entered with 9/11 is an Age of Terror, an Age where an individual at any time can be presumed guilty and blacklisted from a job, dragged out of a line, denied the right to travel, listened in on, detained and even kidnapped, tortured and killed without ever knowing the allegations made against him or the criteria by which he is being judged."[56]

The international human rights framework provides a positive reference point in this maelstrom of forces. It needs to be respected, better known, applied, strengthened and expanded. While we highlight three dimensions here, Amnesty International (Canada) published an assessment late in 2007 which offers a more complete menu of issues.[57] It also provides a menu for those of us who wish to see the system strengthened and made more useful to every person. We must continue to hold the Canadian government up to the measure provided by that standard and evaluate whether it is working to strengthen or to undermine this singularly important framework.

With a Canadian of strong reputation as head of the UN Human Rights system, the Harper government had a clear opportunity to take and support leadership in advancing the cause of international human rights. Instead of working for a further term for Louise Arbour, it expressed faint praise conveying lack of support. The world community faces dire and destructive forces. Strong leadership reinforcing the human right to health, to food and adequate nutrition, and to water is urgently required. The rights of long marginalized peoples, particularly indigenous nations and GLBT populations, need to be brought into full recognition, protection and advancement.

The challenge of advancing the full family of human rights against the claims of private profit and corporate privilege is ever greater. We are clearly in need of a renaissance of Canadian conviction and action for human rights. An agenda grounded in that rebirth needs to be fully integrated into the program agenda for political change in this country and the movement that will achieve it.

Harper and Iraq War Resisters

Joel Davison Harden

> Mr. Speaker, last night the House voted to hold a public inquiry into the Air India tragedy... The Prime Minister has the moral responsibility to respect the will of the House and the wishes of the families. Will the Prime Minister respect the will of the House and the wishes of the families?

ON APRIL 13, 2005, Stephen Harper offered these words as the Leader of the federal Opposition. His goal, understandably, was to communicate a majority sentiment for a public inquiry into the Air India tragedy.

Only three years later, however, Harper leads a minority government where majority sentiment remains ignored. On June 3, 2008, a motion was passed in the House of Commons calling for a provision to allow conscientious objectors to illegal wars the right to stay in Canada. At issue, in particular, were American Iraq war resisters who have come to Canada in recent years. The motion demanded that all deportations of Iraq war resisters be ceased immediately.

Several hundred Iraq war resisters currently live in Canada, and a few dozen have chosen to do so publicly. They have shown the courage to stand up for the principles of international law violated under the U.S. presidency of George W. Bush, but which Canada claims to hold dear.

Iraq war resisters pose a central question, one that tests our federal government's commitment to due process and international law: when a nation goes to war on false pretences and against the interests of the global community, what democratic force exists as a counterbalance?

For those of us who support Iraq war resisters, that force is the collective influence of citizens, governments, and organizations "walking their talk" on human rights and international law. Canada chose to "walk its talk" during the Vietnam War and let over 50,000 war resisters find refuge here. Canada "walked its talk" again in 2003 by choosing not to mobilize a full-scale military presence in Iraq without a mandate from the United Nations. At the time, the federal Conservative party opposed this decision. But today, many early Iraq war supporters now realize that Canada made the right call.

Consider the recent lament of Scott McLellan, former Press Secretary to President Bush. He now regrets being party to decisions that ran afoul of the transparency and due diligence that voters expect from political leaders. Hilary Clinton and Colin Powell have offered similar *mea culpas.*

Belated apologies, of course, are not enough. Supporting U.S. Iraq war resisters today is a much better way to make amends for ill-advised earlier decisions. Canadians respect leaders who acknowledge their mistakes. Should Harper, like Michael Ignatieff, change his mind about the Iraq war, voters will reward him for it.

Let me add a personal note to this reflection. As someone who has worked with five war resisters in the Ottawa area, I can attest to their courage and strength of character. One resister I have helped came to Canada because he opposed being part of "small kill teams" in Baghdad. In essence, his unit would perch on a rooftop and shoot anyone near a U.S. camera positioned in the street below. According to military officers, this practice was encouraged as a means to increase the number of "kill targets" set by U.S. Central Command. Small children or interested passers-by would often approach the camera, and this alone would merit a sniper's bullet. After witnessing this practice once, this resister refused to participate. Not long after that, he came to Ottawa and sought protection from the War Resisters Support Campaign.

This same resister spoke publicly in Canada about "small kill teams," drawing international attention to this issue. I am proud to say that, with this publicity, soldiers in his former unit now say that the practice of "small kill teams" has stopped. Other military units are likely still using "small kill teams," but this example shows what is possible when people of conscience help war resisters.

The War Resisters Support Campaign has given reprieve to one corner of Baghdad. Readers should think of what could happen if Canada welcomed Iraq war resisters. Think of the lives that could be spared, the mental anguish avoided, and the message it would send worldwide.

South of Canada's border, the tide is already turning. Most Americans want their troops to come home, and want to make amends for the disaster visited on Iraq. Canada's support for Iraq war resisters can play a decisive role to encourage this process.

Iraq war resisters face imprisonment and a life of hardship if Prime Minister Harper chooses to hand them back to the U.S. military. This has already happened to Robin Long, who was shamefully deported back to the U.S. on July 15, 2008, before exercising all legal and political forms of appeal. Long faces up to five years in military prison, and, at a minimum, a less than honourable discharge. The latter ensures Long will never have access to gainful employment (even McDonald's refuses to hire applicants with similar records).

That fate is no reward for the bravery war resisters have shown in upholding the values of the U.S. Constitution, international law, and basic principles of human decency. That does not fit the majority view of MPs in Canada's Parliament, or a majority of the Canadian population. A 2008 Angus Reid poll shows that 82% of Canadians oppose the Iraq war. It does not reflect a July 4, 2008 Federal Court ruling that "... officially condoned military misconduct falling well short of a war crime may support a claim to refugee protection."

Harper now faces a choice: Will Canada "walk its talk" on human rights, even if it means angering the current White House, or will Canada follow the Bush crowd and punish those resisting an illegal and immoral war? The ball is now in Harper's court. Without question, his choice will follow him into the next federal election.

Peace and Democracy for Afghanistan

John W. Warnock

ON SEPTEMBER 12, 2001, the government of Jean Chrétien pledged Canada's full support to any action by the U.S. government to confront the al-Qaeda organization and the Taliban regime in Afghanistan. The United Nations passed resolutions calling for all countries "to work together urgently to bring to justice the perpetrators, organizers and sponsor of these [9/11] acts." But George W. Bush's administration rejected this proposal and refused to seek the approval of the UN Security Council for the planned attack on Afghanistan.

On October 2, 2001, NATO gave full political support to the assault on Afghanistan. Prime Minister Chrétien announced Canada's support and began to send Canadian Forces naval vessels to participate in the U.S.-directed Operation Enduring Freedom, charged with bringing about "regime change" in Afghanistan.

The assault began on October 7, 2001. The war was short, given the overwhelming military superiority of the U.S. military and its massive bombing campaign. The Taliban fled Kabul on November 12, and the U.S. allies, the Islamist Northern Alliance, assumed the role of *de facto* government. Kandahar fell in early December and the war was over.

The Liberal government pledged 2,000 Canadian troops to Operation Enduring Freedom (OEF) in Afghanistan, and Joint Task Force 2 special forces were engaged in military conflict near Kandahar as part of the last campaign to destroy al-Qaeda and Taliban forces.

From this time on, Canada's role in Afghanistan escalated. In February 2002, Canadian forces were assigned to Kandahar to defend the city and the airport, and to engage any remaining Taliban forces.

Creating the International Security Assistance Force

On December 20, 2001, the UN Security Council agreed to sanction the creation of an International Security Assistance Force (ISAF) under Chapter 7 of the UN Charter, an enforcement mandate. The ISAF is completely outside the United Nations, part of the "coalition of the willing" created by the U.S. government. This "stabilization mission" was to support the UN humanitarian assistance program. Canada was to be part of the ISAF, under British command.

Between 2001 and 2003, the ISAF was confined to Kabul in a peacekeeping role. By early 2003, the rebellion against the interim Afghan government and the occupation forces had begun. Under direction from the Bush administration, which was preparing for an attack on Iraq, NATO assumed the responsibility for the ISAF. Canadian forces served in Kabul between October 2003 and November 2005. They were then moved to Kandahar, first under OEF and then in July 2006 under the authority of the ISAF. Canadian military forces made a major shift from a peacekeeping role in support of humanitarian assistance to fighting a counter-insurgency war.

Over this period, the governments of Jean Chrétien, Paul Martin, and Stephen Harper all gave full support to the Bush administration's position on Afghanistan. In April 2008, a resolution was passed in Parliament authorizing Stephen Harper's government to extend Canada's role in the counter-insurgency war through 2011. The resolution by the Conservative government received the support of the Liberal opposition headed by Stéphane Dion.

According to public opinion polls, a large segment of the Canadian public is opposed to the participation of Canadian Forces in this counter-insurgency war, ranging between 45% and 50%. An Angus Reid Strategies poll, released on March 26, 2008, found that 58% of those surveyed were opposed to extending the Canadian military mission until 2011. The political breakdown showed that only supporters of the Conservative party (72%) supported the extension. The majority of supporters of the other political parties were in opposition: Liberal party (63%), New Democratic party (74%), Bloc Québécois (78%), and Green party (68%). Only in Alberta did an overall majority support the extension.

Persistence of the insurgency

Over the past two years, the insurgency by the Taliban and their allies has grown in strength, and the conflict has spread to all parts of the country. The number of attacks on the NATO forces has greatly increased, and the number of deaths by the military forces and civilians increased by 62% in the first six months of 2008. In spite of defeats in direct conflicts with NATO forces, the resistance movement has been able to continue to find replacements and expand operations.

Why is this happening? As the UN Secretary-General pointed out in his report of September 2007, the main problem is the unpopularity of the government of President Hamid Karzai and the country's National Parliament. The government is notoriously corrupt, and drug lords and regional commanders have great power. The economy remains very poor and at least 40% of the people are unemployed. The average Afghan earns only $350 per year. Lack of food and housing is a widespread problem. Public services are very limited.

The United States creates the new Afghan government

The formation of a post-Taliban government began in November 2001, when the U.S. government brought some representatives from Afghanistan together at Bonn, Germany, to create an interim government. The Bush administration chose groups aligned to the Northern Alliance, the Islamists who have been their close political allies since 1979. Five broad groups representing the democratic forces in Afghanistan asked to participate, but they were refused official status and voting rights. This set the pattern for everything that followed. The democratic forces have been excluded from all the operations to create a new constitution and government, as well as from the first elections.

It is widely known that the Afghan people wanted a restoration of the liberal, democratic constitution of 1964, a constitutional monarch with a parliamentary government, political parties, elections by proportional representation, and a federal state. The U.S. government, backed by the Canadian government and representatives from the United Nations, blocked this development. At the Bonn meetings in November 2001, the U.S. government mandated that Hamid Karzai be appointed the new interim president. He named 30 people, mainly Islamists from the Northern Alliance, to form the transitional administration.

An interim Emergency Loya Jirga (or Grand Council) was held in June 2002. Delegates were chosen by local warlords and the regional leaders of dominant ethnic groups. Their proposal for a constitutional monarchy was rejected by the U.S. government.

Karzai and his U.S. and UN advisors then drafted a new constitution through a very secret closed-door process. The general public did not get a chance to see the constitution, and there was no public debate. It was presented to the Constitutional Loya Jirga (CLJ) in December 2003. The majority of delegates opposed the plan for a highly centralized government with enormous power entrusted to the president, and there was also strong opposition to the re-creation of Afghanistan as an Islamist state. When 48% of the delegates walked out in protest, Karzai threatened not to run for president. The constitution was then "unanimously" approved by the delegates even though no vote was held. Representatives from the Canadian government played key roles in helping the U.S. government in this entire anti-democratic process.

Demonstration elections

President Bush insisted that a presidential election be held in Afghanistan prior to the U.S. presidential election in November 2004. But there was no national government and no functioning provincial or local governments. No political parties were allowed to participate. The whole process was deeply flawed. Karzai won by default because Afghans feared a warlord would win or U.S. government aid would be withdrawn.

The election for the parliament, held on September 18, 2005, was worse. No political parties were allowed to participate, which greatly strengthened the regional Islamist forces. The Single Non-Transferable Vote (SNTV) system was used, but there were no party lists. The goal was to prevent the development of new political parties on the democratic left. The Karzai administration refused the request by 34 political parties for a system of proportional representation.

Of the 249 elected positions to the House of the People (the lower house), over one-half were filled by men who had fought in the Mujahadeen war, and one-half were clearly identified as radical Islamists. The large majority of those elected had close ties to regional armed groups. Voter turnout was very low, estimated at 40% overall and 30% in Kabul. The Canadian government was deeply involved in these fraudulent "demonstration elections," as Noam Chomsky has called them.

The Harper-Bush military strategy

Stephen Harper's government and Canada's military leaders insist progress is being made in Afghanistan, but this view is not shared by U.S. and British military commanders. The U.S. Government Accountability Office reported in June 2008 that the Afghan Army cannot operate without the support of NATO. Only 52 of 433 units of the Afghan National Police are capable of being deployed. There are widespread reports that over 40% of all economic assistance funds disappear within the system. NATO governments, mindful of their own public opinion, are refusing to send additional armed forces to Afghanistan.

Stephen Harper's new Canada First Defence Strategy dismisses peacekeeping and promises even further integration of Canadian Forces into those of the United States. Military spending will focus on expanding the capacity to be "interoperable with the U.S. Military." NATO will be Canada's first priority, described by President George W. Bush as a new "expeditionary force" for the First World. The United Nations and peacekeeping are ignored in the new Tory policy statement.

But a large percentage of the Canadian public does not agree with this policy direction. It is time for Canadians to stand up and be counted, to pressure the political parties and the government to break with

U.S. policy in Afghanistan. It is time to switch to supporting the people of Afghanistan who want an end to the war and a chance to improve their lives.

What can be done

An opportunity for change appeared beginning in 2007, when the Shanghai Co-operation Organization (SCO) put Afghanistan high on its agenda and called for regional negotiations to settle the conflict and promote reconstruction. The SCO members are China, Russia, Kazakhstan, Kyrgyzstan, Uzbekistan, and Tajikistan.

At the April 2008 meeting of NATO at Bucharest, the SCO position was advanced by President Islam Karimov of Uzbekistan. He proposed the reconstitution of the old Six Plus Two negotiations (1998–2001), hosted by the United Nations, which included the six countries on the border of Afghanistan plus the United States and Russia. To this group would be added NATO. This body would design a general regional plan for establishing peace and democracy in Afghanistan. The United Nations would then replace NATO as the lead organization to direct peace and redevelopment.

Unfortunately, this proposal was rejected out of hand by the U.S. government, and the Harper government agreed. None of Canada's opposition parties seemed to be aware of this peace proposal, which would have had the broad support of the majority of Canadians and been welcomed by the Afghan people.

Since 2001, our Canadian governments have given complete support to the United States on Afghanistan. But this policy has failed to date and is doomed to fail in the long run. The challenge for Canada is to take a different position: one which puts the interests of the Afghan people first. In public opinion polls in Canada over recent years, a consistent 70% have indicated that they want Canada to return to a role of peacekeeper. Higher majorities want Canada to emphasize humanitarian and economic assistance.

The challenge we face is how to convince our elected governments and political parties to join with this majority opinion.

Harper, the Military, and Wedge Politics

Steven Staples

WHEN THE HARPER Conservatives won the federal election in January 2006, and formed their minority government, they inherited from the previous Liberal government a war in southern Afghanistan, a rapidly escalating defence budget, and a military led by General Rick Hillier, arguably the most charismatic and politically powerful Chief of Defence Staff in living memory.

When Prime Minister Stephen Harper announced his five priorities in his first Throne Speech, fighting a war and spending billions more on arms were not on the list. But it became quickly apparent that bolstering the military — and convincing a skeptical Canadian public to embrace a Canadian war-fighting global role — had indeed become an unofficial sixth priority of his government.

In a more politically astute move, Harper could have accepted the war as something the Liberals started and that he was obliged to prosecute until the end of the Liberals' commitment to February 2007. If things went well, he could claim credit, but if they went badly, he could blame the Liberals. This approach seemed logical, given that he had a minority government and was obliged to navigate carefully or risk being defeated by the other parties — two of which were opposed to the war.

But, rather than governing through compromise and accommodation, the Conservatives chose a different political strategy: aggression and "wedge politics." The theory goes that a politically united and well-organized minority can beat a divided and disorganized majority. In a game of "chicken," the most committed will stare down a less committed opponent and win the stand-off. Aggression is rewarded, and the strategic use of issues to divide your opponent's ranks will give you the upper hand.

That is one reason why the Harper government moved quickly to embrace the military and claim the war in Afghanistan as its own. Harper intended to use the war to rally his base, and widen the divisions between opposition parties — and even within the Liberal party itself.

Harper visited Afghanistan within weeks of taking office, and appointed retired General Gordon O'Connor, a former defence industry lobbyist, as his first Minister of National Defence. These early moves signalled that national defence and the military would be one of his unofficial priorities.

While he ignored or cancelled programs initiated by the Liberals, such as the child care program and the Kelowna Accord with First Nations, Harper pledged to fulfill Paul Martin's 2005 Budget promise to increase defence spending massively, by $12.8 billion over five years. In his own first federal Budget, Harper went further and committed an addition $5.3 billion on top of what was already the largest increase in military spending in a generation.

Today, Canada's military spending is rising above $19 billion a year, sixth highest in NATO and 15th highest in the world, dollar for dollar. When adjusted for inflation, Canada's military spending is at its highest since the Second World War, even exceeding the Cold War peak in the early 1950s.

Conservative party enthusiasts loved it. The moves to wrap the government in camouflage-green garb strengthened Harper's political base. Red-Shirt Friday rallies to "support the troops" were backed by the military, and government officials used them to rally support behind the Conservatives. Remembrance Day ceremonies and other memorials to mark past military milestones, such as the 90th Anniversary of Vimy Ridge, were politicized to glorify the military and the Conservative party's support of it.

Even more, the Conservatives used these opportunities to try to write a new Canadian historical narrative, one that recasts Canada as a war-fighting nation, not as a peacekeeper. Canada is a nation that came into being in the bloody (and pointless) military battles of the First World War, in Harper's historical memory.

The Conservatives view Canadians' support for peacekeeping, the United Nations, soft power initiatives, and disarmament treaties such as the Landmines Treaty as Liberal symbols. It is important for them to create a new national narrative, with new symbols to replace the Liberal ones.

In the future, under a Conservative government, Canada's international standing would be based upon pursuing "national interests," and our influence would rely upon delivering hard military power.

Harper's first Throne Speech mentioned "interests" numerous times, especially in the section called *Canada: Strong, United, Independent and Free,* where it was invoked three times in just four paragraphs:

> Canada's voice in the world must be supported by action, both at home and abroad. Advancing our interests in a complex and sometimes dangerous world requires confidence and the independent capacity to defend our country's sovereignty and the security of our citizens.
>
> The Government will work cooperatively with our friends and allies and constructively with the international community to advance common values and interests. In support of this goal, it will build stronger multilateral and bilateral relationships, starting with Canada's relationship with the United States, our best friend and largest trading partner.
>
> More broadly, this Government is committed to supporting Canada's core values of freedom, democracy, the rule of law and human rights around the world. In this regard, the Government will support a more robust diplomatic role for Canada, a stronger military and a more effective use of Canadian aid dollars.
>
> Just as it honours the past efforts of our veterans, the Government stands firmly behind the vital role being played by our troops in Afghanistan today. The dedicated Canadians in Afghanistan deserve all of our support as they risk their lives to defend our national interests, combat global

> terrorism and help the Afghan people make a new start as a free, democratic and peaceful country.
>
> —*Speech from the throne, delivered by Gov. Gen. Michaëlle Jean, April 4, 2006.*

There would be no room for bleeding-heart sentimentality in the pursuit of Canada's national interests. Soldiers' deaths would be a necessary price for defending our national interests, and so flags would not be lowered to half-mast in Ottawa.

No more mushy, middle-power, "boy scout" foreign policies for Canada. The United Nations would be looked upon askance. When a Canadian soldier died from "friendly" Israeli fire at a UN post in Southern Lebanon, the Prime Minister expressed sadness, but coldly questioned why the soldier and his detachment of UN peacekeepers were there in the first place.

Canada's contribution of soldiers to UN peacekeeping missions would hit rock bottom, continuing a trend started under the Liberals. In July 2008, total Canadian personnel contributions to UN operations were a mere 167, ranking Canada 53rd of 119 contributing nations, next to Slovakia at 52nd and Malawi at 54th. The United States ranked higher than Canada at 47th.

Most of the Canadian personnel were police (112), with military observers (39) and troops (16) making roughly a quarter of Canada's contribution. That month, the total number of personnel participating in UN operations reached 88,634, comprising police (11,517), military observers (2,582), and troops (74,535).

Prosecuting the war in Afghanistan and defending the Arctic have emerged as emblems of the Conservative's policies on security and sovereignty. The Arctic, in particular, became a priority under Stephen Harper and he pledged to deploy the Navy to defend the increasingly accessible Northwest Passage, using armed naval patrol ships. To the surprise of many, he challenged U.S. territorial claims in the Arctic soon after he was elected.

To some observers, the Conservative approach largely carries on trends established by the Liberals, especially when it comes to supporting U.S. foreign policy and the "war on terrorism." However, there is a view that, while Paul Martin's Liberals sought to appease the Bush administration to avoid Canada's being "punished" for not toeing the line, the Conservatives' approach is to emulate U.S. foreign policy and to embrace the war on terrorism as its own.

While subtle, and resulting in largely the same outcomes in terms of Canadian policy, the difference could be described as the Liberals wanting Canada to be an arm of the United States, and the Conservatives wanting Canada to be a clone of the United States.

There is an unmistakable copy-cat effect in the Conservatives' policies when compared to the Bush Administration's policies. Canada should cut taxes, drive up military spending, reject multilateralism, and transform its military into a powerful fighting force to win praise from military allies and invoke fear from "enemies.

Harper's policies begin to mimic Bush's, and even his speeches sound the same when he uses phrases such as "we won't cut and run." But the apparent tiff over the U.S.'s unwillingness to recognize Canadian Arctic sovereignty elicited a rebuke from Harper, as if to say that Canada will defend its sovereignty no less than the U.S. would defend its own. More recently, the Conservatives blocked a $1.3 billion foreign takeover of a Canadian firm that produced satellites for Arctic monitoring, and built the iconic Canadarm. The unprecedented move was supported by many Tories, who argued that the Americans would never allow such a sale to proceed south of the border.

The effect of Harper's embrace of militarism to define his own government's tenure has been costly to Canada.

In terms of dollars, the massive increases to Canadian military spending has siphoned dollars away from social programs. If any Canadian wondered where the national child care program funding went when Harper cancelled Martin's plan, one can find it sitting on military bases in the form of new military aircraft and tanks.

According to the military's own figures, since the Liberals' last Budget in 2005 and the first Conservative Budget in 2006, overall spending on defence has climbed by 30% compared to 2004.

Even Harper's opponents would have to grudgingly admit that he has skillfully used militarism and the Afghan war to his political advantage, though the cost to Canada has been great. What to do about the war, dragging on for more than half a decade, has divided the left and the opposition parties, allowing Harper to steamroll the opposition and push through his agenda.

In May 2006, taking advantage of the fact that the Liberal party was without a permanent leader and several of the leadership candidates were in favour of the war, Harper introduced a motion to extend the mission by two years to February 2009. The NDP and the Bloc Québécois opposed it, but, even though many Liberals also opposed the motion, so many Liberal MPs were absent for the vote that a few dozen hawkish Liberals led by Michael Ignatieff delivered enough pro-war votes to Harper that the motion passed by a slim majority.

The fact that a decision of this importance would be put to a parliamentary vote is a credit to Harper, since the Liberals had never done so themselves and low-balled important decisions about the war when they were in power. (The decision to move Canadian forces from the relative safety of the northern city of Kabul to the volatile southern province of Kandahar was announced practically in passing by the Liberal Defence Minister before a parliamentary committee in the spring of 2005.)

The Canadian public is deeply divided on this issue. Opinion shifts, but more often than not a majority of Canadians are opposed to the war. This opposition, however, has not translated into political victories in Parliament. This is in part because the anti-war sentiment is spread among several parties, each seeking ways to separate itself from the others.

In the summer of 2006, needing a way to sharpen its own position and mollify a vociferous leftist faction in its own base, the NDP adopted the position that troops should be withdrawn immediately, in a "safe and orderly fashion." It was a position supported by a great many Canadians, but rejected as unreasonable and unrealistic by policy elites, opinion leaders, and soft or left-leaning Liberal supporters.

The Liberals supported the mission (while criticizing some aspects of the way it was being conducted), but demanded that the combat role in the south be ended at the specified expiration date of February 2009. This position was loudly championed by the party's new leader, Stéphane Dion (who had voted against the extension in May), and he repeatedly asked if the government had informed NATO that Canadian troops would be withdrawn in 2009.

The Bloc Québécois, suffering from its own internal divisions, adopted essentially the same view as the Liberals. However, the deaths of several soldiers from Québec did not galvanize the generally anti-war Québec public, requiring the weakened Québec based-party to tread carefully.

Harper's "divide and conquer" strategy served him well. Opportunities to unify anti-war positions were missed in 2007 when opposition party motions in Parliament were written to intentionally make it impossible for other anti-war parties to support them. The Liberals, in particular, introduced an opposition motion that explicitly supported the mission in its current form, but called for its end in February 2009. The NDP felt forced to vote against the motion because of its uncritical nature, and, ironically, helped the Conservatives defeat the motion. A subsequent motion by the NDP likewise failed to bridge the gap with the Liberals.

These political misfires occurred at a time when Canadians were realizing that the mission in Afghanistan had become increasingly dangerous for Canadians with the move to the Kandahar, and that our troops were no longer peacekeepers, but engaged in constant combat.

Fatalities in 2006 claimed 36 soldiers and a diplomat, when only eight soldiers had been killed in the previous four years combined (four of those fatalities at the hands of a U.S. fighter pilot). A ground-breaking study by the Canadian Centre for Policy Alternatives showed that Canada was shouldering a disproportionately high number of casualties in NATO, and that Canadian troops were in more danger than their U.S. counterparts in Iraq.

Further controversy erupted in April 2007 over prisoners taken by Canadian troops and handed to Afghan authorities, where they were abused and risked torture. This posed a serious challenge to Harper, but he responded in his characteristically aggressive fashion, accusing the opposition parties of caring more about terrorists than Canadian troops. The controversy, along with other factors, did eventually remove Gordon O'Connor from his post as Defence Minister in an August 2007 cabinet shuffle, but otherwise did not fundamentally jeopardize the Harper minority government or its ongoing prosecution of the war.

Upping the ante in 2007, and putting further pressure on the Liberals, Harper shrewdly chose the hawkish former Liberal minister John Manley to head a panel to review Canada's role in Afghanistan. Along with other Conservative and pro-Bush administration panel members, the Manley panel presented a report in early 2008 that largely endorsed the Afghan war and called for an indefinite extension beyond February 2009.

Harper accepted the report and, when challenged by the Liberals, introduced another vote to extend the Canadian mission to December 2011, extending the war by nearly three years beyond the previous expiration date of February 2009. With his foot on the neck of the Liberals, who were beset with continuing internal divisions and desperately wanted to avoid going into another election, Harper made this a vote of confidence, daring the opposition parties to defeat it and force an election that none of them at that time wanted. (This was the same tactic he used to push through other controversial policies in Parliament that a minority government normally wouldn't even attempt.)

The weak Liberal leader, Stéphane Dion, who had been so confidently calling for an end to the mission when it expired in February 2009, reversed his previous position and gave Harper the support he wanted to prolong the war to December 2011. It was a momentous victory for Harper, a great tribute to his aggressive and divisive political strategy. It was also an effective way to muzzle a Canadian public, increasingly growing weary of a war that clearly was now going badly

While Harper was using the Afghan war and national security as political hammers in Parliament, the military and defence establishment was exploiting his militant posturing to extract billions in military contracts — so much so that today the defence lobby wields power and influence in Ottawa on an unparalleled scale.

Harper's embrace of the military and his government's lavish allocation of nearly $20 billion a year on the military has been a bonanza for the defence industry.

In June 2006, the government announced $17.1 billion of planned spending for long-range and medium-range military transport aircraft, helicopters, trucks, and three new support ships. Later, in a surprise move, the government announced more than $1 billion more for Cold War-era tanks.

The military spending tap remained open. In the subsequent months, new programs were announced, amounting to billions more for warship upgrades, Arctic patrol vessels, unmanned aerial vehicles, and a plethora of new equipments programs. Many of these programs didn't even require public disclosure if their price tag was less than $100 million, but several were in the $1 billion range, and a few – such as the helicopters and medium-range aircraft — will involve expenditures as high as $5 billion.

When the Conservatives finally released publicly their Canada First Defence Strategy, the total price tag for their plans amounted to $490 billion over the next 20 years in defence spending. Could we ever expect to hear that the Harper government was committing such vast sums to improving health care or the environment?

The rush to commit money for the military quickly, while Harper's Conservative minority government remained in power, has meant that 20-year commitments of massive amounts of government spending are being made with little long-term planning.

Even worse, some of the spending is meant to avoid political conflicts and satisfy special interests rather than to meet legitimate defence needs. For instance, in 2006 there was a difference of opinion between Chief of Defence Staff General Rick Hillier and Defence Minister Gordon O'Connor. Hillier reportedly preferred a larger fleet of medium-range transport aircraft, and O'Connor wanted a smaller fleet of much more expensive long-range aircraft. Rather than resolve the difference, the decision was to purchase both fleets of aircraft. This was only possible because so much money was flowing to defence that hard political choices could be avoided.

Even worse, taxpayers are being fleeced because the government has sidestepped competitive contracting procedures, tacking untold billions onto the costs of these programs because sweetheart deals are being made with preferred companies, almost all of which are American-based. A study by the Canadian Centre for Policy Alternatives, for example, revealed that more than 40% of defence contracts in 2006–07 were deemed "non-competitive" by the government.

Internationally, NATO allies are reported to be privately offended or amused by Canada's podium-banging calls for more troops to be sent to the south of Afghanistan. Canada had sought out the dangerous mission in part to impress the United States, according to Liberal government officials at the time the decision was made in 2005, even though they had little knowledge of the danger threatened by the new role. More sophisticated European allies were wisely cautious about taking up a mission so heavily under U.S. influence and in a very dangerous region.

As well, whatever greater influence the Conservatives had hoped to gain from such a lethal and "hard power" military operation has not materialized in NATO, where no nation other than the United States has answered Canada's calls for assistance.

But these impacts, as egregious as they are, are just the surface of more significant shifts in Canadian policies. The war in Afghanistan has also had a corrosive effect on Canada's democracy at home.

The military establishment has frequently overstepped its non-partisan tradition and ventured into the political arena. Between 2005 and 2008, Chief of Defence Staff General Rick Hillier used the war and the Defence Department's public affairs machinery, in addition to his own inimitable communications style, to shift the political balance in his and the military establishment's favour. So effective was his influence that even the Harper government felt it needed to rein in the General at times. Hillier changed the nature of civilian-military relations in ways that may not be apparent for years to come.

The Harper government's increased fixation on national security has made it a secretive government. Despite campaigning on greater accountability, the government itself has limited access to information about military activities. The ultra-secret JTF-2 commandos operate outside of proper government oversight. Media complaints that access to information is diminishing are widespread, and in Afghanistan journalists are required to sign conditions on reporting in order to be "embedded" with Canadian Forces. The government is spending millions for military public relations, including funding military front groups such as the Conference of Defence Associations which casts itself as an independent observer while being bankrolled by the military.

The greatest harm, however, is to Parliament itself, where the military, the war, and the lives of soldiers have been used shamelessly for political gain. When Parliamentarians concerned about human rights are labelled as terrorist sympathizers; when critics of the war are castigated as "not supporting the troops" and are put under surveillance; and when billions of dollars needed for social programs are handed out instead to (mostly U.S.) defence corporations, the country's democratic traditions are seriously at risk.

The Harper record on the war and the military should raise an alarm for Canadians who want to protect our democratic values, fund our social programs, and pursue our international traditions of peace and diplomacy.

FOUR

ENERGY AND ENVIRONMENT

Stuck in the Muck

The Harper tar sands legacy

Caelie Frampton and Blair Redlin

NO MATTER THE cost, the Harper government has been relentless in its push for rapid, unchecked development of Alberta's tar sands. The devastating environmental, social, and economic effects of tar sands development for the climate, water, boreal forest, and First Nations communities have done nothing to dampen the enthusiasm of the Conservative government. In line with the Security and Prosperity Partnership (SPP) goal of "energy security" for the United States through a five-fold increase in tar sands production from one million barrels per day today to five million barrels a day by 2030,[1] the Harper government has been aggressive in removing all obstacles to tar sands expansion. Production in the tar sands is planned to double by 2012 and triple by 2018.

Although the Alberta provincial government is the owner and lead promoter of the tar sands, it would be impossible for the tar sands project to move ahead without the active assistance of the federal government. In numerous areas like regulation, pipeline approvals, environmental assessment and Aboriginal policy, both Liberal and Conservative federal governments have been key to increased tar sands production.

Forcing the Kearl Project

A prime example of the determination of the Harper government to drive tar sands projects ahead was a cabinet decision in June of 2008 to override a ruling by the Federal Court of Canada. The court decision concerned the adequacy of the federal/provincial environmental impact assessment for the new Kearl tar sands project sponsored by Imperial Oil and partner ExxonMobil.

The $8 billion Kearl project will denude 200 square km of boreal forest and is projected to generate 3.7 million tonnes of carbon dioxide every year for the 50-year life of the project. The projected greenhouse gas emissions from the Kearl project alone are the equivalent of emissions from 800,000 cars.[2]

Because the environmental assessment panel had deemed that the Kearl project would have "no significant environmental effects," a coalition of four environmental groups — the Sierra Club, the Pembina Institute, Toxics Watch Society of Alberta, and the Prairie Acid Rain Coalition — challenged the validity of that judgment. The federal court held hearings on the application in January of 2008.

On March 3, 2008, federal court justice Daniele Tremblay-Lamer found that the Kearl environmental assessment panel had erred in law by failing to provide a rationale for its conclusions on greenhouse gas emissions. The Harper Conservatives then moved at breakneck speed to overrule the court decisions that were holding up the Kearl project. The federal/provincial environmental assessment panel was immediately reconvened to rapidly submit a new report to the federal government that reiterated its earlier conclusion that new greenhouse gas emissions of 3.7 million tonnes per year for 50 years were not a significant environmental problem. The federal cabinet formally accepted this rationale on June 5, 2008, and the Kearl project was back on track and will be up and running by 2012.

On June 17, 2008, the appellant groups announced they would no longer pursue their environmental assessment challenge in the face of the Harper government's determination to overrule the courts. They said the federal environmental assessment process for the tar sands is an "international embarrassment."[3] Not a single tar sands project application has ever been denied.

Failing the Kyoto Protocol

The tar sands are the largest contributor and fastest growing source of Canada's greenhouse gas emissions.[4] This puts the country in a bind when it comes to meeting the mandatory goals of the Kyoto Protocol to prevent climate change. Since ratification of Kyoto by the Canadian Parliament in 2002, the government has been legally committed to reducing greenhouse gas pollution by 6% below 1990 levels by 2012. Yet, largely due to tar sands expansion, Canada is expected to be 44% above its permitted Kyoto levels by 2010.[5] This isn't surprising when the top five Canadian polluters are tar sands operators.[6]

While the former Martin Liberal government failed to implement meaningful greenhouse gas reductions, the Harper government has reneged on Kyoto altogether. On April 25, 2006, former Conservative Environment Minister Rona Ambrose announced that Canada will not be meeting its Kyoto targets. Instead, Canada will participate in the U.S.-backed Asia-Pacific Partnership on Clean Development and Climate. In May 2006, environmental funding designed to meet the Kyoto standards was cut. The Harper government said it was developing a new plan instead.

In February 2007, Bill C-288 was passed by Parliament. This Opposition-sponsored legislation was intended to force the government to "ensure that Canada meets its global climate change obligations under the Kyoto Protocol." Even though the legislation required the government to prepare a detailed action plan within 60 days, the Harper government has ignored it, citing economic concerns.[7]

In May 2007, Friends of the Earth sued the Canadian federal government for failing to meet its Kyoto Protocol obligations to cut greenhouse gas emissions. This was based on a clause in the *Canadian Environmental Protection Act* that requires Ottawa to "prevent air pollution that violates an international agreement binding on Canada."

The Harper government's refusal to implement the Kyoto Protocol sends a signal to the world that Canada doesn't care about international treaty obligations, let alone climate change. Further, the federal government is ignoring non-industrialized countries, and indeed the effects on Canada's own Arctic, where only a small portion of greenhouse gases are produced, but where climate change damage is already most severe.

Carbon capture spin

While skipping out on Kyoto, the Harper government has placed its bet on storage of carbon underground as a way to reduce atmospheric emissions so that tar sands production can expand unabated. Tar sands production generates three times as much greenhouse gas as conventional petroleum production,[8] so if the federal government says carbon capture is going to do the trick, we should expect lots of it and soon. But carbon capture and storage is mostly unproven and untested.

On March 10, 2008, federal Environment Minister John Baird announced regulations for tar sands plants and other industrial emitters. These regulations were trumpeted as a signal that new tar sands plants must implement carbon capture and underground storage. But the details of the announcement show that many more new plants — like the Kearl project — will be up and running before any carbon capture rules take effect. There is no requirement for the Kearl project to capture or store carbon, even though it is a new project slated to be running in 2012.

Details of the actual regulations will be finalized in 2009 and will start to take effect in 2010, but only apply to tar sands facilities built after 2012. Those regulations will require "...oil sands upgraders, in-situ plans and coal-fired electricity plants that come into operation in 2012 or later to meet carbon capture and storage standards by 2018."[9]

In other words, all new facilities that start operating after 2012 will only have to meet an unspecified carbon capture standard by 2018 — ten years from today. This is a very long lead time, far in the future. It's as if we have all the time in the world to deal with global warming and are not facing a climate emergency today.

The new standards continue to rely on the discredited concept of "intensity" targets which reduce the amount of emissions per unit of production while still permitting overall increases in greenhouse gas emissions as production levels increase.

The overall result of the Harper government plan is that annual emissions from the tar sands will triple over the next decade, from 25 million tonnes today to 75 million tonnes in 2018.[10]

Fort Chipewyan health crisis

Another example of the federal determination to let nothing stand in the way of tar sands development is the callous way the Harper government has responded to the health crisis facing the Cree people of the Fort Chipewyan, Fort MacKay and Fort Fitzgerald areas north of Fort McMurray. Fort Chipewyan is located beside Lake Athabasca, downstream from the many tar sands facilities located close to the Athabasca River.

Since tar sands production started to ramp up in the 1970s, the people of Fort Chipewyan and nearby communities have been faced with a plague of unusual cancers (such as liver, blood and bile duct cancer), as well as other diseases, an ever-increasing death rate, and a steadily worsening health crisis.

The federal government has a fiduciary obligation for First Nations health care, so Aboriginal health services are a federal responsibility. This obligation is confirmed in some numbered treaties and reflected in section 73(1) of the *Indian Act* (1874).[11]

Despite this responsibility, the federal government has firmly resisted instituting the baseline epidemiological health study long demanded by the people of Fort Chipewyan. Indeed, doctors from the Harper government's Health Canada went so far as to file complaints with the College of Physicians and Surgeons against a local doctor, John O'Connor, when he spoke out publicly about the serious cancer and health emergency facing the Fort Chipewyan community.[12] Fortunately, the College cleared Dr. O'Connor in early 2008, but O'Connor had already moved to Nova Scotia in 2007.[13]

An independent scientific study by the Athabasca Chipewyan First Nation confirmed the presence of elevated levels of arsenic and mercury in local water and wildlife. The Cree people of the area rely for food on fish and animals which are likely contaminated, and their local water supply comes directly from the Athabasca River and Lake Athabasca, downstream from where Suncor (for example) continues to send into the river what is called "process water."[14]

If the federal government was taking its fiduciary responsibilities for Aboriginal health seriously, it would at a minimum fund a new water supply for Fort Chipewyan from nearby inland lakes, and would launch a comprehensive baseline health study immediately.

The government's resistance to the baseline health study reflects a reluctance to develop any information which might create difficulties for tar sands corporations. The health of the First Nations people of the area ranks far behind promotion of new tar sands developments in the priorities of the Harper government.

Temporary foreign workers

Since 2006, the federal government has rapidly expanded the Temporary Foreign Worker (TFW) Program. Increased use of temporary foreign worker programs is one of the goals of the Security and Prosperity Partnership. According to the Alberta Federation of Labour, a construction workforce of more than 200,000 will be needed to meet upcoming development demands in Alberta. A disposable workforce is not new to Canada, with the Seasonal Agricultural Workers Program and the Live-in Caregiver Program, but the growth and size of the TFW Program helps ensure that tar sands labour is provided in the cheapest way possible.

The federal government now makes it very easy for employers to bring in temporary foreign workers. In 2007, the Minister of Human Resources announced that, in B.C. and Alberta, approval for TFW's will be granted within 3–5 days, if the employer falls within 12 designated occupations. The list of eligible occupations was traditionally geared towards highly educated international workers. That group has recently been expanded to include "semi-skilled" and "low-skilled" occupations, including fast food and retail. Most importantly, these workers are not eligible for permanent or regular immigrant status.

Temporary foreign workers have great difficulty insisting on basic employment standard protections since they can be sent home quickly at the whim of an employer. Foreign-worker programs are being used to increase the labour pool by creating a population of exploited and vulnerable workers, all while keeping wages down.

In 2006, Citizenship and Immigration Canada issued a total of 15,172 new temporary work permits for Alberta, bringing the total number of temporary foreign workers in the province to 22,392. By comparison, in 2005, 15,815 were working in Canada.[15] There are now more Temporary Foreign Workers than permanent immigrants entering Alberta each year.

In April 2007, two temporary workers from China were killed when a tank collapsed at a Canadian Natural Resources Ltd. tar sands site. The two had been part of a crew of 300 workers brought to Alberta by a Chinese contractor. When a second tank collapsed soon after the first, the contract was quickly cancelled and all the Chinese workers were sent home,[16] highlighting the disposable and unstable nature of temporary foreign worker employment. At a minimum, the federal government should ensure the health and safety of temporary foreign workers and should permit them to become permanent immigrants.

Security and Prosperity Partnership

The Security and Prosperity Partnership of North America (SPP) is the crucial context for the Harper Conservative plan to expand tar sands development.

The core of the SPP structure is the North American Competitiveness Council (NACC), made up of 30 top Chief Executive Officers, ten from each of the three North American countries. The CEO of major tar sands producer Suncor is one of the members of the NACC. Each year, the NACC issues a report for the political leaders of the three countries, with a recommended policy menu that is almost invariably supported and implemented quickly.

The SPP is also structured to receive corporate advice on a number of specific issues through topic-specific working groups. One of the most influential is the North American Energy Working Group and its sub-committee, the Oil Sands Experts Group.[17] The Oil Sands Experts Group held a workshop in Houston in January of 2006 which developed a policy agenda that is now being implemented.[18] In explaining the project, the workshop report said: "Through the SPP, Canada, the United States and Mexico agreed to collaborate on the development of oil sands resources..."

The report sets out a "plan for a smooth transition towards bitumen production that could be as high as 5 million barrels per day (by 2030)..." (up from approximately one million barrels per day today). The report goes on to say, "If oil sands production is to realize its full potential, new markets must be developed in the U.S. and possibly offshore via the west coast."

> New pipelines and pipeline expansion plans are already in place to meet the certain doubling of oil sands production to two million barrels per day by the 2010 to 2012 timeframe. This includes extensions of the market via a west coast port and more deeply into the U.S.
>
> The five fold expansion anticipated for oil sands products in a relatively short time span will represent many challenges for the pipeline industry. New and expanded pipelines will move more volume into existing and expanding interior U.S. markets and offer shipments to California via the Canadian west coast.

Now, only two years later, we see a plethora of applications for tar sands pipelines to the U.S., as well as to an expanded port at Kitimat on the B.C. coast. The SPP vision for a five-fold expansion of tar sands production is well under way.

But the SPP is about more than economics. At its core, it is also about "security" and military integration. The tar sands help to feed the U.S. military machine. The U.S. Department of Defense burns up approximately 395,000 barrels of oil per day and is the largest single consumer of oil in the world. The Pentagon consumes an estimated 85% of the U.S. government's total use of oil.[19]

Given that Canada exports some 750,000 barrels of oil per day to the U.S. and is now the major foreign source of oil for the U.S., much of the U.S. military's demand for oil is being supplied from the Alberta tar sands. Canadians opposed to the war in Iraq can reflect on our own role in supporting the U.S. military with tar sands oil.

Stephen Harper is a strong believer in deep North American integration, corporate influence over government and the SPP. His government's agenda of aggressive tar sands expansion is reflective of all that.

Pipelines, pipelines everywhere — except to Eastern Canada

As per the recommendations of the SPP working group, new export pipeline projects are moving ahead rapidly. Because tar sands bitumen is meant to be exported, rather than used or refined in Canada, the rapid expansion of export pipelines is key to the overall plan.

It is incredible that there is no pipeline to transport Alberta petroleum to Eastern Canada. Canada currently imports 40% of the oil that it uses. While a small amount of tar sands product is used in Western Canada, the vast bulk of it goes south to the U.S.

The National Energy Board and the Harper cabinet have recently been considering three major new export pipeline proposals. They are Trans-Canada Corporation's Keystone pipeline, Enbridge Inc.'s Southern Lights Pipeline, and the Alberta Clipper Expansion.

Taken together, the three pipelines to the U.S. will have an initial capacity to ship 1.07 million barrels per day of tar sands bitumen to the United States, with potential for that to increase to 1.57 million barrels per day.[20] None of that bitumen will be refined in Canada.

In order to move highly viscous bitumen through pipelines efficiently, it is necessary to mix it with diluent. Diluent is sometimes called condensate and is similar to kerosene or paint thinner.

The Southern Lights pipeline will transport diluent from Chicago to Edmonton, where it will be mixed with bitumen and shipped south. The diluent will then be stripped out from the bitumen in the U.S., recycled and transported back to Alberta again. The entire concept is based on the idea that the bitumen will be refined into oil in the United States. If the tar sands were being refined in Canada, there would be no need to transport the diluent in this way.

As for the Keystone pipeline, the Communications, Energy and Paperworker's union has dubbed it a "...lost opportunity to create 18,000 refining jobs in Canada," based on a report it commissioned from the economic consulting firm Infometrica Ltd. for National Energy Board hearings on the Keystone proposal.[21] The Keystone pipeline is projected to start operations in 2009 and will eventually export 590,000 barrels of bitumen per day, which will be 100% of all incremental tar sands production at that time. Tar sands bitumen is now, or will shortly, be refined in Indiana, South Dakota, Ohio, Colorado, Michigan, Wisconsin, Pensylvania, and along the U.S. Gulf Coast.[22]

The Harper government has made it a priority to expedite approval of these pipeline projects. Despite an appeal to the federal cabinet of the National Energy Board's approval of the Keystone pipeline in October 2007, the Harper cabinet gave final approval in December 2007.

The House of Commons Standing Committee on Natural Resources requested that approval of the Southern Lights and Alberta Clipper projects be delayed until the Committee had an opportunity to review their implications for energy security and the public interest; but the Harper cabinet ignored the Committee's request and gave final approval to both projects on May 13, 2008, just three months after the National Energy Board's preliminary approval. As with other aspects of the tar sands expansion plan, the Harper government has tolerated no delay in development of new export pipelines.

In addition to the pipelines pointing south from Alberta and again in keeping with the plan scoped out by the SPP working group, there are also major proposals for pipelines to the British Columbia west coast.

The most significant of these is the $4.2 billion Gateway pipeline project sponsored by Enbridge. The Gateway proposal consists of an export pipeline to take at least 400,000 barrels per day of tar sands bitumen from Alberta to an expanded port at Kitimat, B.C., and a second pipeline to take 150 thousand barrels per day of diluent condensate back to Alberta from Kitimat. The export pipeline will feed oil tankers that will take tar sands bitumen to China, India, and California for processing there. The condensate will come to B.C. in tankers from Russia. Enbridge intends to seek regulatory approval of the Gateway project in early 2009.

If the Gateway proposal goes ahead, oil supertankers will ply the fragile coastal ecosystems of the B.C. Inside Passage, which is where the Harper government comes in. Since 1972, the federal government has had a moratorium in place to prevent oil tanker traffic off the B.C. north coast. The disastrous Exxon Valdez oil spill in nearby Alaska in the late 1980s reminded Canadians of the need for the moratorium. In 2003 and 2004, Natural Resources Canada reviewed the moratorium and concluded it should stay in place.

Under the Harper administration, however, the moratorium on north coast tanker traffic is under significant threat. Since January of 2006, tankers have been allowed to offload condensate at Kitimat, where it is transferred to rail-cars and transported by train to Alberta.

The B.C. Liberal government of Gordon Campbell has been quietly advancing to the federal government an absurd interpretation of the moratorium, claiming it is only meant to cover foreign oil tankers transiting the B.C. coast and is not directed at tankers sailing to and from B.C. ports.[23] The Harper government has done nothing to defend the tanker moratorium against the condensate tankers and is doubtless looking for ways to similarly "re-interpret" its prohibition of oil supertankers.

The Gateway pipelines faces significant concern and potential opposition from many of the 40 First Nations whose unceded traditional territory the pipelines will pass through. The Carrier Sekani Tribal Council and the Haida Nation are among 18 Aboriginal nations participating in a formal review process of the pipelines that the First Nations themselves have set up.[24]

Energy giant Kinder Morgan has recently announced that it too wishes to build a tar sands export pipeline to Kitimat, B.C. It is advancing plans to build a northern leg from its existing Trans-Mountain line, connecting to Kitimat from Valemont.[25] This extensive network of tar sands export pipelines is bringing to reality the vision of the SPP working group. The Harper government is doing everything it can to rapidly facilitate the export of huge volumes of unrefined tar sands bitumen.

Economic considerations

Though the tar sands are creating thousands of jobs, mostly in construction and many staffed by temporary foreign workers, there are negative implications for the economy and finances of Canada as a whole.

High value of the Canadian dollar and decline in manufacturing

Canada has lost 400,000 manufacturing jobs since 2002 — 15% of all manufacturing jobs in the country — with the pace of losses recently accelerating even more. The loss of manufacturing jobs can be attributed to the currently high value of the Canadian dollar, which lately has been close to par with the U.S. currency for the first time in decades. The competitive export advantage of a lower dollar has been lost for industries like auto and forestry.

With world oil prices averaging $120 (U.S.) per barrel, huge demand for Canadian oil and gas in the U.S. and record profits, the value of Canadian oil companies and their assets has skyrocketed. As Canadian Auto Workers economist Jim Stanford put it: "High global prices for oil minerals lead to incredible profits for those companies, boosting their stock value and attracting foreign investors."[26] (See Stanford elsewhere in this volume.) This, in turn, has made the Canadian dollar extremely attractive to currency speculators.

Big public subsidies

Incredibly, given the high world price of oil and oil company profits that are hitting the stratosphere, the government of Canada continues to provide subsidies to tar sands development.

The main form of subsidy is the tax expenditure known as the Accelerated Capital Cost Allowance (ACCA). The ACCA allows oil companies to defer all federal and provincial taxes until 100% of project capital costs have been paid off. According to recent reports by Kairos Canada and the Pembina Institute, the value of this subsidy for the tar sands developers is $1.5 billion over five years (i.e., $300 million per year from 2007 to 2011).[27] The 2007 federal budget announced that the ACCA will be phased out, but only very slowly. For new projects, the phase-out will start in 2011 and be complete in 2015.

Other examples of subsidies include full deductibility for exploration expenses and $596 million in federal funds set aside for mitigation and socioeconomic review related to the Mackenzie Valley gas pipeline, which is meant to supply gas to tar sands facilities.

Draining of Canada's natural gas reserves

The tar sands are a voracious consumer of natural gas. Each tar sands barrel requires 250 cubic feet of natural gas if mined, 1,000 cubic feet if produced in-situ, and another 500 cubic feet if the bitumen is upgraded to synthetic oil. Given planned expansions, it is projected that tar sands plants will be using four times as much natural gas in 2018 as they used in 2004. Tar sands, of course, are not the only reason for depletion, but by 2018 Canada's proven reserves of natural gas will have been exhausted and an estimated 24% of additional discovered reserves will be in use.[28]

Burning so much comparatively clean and valuable natural gas to create dirty tar sands oil has been compared to using gold to make lead. Canadians require natural gas for heating and a variety of other needs, but tar sands demand will contribute to a rapid depletion of reserves.

Given general construction inflation (in part caused by unchecked expansion of tar sands plants), the cost of the 1200-km Mackenzie Valley gas pipeline has shot through the roof and is now estimated at $16.2 billion. The consortium of oil companies sponsoring the project have been in discussion with the federal government seeking special royalty and tax breaks.

Environmental implications

As concerns from First Nations communities like Fort Chipewyan demonstrate, the tar sands are already taking a huge toll on the ecology of northern Alberta. Unfortunately, industry has been left to monitor the environmental impacts itself. Because most research is conducted by corporations, the federal Standing Committee on Natural Resources has called on government agencies to step up public research to determine the true impacts on the Athabasca water system.

The federal government largely defers to Alberta on tar sands management. As a result, Canadian federal laws like the *Fisheries Act* and the *Canadian Environmental Protection Act* are not being properly enforced and jurisdiction is a blur. Environmental protection, however, is a shared responsibility, which is why federal laws should apply. A federal government so heavily involved in the approvals process for development is also accountable for environmental impacts.

Water Depletion

Tar sands production requires massive and unsustainable quantities of water. Tar sands plants use between 2 and 4.5 barrels of water for every barrel of tar sands bitumen. Although some of that water is recycled, considerable quantities end up in massive toxic tailing ponds, some of which are so large they can be seen from outer space.

In 2006, an Alberta government Ministerial Strategy Committee warned that there may not be enough water in the Athabasca system to support planned tar sands expansions. The committee report said: "Over the long term, the Athabasca River may not have sufficient flows to meet the needs of all the planned operations and maintain adequate in-stream flows."[29]

The federal government has direct responsibility for a number of the issues related to this unsustainable water depletion, including protection of fisheries, groundwater issues, general environmental responsibilities of Environment Canada, and protection of wildlife, let alone inter-provincial and territorial implications for the Peace-Athabasca delta, Lake Athabasca, and connected river systems such as the Mackenzie and the Slave. As with so much else, the Harper government has been missing in action when it comes to ecosystem implications of Athabasca river system depletion.

Nuclear Reactors

Because of concerns about the amount of natural gas needed to power the energy-sucking tar sands, the option of using CANDU nuclear reactors has surfaced. Royal Dutch Shell and Husky Energy are working with the private Energy Alberta Corporation, as well as the federal Crown corporation Atomic Energy of Canada Ltd., to explore nuclear potential. There are currently no nuclear reactors west of Ontario.

The House of Commons Standing Committee on Natural Resources reviewed the nuclear ideas in a 2007 report.[30] The committee estimated that, based on current plants and proposed tar sands expansion, 20 nuclear reactors would be necessary to replace natural gas. They recommended that nuclear plans be put on hold.

Nuclear power in Northern Alberta would have all the damaging results experienced elsewhere, including great difficulty in disposing of nuclear waste, other safety issues, and big costs. Yet it is a tempting option for some because nuclear plants do not produce greenhouse gases. If nuclear goes ahead, the federal government will have a key role, particularly because AECL is interested in selling reactors.

Boreal forest

Canada's boreal forest stretches between several provinces and represents one-quarter of the world's remaining intact forest. The national government owes an obligation to the world to steward it with care. But, according to Environment Canada, development of the tar sands is "staggering for forest conservation and reclamation".[31]

When bitumen is extracted from the soil, large tracts of forest are cut down. But it isn't just trees that are lost, since the forest ecosystem supports wetlands and lakes. After 40 years of mining, only one operation, Syncrude (March 2008), has received a reclamation certificate from the government of Alberta.

Alberta tar sands deposits cover an area the size of Florida. Approximately 3,000 square kilometres of boreal forest could be cleared if development goes ahead as planned. A further 137,000 square kilometres could be fragmented to accommodate infrastructure like roads and pipelines.[32] The Northern Alberta boreal ecosystem is at risk of being forced beyond its tipping point, resulting in unalterable damage.

Conclusion

Unplanned and unfettered development of new tar sands facilities needs to be resisted, as it will only worsen already critical environmental, economic, and social problems.

Rather than merely being a tar sands booster, the federal government should be taking pro-active steps to protect the public interest. Just a few examples include:

- respecting proper environmental assessments;
- using laws designed to protect ecosystems;
- honouring federal obligations to First Nations; and
- restoring justice to temporary foreign workers by allowing immigration to Canada and monitoring to ensure that working conditions are safe.

But if the government is going to be moved to take even those simple steps, there is an urgent need for community organizing on tar sands issues. Whether the demand is for a moratorium, "no new approvals," or a complete halt to tar sands production, there is much work for activists to do:

- Canadians should insist the federal government take urgent steps to resolve the cancer and water crisis facing Fort Chipewyan. The federal government should get started on a baseline health study and move quickly to fund a new, healthy water supply for the Fort Chipewyan community.
- Canadians need to demand a comprehensive energy strategy that includes government regulation. This means re-negotiation or abrogation of the North American Free Trade Agreement, and an end to Canada's participation in the SPP discussion of an energy

strategy should be driven by the urgent need to curb climate change.

- The tar sands have connections throughout Canada. Campaigns are needed to stop pipelines and supertankers on the B.C. coast, to protect Aboriginal rights and ecosystems in Alberta, and to prevent expansion of export pipelines to the U.S.[33]

Rapid, unrestrained, and unsustainable tar sands development is a major legacy of both the Martin and Harper administrations. Canadians who care about the environment, Aboriginal rights, democracy, or worker rights have much to do to resist and reverse the damage already done.

Downstream From the Tar Sands, People are Dying

Jessica Kalman

> There's deformed pickerel in Lake Athabasca... Pushed-in faces, bulging eyes, humped back, crooked tails... never used to see that. Great big lumps on them... you poke that, it sprays water... A friend caught a jackfish recently with two lower jaws... He had seen deformed jackfish before, but never one with two jaws.
>
> —*Ray Ladouceur, Elder of Fort Chipewyan, Alberta.*[1]

THERE IS A massive development occurring in Northwestern Alberta, covering an area the size of the state of Florida. This scale of project has never been seen in Canada before. The Alberta "tar sands" is the single largest industrial development complex in the world. With corporations like Suncor, Syncrude, Shell, Exxon-Mobil and BP getting into the mix, development in the region is at an all-time high, and even more is still to come.

Along with the promise of jobs and a strong dollar, Prime Minister Stephen Harper is promoting the tar sands as the main avenue for Canada to become an international energy superpower, and is pushing Canada even further toward a completely fossil-fuel-based economy. He has even dared to claim Canada can be a "clean energy superpower," a blatant lie and impossibility when the tar sands, the backbone of his agenda, are in the mix.

As the people who live along the Athabasca River attest, tar sands extraction is far from "clean." The process emits three times the amount of greenhouse gases as conventional oil extraction, and uses an average of three barrels of water per barrel of oil. The extraction process results in the accumulation of tailings into lakes of toxic sludge, which currently cover $55km^2$ in Northern Alberta. These lakes are so toxic that cannons must be set off and bright orange figures called "Bitu-Men" dot the lakes to prevent bird and wildlife from drinking the sludgy water. Despite these preventive measures, 500 ducks died in one of Syncrude's "tailing ponds" in April 2008.

Add to this the admission by Suncor that the lakes leach toxins into the groundwater, leading to what Environmental Defence has called "a slow motion oil spill in the region's river system, [which] may be worse in many respects than the *Exxon Valdez* oil spill."[2]

All of this development is creating destruction to Albertan and northern Canadian boreal wetlands and wildlife, and it affects the health of the entire Northern ecosystem. In particular, the development of the tar sands has created a life-and-death health crisis for Fort McKay, the Mikisew Cree and Athabasca Chipewyan First Nations community downstream from the major tar sands developments on the Athabasca River.

The community of Fort Chipewyan has reported extremely high incidences of illnesses. In particular, Dr. John O'Connor noticed unusual rates of cholangiocarcinoma, an extremely rare bile duct cancer. He also reported auto-immune diseases, high rates of diabetes, renal failure, hypertension, and other rare types of cancer.[3] Since publicly ringing alarm bells in 2001, O'Connor has come under criticism from Health Canada about raising "undue distress" in the community. O'Connor stands by his statements and concerns.[4]

"The elders are saying 'Why are we burying our children?' Nobody here can give us answers," says Chipewyan elder Pat Marcel. "It is speculation to say it's the water. But for me it's common sense."

Lorraine Mercredi, after her cousin and aunt died from digestive cancer, bought a water filtration system.

"It had to have been something from the water, air or land," says Ivy Simpson, who was only 17 when she contracted cancer. Her cousin has testicular cancer; her aunt died of uterine cancer, and her sister has terminal cancer.[5]

A recent report written on behalf of the Nunee Health Board Society in Fort Chipewyan found some chemicals with levels that exceed prescribed guidelines at various places and times downstream of the tar sands "digging zone."[6] Chemical constituents found in water include arsenic, total phenols and lead.[7] The risk of adverse health effects from these chemicals is increased for people consuming untreated surface water and eating plants, fish, and other wildlife.[8]

Fort Chipewyan lies 600km north and east of Fort McMurray, the centre of the Athabasca tar sands development. During the spring, summer and autumn months, the community can only be reached by air or water, with winter roads reaching the community as weather allows. The town is located on the south-western tip of Lake Athabasca. The small community of 1,200 has been sounding the alarm for years about the adverse health effects of the tar sands development. Until recently, the community's residents felt their concerns fell on deaf ears. Even their doctor, Dr. John O'Connor, a hero in the community, was accused of creating panic in the community and was investigated by Health Canada, rather than having his concerns properly addressed.

Since then, both the Athabasca Chipewyan and Mikisew Cree have spoken out and called on the government to address the needs and concerns of the community before any more of their people die. They have been joined by many other groups, who recently met in Fort Chipewyan in August 2008 at the gathering of Keepers of the Water III.[9]

The situation has prompted the community to redouble its political efforts:

> On behalf of all citizens of Fort Chipewyan, I am begging for your help in providing the strategic turnaround to stop the destruction that is costing our community so much and that is robbing our children of a future. Those who call Fort Chipewyan and the lands and waters around it home have a sacred responsibility to be keepers of the land and water, and we have a fundamental right to live here and to survive as peoples. Please stand in solidarity with us all and call on your government to say No to new approvals for tar sands and demand that they deal with the

pollution that is killing the people of Fort Chipewyan and the environmental impacts that are destroying our way of life. We need your voice and we need a time-out of the tar sands now!

—Peter Cyprien, Keepers of the Athabasca Watershed Council, Fort Chipewyan, Alberta.[10]

A legislative firewall around Alberta

In order for Canada to become an "energy superpower," with the tar sands as its prize, the Harper government has taken preventive steps to ensure that the experience of the National Energy Program of the 1980s is not repeated. To do so, the Harper team has been quietly building a firewall around the tar sands, in collaboration with the oil companies and the Alberta government.

Laws enacted on both a national and provincial level are framed in such a manner as to protect the industry. For example, national greenhouse gas emission legislation initiated under the Harper government in the spring of 2007 requires per-barrel reduction in emissions, but allows the industry to increase its overall emissions, ensuring that industrial growth is not affected. Harper has taken extensive measures to make certain that the "Alberta Agenda" is guaranteed.

Further, while the Alberta and Canadian governments have an obligation to keep mega-industrial projects like the tar sands accountable in terms of their health and environmental impacts, they have largely abdicated this responsibility and opted rather for industry self-regulation. This is particularly true in the case of water contamination. When it comes to monitoring water pollution, the tar sands industry mainly funds and runs the Regional Aquatics Monitoring Group (RAMP). According to independent scientists, RAMP's monitoring and testing programs are highly questionable. Erratic and inconsistent testing doesn't allow for proper management of water resources. Both the Mikisew Cree and the Athabasca Chipewyan have withdrawn their participation in RAMP because of its failure to adequately monitor and test the water pollution.[11]

This is not the first time First Nations health and livelihood have been sacrificed in the name of resource development, nor is it likely to be the last. Canada has a long and sad history of mistreatment of indigenous peoples, from first contact, to the residential school system, to massive resource development of oil, timber, hydro-dams, and everything in between. Previous national governments have largely failed to rectify past wrongs. Many First Nations communities struggle to access safe drinking water, proper sanitation, and health care.[12] Resource development in many regions has left communities without the environmental integrity to maintain traditional livelihoods.

Stephen Harper has not only failed to right past wrongs, but since becoming Prime Minister, has also abrogated the $5 billion Kelowna Agreement that was signed between the previous government and First Nations, and has voted against the United Nations Declaration on the Rights of Indigenous Peoples.

Further, far from the common and misguided notion that treaty rights give land title to indigenous peoples, the treaty process allows Canada *some* rights to land, which is populated currently by descendants of the original inhabitants. Indigenous peoples have lived on the land long before the arrival of European and other settler populations and therefore are entitled, legally and morally, to determine the future of their people and their territory.

While treaty rights allow Canada to have some say in determining how the land is used, these rights do not trump the entitlement of the First Nations and Métis populations. The rights of indigenous peoples supersede the rights of either the provincial and national governments or the rights of corporations operating in Canada. However, the Canadian government has continued to undermine these rights, and denied indigenous peoples the proper human rights, dignity and respect they merit in determining their own future.

Both Mikisew Cree and Athabasca Chipewyan band councils have called for a moratorium on tar sands development.[13] The calls are becoming louder, with groups from a variety of backgrounds (including some industry) calling for planning and sanity to the disaster being created in Northern Alberta. Clearly, the management plan — or, more astutely, the *lack* of a management plan — proposed by Stephen Harper and the Alberta government cannot substitute for economic justice and democratic governance. Canada is endangering the health and well-being of these communities, and the eyes of world are watching.

The Harper Government and Climate Change

Lost at sea?

Toby Sanger and Graham Saul[1]

OF ALL THE issues confronting the Harper government, climate change has caused it the most trouble. In fact, for the communications tsars in the Harper government, the issue of climate change must represent a continuing storm that they are struggling to sail through, with a leaky platform, little public credibility in their direction, and a crew that often loses its footing.

The climate change storm hasn't sunk Harper's ship of state yet, but it may remain one of his greatest impediments to majority rule. At the same time, his reaction to this issue provides a good illustration of Harper's overall approach to the role of the federal government.

The Harper view

Before he was elected prime minister, Stephen Harper's view on climate change and the Kyoto protocol was perhaps best articulated in a fund-raising letter for the Canadian Alliance party in 2002:

> We're gearing up for the biggest struggle our party has faced since you entrusted me with the leadership. I'm talking about the "battle of Kyoto" — our campaign to block the job-killing, economy-destroying Kyoto Accord.

It would take more than one letter to explain what's wrong with Kyoto, but here are a few facts about this so-called "Accord":

— It's based on tentative and contradictory scientific evidence about climate trends.

— It focuses on carbon dioxide, which is essential to life, rather than upon pollutants.

— Implementing Kyoto will cripple the oil and gas industry, which is essential to the economies of Newfoundland, Nova Scotia, Saskatchewan, Alberta and British Columbia.

— As the effects trickle through other industries, workers and consumers everywhere in Canada will lose. THERE ARE NO CANADIAN WINNERS UNDER THE KYOTO ACCORD.

— The only winners will be countries such as Russia, India, and China, from which Canada will have to buy "emissions credits." Kyoto is essentially a socialist scheme to suck money out of wealth-producing nations.[2]

Harper's hostile perspective was in quite stark contrast to the approach of former Conservative Prime Minister Brian Mulroney. Mulroney emphasized the environment so much that he was proclaimed the "greenest prime minister in Canadian history" by *Corporate Knights* magazine in early 2006 by a group that included the leader of the Green party, Elizabeth May.

Mulroney made the environment a high priority within his cabinet with the appointment of Lucien Bouchard as a high-profile minister. His government developed a first-ever *Green Plan,* and Canada was the first industrialized country to ratify the *United Nations Framework Convention on Climate Change (UNFCCC),* under which the Kyoto Protocol was developed. His government also ratified the Montreal protocol on ozone, the *Rio Convention on Biodiversity,* created the *Canadian Environmental Protection Act,* and established a number of new national parks.

In the 2004 election, the Conservative party, newly merged with the former Canadian Alliance party, made a commitment that it would withdraw from the Kyoto Protocol. Going into the 2006 election, the Conservative party platform had little about climate change, but what was there suggested Harper's views hadn't changed much by that time:

> For all the Liberal talk about the environment, they have done nothing to clean up the environment here in Canada. They sign ambitious international treaties and send money to foreign governments for hot air credits, but can't seem to get anything done to help people here at home.
>
> A Conservative government will implement a "made-in-Canada" plan focused on ensuring future generations enjoy clean air, clean water, clean land, and clean energy here in Canada.[3]

According to the platform, the Conservatives' made-in-Canada plan was to include a *Clean Air Act*, a requirement for 5% ethanol or biodiesel fuel content in gasoline fuels, and addressing greenhouse gas emissions with a plan emphasizing new technologies developed in concert with the provinces and with other major industrial countries.

Then federal Environment Minister Stéphane Dion hosted a United Nations climate change conference in Montreal during the federal election campaign, but none of the political parties focused on it as a major election issue.

When the Harper government came into office in January 2006, they had their own made-in-Canada plan to address climate change, whatever that was going to entail. What they didn't plan on was the forceful rise in the public's concern about climate change and about the future of our environment in global terms.

A gathering storm

Hurricane Katrina, which killed over 1,800, displaced millions, and caused over $80 billion in damages when it struck New Orleans in August 2005, convinced many that the impacts of climate change were real and could be extremely devastating, especially for the poor. Europe had already suffered from a record heat wave two years before that caused an estimated 35,000 deaths.[4]

Concerns about climate change continued to rise in early 2006 as Canadians lived through the country's warmest winter on record, followed by a searing heat wave throughout North America and Europe in the summer.

Al Gore's documentary film about global warming, *An Inconvenient Truth*, premiered in May 2006 and quickly became a sensation, breaking box office records and helping to spawn a popular movement to take action on climate change. The following year, the film propelled Gore to win both an Academy Award and the Nobel Peace Prize for his work.

As if this wasn't enough, the UK government published the *Stern Review on the Economics of Climate Change* in October 2006. This comprehensive review by one of the world's top economists concluded that nations should invest 1% of their economic output per year now to prevent an estimated 5–20% loss that would result from climate change if nothing was done.[5]

Stern's Review was followed by the publication of the *Fourth Assessment Report* by the *Intergovernmental Panel on Climate Change* (IPCC) throughout 2007.[6] The IPCC report, prepared in cooperation by thousands of scientists and experts around the world, outlined the consensus scientific view on the physical science evidence of climate change, its likely impacts, and actions that could be taken to mitigate it.

In Canada, it was revealed that the nation's greenhouse gas emissions had increased by 27% from 1990 to 2004. This was one of the largest increases of all the countries bound by the Kyoto Protocol, and far beyond the 6% reduction that Canada had committed itself to for the 2008 to 2012 period.[7]

The *National Roundtable on the Economy and the Environment* and an increasing number of economists began to argue more forcefully that Canada needed to put a price on greenhouse gas pollution to achieve reductions.[8] This was something that the former Liberal government's climate change plans had all failed to do with their emphasis on subsidies and voluntary actions, resulting in a growing gap between their rhetoric and action.[9]

In September 2006, the Commissioner of the Environment and Sustainable Development, a position under the Auditor General, issued a damning report on the federal government's progress in reducing Canada's emissions. She outlined a number of the failures and emphasized that a "massive scale-up of efforts is needed."[10]

The evidence accumulated among scientists, policy-makers, and the public that climate change was a growing and devastating threat to the planet and that strong action urgently needed to be taken. Polling showed the environment rapidly rising to an almost unprecedented top concern for the public.

Year one: The battle of Kyoto

Most governments would probably have responded by taking positive action to address this concern. Instead, the Harper government stood its ground and tried to fight the growing storm of scientific evidence, public concern, and policy pressure.

In April 2006, newly appointed Minister of the Environment Rona Ambrose stated that it was "impossible, impossible for Canada to reach its Kyoto target."[11] Other Conservative government ministers and spokespeople talked about the flaws and problems with the Kyoto protocol. Ambrose said they wouldn't meet their commitments, but wouldn't pull out of the Accord either.

The assault continued in Harper's first budget, even though climate change and the environment were barely mentioned. Despite having just registered an $8 billion surplus, the federal government slashed funding for its climate change programs by 40%. This funding was "re-allocated" to cover the cost of a new tax credit for public transit passes at a projected cost of $220 million a year.[12] Environmental groups and others had proposed the idea of making transit passes a non-taxable benefit for employers, not realizing that a redesigned plan would mean the slaughter of many effective federal climate change programs.

A memo prepared by department officials had told the environment minister that the Conservative transit pass tax credit would have little effect and would be a very expensive and inefficient way of reducing emissions, but the Harper government forged ahead with its ideological belief in tax cuts at any price and a hostile aversion to effective government programs. This pattern of cutting government spending and replacing targeted public programs with expensive and inefficient "boutiquey" tax measures that complicated the tax system would soon be repeated in many other areas of policy.

This first budget contained virtually nothing else for the environment and climate change. Behind the scenes, almost all the climate change programs from the Liberal government's *Project Green* plan were eliminated, including the *Large Final Emitter System*, renewable energy programs, a provincial partnership fund, the one-tonne challenge, the *Climate Fund*, the *EnerGuide* program for houses, low-income retrofits, information offices, and scientific and research programs.[13]

By virtue of Canada hosting the latest meeting of the *United Nations Framework on Climate Change*, Ambrose was appointed the titular head of an organization that her government was fundamentally opposed to. Canadian negotiators at a conference in Germany were ordered to delay negotiations, block discussion of tougher targets, and push for an abandonment of Kyoto after 2012.[14] Calls soon came for Ambrose to resign.

The opposition in the minority Parliament united around a Liberal private member's bill, the *Kyoto Protocol Implementation Act (C-288)*, designed to force the federal government to meet its own emission reduction commitments.

The introduction of the *Clean Air Act* in Bill C-30 in October 2006 was designed as the Harper government's first positive advance on this issue, but it was met with immediate and near-universal derision. The bill was a botched and confused attempt at appearing to do something — shifting around responsibility for greenhouse gases and pollutants — but was attacked as counterproductive and possibly unconstitutional.[15]

In what was one of the most interesting parliamentary manoeuvres in years, instead of killing the bill, the NDP led a cooperative move with the opposition to take control of the bill. Over the next seven months, opposition MPs rewrote the bill into forceful legislation that established reduction targets consistent with Kyoto, deep long-term reductions, a cap-and-trade system for industry, leading fuel efficiency standards, and funding for building retrofits.

Harper's government continued to flounder further. Ambrose's performance at a UN climate change conference in Nairobi in November was considered to be particularly embarrassing. She made partisan attacks on the former Liberal government and betrayed a repeated lack of knowledge on the file. International environmental groups rated Canada second-last in a comparison of national government policies to reduce greenhouse gas pollution, and yet Canada continued to demand emission reductions from large developing countries.

The environment took centre stage again at the end of the year when the Liberal party cast aside its traditional red colours and selected Stéphane Dion as leader in a surprise election on a green platform.

Year two: A new aggressive approach

In early January 2007, a poll was released showing that three-quarters of Canadians felt that the federal government's effort on the environment was lacking: its worst showing. Later that month, another poll showed the environment had ascended to the top of Canadians' list of priorities.

Over the winter break, the Harper government retreated. Early in the New Year, it attempted to launch a new approach with a new brand and a new face at the helm of the climate change file.

Ambrose was summarily sacked as environment minister in early January 2007 and replaced with the more experienced and aggressive John Baird.

Baird's appointment was followed with a flurry of announcements of new programs, most announced by Harper and Natural Resources Minister Gary Lunn: the *ecoENERGY Technology Initiative*, the *ecoENERGY Renewable Initiative*, the *ecoENERGY Efficiency Initiative*, and the *ecoTrust* program.

Many of these were simply rebranded versions of programs that had been cancelled the previous year and criticized by Lunn as inefficient. In a number of cases (such as for the EcoTrust program that was modelled on the provincial partnership program), the funding was cut in half. In other cases (such as the EnerGuide program that provided funding for energy retrofits to 130,000 low income households), funding was never restored.

In Ottawa, the climate change file is largely shared between Environment Canada (EC) and Natural Resources Canada (NRCan). The environment minister almost always takes the higher public profile and their department has primary responsibility for regulating pollutants. Natural Resources is responsible for most of the federal government's energy efficiency and technology programs, but, because it also has close relationships with oil and gas and mining industries, politicians like to keep its profile low on climate change and environmental issues. NRCan Minister Gary Lunn, while exercising great influence over major polluting industries, energy efficiency and technology programs, has been the master of low profile on the climate change file.

Baird organized meetings with prominent environmentalists and made a point of welcoming, rather than attacking, each new report from the IPCC. The makeover was well under way, but did it really represent a substantial change in direction?

Harper's second budget, tabled in March 2007, also appeared to signal a new-found concern for climate change. Programs that had been eliminated a year before and then revived and rebranded by "Canada's New Government" were highlighted as evidence of the Conservatives' concern for climate change.

This budget also included a number of new announcements responding to pressure from environmental organizations. Hundreds of millions of dollars in federal tax subsidies to new developments in the tar sands would be phased out, but very gradually. A new vehicle efficiency incentive for low-fuel-consumption vehicles was also announced. This proposal came under attack when it was revealed that it would preferentially benefit certain vehicles manufactured close to Finance Minister Flaherty's riding, but exclude other much more efficient vehicles.

The most significant environmental measure in the March 2007 budget was a measure that was met with general support from the public and all political parties at the time, but is likely to be highly damaging for the environment and very costly for the poor: regulations requiring a minimum percentage of ethanol, bio-diesel, or other "renewable fuels" content in gasoline, and direct federal subsidies to producers of these fuels.

Regulations and subsidies that promote turning food, and especially corn, into fuel have shown to be especially ineffective in reducing greenhouse gases: both are very costly and potentially more environmentally damaging than the alternatives.[16] Use of food for fuel has also forced up the price of food around the world, hurting the poorest around the world the most. While promoted as an environmental measure, until alternatives to food-based ethanol and bio-diesel are economically feasible, these measures really involve the transfer of billions to the agricultural industry, paid for through taxpayer subsidies and higher prices on food by the public.

What's more, the 2007 budget included a little-noticed change from an exemption to the fuel excise tax for ethanol to an equivalent producer subsidy. This change could be worth hundreds of millions to Canadian ethanol exporters, and betrayed the increasingly cozy relationship between the Harper government and its most enthusiastic industry supporters: the Renewable Fuels Association.

Despite all these new manoeuvres, the battle of Kyoto continued in Ottawa.

In April 2007, Baird released a report with the crest of the Canadian government on its cover in an unprecedented direct attack on a private members bill. The opposition-supported *Kyoto Protocol Implementation Act* had been approved by the House of Commons and was proceeding through the Senate.[17] Baird's report, *The Cost of Bill C-288 to Canadian Families and Business,* was a peculiar attempt to highlight the devastating economic consequences that would result from Canada complying with its Kyoto commitments.[18] The study included "validation" from a number of well-known economists, but was widely criticized for its scaremongering and contrived and misleading analysis that was based on faulty assumptions.

Later in April, Baird announced the *Turning the Corner* regulatory framework to reduce greenhouse gases and air pollution.[19] This is by far the most significant climate change measure announced to date by the Harper government. It was notable for a few things.

First of all, the plan connected regulation and reduction of greenhouse gases with the reduction of smog-producing air pollutants, such as nitrogen oxides, sulphur oxides, volatile organic compounds, and particulate matter (or NOx, SOx, VOCs and PMs). Others don't often link greenhouse gases, which have impacts over the long-term on a global scale, with these pollutants which have mostly immediate and local impacts, but for Harper, who has asthma, these local air pollutants have always been a policy priority. There may be co-benefits to this form of co-regulation, but it may lead to co-implications as well.

Secondly, the proposed regulations are based on intensity-targets instead of absolute caps on emissions. Kyoto and virtually all other cap and trade systems around the world are based on reductions of actual levels of emissions. Harper, in his often vociferous opposition to Kyoto, has always insisted on intensity targets, which specify greenhouse gas emissions as a share of production. Intensity targets benefit fast-expanding industries, such as the tar sands, but are usually worse for slower growing or shrinking industries.

Even more troubling, intensity targets cannot guarantee actual emission reductions and are not compatible with any other international greenhouse gas regimes. This was a serious problem for international businesses, who prefer greater certainty as well as clear, simple, and internationally compatible regulations.

Thirdly, the plan included a multitude of ways for polluters to avoid actually reducing their emissions or to suffer any penalties for doing so. These include credits for early action, exemptions for small or new facilities, a "flexible approach" for some facilities, leniency for the oil and gas industry, payments to a technology fund, credits for certified investments, credit for emissions trading with non-Kyoto countries, and a domestic offsets system.[20] With the intensity targets and complicated array of loopholes, it was impossible to tell, and very hard to believe, that the proposed regulations would actually result in the emission reductions suggested, or perhaps any at all. Independent assessments by four different organizations, including international banks, business groups and environmental groups, reported that this plan wouldn't provide the reductions required.

For all these problems, the framework actually did represent a symbolic advance. After years of emphasis on failed voluntary targets and subsidies for industry, the framework represented the first time that the Harper government actually proposed specific mandatory regulations for industry. The plan very likely wouldn't achieve any reductions and was roundly condemned; Al Gore proclaimed the plan "a fraud," and Baird shot back. Still, the plan represented a tiny step ahead for Ottawa, even if it was out of step with the rest of the world.

Harper made a larger symbolic step when he acknowledged to a business audience in Germany that climate change was "perhaps the biggest threat to confront the future of humanity today."[21]

Following this less than enthusiastic reception to the Harper government's principal piece of climate change legislation, Baird appeared to uncharacteristically lower his profile for some time, reappearing occasionally to make a feel-good announcement or to try and assure the public that his department wouldn't be cut again.

Two months after the *Kyoto Protocol Implementation Act* was passed through Parliament by the opposition, it compelled the federal government to prepare a climate change plan to describe the measures it was taking to meet its obligations under Kyoto. As required by law, the federal government produced a document, but it was filled with all the reasons why it couldn't meet the Kyoto targets.

Instead of facing another embarrassment with the rewritten bill C-30, the *Clean Air and Climate Change Act*, Harper made the decision to prorogue Parliament and start a new session in September. This effectively killed bill C-30 and gave Harper the opportunity to start again with a clean slate and a new Throne speech. The Throne speech, delivered on October 16, stated explicitly that Canada could not meet the reductions required under Kyoto. This was a clear attempt to embarrass the Liberals, who had decided not to vote against it and provoke an election on a matter of confidence.

From now on, Harper proclaimed, he would consider a much wider range of votes matters of confidence, effectively requiring the Liberals to vote with the government if they didn't want to trigger an election. Harper was clearly angry at not being able to get his way and being outmanoeuvred by the opposition, particularly on climate change issues.

This destroyed the opposition unity that had been so effective working together on the *Kyoto Protocol Implementation Act.*

In September, Harper and Baird further tried to undermine the UNFCCC and Kyoto process by desperately trying to establish public credibility with alternative organizations of nations. Harper announced that Canada would formally join the *Asia-Pacific Partnership on Clean Development*, a U.S.-led group with voluntary emissions targets. The organization was also dubbed the "coalition of the emitting" and the "coal pact," as it was aimed at undermining Kyoto and making it easier to sell coal to China.[22] Baird also joined another U.S.-led group in Washington to strategize about post-2012 global agreements.

At a Commonwealth meeting in November, Harper yet again refused to accept binding commitments on emission reductions by developed countries unless developing countries — with a fraction of the per capita emissions of Canada — did the same.

These meetings were all a prelude to the major UN Climate Change conference in Bali, which was designed to start negotiations for the post-2012 global climate agreement or "Kyoto Phase 2." EU heads of state had already agreed to a binding target of 20% reductions from 1990 levels by 2020, and were considering a green import tax on countries that don't sign up to emission treaties. Harper often claimed that he was trying to have Canada act as a bridge to bring the United States closer to the EU countries. But a summary of Canada's actual positions leading into the Bali negotiations shows that Harper's position was firmly with that of George Bush on most of the key issues.[23]

The Bali negotiations almost ended in failure, thanks to Canada working closely with the U.S. to oppose key parts of the "Bali roadmap."[24] Canadian negotiators were under explicit instructions to demand that poorer countries accept the same binding reduction targets as rich countries. Baird excluded environmental groups, but included industry as part of the official Canadian delegation.[25] With support from Canada and Japan, the U.S. pushed for post-2012 targets to be voluntary, which would have made them meaningless. The meeting was extended and, under intense pressure, Canada agreed to not oppose a consensus position calling for 25%-to-40% emission reductions below 1990 levels by 2020 for developed countries.

Year three: Harper becoming isolated at home

In 2008, the focus of the climate change debate shifted to another level. The federal advisory *National Roundtable on the Environment and the Economy* released a report stating that Canada needed to put a broad-based price on carbon pollution through a carbon tax and/or a cap-and-trade system to meet its targets for emission reductions. The NRTEE stated that Canada could achieve a 65% cut in reductions by 2050 without too much economic damage, but only if a strong carbon price signal was put in place across the entire Canadian economy as soon as possible.[26]

A number of environmental advocates had been reluctant to explicitly propose carbon taxes before, fearing a negative public reaction, but with this support from an eminent organization, it became a priority.

The climate change debate in Canada shifted to a different level in another way as well. In early February, the British Columbia government presented a budget intensely focused on climate change, including the first carbon tax to be put in place in North America. It also announced that B.C. would put a cap-and-trade system in place by joining the Western Climate Initiative.[27] Federal Finance Minister Jim Flaherty responded, saying that a national approach was preferable to a patchwork of provincial carbon taxes and greenhouse gas regimes — but then didn't say when the national approach would be revealed.[28]

Flaherty's federal budget later that month provided virtually no additional support for climate change measures. The only two main measures were funding for a carbon capture demonstration project and for nuclear energy, together with accelerated depreciation tax measures for a wider range of investments. This reflected the Harper view that the emissions problem could be easily solved by technology on its own.

Instead of demonstrating a commitment to seriously deal with the growing problem, Harper's government continued to delay and obstruct. Conservative MPs filibustered environment committee hearings to delay any progress on Bill C-377, the *Climate Change Accountability Act* tabled by NDP leader Jack Layton. This first-ever filibuster by a governing party at the committee level continued for over a month.

New measures announced for the government's *Turning the Corner* climate change plan provided new operations in the tar sands with minimal obligations for another decade and a number of other loopholes.[29]

Other provinces also showed leadership on climate change in the New Year. Manitoba turned its back on the federal government's *Turning the Corner* plan when it passed legislation to commit to Kyoto targets and achieve longer-term reduction goals for 2025. Its climate plan included a focus on public investments and energy efficiency regulations and joining the *Western Climate Initiative* cap-and-trade system. Québec and Ontario also signalled rejection of the federal government's intensity approach when they announced that they would also join the *Western Climate Initiative*.

Harper's government continued to announce new ecoACTION initiatives: funding for the freight industry, amendments to the *Energy Efficiency Act*, more funding for ethanol producers, and numerous other announcements to provide positive grist for the news services.

But on the main bill — requiring broad-based emission reductions — they were becoming increasingly isolated at home and abroad.

Harper lost a key ally when his mentor, Australian Prime Minister John Howard, lost an election to Labour with climate change as a prominent issue. With George W. Bush set to leave the White House by the end of the year, Harper would soon be almost completely isolated on the world stage. Both contenders for the U.S. presidency, Barack Obama and John McCain, have said they would implement a cap-and-trade program to enforce absolute emission reductions on industry.

Harper's government did maintain some close friends at home, especially among members of the Renewable Fuels Association, the ethanol industry's lobby group. There has been a revolving door of staff between this organization and Conservative politicians' offices.[30] The most notable recent appointment is of its former executive director, Kory Teneycke, as chief spokesman for the Prime Minister.

The Canadian government under Harper continued to obstruct and delay progress on climate change negotiations in Bonn in June. Harper then pushed G-8 leaders to adopt weakened commitments at their July meeting in Japan.

In-depth polling showed that Canadians continued to express a strong concern for environmental issues, with almost 90% agreeing that Canada should do what it can to reduce emissions, even if countries such as China and India do not take similar action.[31]

When Liberal leader Stéphane Dion released his "Green Shift" carbon tax proposals, the reaction of the Harper government was so over the top, it seemed to hit a raw nerve. Baird's initial reaction was so incoherent that he was replaced on the top of their reaction roster by Jason Kenney, Harper's parliamentary secretary.[32] Harper attacked the carbon tax proposal by saying, "This is crazy economics. It's crazy environmental policy" that will "screw everybody."[33] The attack ads they prepared were even rejected as inappropriate by the advertising company.

Harper's next act on climate change

It is difficult to predict what the Harper government's next act on climate change will be. Despite Harper's apparent conversion from a full-force sceptic to acknowledging the severity of the threat, his government's actions have not made a similar progression. All the Harper government's major policies on climate change remain entirely consistent with their election platform. It is hard to imagine any 11th hour conversion.

Harper's government is likely to continue to obstruct and delay progress at the international level, even though Canada may be increasingly isolated in doing so. We can also expect very significant promotion of their made-in-Canada *Turning the Corner* emission reduction plan — even though provinces with a majority of the Canadian population have abandoned this proposal for something more forceful.

The Harper government might be tempted to see the price of fuels and a declining economy as its No. 1 ally in an election focused on climate change. Unfortunately, Canada's lack of progress in reducing our fuel dependency has made us more vulnerable to rising prices for oil and other fuels. Higher fuel prices are now leading to lower fuel use and emissions through the market system, but instead of this resulting in more revenues for governments through carbon taxes, it has meant more profits for oil and gas companies. Polling has shown that a two-to-one majority of Canadians feel that the rising price of fuels is a reason to move more aggressively, rather than more slowly, on climate change issues.[34]

The Harper record on climate change is interesting for what it reveals about Harper as a person. It appears to show a person utterly convinced about the superiority of his own positions and unwilling to compromise or reach consensus, even when virtually everyone in the rest of the world agrees with a different approach. This steadfastness could be a positive quality if the positions were based on solid principles, as they often were for Harper's mentor, Preston Manning, no matter how much one may have disagreed with his principles.

Unfortunately, Harper's positions do not appear to be based on any broad or solid principles. While Harper is sometimes described as an economist, many of his climate change policies are actually damaging to the economy. Virtually all economists support carbon pricing — an effective cap-and-trade system, and/or carbon taxes — as a means to reduce greenhouse gas emissions. Industry wants certainty and straightforward national level regulations that are internationally comparable, but, under Harper, Canada's approach has degenerated into a complicated and byzantine array of regulations at many different levels. Tax credits and loopholes are expensive and inefficient and complicate the tax system, yet these have proliferated under Harper.

Canada's economy will suffer tremendously by being a laggard on climate change, with uncertainty preventing greater investment in the economy, and no national leadership. Large industrializing countries will need to be brought into an international climate change regime, but this is already happening in different mechanisms under the UNFCCC. Insisting on immediate hard targets from them becomes just a stalling tactic.

Ultimately, Harper's fundamental climate change policies haven't shifted much at all during his time in office, even though the script and actors may change. In many ways, they appear to be based more on parochial interests: defence of the interests of the domestic oil industry, Western agricultural producers, and concern for ground-level air pollutants.

These climate change policies also provide a good reflection of the Harper government's approach to the role of the federal government for many social and environmental issues. They illustrate an overwhelming preference for tax cuts and tax incentives over public programs, even where tax cuts are shown to be highly inefficient. Climate change policies have generally been developed without much consultation, except with industry, and also include considerable opportunities for privatization and steering benefits to corporations. Communications have been aggressive both in promoting their policies and in containing other information and reports from the public.

At a more fundamental level, they also represent a lack of interest in using the potential of the federal government to achieve positive progress on most social and environmental issues, leaving these largely to the provinces. Harper's government hasn't actually said that the provinces should have primary responsibility for the climate change issue, but this is effectively what has happened.

Provinces have moved far into the lead on climate change policies in Canada. A number have adopted significant emission reduction targets, have developed provincial climate change plans, and have implemented or are considering carbon taxes. Perhaps most significantly, by the summer of 2008, provinces representing over three-quarters of Canada's population had joined the Western Climate Initiative (WCI). The WCI's cap-and-trade program, with its absolute limits for emissions, would effectively make the Harper government's weaker proposals for intensity-based emission regulations irrelevant.

The WCI is likely itself to become subsumed by the introduction of a federal cap-and-trade program in the United States, which both presidential candidates have explicitly supported. At that time, the Harper government's current set of climate change policies could become truly lost at sea.

Policy Drought

The Harper government's mismanagement of Canada's water

Maude Barlow and Meera Karunananthan

AS MARTIN LUTHER King once said, "legislation will not change the heart, but it will restrain the heartless."

When it comes to fresh water in Canada, the Council of Canadians has long lamented that, without a national water policy, Canada's water has very weak or non-existent safeguards to protect against bulk exports, contamination, and unsustainable commercial exploitation.

As University of British Columbia Professor Karen Bakker explains, Canada is one of the few industrialized countries in the world that does not have legally enforced water quality standards.[1] In addition, the Great Lakes are polluted and being drawn down faster than recharge can replenish them. Lake Winnipeg is deeply polluted. The Athabasca River's very existence is imperilled by unsustainable consumption in the production of heavy oil in the Alberta tar sands. A leaked Environment Canada memo acknowledged in 2005 that Canada had a "looming freshwater crisis," but that no one was minding the store.[2]

Today, under the neoconservative agenda of the Harper government which has given increasing power to corporations, there is a more urgent need to "restrain the heartless" than ever before.

The drinking water crisis and the privatization of water services

Continued negligence of the infrastructural needs of municipalities and Aboriginal communities has led to a drinking water crisis that is shameful in a rich country like Canada.

Since the Conservative government first announced its national water strategy — largely a patchwork of funding proposals — in its October 2007 Throne Speech, it has done very little to improve access to safe drinking water in Canada.

A strategy for safe drinking water in First Nations communities was launched in March 2006, but, according to the May 6, 2008 Canadian Medical Association Journal (CMAJ), a staggering 93 advisories about unsafe water were in place in First Nations communities as of February 29, 2008. The Conservative government promised a clean water strategy in March 2007. Yet a year later, the CMAJ revealed that there were 1,766 boil-water advisories in effect across the country.

The drinking water crisis is seen as an opportunity for big business involvement. The CIBC, one of Canada's largest banks, released a report in November 2006 peddling the benefits of investing in water. While those of us who see water as a fundamental right are outraged that our governments have neglected water infrastructure in communities across the country, the CIBC sees crumbling infrastructure as a great opportunity for private corporations to make profits, and the Conservative government is committed to facilitating the process. It announced this year that it would be placing public money destined for water infrastructure into the hands of water profiteers.

Municipalities were once again denied much-needed funding for crumbling infrastructure in the Harper government's 2008 budget, which announced a $1.26 billion investment in a new Crown corporation to build private-public partnerships called PPP Canada Inc.[3] *Invest in Canada*, a government website aimed at promoting business opportunities in Canada to foreign investors, touts this development as an added incentive for foreign corporations. In other words, rather than using public funds to support municipalities struggling to meet the needs of their communities, the Canadian government is promising subsidies to foreign multinationals, enabling them to profit from water distribution and treatment, and other essential services in Canadian communities.

Invest in Canada also boasts that Canada reported an 11th consecutive annual surplus in the fiscal year of 2007–08. In 2006, Canada was the only G-7 country to have a surplus.

Bulk water exports

The Harper government continues to deny the threat of growing pressure from the United States to import Canada's water, and has disregarded repeated calls from the Canadian public to ban bulk water exports.

In April 2007, the Council of Canadians obtained a leaked document produced by a Washington think-tank revealing that business and government leaders in Canada, the U.S. and Mexico were actively discussing bulk water exports within the context of the Security and Prosperity Partnership of North America (SPP), a plan to harmonize policies and regulations and to facilitate corporate access to natural resources in Canada, the United States and Mexico.[4]

When information about a closed meeting to take place in Calgary involving high-ranking government officials and business representatives from all three countries was released to the media, it generated a strong public outcry. The Conservative government was forced to withdraw its delegation from the meeting.

However, Environment Minister John Baird not only denied the federal government's involvement in the meetings, but also argued that existing legislation provided adequate protection against bulk water exports. He erroneously told the media: "Canada has restrictions in place to prohibit bulk removal of water, including diversion, backed by serious fines and/or imprisonment."[5]

Fortunately, the Conservative government is now increasingly isolated in this view. Prompted by the evidence obtained by the Council of Canadians that the SPP would force Canada to export water to the United States, the House of Commons passed a motion in June 2007, requesting that the federal government begin talks with our United States and Mexico partners to have water excluded from NAFTA. Over a year later, the Conservative government has yet to follow through on this motion.

The reality is that Canada does not have jurisdictional control of its water resources under NAFTA, which means our federal government has to rely on weak environmental "exemptions" to NAFTA rules to protect water. These have proven to be inadequate in preventing bulk water exports, as have the voluntary provincial bans often cited by Environment Minister John Baird.

In a winter 2003 paper in the *Canadian Public Administration Journal*, Timothy Heinmiller of McMaster University reported that free trade agreements brought a series of new institutional constraints that have seriously limited the role of the Canadian government in determining water policy.[6]

NAFTA defines water as a "service" and an "investment." This means that, once a province lifts its voluntary ban on bulk water exports, NAFTA rules will take effect to prevent our governments from restricting such exports.

Both Ontario and Newfoundland, at different times, have attempted to lift the ban in order to allow corporations to export water in bulk. Both provinces eventually backed away from the plan, but only after intense public pressure.

Another incident that exposed the precarious state of Canada's water under NAFTA was the challenge launched by Sun Belt Water Corporation of Santa Barbara, California, against the Canadian government when the government of British Columbia banned bulk water exports in 1991.

Environmental exemptions could not prevent Sun Belt from invoking NAFTA's chapter 11 provision, which allows corporations from one NAFTA country to sue the government of another NAFTA country for financial compensation if that country changes the rules of business in a way that adversely affects the company. The company claimed US$10 billion in damages from the Canadian government.

Jack Lindsay, Sun Belt's CEO, put it bluntly when he stated: "Because of NAFTA, we are now stakeholders in the national water policy of Canada."[7]

If not for unflagging public opposition, there is no doubt that corporate-driven trade deals would have precipitated the establishment of a lucrative industry of bulk water exports to a thirsty U.S. market a long time ago.

The right to water

The Canadian government's corporate-centred approach to water has also directly affected the global movement for water justice.

The rapidly growing international crisis of water shortages, water pollution, and lack of access to safe clean drinking water and sanitation, broadly referred to as the global water crisis, has prompted a call amongst water activists for a new international framework that would protect water from corporate takeover by ensuring formal recognition of water as a human right in international law.

The Canadian government has consistently opposed the recognition of water as a right at the United Nations. Most recently, the Harper government played a key role in watering down a motion by Germany and Spain to officially recognize water as a human right at the UN Human Rights Council in March 2008.

This was the third time in six years that member nations of the UN have pushed for recognition of the human right to water. On each occasion, Canada blocked these efforts.

At a 2002 meeting, Canada stood alone among 53 countries by voting against the appointment of a special rapporteur on water. More recently, Canada reacted negatively to an October 2006 resolution of the UN Human Rights Council to conduct a study on the right to water.

In March 2008, Canada worked to weaken the resolution by demanding that references to the right to water and sanitation be removed and that the scope be reduced. The initial resolution called for the appointment of a "special rapporteur," but Canada saw to it that this position was downgraded to that of an "independent expert," serving only a one-year term instead of the proposed three years. Canada also opposed visits by this expert to individual countries and the granting of a mandate enabling the expert to clarify the content of the right to water and sanitation.[8]

The Liberal party defended the Harper government's position in the media, claiming that a right to water would make Canada vulnerable to bulk water exports. This is utterly untrue.

All trans-boundary water issues were explicitly excluded from the scope of the 2008 resolution. In addition, a human rights convention is between a government and its citizens. Recognition of the right to water in no way affects a country's sovereign right to manage its own resources.

The reality is that the resolution would be at odds with NAFTA, which defines water as a service and an investment. The real issue is that the Conservatives refuse to reopen NAFTA to remove water. They would rather deny Canada and the world the right to water.

Recognizing water as a human right is vital to ensuring that governments address the reality of more than a billion people who are currently without access to clean water.

Lakes and tailing impoundment areas

The privatization of water achieved a new height in Canada when Environment Canada announced in 2005 that 11 lakes would be used as tailing impoundment areas, or dump sites for the toxic waste of metal mining corporations.[9]

According to a June 2008 CBC report, a total of 16 Canadian lakes are already "slated to be officially but quietly 'reclassified' as toxic dump sites for mines. The lakes include prime wilderness fishing lakes from B.C. to Newfoundland."[10]

Mining Watch Canada predicts that number will soon increase. "The fate of many of these lakes has yet to be decided, but there is currently a strong bias within the government toward allowing the use of water bodies to receive mine wastes," says the organization. Once a lake is considered a "tailing impoundment area," according to Mining Watch, it is no longer protected under the federal *Fisheries Act*. Public consultations so far have been inconsistent and inadequate.

The long-term responsibility of dealing with the social and environmental consequences of the destruction of a lake will undoubtedly lie with the community and local government, not the company.

Furthermore, the contamination of a water body will have devastating consequences on entire watersheds, and the building of dams and diversions to contain the contamination will only make things worse in the long run.

Canada needs a national water policy

Two years under the Harper regime have made it clear that we need a national water policy that affirms the right to water. Harper's patchwork of funding proposals are not a substitute for robust legislation that protects Canadian water from commodification, diversion, bulk exports, and privatization.

An April 2008 survey conducted by Environics for the Council of Canadians disclosed that 89% of Canadians want a national water policy that would ban bulk water exports and recognize water as a human right. The growing push for private sector involvement in water services, the destruction of Canadian lakes, and the alarming rates of boil-water advisories underscore the urgent need for such a policy.

Core elements should include:

- watershed management and restoration;
- national drinking water standards;
- groundwater mapping and protection;
- an assessment of the viability of the virtual water being used in commodity exports;
- strict enforcement of laws against polluters;
- a serious climate change policy;
- protection of mountain habitat (the source of 50% of our water);
- sustainable food production policies;
- taxation to reflect the real environmental cost of commercial water extraction;
- a moratorium on new production in the tar sands;

- the removal of water as a service and an investment from NAFTA;
- a ban on the commercial export of Canada's water;
- a high-level emergency colloquium on the Great Lakes;
- strategies to reduce bottled water consumption and a re-investment in public water infrastructure;
- re-investment in research and scientific oversight of our freshwater supplies;
- adoption of the public trust doctrine to oversee our surface and groundwater sources as a commons;
- a water service charge regime based on the principle of equity as well as conservation; and
- support for the right to water at the United Nations.

Importantly, Canada needs to replace the current model of planning for massive growth and then trying to find the resources to accommodate this growth with a model that builds our economy around the need to protect water. Such a policy would likely mean a new emphasis on local food production and manufacturing, and more sustainable living in every aspect of our lives.

Putting Commerce Before Safety in the Nuclear Industry

Marita Moll

BREAKING NEWS: AN ageing nuclear reactor is ordered closed by a safety regulator against the wishes of the government. The regulator disappears and is replaced by a loyal servant. The reactor is restarted without the safety upgrades. This doesn't happen in Canada, right? Wrong!

This, unfortunately, is a snapshot of the Harper government's "nuclear meltdown" that occurred in late 2007. A 50-year-old nuclear reactor in Chalk River, Ontario, which produces medical isotopes used for diagnostic purposes, was not in compliance with safety upgrades requested by the Canadian Nuclear Safety Commission (CNSC). The CNSC ordered the facility to close despite pressure from the Harper government.

In the circus that ensued, Prime Minister Stephen Harper accused Linda Keen, President of the CNSC, of being a Liberal partisan. Harper, Health Minister Tony Clement, and Environment Minister Gary Lunn all became instant experts on nuclear safety, assuring parliamentarians that there would be no nuclear accident as a result of their passing an emergency bill to override the decision of the Commission and restart the reactor.

Ms. Keen testified later at a parliamentary committee hearing that, without the requested upgrades, the safety risk at the reactor was 1,000 times higher than accepted international standards. For her efforts, she was summarily fired from her position as president (she remains a commissioner for the time being) via a late night telephone call just before her scheduled appearance before the Commons committee.

At the hearing, Gary Lunn was clear about the reason for his actions: Ms. Keen refused to comply with a government request to keep the reactor open to maintain the supply of medical isotopes. She insisted that the CNSC was mandated to ensure safety, not the production of isotopes. To observers, it was clear that the government was reacting to industry pressure over potential damage to the very lucrative medical isotope business — Canada produces an estimated 45% of the world supply.

The firing of Linda Keen raised eyebrows around the world. This government has bullied other regulatory bodies, including the CRTC, without any public backlash, but firing (they called it a "rescinding of her designation") the nuclear safety regulator for doing her job was denounced across the country, by citizens through open-line radio programs and letters to the editor, by editors of major newspapers, and by the international nuclear safety community of which Keen is a respected member. Shawn Patrick Stensil, energy campaigner for Greenpeace, called the firing "a frightening lesson in an industry where safety is paramount. It's very unlikely that the regulator will have the courage to stand up to the industry again."[1]

Harper quickly replaced Keen with Michael Binder, who has an unblemished record as a "no nonsense, don't waste my time with arguments that don't reflect the current political reality" bureaucrat. Binder served for years under Kevin Lynch — recently named Clerk of the Privy Council, the most powerful non-elected position in the country — when Lynch was deputy minister at Industry Canada. So who's partisan now? You might be tempted to ask.

In its handling of this issue, the Harper government made it clear that, with respect to the nuclear industry, it takes a risk management approach: basically, they guess how much risk Canadians are prepared to accept to keep the lights on or keep the isotopes flowing and proceed accordingly. If the international standards are "too high," they adopt their own standards.

Here's the present danger. For some time, the nuclear industry has been lobbying for lower standards at the CNSC in order to continue operating aging reactors in Ontario and Québec, as well as build new ones with as yet unproven technologies. With CNSC now effectively "politicized," many observers fear that the fastest way to give the industry an economic boost will be to tinker with the safety margins. This is the kind of thinking that led Ontario, under the Harris government, to the Walkerton tainted-water crisis.

The alternative approach is to respect the precautionary principle: "If an action or policy might cause severe or irreversible harm to the public or to the environment, in the absence of a scientific consensus that harm would not ensue, the burden of proof falls on those who would advocate taking the action."[2] But chances of getting there from here under the current regime are pretty slim.

There are many other issues brewing in the nuclear arena which implicate the federal government:

- the shelving of the Maple 1 and 2 reactors which were supposed to replace the aging Chalk River reactor;
- a decision by MDS Nordion, which markets and distributes Chalk River's nuclear isotopes, to sue Atomic Energy of Canada Ltd. (AECL), a Crown corporation that designs CANDU-style reactors, and the federal government for $1.6 billion for failing to live up to its commitment to secure a 40-year supply of isotopes;
- the possible privatization of AECL;
- the safe burial of nuclear waste already accumulated; and
- the proposed new reactors in Alberta and Saskatchewan.

The industry, backed by the government, likes to say it is experiencing a renaissance. Critics say it's a carefully constructed illusion and a swamp we ought to recognize by now.

In firing Linda Keen, however, this government has tipped its hand and given us a very good idea of what we might expect from them in the future: lower standards, both technical and environmental, for nuclear installations; accelerated processes for approving new reactors; further privatization in the nuclear industry; and considerably less attention to public concerns which generally arise from the precautionary principle.

The public trust in our nuclear installations has been seriously damaged by a government which has shown its willingness to trade safety and security for commercial interests. That's a very dangerous situation, indeed.

Harper and Biofuels[1]

In Budgets 2007 and 2008, the Harper government allocated more than $2.2 billion to support the increased use of biofuels.[2] This financial commitment of public funds was accompanied by legislation. Bill C-33 will require all gasoline sold in Canada to have a minimum amount of 5% biofuel content by 2010. By 2012, all diesel and heating oil will have 2% biofuel content.[3] The Senate of Canada voted in favour of the bill on June 26, 2008, the day after Pat Mooney testified urging the Senate "to delay a decision here and spend more time looking at this issue. I think the scene is changing day by day and week by week..." The following is his testimony.

Pat Mooney

AT THE BIODIVERSITY convention meetings in Germany, we had this strange feeling that all of Africa as a block was asking for a moratorium against any development of biofuels. They were saying, "please go no further." They are asking for an end to subsidies in Europe. On the other side, we had the European Union, 27 countries, that wanted to change their position. We talked to them individually. They wanted to shift from supporting biofuels, but they could not. Brussels, as a group, had made the decision months before for the negotiations and they could not turn the ship around that fast.

One country after the other is saying they know it is a problem and they know they have to address it.

Africa is the hungry continent — the continent for which it was a problem. The world is saying to them that this is an industry that they can develop and take to their hearts as Africans. Africa is saying, "We do not want this. We do not trust how this will play out for us."

Everyone basically ignored Africa. It was Brazil, the United States, Canada, and the European Union that pushed through their position. Even then, with enormous caveats saying "We are not so sure about this; it needs to be studied more," and so on. However, they did not agree to the moratorium...

First is that we always tend to want to say we are only doing something for our country. It will only be for Canada or Brazil, and will not have an impact beyond that. Having dealt with agricultural commodities for the last 40 years, I find that remarkable. There is never a time when what we decide to do about agriculture in Canada does not affect the rest of the world. There is always a knock-on effect from what Canada does in wheat, corn or canola production, etc., that affects global food prices and stocks and who grows what where.

I recently talked to a colleague from Paraguay who told me that soybean production is moving into the forest lands in Paraguay. Soybeans are not used for biofuels, so I failed to see the connection. She explained that the connection is that corn is being grown in the old soybean-producing areas for biofuels, and soybeans are being pushed into the forest areas.

Those kinds of links and connections are happening around the world, and they can have an enormous impact. Unless we can be assured that the unimaginable has happened — that we can somehow isolate Canadian agriculture from the rest of the world — whatever we decide in Canada regarding fuel and food crops will have an impact on the rest of the world, and an impact on food prices.

Looking at the arguments about pricing in the world's food supply and how much of it is influenced by biofuels, look at who is saying what on this topic. On one side, you have the United States government and the fuel industry saying that only 2% or 3% of the increase in food prices can be traced back to biofuels. On the other side, you have the IMF, the International Food Policy Research Institute which is supported by the Consultative Group on International Agricultural Research affiliated with the World Bank, and the World Bank itself all saying that the impact of biofuels on food prices is 30%, and up to 65% under some conditions...

The second issue is that of climate change.

We see ourselves in a food emergency, which will last for a decade by all considerations. It is not only a year or two. It will last for the next 10 or 20 years.

Within that time-frame, we know there is this food emergency and we know that food stocks are the lowest they have been in decades. We also know, however, that climate change is coming and we do not know what will happen to food production because of climate change...

In regard to the Canadian Prairies, I was in Saskatchewan a few weeks ago. People there were telling me that the bottom half of the province will be a dust bowl.

When someone says do not worry, we have extra land and opportunities here, we do not know what will happen with climate change. Therefore, to impose upon an extraordinarily fragile food security situation by adding a whole new factor is simply incredibly risky and dangerous. It is a new pressure that we will not be able to reverse once it is established, because the demand in the industry will be structured for it.

We must be sure what we are doing because, if we are not sure, people will starve. The estimate now is that we have 100 million more people who are hungry in the world than we had six months ago. Some estimates indicate that it will increase to 290 million more hungry people by the end of this year.

To add to that pressure and to throw the factor of biofuels into this equation does not make sense to me.

Whether it is at scientific or biodiversity conferences or the World Food Summit, there seems to be a consensus emerging that the current situation is not good. Generation-one biofuels do not work very well, but we should not worry, we're told, because generation-two biofuels are coming down the road. We can relax because that will take care of all the problems for us.

I have some worries about that. It was interesting to hear the industry representatives here talk about how you can convert rubbish and algae into fuel. Without question, that is very interesting. It is absolutely fascinating. I hope it works, but we do not know for sure that it will.

That is not what is being done now. We are talking about the land area in corn and canola production, which is the big issue. It was unusual to have an industry lobbyist present to you what is not happening yet. He did not talk to you about what is happening, which is about corn, canola, and sugar cane production around the world today. This is where the impact will be for the next 15 to 20 years. The scientists and governments I talk to about these generation-two biofuel developments believe that commercial yields — if the process works at all — are far down the road. We will continue to have the current problem of taking biofuels from major food crops for a long time to come. This will all occur in the context of the current food emergency and climate change...

How can we do this to ourselves? I have sat through and been part of many food summits over the decades. I have heard these forecasts not to worry, that hunger will not be a problem in the future, and we will take care of that. I was in high school in Winnipeg in the 1960s, when I heard John F. Kennedy say we have the means and the capacity to wipe hunger and poverty from the face of Earth in our lifetime; we need only the will. He was wrong. It did not happen.

I was at the World Food Summit in Rome in 1974, which was a very political summit during the last food crisis, and heard Henry Kissinger say that within 10 years no child will go to bed hungry. That is not true. That did not happen.

I was at the World Food Summit in 1996 in Rome when our government joined other governments in saying that by the year 2015 we will have half the number of hungry people we have today. It was to go down to 415 million from 830 million. Today, the number of hungry people is 862 million. It has gone up, not down. The estimate is that by the year 2020 there will be 1.2 billion people who are hungry on this planet. Instead of reducing the number by half, we will increase the number of people who are hungry by one-and-a-half times.

I have heard governments say for a long time that they will solve the problem of world hunger, that there is lots of land, that they will increase crop yields, or that they will take care of the water problem. It has never happened.

What *has* happened is that energy consumption has increased and the hungry have increased in numbers during that time. I would like to see proof that what is being decided today, perhaps by the Senate, will truly be something that will not impair the health and well-being of those 1.2 billion people who are becoming hungry. I doubt that will happen. I worry that we will grab at straws and hope our usage of fossil fuels will be reduced by 0.65% or 0.70% by the biofuels industry because of this bill. It is so marginal. We could reduce fossil fuels that amount by simply slowing down our cars by one mile per hour. But it would cost $2.2 billion to do it in terms of the bill. Pumping up our tires could have the same effect without costing that kind of money.

With this bill, we would be setting in place the infrastructure and an industry that will not get rid of the problem in five or 10 years. It will still be there. If Saskatchewan or Alberta were to dry up and could not produce the required yields, the infrastructure would disappear and we would have to turn to California or Brazil or Indonesia. Some of the governments in Africa at the food summit said to us, please do not do this.

Harper's Attack On the Canadian Wheat Board

Helen Forsey

THE CANADIAN WHEAT Board is fighting for its life.

Ever since 1935, when a rather different Conservative government listened to farmers and passed the Canadian Wheat Board Act, the Canadian Wheat Board (CWB) has been working to bring Western Canada's grain to the world. The largest of our farm marketing boards, it is also one of the biggest, oldest, and most stable collective bargaining units in the country. As such, it represents a ripe field of temptation for Stephen Harper and his corporate backers to swing their ideological scythes and try to make off with the harvest.

If they succeed, the impact will be enormous. The gutting of the Winnipeg-based Wheat Board and its sister agency, the Canadian Grain Commission, would be a disaster — and not only for prairie grain growers. It would be a giant step towards the dismantling of orderly marketing systems in other farm sectors, a further weakening of collective bargaining, a devastating blow to Canadian democracy, and a threat to workers and consumers across Canada and even beyond. The current fight to save the CWB is a crucial one for all Canadians.

CWB represents 75,000 grain growers

Since many non-farmers know little about the issues involved, some background facts will help. The Canadian Wheat Board represents some 75,000 grain growers, and handles all Western wheat and barley destined for export and human use. The CWB is 100% self-supporting, and, with $5 billion in annual sales, is a real power in the international marketplace. Backed by the Canadian Grain Commission's excellent quality assurance, the Board uses its exclusive "single-desk selling" power — its much-maligned "monopoly" — to get the best possible prices, transportation rates, and quality premiums for its producers. The CWB is worth $700–$800 million annually to farmers, averaging almost $10,000 per farm.

And it's not just farmers who benefit. A 2005 Price-Waterhouse-Coopers study credited the Board with a "huge" economic impact totalling $1.6 billion annually, including some 14,000 non-farm jobs. The CWB moves 20 to 30 million tonnes of grain a year over Canadian rail lines and through Canadian ports in British Columbia, Manitoba, Ontario and Québec, making it one of Canada's biggest rail shippers and one of our strongest East-West links. The Board has also been a crucial player in protecting grain customers — including Canadian consumers — from the risks of GM (genetically modified) wheat.

U.S. agribusiness wants Wheat Board gone

For years, the big American grain interests have been trying to destroy the Wheat Board and grab control of our grain industry for themselves.

"They'd just love to add grain to the list of Canadian resources and jobs leaving Canada for bigger profits elsewhere," says Ken Sigurdson, former Manitoba coordinator for the National Farmers' Union and a co-founder of the *Save My CWB* Campaign. "They've tried NAFTA challenges, they've tried the WTO, they've tried propaganda and political pressure. And time after time they've failed."

But now, in Stephen Harper, those giant corporations have an ally. "Ever since coming to power, this Conservative minority government has been using every sneaky and undemocratic method imaginable to undermine the CWB and betray the farmers and workers who rely on it," says Sigurdson, who farms with his family near Swan River, Manitoba. "There's a whole raft of issues about how the government has attempted to manipulate this process."

That the Harper government carefully planned this manipulation became crystal clear in mid-June 2008, when lawyers for the Board made public a secret Cabinet document from August, 2006. The plan, which has been systematically implemented, recommended firing the CWB's highly capable and respected CEO, Adrian Measner, and replacing appointed pro-Board directors with anti-Board grain industry hacks. It urged government use of Orders-in-Council to get around legal democratic requirements, and eventual legislative changes to eliminate those requirements permanently.

The October 2006 gag order forbidding Board directors and staff from spending a penny to defend the single-desk system was a key element of that plan. The 2007 "non-binding" producer plebiscite on removing barley from CWB jurisdiction was part of the same scheme.

Farmers fought back. The Board challenged the gag order in Federal Court, and the case began wending its way through the legal system. Then, when the Harper cabinet followed up its dubious plebiscite with an Order-in-Council to remove barley from the CWB's marketing authority, the Friends of the Canadian Wheat Board, a producer group, went to court to stop it.

Meanwhile, the government had been practising its election tampering skills. CWB director elections are the key to farmer control of the Board, with 10 of the 15 directors elected by grain producers and the other five appointed by government. Every two years, elections are held in five of the 10 Wheat Board districts, staggering the four-year terms. Right in the middle of the 2006 director election campaign, the Minister issued an order removing almost 40% of the names on the producer voting lists. Later, in the barley plebiscite, the government's techniques included ambiguous wording of the options, traceable numbered ballots, no scrutineers, and predetermined interpretation of the results.

"Illegal and immoral"

Colleen Ross of Iroquois, Ontario, the NFU's Women's President, calls what the government is trying to do to the Wheat Board "both illegal and immoral. It just flies in the face of the principles of food sovereignty: people's control over food, including how it is marketed. This government is once again putting corporate profits before the interests of people, and they're doing it through fraud and lies."

And all paid for by the taxpayer. During the 2007 plebiscite campaign, with pro-Board staff and directors muzzled by the gag order, the government spent $1.2 million in public money on propaganda promoting its "dual marketing" option — what it likes to call "producer choice."

"'Dual marketing' is a fraud if ever there was one," says Bruce Dodds, national organizer for the grassroots *Save My CWB* campaign. "Even the government's own anti-Board task force confirmed in 2006 that, without its single-desk selling power, the CWB would not survive as an effective bargaining agent for farmers. It would be like having a trade union without a check-off or the Rand Formula. Take the Rand Formula away from labour and call it 'worker choice.'"

"This is all about money and control," says Sigurdson. "U.S. agribusiness wants to 'integrate' Canada's grain industry with their own, and cherry-pick our prime production. Without the Wheat Board, the big grain companies would totally take over. Farmers would just be contract growers, restricted to the company's varieties, their chemicals, their prices and conditions. For transportation rates and service we'd be at the mercy of the railroads, with no representative body strong enough to take them on." Little wonder most grain producers — even Conservatives — continue to support the Board.

And they've won some important battles. In July 2007, the Federal Court ruled in favour of the farmers and stopped the government from removing barley from the Wheat Board's marketing authority, a power explicitly reserved for Parliament. The government appealed — forcing the litigants to spend thousands more on legal costs — and lost again. Then, last June, another judge quashed the ministerial gag order that had prevented the Board from effectively defending its role. Thwarted, a furious Harper vowed to continue his push for "marketing choice," threatening that anyone standing in the way "is going to get walked over."

Three bills threaten Board

Harper's walking boots include three bills that were on the order paper prior to the election call. Bill C-39 would severely undermine the Canadian Grain Commission's long-standing mandate to inspect and regulate the grain industry "in the farmers' interest." Bill C-46 would take away the right of barley producers to a vote on the CWB's role, and would tie the Board up in frivolous arbitration processes. The most recent Bill, C-57, would revamp the voters' list for Director elections, disenfranchising even more farmers, notably smaller producers.

Harper's intent is clear: if he wins a majority government, the Canadian Wheat Board will be history.

What would that mean? The Canadian grain industry, with its associated jobs and economic spin-offs, would go south — literally and figuratively. The huge economic benefits provided by the Board and the Grain Commission would be gone, leaving farmers and workers more dependent than ever on the grain companies and the railroads. Unions in the transportation, shipping, and administration sectors would soon feel the impact. With companies shipping where and when they pleased, much prairie grain would go overland to the U.S., seriously reducing east-west shipments and business at Canadian ports. The port of Churchill and the Hudson's Bay Railroad, both 80–90% dependent on CWB shipments, could face bankruptcy, stranding many small northern Manitoba communities.

With the Board gutted and the Grain Commission hobbled, foreign grain markets would no longer be able to count on Canadian quality and reliability. Much of our harvest would be mixed with American grain, and customers in Europe, Asia, and here at home would lose a strong bulwark against the risks of genetically modified (GM) wheat. And transnational corporations would get a global lock on grain supplies at a time when skyrocketing prices and shortages are already causing a massive global food crisis.

"Do or die" election for farms and food

As for the rest of organized agriculture, all this is a foretaste of what a Harper majority would do to Canada's supply-managed sectors: dairy, poultry, and egg farming. In a brutally competitive global market, without the "cost of production" pricing maintained by supply management, Canadian farmers in these sectors would not be able to make ends meet. Industrial-style contract farming, like what we see already in pork production, would take over, with corporate agribusiness calling the shots and scooping up the profits. Regardless of the impacts on local production, food safety, or the environment, even more of our food would be imported, and Canadians' shaky hold on food sovereignty would become even more tenuous.

What we're seeing in the Harper government's anti-Wheat Board vendetta is the familiar spectre of privatization and deregulation, the familiar systematic attack on the public interest.

"The threat to the Wheat Board is really an attack on collective bargaining and democracy," says Dodds. "In the first half of the 20th century, two great social movements — for farmers and workers — struggled to win the right to control their own institutions and the products of their labour. Now we're defending what they won."

This is a critical year for the Wheat Board and the Grain Commission. "It's do or die," says Sigurdson. "We're fighting hard, in the courts and on the hustings. We've got to win the upcoming CWB Director elections this fall, and make sure voters across the country stop Harper from getting a majority in Parliament. If people understand the importance of this fight, and back us up, I think we can win. After all, it's really a fight for Canada and our place in the world."

FIVE

(*IN*)EQUALITY AND PUBLIC SERVICES

Women's Equality and Human Rights

The Ad-Hoc Coalition for Women's Equality and Human Rights

> Yes, I'm ready to support women's human rights and I agree that Canada has more to do to meet its international obligations to women's equality. If elected, I will take concrete and immediate measures, as recommended by the United Nations, to ensure that Canada fully upholds its commitments to women in Canada.
> —*Stephen Harper, January 18, 2006.*

DESPITE STEPHEN HARPER'S apparent enthusiasm for women's rights during the election campaign, his government, by September 2006, had committed itself to a course of action that undermines rather than improves women's equality in Canada.

Fall 2006 was a bleak time for women's equality activists, as the government announced significant cuts and changes to the Women's Program of Status of Women Canada. The budget was cut by 43% ($5 million), 12 of the 16 regional offices of SWC were closed, funding for women's equality research and advocacy was eliminated, and the word "equality" was removed from the Program's mandate. Funding to the Court Challenges Program, which had supported many women's equality legal challenges, was also eliminated.

Thanks to ongoing public education and advocacy by those committed to women's equality, some of these cuts were later reversed. The

Women's Program budget was restored and the word "advocacy" was reinstated in to its mandate.

In the past 12 months, the Women's Program has provided significant financial support, through grants and partnership agreements, for programs and projects across the country, many of them aimed at extremely vulnerable women from marginalized communities. The funding that is now flowing supports important work that will have a direct and positive impact on women's ability to leave violent or abusive relationships, to find appropriate safe housing, and to become employed. However, the offices that were closed in 2006 remain closed, the Women's Program still does not fund women's equality advocacy work in Canada, and the Court Challenges Program did not get its funding reinstated. Without funding for women's equality advocacy work, women's essential inequality remains entrenched in Canadian and Québec culture.

Further, the drastic steps taken in September 2006 have had a significant chilling effect. Some women's equality organizations have closed their doors or have had to cut back on their activities (the National Association of Women and the Law, and the Canadian Research Institute for the Advancement of Women, among others) because their research and/or advocacy work will no longer be funded. This has had a trickle-down effect for women's organizations and others (including politicians) across the country who have for decades relied on these organizations to provide the research and advocacy tools that they use in their work.

Women must work with the challenging reality of a Conservative government. This is a government that supports programs and projects that contribute to women's equality, but does nothing to address the framework of institutional and systemic inequality faced by women in this country.

Are we all equal now?

Long-time activist and social theorist Janine Brodie argues that "despite the persistence of gender inequalities, the idea of gender equality has been progressively erased from Canadian political rhetoric, policy goals and bureaucratic machinery." In her recent article in *Feminist Theory*,

Brodie elaborates how the Harper government has waged the battle over ideas:

> In the fall of 2006, the Honourable Beverley Oda, Minister of Canadian Heritage, a catch-all portfolio that includes the Status of Women, confidently informed a House of Commons standing committee that "this government does fundamentally believe that all women are equal."[1] Oda had been called before the standing committee on the Status of Women to explain why Stephen Harper's Conservative government's recent two-billion-dollar "fat trimming" exercise, conducted within the context of a ballooning federal surplus, had been achieved largely at the expense of Canada's equality-seeking groups, and especially Canadian women....
>
> In the eyes of many observers, the minority Conservative government appeared bent on silencing a diverse range of governmental and non-governmental organizations that had, over the course of a generation, advocated for citizenship equality both in the courts and in the policy process....
>
> "Equality," Oda explained, "is enshrined in the Charter and there was no need to repeat it in the mission statement of Status of Women Canada.[2] Every part of the federal government has to be founded on the belief of equality," she continued, and thus the government as a whole, rather than designated agencies, was "responsible for the development of policies and programs that address the needs of both men and women."[3]...
>
> If we are all equal now, it is because we are all invited to become enfranchised and empowered by the market, to become self-sufficient Canadians and citizen-taxpayers, who neither expect nor tolerate the recognition of systemic barriers or the inefficiencies of collective redress. But this invitation to neoliberal citizenship is also a platform for contestation, reversals, and invention.[4]

How women vote

The gender gap in politics is no secret. Traditionally, women who vote lean left of centre while male voters lean towards the right. The gender gap is especially distinct when considering hot-button political issues.

In 2004, health care was the main issue, especially for women voters. From a list of issues that also included taxes, social welfare programs, the environment, and corruption, 61% of women but only 41% of men chose health care as their priority issue.[5]

In 2006, in the wake of the federal Liberal government's "sponsorship scandal," polls showed that corruption rivalled health as a key issue. This scandal was born of the federal government's sponsorship program, which ran from 1996 until 2004. It was established to highlight federal investment in Québec and reduce support for separatist parties. Illegal activities surrounding the administration of the multi-million-dollar program included misdirecting public funds to advertising firms with Liberal organizers and fundraisers on their payrolls, or firms that donated part of these public funds to the Liberal party of Canada.

Nonetheless, according to the 2006 Canadian Election Study (CES) and surveys conducted by the Institute for Social Research at York University, 47% of women still cited health as their most important political issue, while the percentage of men who did so dropped to 30%.[6]

Men and women traditionally differ on issues mirroring the partisan divide in Canadian federal politics. Women more than men are concerned with tackling issues like poverty, health care, and the public provision of services. Men tend to be more conservative on social issues generally, and are more likely than women to oppose same-sex marriage. More men than women support the death penalty, and men are less likely than women to support gun control.

Women are clearly to the left of men on all of these issues, which may explain why, in polls leading up to the 2006 election, women were more likely to evaluate the Conservative party and Stephen Harper negatively. As the 2006 campaign was coming to a close, one in three women outside Québec, compared to one in four men, named the Conservative party as the party they absolutely would not vote for.[7]

Women juggling full-time (in many cases, underpaid) work and family responsibilities rely more heavily on public services. Women have traditionally been less convinced than men of arguments favouring the market economy over government intervention. Indeed, the increased feminization of poverty means that more women than men must de-

TABLE 1 *Candidates nominated and elected in the 2006 election*

	Bloc Québécois	Conser-vatives	Liberals	NDP	Green Party
Total candidates					
Nominated	75	308	308	308	308
Elected	51	125	101	29	0
Male candidates					
Nominated	52	270	229	200	236
Elected	34	111	80	17	0
Female candidates					
Nominated	23	38	79	108	72
Elected	17	14	21	12	0
Female candidates (%)					
Nominated	30.6%	12.3%	25.6%	35%	23%
Elected	33%	11%	21%	41%	0%

pend on the government to provide supports and service to enable them to better care for their families.

The gender gap was evident in the 2006 election, where voting patterns showed that the women's vote ensured that Stephen Harper and the Conservatives were held to a minority government.

Where are the women?

The United Nations has noted that, for public policy to reflect women's priorities and to see management and organizational change, women elected to public office must reach a critical mass of 30 to 35%.[8] Canada, a signatory to CEDAW, the Convention to End All Forms of Discrimination Against Women, and the Beijing Platform for Action, has committed to ensuring that women in Canada are better represented in the House of Commons. While women's representation has improved since signing these agreements, the improvement is marginal.

In fact, the 2006 election which brought the Harper government to power saw a slight decrease in the number of women elected to Canadian federal politics. In 2006, only 64 of the 308 elected MPs

(20.7%) were women, compared with 21.1% in the 2004 election. Table 1 presents a breakdown of female representation by political party as of the 2006 election.[9]

Some political parties have agreed to increase their numbers of female candidates and, while they may hold true to that commitment, women are too often nominated in ridings deemed "unwinnable" by the party, while surefire seats are reserved for prominent male candidates.

Following his 2006 election, Stephen Harper appointed six women to cabinet out of a total of 27 positions (about 22%). This is a slight decrease from the previous Liberal government, in which 24% of cabinet positions were filled by women. Both of these statistics are considered unacceptable by United Nations standards.

Pay equity

> For taxpayers, however, [pay equity] is a rip-off and it has nothing to do with gender. Both men and women taxpayers will pay additional money to both men and women in the civil service. That's why the federal government should scrap its ridiculous pay equity law.[10]

More than 30 years after the adoption of the *Canadian Human Rights Act,* the average annual earning of Canadian women is only 64% of what men earn.[11] Respect for the fair value of women's work is a very important concern in public opinion, yet it is not being addressed. It is unacceptable that Canada has one of the highest wage gaps among the advanced industrial countries in the Organization for Economic Co-operation and Development (OECD).

Today, women working full year and full-time in Canada earn an average of 70.5 cents for every dollar earned by men. Concretely, this means that women working full-time, full year, earn an average of $39,200 while men earn an average of $55,700.[12] If we look at all workers, including part-time workers, the gap is even greater, women earning only 64% as much as men. This wage gap is even greater for Aboriginal women, women of colour, new immigrant women, and women with disabilities. Racialized women make only 64 cents and Aboriginal women an appalling 46 cents for each dollar earned by men.[13] Even when women retire, they continue to be victims of wage discrimination, as they will make just 58% of the income made by their male counterparts.

The gap between men's and women's wages narrowed in the 1990s, when women earned 72% of the male dollar, but it is now back to 70.5% — even though women are more educated than ever before. More women than men now go to university or college. Almost half (49%) of women aged 25 to 45 have a post-secondary qualification. Women make up the majority of university graduates, and almost 60% of those with a community college qualification. In several undergraduate fields of study that have traditionally been male-dominated, such as medicine, law, and commerce/business administration, women now outnumber or equal men. It is particularly disturbing that university-educated women face an even larger wage gap than the national average, that women with university educations are now only earning, on average, 68% as much as men.

Women's pay inequity continues even though they are working in greater numbers and for longer hours than ever before. Mothers of young children are working: two-thirds of women with children under the age of 6 are in either part- or full-time paid employment. While women are working for less pay than men in the job market, they continue to take on most of the child care and domestic work for their families. As the population ages, many women also now find themselves providing care to aging parents, including their partner's parents.

Pay equity is a human right protected by the *Canadian Human Rights Act*, the Canadian Charter of Rights and Freedoms equality provisions, and a number of international human rights conventions that Canada has signed. In response to pressures from organized labour and the women's movement, the previous Liberal federal government created the Task Force on Pay Equity, which conducted widespread consultations with key stakeholders, including women's organizations. During the Task Force study, all participants, including employers, unions and women's groups, agreed that a new law requiring positive employer action, clear standards, and an adjudicative body was required. The current complaint-based system, in place for the past 25 years, has proven to be ineffective, time-consuming and costly to both employers and unions.

In May 2004, the Task Force released its final report entitled *Pay Equity: A New Approach to a Fundamental Right.* In this report, the Task Force recommended that the federal government develop and implement a stand-alone, pro-active pay equity law that would include an obligation for employers to review pay practices, identify gender-based wage discrimination gaps, and eliminate pay inequities within a specific time frame.

The Task Force also recommended that, to be effective, pay equity legislation should recognize the discrimination faced by Aboriginal peoples, persons with disabilities and visible minorities, as well as women. It urged that the legislation should protect all employees, unionized or not, and should recognize that pay equity is a non-negotiable human right.

The Task Force also recommended the creation of a new Canadian Pay Equity Commission that would administer the new pay equity law. This Commission would provide education and assistance to employers, unions and employees, review complaints, and conduct investigations and random workplace audits. It would offer advocacy services for unrepresented workers, and would conduct research and issue orders to ensure the law is enforced. The government should provide enough human and financial resources to allow the Commission to effectively administer the pay equity legislation.

The Task Force also recommended that a new Canadian Pay Equity Hearing Tribunal be set up to adjudicate disputes on any issues as they arise in the implementation or maintenance phases of pay equity.

These recommendations of the Task Force have been disregarded by the Conservative government for four years and have not yet been implemented, with women workers paying the highest price for this inaction.

The all-party Standing Committee on the Status of Women has twice recommended that the government introduce pro-active legislation. In its response tabled September 18, 2006, the government ignored both the consensus achieved during the Task Force process and the widespread support for pay equity law reform. Instead it is going back to a system that has proven to be totally inadequate over the last 25 years, promising to make the current law effective through education, inspections, and mediation.

But education, mediation and compliance inspections have all been components of government policy since the early 1980s. Labour Canada, as it then was, ran this program for years, with no tangible results. Leaving individual women and their unions with only the right to complain has repeatedly proven ineffective, time-consuming, and extremely costly.[14]

Fiscal policy and women

Tax cuts

Recent financial policies have made clear the government's key priorities: tax cuts, debt reduction, and shrinking government. All of these erode Canada's revenue base and social safety net. Despite Canada's claims on the international stage that it is committed to a high level of gender-responsive budgeting, recent budgets have allotted paltry amounts to those issues that are traditionally more pertinent to women, such as housing, education, health care, and public transit.

Over a 15-year period, federal governments have chosen to spend $340 billion on tax cuts, rather than investing in a comprehensive anti-poverty strategy, combating climate change, or strengthening the public health care system.[15] An aggressive tax cut agenda is worrisome to women's equality-seeking groups. Not only does such an agenda fail to reach many low-to-middle-income women, but it also greatly reduces the spending capacity of the government.

The tax expenditures that directly benefit women, such as the Working Income Tax Credit and the Child Care Expense Deduction, have remained virtually stagnant from 2004 to 2008. In contrast, tax credits made available to high-income earners, owners of capital assets, and corporations are rapidly increasing.

Women's incomes typically fall in the two lowest tax brackets for incomes of $38,000 and less. Nearly 40% of women and 24% of men do not pay taxes at all because their incomes are so low. Delivering policies through the tax system is simply impractical, as it does not target poverty and income inequality. For example, in Budget 2008, 78.8% of tax expenditures (cuts) go to taxpayers in the top three quintiles, while only 21.2% of tax cuts go to the lowest two quintiles. This lost revenue benefits the higher income groups in which most women are not traditionally represented.

Many would argue that women benefit from the GST tax rate cut from 7% to 6% to 5%. But women, because of their typically lower income levels, generally make less costly purchases and so benefit less from the consumption tax rate cuts. Personal income tax rate cuts also do not tend to benefit women due to their traditionally low income levels and consequent low taxation levels; and cutting the personal income tax rate clearly does nothing to help those 40% of women who earn so little they do not pay taxes at all.

Under the current taxation agenda, low-income individuals, most of them women, will pay a higher income tax rate than do large corporations. Aggressive corporate income tax rate cuts announced in 2008 will undoubtedly shift the overall tax burden to low-income individuals while draining revenues needed to invest in infrastructure and public services.

Pension income-splitting

In 2006, the Conservative government introduced pension income-splitting, which allows a higher pension income earning spouse to transfer tax liability (not income) to the lower earner to lower the family's taxes. This is of grave concern to many women's equality-seeking groups because it clearly discriminates against women and opens the door to full income-splitting.

Full income-splitting and joint taxation is a very discriminatory policy and would cost the public treasury billions of dollars — monies, many would argue, that would be better spent on such services as a national child care program.

The benefits of income-splitting go mainly to higher income men. Unpaid care-givers do not get any direct benefits and could suffer additional financial burdens by appearing to the Canada Revenue Agency to earn more than they actually do, thus making them ineligible for income-tested programs. Income-splitting can also discourage women's paid workforce participation, as the family could lose tax benefits if the secondary earner increases her income. As with many social and financial policies of this government, income-splitting favours traditional one-income-earner families.

Because recent budgets and the tax cut agenda do little to help women, they do very little to comply with Canada's international commitments. An aggressive tax cut agenda can disadvantage women because it is inaccessible and also depletes revenues for the public programs on which many women rely.

In 1981, Canada ratified the United Nations Convention to End All Forms of Discrimination Against Women (CEDAW). In 1995, the federal government developed a federal plan for gender equality in response to the Beijing Platform for Action. Neither CEDAW nor the federal plan encourages the use of tax cut strategies to eliminate poverty and strengthen women's economic security.

In order to truly address the increasing income gap and the feminization of poverty in Canada, we need a strategy with the key objective of alleviating poverty. The commitments have been made. The infrastructure and analytical support are in place. The key impetus still needed is the political will and a desire to help those who need it most.

Bill C-484

Last March, Bill C-484, the *Unborn Victims of Crime Act*, passed Second Reading in the House of Commons. This bill seeks to amend the Criminal Code to create a separate offence for causing injury to or the death of an "unborn child" when a pregnant woman is the victim of a crime.

On its face, this bill is a compassionate response to the tragic murders of pregnant women. However, it carries with it significant threats to the rights of women while not significantly addressing the issue of violence against women.

Bill C-484 would grant a type of legal personhood to fetuses. This conflicts with section 223(1) of the Criminal Code, which states that fetuses are not persons until they exit from the birth canal alive. The Supreme Court has found that a woman and her fetus are "physically one" person under the law.

This bill is not an effective way to address violence against women, including pregnant women. Spousal violence and pregnancy are already recognized as aggravating factors in sentencing. Any future legislative reforms intended to respond to violence against women must focus on the woman and not the fetus, if they are to be effective.

By legally separating a pregnant woman from her fetus, this bill creates an adversarial relationship between them, as well as one in which fetal rights are elevated above women's rights. This can — as it has already in the United States — lead to women being prosecuted for perceived misconduct or illegal activity during their pregnancy. If passed, Bill C-484 would set back women's equality rights by decades, in particular a woman's right to control her own body and her own reproductive capacity.

Women have made some gains over the last century. But, with regressive bills like this being brought forward by Conservative MPs, it is evident that those gains are in jeopardy. There is still a long way to go before women's full equality becomes a reality.

Conclusion

Under Stephen Harper's Conservative government, women in Canada are witnessing a steady encroachment on the hard-won and still fragile equality rights for which they have fought long and hard. Canadians, both women and men, expect more than lip service and window-dressing to ensure that substantive equality for women becomes a reality and not simply an election promise.

Harper and Child Care

Morna Ballantyne

FEBRUARY 6, 2006 was a big day for the newly elected minority Conservative government. Stephen Harper introduced his new cabinet, set the date for the start of the new Parliament, and was sworn in as Prime Minister. Moments later, he terminated the early learning and child care agreements that would have provided $5 billion as a first step to building a national child care system in Canada.

Harper declared that his government would meet the needs of children through a new taxable monthly allowance of $100 for children under six, as promised in the election campaign — and ridiculed by Liberal spokesperson Scott Reid as "beer and popcorn money."

Clearly, child care was at the very top of the government's list of five priorities. As long-time child care advocate Jamie Kass recalls, "it was the first time ever that we were hoping to be ignored by government. Instead, child care was the first target."

Advocates and defenders of child care were quick to react. Within days, a large contingent of parents, children, and child care workers gathered outside the Prime Minister's residence. Taken by surprise, the RCMP officers on duty urged the crowd to go home, arguing that the Harper family had not even had time to move in.

Coalition formed

In a few weeks, a new coalition of groups and individuals came together to launch the Code Blue for Child Care campaign. Some organizations had never before made child care a focus of political work, but they were convinced that a significant setback for Harper on this front would make it more difficult for him to move his agenda forward on other fronts. Within two months, Code Blue had the active support of more than 80 groups representing a broad cross-section of interests and constituencies. More than 100,000 Canadians had signed petitions opposing Harper's child care proposals.

The government's plan had three components: cancel the early learning and child care agreements; institute a monthly federal transfer to individual families with young children and market it as "universal child care"; and allocate $250 million in a future budget to create new child care spaces through businesses or community groups.

Code Blue made the strategic decision to zero-in first on the cancellation of the child care agreements.

"The cancellation represented a massive reduction of more than $1 billion in transfers to the provinces for early learning and child care, starting in 2007–08," explains Jody Dallaire, chairperson of the Child Care Advocacy Association of Canada, a leader of Code Blue. "We knew that Canadians would be furious about the magnitude of the cut when child care programs are so desperately needed."

This is not to say that Code Blue or others ignored Harper's so-called child care allowance. For example, the Caledon Institute of Social Policy, a well-respected Ottawa-based think-tank, had already produced an analysis during the federal election exposing the allowance's flaws:

> The scheme's true value would be less than $1,200 because it would increase families' taxable allowance income and thus trigger both reductions in federal and province/territorial income-tested benefits and increases in taxes... The biggest losers would be modest-income families earning in the $30,000–$40,000 range... It is doubly unfair because it would favour one-earner families over single-parent families and two-earner families.

Most Canadian families need and use child care outside the home so that parents can work in the paid labour force or study. The proposed Choice in Child Care Allowance would do little if anything to increase the supply of affordable, quality child care. Nor would the scheme do much to help families pay for child care, since it would offset only a fraction of the cost of child care.[1]

While there was a lot wrong with the monthly allowance, Code Blue came to the conclusion that it would not be possible to organize massive opposition to a program that would give families some extra cash. To make things even more difficult, the government was determined to move quickly on the allowance, getting it approved through the first Budget and cheques mailed out by July 1.

"We decided to focus on the cancellation of the agreements because we had more time to organize on that front," says Code Blue Steering Committee member Sue Colley. "The terms of the agreements required Harper to give one year's notice. Also, we figured we needed the powerful voices of the provincial and territorial governments to turn things around. We knew they would be more likely to speak out against the transfer cuts."

Premiers disappoint

In fact, only five provinces — Saskatchewan, Manitoba, Ontario, Québec, and Nova Scotia — came out publicly against the cuts, and even their muted opposition quickly dissipated. By the time the premiers gathered for their annual meeting in July 2006 in St. John's, not one of them would step out of the hotel to accept Code Blue's 85-foot petition urging them to take a strong stand against the cuts. Ian Urquhart, *Toronto Star* political commentator, gave this astute explanation for their hesitancy to take on the issue:

> ... The premiers' preoccupation now is with lobbying Ottawa for more money with no strings attached — through either equalization payments or, in the case of Ontario, per capita grants. A simultaneous push for restoration of funding with strings attached to child care might be counterproductive. Whether the provinces would spend any no-strings-attached

funding on child care is another question. They all have competing priorities — from post-secondary education to infrastructure. Better for the premiers, then, to put the child-care issue behind them. But not better for the cause of public debate.[2]

Rebuffed by the provinces, Code Blue turned to the federal opposition parties to take action against the Conservative child care policy, but here too they ran into roadblocks. For one, the parties were more interested in differentiating themselves from each other than in taking a unified position on child care. The Liberals championed the federal-provincial agreements as a reminder to Canadians of what they had lost in electing the Conservatives. The NDP focused on the massive federal transfer cut that would result in terminating the agreements, arguing that the previous Liberal government had not gone far enough in its negotiations with the provinces. The Bloc Québécois took issue with the new government's unilateral decision to end the agreements, but at the same time stuck to its position that all federal transfers be unrestricted. The biggest problem, though, was that none of the parties was willing to trigger another federal election on this or any other issue.

Budget passes

Child care advocates were frustrated by the political quagmire on Parliament Hill. An Environics public opinion poll prepared for the Child Care Advocacy Association of Canada revealed that only a minority of Canadians supported Harper's child care program,[3] yet the opposition parties, representing a majority in the House of Commons, could or would not block it. The 2006 federal budget, including the new monthly allowance, passed easily.

The federal-provincial early learning and child care agreements expired without fanfare in early spring of 2007, but Code Blue continued to lobby against cuts in federal transfers for child care. Under the Harper plan, $250 million was to be transferred to business and other groups to subsidize capital investments in child care spaces. Code Blue argued that to divert previous federal dollars to private child care ventures, divorced from provincial capital and operating program funding, would result in making child care services even less affordable and less available to most Canadian children.[4]

Child care advocates wanted to see the Conservative government's $250 million program replaced with a dedicated transfer payment to the provinces and territories for capital expansion, along with an increase in transfer payments for operating funds such as those that had been committed in the now-defunct federal-provincial agreements.

Harper flip flops

The Conservative government did in fact backtrack by the time it introduced its March 2007 federal budget, abandoning the ill-conceived Child Care Spaces Initiative in favour of a $250-million direct transfer to the provinces, distributed on a per capita basis.

"It was the first Harper policy flip-flop," says Margot Young of the Canadian Union of Public Employees, one of the many trade union supporters of Code Blue. "Giving financial incentives to businesses to create spaces had been tried before and failed. It was such bad policy that even members of the Minister's hand-picked advisory group raised objections, and it was roundly criticized when the government's policy folks conducted cross-country consultations on how it could be made to work."

Child care advocates celebrated the government's retreat, but recognized that it was a minor victory in the larger scheme of things. It meant a quarter of a million dollars for child care, but the $1.2 billion for child care committed for 2007–08 and the following year by the previous government through the federal-provincial agreements was wiped out.

The fallout from Harper's child care policy will be felt for years to come. Federal transfers specifically designated for early learning and child care were reduced by almost 37% in 2007–08.[5] The $1,200 taxable allowance cost the federal government an estimated $2.4 billion in 2007–08[6] and the price tag will keep going up. This is money that should have been used to begin to build an accessible, affordable and quality early learning and child care system.

In 2006, only 19.3 %[7] of children five and under had access to a regulated child care space, leaving more than 2.4 million children in that age group without one. The Harper Conservatives have no interest in closing the gap. Since their election in 2006, growth in child care slowed as Canada has seen an increase of only 26,661 regulated child care spaces, the smallest since 2001.[8]

Advocates targeted

Another crucial victim of the Conservative government is the child care advocacy movement itself. In the fall of 2006, a major shift in federal policy ended government grants to women's and community groups for research and advocacy. The Child Care Advocacy Association of Canada, one of Harper's most vocal and high-profile critics, was hit hard, as were other child care advocacy groups across the country.

However, the child care movement in Canada is resilient, and advocates are determined to make child care an issue in the next federal election. The Liberals and BQ both supported the NDP's private member's bill to create a public, non-profit child care system by attaching strings to federal transfers for child care.[9] Code Blue, the Child Care Advocacy Association of Canada, and others are pushing these parties, along with the Green party, to stay firm in that commitment should there be a change in government.

"We can't overstate the damage Harper has done to early learning and child care in Canada," says Kass. "The situation, outside of Québec, has never been good, but we were seeing some real interest by governments to make things better. Just as we were getting started, the Conservatives got elected and derailed things. With a change in government we could get things back on track. Child care advocates are a tenacious bunch."

Retro-Social Policy

Child benefits under the Harper government

Ken Battle

GOOD SOCIAL POLICY is a rare and endangered species. It took the Harper government just two years to unravel decades of hard-won progress under both Liberal and Progressive Conservative governments towards a rational, progressive and fair child benefit, the Canada Child Tax Benefit. Families now must contend with a child benefits system that is complex, irrational, and unfair.[1]

"Child benefits" are government payments in the form of cash or tax savings to families with children. Child benefits serve two core purposes: reducing child poverty and helping parents with the cost of raising children. Child benefits have proven to be a powerful instrument in poverty reduction initiatives in the U.K. and Ireland, and are being advocated by a growing number of governments and political parties in Canada.

Child benefits under the Liberals

When the Conservatives came to power in 2006, they inherited a federal child benefits system composed of a single program, the Canada Child Tax Benefit (CCTB). Launched in 1998, the CCTB is an enriched version of the Child Tax Benefit created in 1993 as a replacement for three programs that did not mesh well together: family allowances, the refundable child tax credit, and the non-refundable child tax credit.

The Canada Child Tax Benefit boasts several strong features. It is a non-stigmatizing, inclusive program that delivers benefits to the large majority (9 in 10) of Canadian families across the country, excluding only those with high incomes. It is "portable," providing a stable and assured supplement to income no matter where families live or work (or do not work, in the case of families receiving Employment Insurance, social assistance or other benefit).

The CCTB is progressive; its payments decline as incomes rise. It provides the same amount to all families with the same income, regardless of the source of that income, jurisdiction in which they live, or family type.

The Canada Child Tax Benefit has enjoyed substantial increases over the years, from a maximum $1,605 in 1998 to $3,332 by 2008 — significant progress towards the target of $5,000 proposed by social groups.

Back to the future

The major social policy plank of the Conservatives' 2006 election campaign was the Choice in Child Care Allowance, renamed the Universal Child Care Benefit (UCCB) after they won office. The UCCB pays $1,200 for every child age 5 or younger, regardless of family income. In 2007, Ottawa added a non-refundable child tax credit providing federal income tax savings up to $300 per child under 18 to all except the poorest families, which get nothing.

These two "new" child benefit programs are basically social policy dinosaurs from the past. Unlike the Canada Child Tax Benefit, the UCCB and non-refundable child tax credit bestow sizeable benefits upon high-income families, re-introduce serious inequities, and embody social policy by stealth.

Because the Universal Child Care Benefit is subject to federal and provincial/territorial income taxes, most families do not end up with the much-touted $1,200 per child. For example, the UCCB for a Manitoba two-earner couple with net family income of $60,000 and two children is $889 after tax. In some provinces, even poor families get less than $1,200 (see Figure 1).

Another stealthy aspect is the elimination of the Canada Child Tax Benefit's young child supplement of $249 per year, paid mainly to low- and modest-income families. Few households that received the supplement would be aware of this loss.

Despite its name, the Universal Child Care Benefit is not tied to use of child care. Even if used for this purpose, its annual maximum $1,200 buys little in the way of child care, decent or otherwise.

There is also less than meets the eye to the non-refundable child tax credit. When introduced in 2007, it was billed as "$2,000" per eligible child. The federal budget went on to acknowledge that the real value is $2,000 times the lowest tax rate of 15%, but makes readers do their own math. The missing answer is $300, a lot less than $2,000.

Inequitable

The actual value of the Universal Child Care Benefit varies according to family type. One-earner couples and two-earner couples with the same income get different benefits because the latter are based on the income of the lower-income parent. Moreover, families with the same net income but living in different jurisdictions end up with different after-tax benefits because their UCCB is subject to variable provincial/territorial income tax regimes.

All non-poor families receive $300 per child from the non-refundable child tax credit, including the very rich. Some low-income families with small federal income tax liability (less than $300) get smaller tax savings, while the poorest get nothing at all because they do not owe income tax.

The three federal child benefit programs each operate differently. Unless employed as tax accountants or in finance departments, few families have any idea what they actually get from federal child benefits. Confusion reigns — and probably not by accident: social policy by stealth is alive and well in the nation's capital.

The Canada Child Tax Benefit sends out monthly payments on behalf of children under 18 that vary according to the family's net income. Benefits are non-taxable, so what families see is what they get.

The Universal Child Care Benefit delivers monthly payments for children under 6 that are the same for families at all income levels. But benefits decline in value as the marginal tax rate of the lower-income parent (or single parent) rises.

The non-refundable child tax credit delivers payments once a year for children under 18 in the form of a federal income tax reduction. Most eligible families get the same tax break, worth $300 per child; low-income families get less or nothing.

A bigger and better child benefit

The only positive aspect of the Harper government's child benefit changes is the fact that it raised payments not only to low-income families, but also to those with modest and middle incomes. A mature and effective child benefits system should serve both its poverty reduction and parental recognition objectives.

There is a better way to design child benefits than the Conservatives' problem-ridden approach, illustrated in Figure 2. The Caledon Institute of Social Policy has developed a proposal that would abolish the UCCB and non-refundable child tax credit, using the savings to help finance a stronger Canada Child Tax Benefit. The maximum amount, payable to low-income families, would be $5,000 per child, up from the current $3,332 for a first child.

A $5,000 CCTB would reduce the family poverty rate by a full percentage point, from 9.3% to 8.3%, moving 40,000 families above the poverty line. It also would improve child benefits for the majority of families with modest and middle incomes.

The current child benefits system costs Ottawa $13 billion. Caledon's proposed $5,000 Canada Child Tax Benefit would require only an additional $4 billion. This is certainly an affordable way to strengthen one of the most powerful and proven tools for reducing child poverty.

Prescription for Trouble

The Conservative government and big pharma

Julie White and Michael McBane

> The burden of a loved one being sick in front of you and going down with dementia, is enough. Last year we were $6000 in debt with drug bills. Now we are faced with losing our home. We both worked hard all our lives and I don't think that's right.
> — *Gretta Ross, Sarnia, Ontario.*

DOES ANYONE REMEMBER that the Conservative party promised, just four years ago, to implement a national drug plan? During the 2004 election, with health care a top priority for Canadians, the Conservatives made a commitment of $2.8 billion for a federal program to cover drug costs for individuals who had to pay more than $5,000 a year for their prescription drugs. It was part of a promise to spend a total of $13 billion of new federal money over five years on health care.

Given the record of the minority Conservative government since it took office, it's hard to imagine that the Harper Tories once proposed a new federal social program. It runs counter to all that this government has done since January 2006 to undermine the role of the federal government in providing national programs that benefit all Canadians. Conservative policies have ensured a minimalist federal government by implementing massive tax cuts, thereby reducing revenue and leading inevitably to the curtailing of national programs.

Since October 2007, the Conservative government has committed to $60 billion in tax cuts through to 2012. Corporations in particular have had a bonanza of government support, with tax cuts that will reduce their tax payments by one-third from 2006 to 2012. The latest budget of February 2008 deepened the erosion of public finances, and Finance Minister Jim Flaherty boasted that he had reduced taxes to the level they were at 50 years ago. He did not mention that 50 years ago there was no national Medicare, no Canada/Québec Pension Plan, and no subsidized post-secondary education.

In the Speech from the Throne in 2007, Prime Minister Stephen Harper went further and outlined his government's intention to legally restrict federal involvement in social programs for all Canadians. He announced: "Our government will introduce legislation to place formal limits on the use of the federal spending power for new shared-cost programs in areas of exclusive provincial jurisdiction." Such legislation would prevent the federal government from introducing further nation-building programs, such as child care or Pharmacare. It also ignores the reality that provinces have chosen to opt into national programs with federal standards, both to access federal funds and to provide country-wide benefits and equality to Canadians. Provinces have not given up jurisdiction over health care, for example, by participating in the national Medicare system.

Moreover, in the case of prescription drugs, the provinces have been calling for federal leadership. In 2003, a meeting of First Ministers identified prescription drugs as a problem that needed to be resolved. A year later, the First Ministers from both levels of government established a Ministerial Task Force to develop a national strategy for prescription drugs. So, at the time of the election of the minority Conservative government in 2006, a process to increase federal involvement in prescription drugs was already underway, initiated by the provinces, with Québec attending meetings as an observer.

The Conservative government has withdrawn from its promise to initiate a national drug program, has systematically undermined the capacity of the federal government to implement such a program, and has wrongly argued that national social programs undermine provincial jurisdiction.

Why we need national Pharmacare

There are two major problems with prescription drugs: rapidly rising costs and unequal access. Solving these problems requires federal government involvement.

1. Paying for drugs

The rising cost of drugs is driving provincial and territorial governments to call for federal help. Between 1997 and 2005, expenditure on prescribed drugs by the public sector grew at an average annual rate of 12.2%,[1] sucking money away from other areas of health care expenditure and straining provincial budgets. This might be acceptable if these expenditures were cost-effective and appropriate, but they are not.

The way it works is that a drug company develops a so-called "new" product, which is not actually new. About 85% of all drug approvals by Health Canada are drugs that are the same, or similar, to drugs already on the market, with no therapeutic advantage.[2] It should be noted that drug companies pay for more than half the cost of the approval process at Health Canada; that research on drug safety is not made available to the public or to health professionals; and that, to be approved, a drug need only be better than a placebo, not better than an existing drug. It is hardly an independent, transparent, or cost-effective process.

These so called "new" drugs are also substantially more expensive than existing brand name or generic drugs. Why buy more expensive versions which are no more effective? Because of massive marketing and promotion by the drug companies. The big pharmaceutical companies (known as Big Pharma) spend three times more on marketing than on research. It's not just bombardment advertising on television and in magazines, but also direct promotion to doctors through sales reps, giveaways, samples, trips to conferences, payment for papers, and so on — an estimated $30,000 per doctor per year.[3]

Research has shown that marketing is effective in influencing what doctors prescribe.[4] Research has also shown that prescribing less expensive but therapeutically equivalent drugs, either brand name or generic, would save millions of dollars.[5]

A huge issue for the provinces is that the federal government has major control over the cost of drugs, but the provinces pay the bills. The federal government approves drugs, regulates price protection for drug companies through patents, and is supposed to control drug advertising. However, the feds contribute just 3% of total national expenditure on drugs. Big pharmaceutical companies are among the most profitable companies in the world, and they continuously lobby governments to influence policy — in this case, a government that does not pay for its decisions.

A national drug plan with meaningful federal involvement would rectify this imbalance and give the federal government a reason to bring Big Pharma under tighter control. We need a more rational approval process, stricter controls on advertising, and more independent information for doctors on both research and costs.

2. *Getting drugs*

Canadians are not well served by our patchwork of provincial programs and work-based plans that offer inequitable and/or partial coverage. Getting the drugs you need depends upon where you live and where you work. Some provincial drug programs are more generous than others, and work-based plans vary from one employer to another. Recent public hearings across the country by the Canadian Health Coalition found that many Canadians are in serious difficulty, facing high costs for drugs that they cannot afford.[6]

Drugs should be a part of our universal health system, as is the case in nearly all other Western countries. Prescription drugs should be publicly provided to all Canadians, with some national standards and federal financial involvement, under provincial administration. There is no reason why this should not be a reality, and it would also be cost-effective. Currently, half of all Canadians are covered by work-based plans through private insurance. This means thousands of different work-based plans and millions of individual claims that have to be processed. Clearly, a single universal plan would be both more equitable and more cost-efficient. Other countries with national systems use their single-payer buying power to negotiate significantly reduced prices from the drug companies.[7]

The unhealthy Harper record

1. Government under the influence

One of the disturbing characteristics of the Harper government is the close personal relationships of the government with corporate interests. For example, Minister of Health Tony Clement owned a 25% stake in a pharmaceutical chemicals company, Prudential Chem Inc. Even as Health Minister, Clement initially saw no conflict, saying he would absent himself from decisions affecting the company. This caused a torrent of protest, given that policy affecting pharmaceutical companies is a major part of the work of Health Canada. "It is hard to think of a more flagrant conflict of interest," was one newspaper comment. "Hardly a week goes by during which Clement does not deliberate over an issue affecting the pharmaceutical industry."[8] After pressure both in and out of Parliament, Clement's chief of staff, Bill King, reported that the Minister had transferred his interest to the company's president with no compensation.[9]

Similarly, the government appears to be highly responsive to the influence of certain well-known and well placed lobbyists for the pharmaceutical industry. For example, in March 2007, the Harper government announced a $300 million fund for the controversial HPV vaccine called Gardasil, made by Merck Frosst Canada. This is the vaccine for young women that can prevent some types of cervical cancer. There has been criticism that not enough is known about the drug's long-term effects and that there was no public health crisis warranting such a decision.[10]

The funding was provided with remarkable speed. It took just eight months from approval of the drug by Health Canada to the announcement of a $300 million federal contribution for provinces wanting to provide the vaccine to young women. This was no accident. Merck Frosst hired the public relations giant Hill & Knowlton to push the immunization approach. Ken Boessenkool, a vice-president at Hill and Knowlton, worked on the vaccine campaign, but, as reported by *The Toronto Star,* he is also a close friend and advisor to Stephen Harper. He was the architect of the unpopular flat-tax proposal by Stockwell

Day and a chief advisor to the Conservatives during the 2004 federal election campaign.[11]

After his successful involvement in the cancer drug lobby, Boessenkool moved on to register as a lobbyist for Taser International, promoting the controversial police weapon.[12] Such close relationships between lobbyists for the pharmaceutical industry and the Conservative government are cause for concern.

2. *Undermining the national initiative*

It is discouraging to conclude, after a review of the record, that Harper`s minority Conservative government has undermined provincial and territorial movement toward a cross-Canada program for prescription drugs.

In 2004, federal, provincial and territorial First Ministers agreed to work on a national approach to drugs, called the National Pharmaceutical Strategy (NPS). A nine-point list of goals was developed to improve access to drugs, relieve financial hardship, and obtain better value for money. A Ministerial Task Force was established to determine how to implement the goals, with the federal government as co-chair and Québec as an observer.

In July 2006, a conference of Ministers of Health released a progress report on the NPS and discussed its future.[13] It was obvious that the process was in trouble when Tony Clement, Harper's Minister of Health and Co-Chair of the Task Force, did not attend the conference. Under Clement's care, the NPS has languished. Provinces and territories continued working in good faith, but now acknowledge that the NPS can go nowhere without the federal government at the table to provide leadership and discuss the federal contribution. Clement no longer convenes regular meetings of health ministers.

According to a recent report issued by the Health Council of Canada in June 2008:

> Significant gaps in coverage are still evident across Canada, and too many Canadians are vulnerable to personal hardship from needed drugs that cost more than they can afford. Canadians are also not adequately protected from inappropriate prescribing because we do not have the

necessary systems in place to keep health care providers and consumers informed about drug safety and effectiveness. Governments have not made acceptable progress in creating the National Pharmaceuticals Strategy that was promised in 2004.[14]

Instead of providing leadership to implement the NPS, the Harper government is sabotaging the process by neglect.

3. More price protection for Big Pharma

In April 2008, the government made a blatant move to favour the bottom line of Big Pharma by extending its patent protection. Brand name drug companies already have 20 years patent protection, giving them a monopoly for that period to set prices with no market competition. But they had been extending this protection with court challenges against generic copies, obtaining an automatic two-year patent extension. Generic drug companies contested this artificial extension of the patents, and the Supreme Court agreed with them in a decision in November 2007.[15]

The Conservative government moved quickly to undermine the Supreme Court decision by proposing amendments to the regulations of Canada's *Patent Act*. The changes would allow the drug companies to continue to get automatic injunctions, thereby preventing Health Canada from approving lower-cost generic drugs. The federal government proposed its new regulations on April 26, 2008, with no prior consultation with the provinces or the public and providing just 15 days for comments.

Provincial governments objected to both the change and the process. New Brunswick asked for further consultation, stating that "delays in accessing those generic drugs will have a direct cost impact on the provincial drug plan." The British Columbia Health Minister also asked for an extension to the deadline (which was refused) and said, "One can probably predict that this will not be a happy eventuality for budgeting."[16] The patent extensions are a multi-million-dollar gift to Big Pharma and an added cost burden to provinces, employer drug plans, and individuals.

4. New legislation for the drug companies

The most troubling concession to Big Pharma by the Harper government comes in the form of Bill C-51, which was introduced in the House of Commons on April 8, 2008. The proposed legislation amends the *Food and Drugs Act,* in essence replacing the entire text on drugs. It is likely to adversely affect both cost and safety by:

- speeding up drug approvals with lower standards for drug safety and effectiveness;
- removing barriers to advertising of prescription drugs;
- restricting access to natural health products;
- enshrining corporate secrecy about the health effects of drugs; and
- eliminating liability for regulatory negligence by Health Canada.

First, the proposed legislation permits bringing new drugs to market before research on effectiveness and safety are complete. Instead, research on safety would continue after drugs are widely prescribed and used. Usually, post-market studies are carried out by manufacturers. This introduces a bias, as manufacturers have an interest in presenting their products in a positive light, and there are fewer rules to ensure rigorous scientific methods in post-market studies than in pre-market clinical trials. In effect, Canadians will be exposed to drugs that have not been adequately tested.[17]

This is unacceptable because, even in the current system, drugs are sometimes found to be dangerous. Thalidomide is remembered as one of the most tragic examples. Vioxx was recalled in 2004 in both Canada and the U.S., and is estimated to have caused between 88,000 and 139,000 extra heart attacks in the U.S.[18] Recent research in the U.S. has shown that drugs that are approved faster are more likely to cause problems once on the market than drugs approved under less pressure. This research compared drugs approved under a deadline to speed up the process with drugs approved at other times. The deadlines produced "adverse effects," including more drugs recalled for safety reasons, more drugs later carrying warnings about negative side-effects, and more drugs voluntarily discontinued by the manufacturers. The research concluded that drugs subject to the deadlines "have a higher likelihood of unanticipated safety problems once they are in widespread use."[19] This highlights the need to strengthen, rather than erode, safety standards for approval for marketing.

The second problem with Bill C-51 is that it will eliminate the current restrictions on direct-to-consumer advertising of prescription drugs. As it stands, the *Food and Drugs Act* recognizes that drugs are not the same as clothes or soap powder or autos. Someone with a grim diagnosis or a seriously ill child needs accurate information about treatment options, not advertising hype that can lead them to less effective, less safe, or more costly products.

The massive advertising of drugs allowed in the U.S. has added enormously and unnecessarily to drug costs.[20] In Canada, we are bombarded with ads on U.S. television channels, but this should be controlled to comply with our more restrictive legislation. We should strengthen and enforce our controls on drug advertising, not weaken them.

Third, Bill C-51 will impose severe restrictions on natural health products that are low-risk, while it weakens the regulation of prescription drugs. The legislation would give Health Canada officials unprecedented and arbitrary enforcement powers to force natural health products off of the market and impose fines up to $5,000,000 on family-owned businesses. Many Canadians rely on natural health products to help prevent disease and illness.

Fourth, Bill C-51 will enshrine secrecy and commercial confidentiality for the first time in the *Food and Drugs Act*. It introduces a definition of confidential business information into the Act, so that anything that affects a company's bottom line may be kept secret. Bill C-51 defines as confidential any information —

> a) that is not publicly available,
>
> b) in respect of which the person has taken measures that are reasonable in the circumstances to ensure that it remains not publicly available, and

> c) that has actual or potential economic value to the person or their competitors because it is not publicly available and its disclosure would result in a material financial loss to the person or a material financial gain to their competitors.[21]

In other words, pharmaceutical companies will have the right to keep information secret if it is already secret, if the company is actively keeping it secret, and if making it public could affect their bottom line.

Access to independent research information is already limited, leaving doctors prescribing drugs on the basis of information from drug companies. This Bill will make the situation worse. Instead of enshrining rights for Canadians and health professionals to information about drugs, Bill C-51 gives drug companies the right to maintain secrecy about key health and safety information, including less than stellar clinical trial results and serious side-effects.

Last but not least, Bill C-51 will lower the Minister of Health's "duty of care," so that Health Canada can evade liability for regulatory negligence when Canadians are harmed by inadequately tested prescription drugs. If this Bill becomes law, Canadians could lose recourse to the courts for claims of regulatory negligence. This is of particular concern, given the lower standards established by other parts of Bill C-51, which increase the likelihood that Canadians will need recourse to the courts.

Bill C-51 poses a threat to the safety of Canadians. It denies the public's right to information on drug research, adds to the high cost of drugs through advertising, restricts access to natural health products, and decreases the responsibility of Health Canada for protecting our health.

Conclusion

The Canadian Health Coalition has just completed hearings across Canada on the problems of access to affordable prescription drugs. Many Canadians went to the hearings to explain how their health is being put at risk because of the high cost of drugs.

Stories were told by people seldom heard in the corridors of Parliament Hill:

> According to the government, we make too much money to qualify for drug coverage. But I don't know too many people who can take $1000 a month off their net income and not have it have an effect. I think there's something wrong. And I also think I'm not unique. We need to start to look at the stories behind the numbers...Generally it's the sickest of the sick that have to deal with all this stuff. The people that need it the most are the people least able to fight for it. And it's a fight.
> — *Tracy Gilles, Charlottetown,* PEI.[22]

Prime Minister Harper and his Minister of Health, Tony Clement, are failing to provide for the well-being of Canadians. They are systematically placing the profits of pharmaceutical companies ahead of the needs of people like Gretta Ross and Tracy Gilles.

Harper and Public Health Policy

John Hugh Edwards

IN THE FALL of 2007, almost two years after the Stephen Harper Conservatives came to power, I had the opportunity to sit with a group of public health advocates to discuss the direction of public health care policy in Canada. At the meeting, there was concern about how the Harper government appeared to be shaping a new agenda that centred on a move away from the systemic approach to population health toward a regime placing individual responsibility at the centre of health policy.

Meeting participants had two major concerns. First, people worried about the direct effects of health policy changes. Second, there were worries that the direction of the federal government in a broad range of policy areas, including economic and social development, would have a negative effect on the health of Canadians and their ability to cope with the circumstances affecting their lives.

By the fall of 2007, some of these changes were already clear. As early as August of 2006, in a speech to the Canadian Medical Association, Health Minister Tony Clement signalled the new government's approach by calling for a "get tough on drugs" policy. It appeared that the government was now leaning toward enforcement and incarceration as key elements of its policy on drug addiction.

In the same speech, Clement made it clear that the use of harm reduction programs as part of a range of initiatives, also including treatment, rehabilitation and community support, was no longer acceptable. The subsequent controversy over the federal government's efforts to close Vancouver's safe injection site for drug users showed just how serious this government is in its opposition to harm reduction policies and programs.

In September 2006, nurses in Ontario warned the Harper government about its cutbacks to federally funded programs, including research programs on the health of visible minorities; programs aimed at improving adult literacy and workplace skills; and support for voluntary based programs. Such cutbacks, the nurses warned, would have an adverse effect on the health of Canadians, particularly the poor and most vulnerable.

Since then, people across the country involved in community-based responses to population health issues felt a chill as it became clear that Harper and his government were moving away from a collective response to the root causes of ill-health toward a stance that suggested that health is the responsibility of the individual. And yet, since the 19th century, thousands of studies have shown that health is determined by a series of social and economic factors, including income and social status, social support networks, education and literacy, and working conditions. Simply put, people in more privileged social and economic positions are healthier and live longer than people in lower income classes. Thousands of hours of scholarly studies have been devoted to understanding how class and socioeconomic circumstance determine health outcomes.

These social determinants of health are at the core of most progressive thinking on improving the health of populations. The key is to seek to remove the conditions which serve to make people ill and to promote policies and practices which assist people to remain healthy. While it is clear the current federal government is not convinced of the efficacy of this approach, most progressive public health advocates would contend that the largest increase in improved health outcomes would be achieved by reducing poverty and social exclusion.

In my own work in Cape Breton, I have found that people with little or no formal training in population health have clear understandings of the ways in which poverty can impact health. In 2005, at the request of the Public Health Agency of Canada, I was involved in a community examination of the link between economic and social conditions and chronic disease on Cape Breton Island. The PHAC had found that three areas in Atlantic Canada — Labrador, Northern New Brunswick, and Cape Breton — had a high incidence of chronic disease.

According to recent data, Cape Breton had a very high occurrence of chronic disease, disability, and premature death. It had the highest age standardized mortality rate in the Maritime provinces and a death rate from circulatory disease and heart disease that was 30% higher than the national average. Of the 21 health regions in Atlantic Canada, Cape Breton had the highest death rates from cancer (25% higher than the national average), bronchitis, emphysema, and asthma (more than 50% above the national average). Cape Breton also had the highest rate of high blood pressure in Atlantic Canada, 72% above the national average.

Along with these alarming health outcomes, Cape Breton also records poor performance on a number of economic and social indicators. Over the last several decades, as the coal and steel industries declined and closed, Cape Breton, and specifically the Cape Breton Regional Municipality (CBRM), has experienced a pronounced economic decline. According to the analysis of the planning department of the Regional Municipality, economic indicators have continued to drop in the last inter-census period.

The average income for individuals 15 years and older living in the CBRM, in 2000, was $20,766, while the median income was $15,862. This compares with Nova Scotia's average personal income of $25,297 and median income of $18,735, in the same period. In 1995, the average individual income in the CBRM was $6,892 below the Canadian average. By 2000, the gap between the CBRM and the Canadian average had grown to $9,003. Based on the low-income cut-offs used by Statistics Canada and excluding people who reside in First Nations communities, 24.1% of people residing in the CBRM live in low-income households.

According to the planning department of the CBRM, this is the highest level of low income in any county in Nova Scotia.

Cape Breton clearly suffers from both poor health outcomes and dire economic circumstances. To determine how well the link between the two was understood, I decided to speak directly to two groups of people who had been identified as "at risk" in these communities.

First, with the help of a well-established community organization, focused discussions were organized with a group of young people in one of Cape Breton's poorest urban neighbourhoods. An interesting finding was that these young people, ranging in age from 12 to 17, had a holistic understanding of health and its many dimensions. Rather than speaking of health as simply an absence of illness, these young people spoke to me about the health of their body, mind and spirit. Not only that, but they linked the concepts.

One young man said that "if we don't feed our bodies well, we will not be able to do well in school, and if we don't do well in school, our self-esteem will be injured."

When we discussed the things in their lives that could make them ill, many of the young people mentioned the choices that have to be made by people who are economically disadvantaged. Several mentioned the choice between food and prescription drugs when the family income would not allow for the purchase of both. One young person told such a compelling story about the consequences of being forced to make this kind of choice that it was not difficult to believe that he had lived through the experience himself. He spoke of a family being forced to choose between buying heating oil and other family necessities.

"If you run out of oil, your house gets cold and that could make you sick", he said. "What is worse, if there is no heat in the house, the water pipes will freeze. With no water to wash, bathe, cook, and flush the toilet, your chances of illness increase even further. If your family can't afford a plumber to thaw the pipes, your father might try to do the job with a propane torch, which risks setting the house on fire."

In this young person's lucid narrative we see a descent into chaos, precipitated by choices made because a family had inadequate resources to meet their basic needs. Public policy responses to this bleak scenario would necessarily include the provision of adequate and affordable housing and a decent living wage. But perhaps these options would constitute too much intervention in the economy and distortion of the market for the neoliberal mindset of our present policy-makers.

A similar description of a spiralling descent into chaos was given to me by a group of young women, several of them lone parents, who were engaged in an employment re-entry program in another neighbourhood in urban Cape Breton. One of these women spoke of her experience as a mother working in a minimum wage job. The family budget is so tight that any unexpected costs can throw the household economy into disarray. A child arriving home from school with a request from the teacher to purchase additional paper or pencils means little to a family with some economic security. But to these young women it can cause high stress. With no available margins, the only way to respond is to juggle other necessities.

Children are frustrated because every request is met with the same negative response, while many of their friends have no such problems. The next day, a doctor prescribes a medication that throws the family budget into further crisis. Just then, the oil truck arrives and the driver demands payment before delivery.

Through these discussions, I came to understand that not only is the link between social and economic circumstances and health firmly established in the clinical and learned literature, but that people who are experiencing the consequences of poverty and ill-health also understand and can often clearly articulate the links.

Healthy public policy

The social determinants of health are well understood. What is missing is an adequate policy response. This response needs to be focused in both the areas of concern identified by the public health advocates at the 2007 meeting. Direct support of programs which prevent disease and promote wellness are essential. Policies which support the kind of community-based programs run by AIDS/HIV organizations across the country should be central to our public health agenda. It is just as important to recognize that programs which alleviate poverty and improve inclusion are key components of healthy public policy.

Consider the taxable $100 per month child care benefit that is central to the present governments social policy. The "benefit" is an obvious move away from a systemic approach to providing quality, affordable child care to the more ideologically acceptable process of placing responsibility for providing care on the individual and the market. The $100 per month will not come close to providing quality child care. It will, in many cases, become part of a still inadequate household budget where it will often be spent on the most pressing need of the day.

The development of a truly affordable system of child care would allow many primary care-givers to play a more active and productive role in the economy, seek education and training to improve their economic lot, and provide their families with increased resources to meet their essential needs. One hundred and fifty years of study in public health confirm that such a policy initiative would positively affect the health outcomes of Canadian families.

The same can be said about a range of social and economic policy issues. Any adequate analysis of the impact of the Harper government on the health of Canadians will have to look beyond direct health policy and into the full spectrum of government action (or inaction) on the social and economic issues which determine health.

Two Steps Forward and Two Steps Backward

The legacy of disability rights in Canada

John Rae

CANADIANS WITH DISABILITIES are striving to obtain what most Canadians take for granted: attending one's neighbourhood school, getting a job and paying taxes, voting in elections, travelling from city to city, or having children. Usually the discrimination against people with disabilities is not perpetrated maliciously. Rather, rules and practices that create barriers for persons with disabilities have been put in place, and these must be eliminated.

While Canadians with disabilities need leadership from all levels of government to remove existing barriers and to prevent the introduction of new ones, the Harper government has made it clear that it believes in a government that focuses only on "core federal responsibilities."[1] Since Stephen Harper was elected Prime Minister, Canadians with disabilities have been adversely affected by the Harper government's belief in a more limited role for the Government of Canada, and by a number of his government's decisions. Yet, despite these setbacks, some advances have taken place.

Equality-seeking groups need the Court Challenges Program

The Court Challenges Program of Canada (CCP) is a national non-profit organization established to administer funding to help equality-seeking groups pursue important test cases and legal interventions advancing the language and equality rights guaranteed under Canada's Constitution.[2] The Court Challenges Program has supported challenges and interventions of national importance, which have helped define Canada's Charter of Rights and Freedoms, and developed a rich body of equality jurisprudence that is internationally respected.

Cases funded by the Court Challenges Program resulted in the following gains for equality:

- Deaf people can participate fully in Canadian society by requesting that a sign language interpreter be provided to enable them to communicate effectively with their government representatives.
- People found not criminally responsible because of a mental disability are guaranteed a hearing to determine if institutionalization is necessary or if some other form of treatment would be more effective.
- People with mental disabilities who reside in institutions have the opportunity to vote.
- People with various disabilities have gained increased access in the transportation sector through Via Rail and One Person One Fare cases, the latter having positively influenced the recent CTA decision guaranteeing adequate space for persons travelling with a service animal on airlines.

Despite its importance, the Harper Government cancelled this program effective September 25, 2006. This move resulted in the saving of a mere $5.6 million. Assistance for cases already approved is still being honoured, and both the language and equality sectors continue to fight hard for full restoration of the Court Challenges Program.

Without the funding provided by this Program, many of the organizations and individuals that have invoked the guarantee of equality under the Charter would have been otherwise unable to do so. "With the government's decision to de-fund, Canadians who most need the Charter are now effectively denied access to that protection," said

Carmela Hutchison, President of Disabled Women's Network Canada.[3] Without the Court Challenges Program, Canada's constitutional rights are real only for the wealthy. This is unfair, and it does not comply with the rule of law, which is a fundamental principle of our Constitution. As described by Marie White, Chair of the Council of Canadians with Disabilities (CCD), "Rights without remedies are no rights at all."[4]

First human rights treaty of the 21st century focuses on persons with disabilities

On December 13, 2006, the Convention on the Rights of Persons With Disabilities and its Optional Protocol were adopted.[5] When it was opened for signature on March 30, 2007, there were 82 signatories to the Convention, 44 signatories to the Optional Protocol, and one ratification of the Convention. This is the highest number of signatories to a UN Convention on its opening day. To date, some 27 countries have ratified the Convention, and 16 have also ratified the Optional Protocol. Countries that have adopted both are: Bangladesh, Croatia, Ecuador, El Salvador, Guinea, Hungary, Mali, Mexico, Namibia, Panama, Peru, San Marino, Slovenia, South Africa, Spain, and Tunisia.

The Convention was negotiated during a fast-track process over eight sessions of an Ad Hoc Committee of the General Assembly, from 2002 to 2006. The purpose of the Convention is to promote, protect, and ensure the full and equal enjoyment of all human rights by persons with disabilities. It covers a number of key areas such as accessibility, personal mobility, health, education, employment, habilitation and rehabilitation, participation in political life, and equality and non-discrimination. After considerable pressure from Canadian disability organizations, Canada was among the initial signatories to the Convention, but it has not yet ratified either the Convention or its Optional Protocol.

The Convention marks a "paradigm shift" in attitudes and approaches to persons with a disability, from a social welfare to a human rights model, which acknowledges that societal barriers and prejudices are the real barriers facing persons with disabilities worldwide. Throughout the negotiations, the Canadian delegation, which included Steven Estey, chair of the Council of Canadians with Disabilities' (CCD) International

Committee, played a leading role. Other international disability organizations were also front and centre in moving the negotiations at the UN.

The Convention includes many principles that will be very familiar to Canadians. Now it is time for Canada to ratify the Convention. This is a slower process, as many of its provisions cover areas of provincial and territorial jurisdiction, so it is crucial to also bring pressure on our provincial and territorial governments.

A National Disability Act?

While Canada's disability community was solidifying its priorities in the area of disability-related supports, the Conservative party of Canada included the following in its 2005 policy declaration:

> 71. National Disability Act: A Conservative government would introduce a National Disability Act designed to promote reasonable access to medical care, medical equipment, education, employment, transportation and housing for Canadians with disabilities.[6]

The impetus for such a *National Disability Act* stems at least in part from the A*mericans With Disabilities Act.*[7] Canada's government and division of powers between its federal and provincial governments are different from the U.S. system, and this makes importing a "made in the U.S." approach dangerous. Any such act must be tailored to the Canadian reality.

The possible effect of a *National Disability Ac*t in Canada must be considered from three standpoints: what it can do, what it will not do, and what can be accomplished without an Act using existing legislative and regulatory authority.

A *Federal Act* could remove the discriminatory provisions in Canada's *Immigration Act,* make it possible for blind electors to vote independently and in secret in federal elections, ensure that federal office buildings have accessible washrooms, increase audio description on television, get post offices to install visible fire alarm systems, and ensure that Canada's transportation system is fully usable by all Canadians.

By contrast, a *Federal Act* cannot change a provincial benefit program that fails to provide information in alternate formats; towns or cities that do not have accessible municipal voting polls; courts that are not accessible; schools that do not provide accommodation for students with disabilities; municipal planning and zoning rules that do not permit group homes for persons with intellectual disabilities; or provincial health insurance offices that do not have a TTY. Such an Act will not deal with the lack of disability supports and chronic poverty that is the plight of far too many Canadians who live with a disability in our affluent country.

The Government of Canada could make some changes without introducing a new Act. The disability community believes current voluntary codes of practice in the transportation sector could be given the force of regulations, if only the will to do so existed. The *Federal Employment Equity Act* and Federal Contractors Programs could be given added teeth, and the complaint process under the *Canadian Human Rights Act* could be streamlined and made more user-friendly to complainants.

For a detailed discussion of a possible *National Disability Act*, see Phyllis Gordon's paper, *A Federal Disability Act: Opportunities and Challenges*, which advances a set of tools that might be implemented in a *Federal Disability Act* and outlines a model legislative framework to illustrate how proposed strategies and tools might interact.[8]

Disability community develops national strategy

Over the past five years, the Council of Canadians With Disabilities spearheaded a series of meetings that were designed to develop a national agenda for Canada's disability community, and Disability Related Supports emerged as the community's most important priority. The End Exclusion campaign sounded the alarm:

> There is a shared vision for an inclusive and accessible Canada, and an unprecedented consensus exists among the Canadian public, governments, the disability community and experts about the need for national action on disability issues.[10]

Organized collaboratively by CCD, the Canadian Association for Community Living (CACL), and the Canadian Association of Independent Living Centres (CAILC), in November 2006 over 300 people gathered in Ottawa to celebrate the accomplishments of Canadians with disabilities over the past 25 years. Over 100 organizations stood together, signing the Declaration of Principle and joining in the discussions that focused on building an inclusive and accessible Canada.

On November 22, 2007, Canadians with disabilities again gathered in Ottawa. Using the 2006 Declaration as the foundation, partners endorsed a National Action Plan, "From Vision to Action: Building An Inclusive and Accessible Canada A National Action Plan on Disability."[11]

For an inclusive and accessible Canada to be a reality, the National Strategy calls upon the government of Canada to show leadership by enhancing their role in four key areas by including:

- enhanced disability supports to enable Independent Living, active citizenship, and full participation;
- enhanced federal role in alleviating poverty of persons with disabilities and their families, thus freeing up dollars at provincial/territorial levels for new investments in disability supports;
- labour force inclusion measures; and
- a national social development role to promote accessibility and community inclusion.

Representatives of national organizations trekked through the snow to the Centennial Flame on Parliament Hill, and many took the opportunity to make brief statements in support of the National Strategy. John Rae, President of AEBC, stated that:

> Our priority is achieving the elusive goal set out way back during the International year of the Disabled Person 1981, namely, full participation and equality. For our community this would include participating in a meaningful way in the development of all policies and programs that affect our lives; being able to vote independently and in secret like all other electors through an electronic option; having access to a publicly funded assistive devices program in every province and territory across Canada;

being able to travel throughout our communities safe from the dangers of the quiet hybrid automobile; and finally, we must see the implementation of a National Economic Strategy that would address the historic and chronic levels of marginalization, poverty and unemployment that remain the reality for so many Canadians who have a disability.[12]

The future imperative

Since the Harper government was elected, many other issues of concern to the disabled community have been on the national agenda, including the very controversial Latimer decision, improvements to the Canadian Pension Plan Disability (CPPD) provisions for persons with disabilities who work, creation of the Mental Health Commission of Canada, and province-wide anti-poverty mobilization across Ontario in response to the Ontario government's commitment to developing an anti-poverty strategy for Ontario. Any anti-poverty approach must be comprehensive and deal with both income and labour market inequities that continue to plague far too many Canadians with a disability.

Over the past 30 years, much of the work of Canada's disability rights movement has focused on removing existing barriers. Today, that work continues, but our movement now must also fight a rearguard battle to preserve and protect the gains we have made and to prevent the introduction of new barriers. In today's neoconservative climate, pressures are present that are attempting to push us back into an earlier time when voluntarism, paternalism, and decisions made by others were the norm for far too many Canadians with a disability. We succeeded in moving our issues more into a rights-based approach, where more and more Canadians came to support our beliefs that public attitudes, behaviours, and the built environment were our real obstacles and not the effects of our respective disability.

The motto of the disabled community has come to be "nothing about us without us," and this calls on all decision-makers to involve representatives of consumer-based, rights holder organizations in any and all policies, programs and legislation that affect our lives. Persons with disabilities are our own best spokespersons. We know disability best and we know what is needed to help move us from the margins to the mainstream of Canadian society. We seek new allies on this voyage.

Harper and Crime

The great distraction

Dawn Moore and Erin Donohue

CRIME IS A great target in an election strategy. Everyone hates crime. No one wants crime. People are very upset by crime. It is relatively easy, then, to put together a tough-on-crime agenda that will play on people's visceral reactions to the crime segment on the evening news.

This is exactly what the Harper government successfully did in the 2006 federal election. Picking up the momentum of a few flash points — the "summer of the gun" in Toronto, high-profile murders in Ottawa, a serial killer in Vancouver, and climaxing with the boxing day murder of a teenage girl on Yonge Street in Toronto — the Harper camp was exceedingly effective in pulling together a campaign using these crimes to create the impression that Canadian cities were undergoing a crime wave, and offering tailor-made solutions.

True to its word, the Harper government made good on its election promises to "get tough on crime" with the 2008 *Tackling Violent Crime Act*. This omnibus bill ushered in a raft of changes to the *Criminal Code*, all framed by the promise that Harper and his team will get rid of crime.

Getting rid of crime is an interesting promise given that, despite a long history of interventions, crime has never been eradicated from any society anywhere in the world, ever. Flying in the face of all reason and knowledge about crime, Harper in the next election will no doubt ride the tide of his successful crime strategy. The Conservative government already has more "get-tough" plans in the works.

The Harper crime policy is pitched to respond to what we think of as "prime-time crime": serial killers, gangland executions, home invasions, and child abductions. These are all scary crimes, but the reality is that, while most of us will be touched by crime in our lives, these are not the kinds of crimes we are likely to experience. So the Harper crime plan is a piece of legislation set up to respond to a problem that isn't really there and that doesn't really affect the vast majority of Canadians.

Canada is home to a wealth of researchers, scholars, and community leaders who know a great deal about the reality of crime and the impact of law enforcement in our communities. Harper made almost no consultations with any of these crime experts in drafting his legislation, citing his distaste for the "ivory tower" and appealing to "common sense." The problem is that common sense, especially about crime, is usually very far from sensible.

This chapter is an attempt to correct that misinformation by offering readers a brief guide to the "crime scene" in Canada. Here we cover the Conservative crime plan, offer careful criticism of some of its most worrying features, and raise some serious cautions which ought to give every informed voter pause to consider what sort of society she or he envisions when filling out a ballot. It may be a society that uses the justice system as a justice system. Alternatively, voters may choose to support the social, economic, racial, linguistic, gender-based, and geographic interests of those in power.

What is Harper's crime plan?

In the spring of 2008, Bill C-2, the *Tackling Violent Crime Act*, became law. The omnibus legislation included a number of amendments to the *Criminal Code*, including initiating more mandatory minimum sentences and tightening up on parole eligibility criteria. It is worrying that the legislation met with very little resistance in Parliament, signalling an "if you're not with us, you're with the criminals" attitude in the House of Commons. This poses a dangerous threat to the democratic process.

The Harper government indicated the direction of its revision of Canada's drug policy, by re-naming the long-standing *Drug Strategy* the "*Anti-Drug Strategy.*" It shifted responsibility for federal drug policy from Health Canada to the Department of Justice, and virtually erased harm reduction initiatives. Meanwhile, the Conservatives added billions of dollars to law enforcement.

In the summer of 2008, Minister of Health Tony Clement made public his desire to override the B.C. Supreme Court decision protecting the nation's only safe injection site (Insite) in a bid to shut it down. This, despite several reports including the site's independent evaluation crediting Insite with saving hundreds of lives and filling a gaping void in B.C.'s health care services.[1]

In order to accommodate the large-scale social changes that will be the inevitable fallout of this legislation, the Conservative government also plans to build more prisons, hire more police, and create more addiction treatment facilities. At the same time, the plan is to shut down community-based correctional organizations and bind the hands of judges who would apply discretion in sentencing to accommodate different circumstances.

Five problems with Harper's crime plan

1. There is no new crime problem

The major assumption on which Harper's crime agenda rests is that crime, especially violent crime, is on the rise. This simply is not the case. *Juristat,* the arm of Statistics Canada responsible for justice statistics, has reported a *decline* in virtually every category of reported violent crime consistently over the last ten years. Canadians now face less of a threat when it comes to crime. The crime rate is approximately 30% lower than it was in 1991 and continues on a steady decline. Crime rates haven't been this low in Canada since the 1950s.[2]

One exception to this overall trend is a moderate rise in youth-accused homicide (up 3% as of 2006). Even as we see a rise in the number of youth accused of the most violent crimes, note that an accusation is quite different from a conviction. The overall rate of youth crime follows the same trend as adult crime in Canada. The rate of youth crime in 2006 was 12% lower than that of a decade earlier, and is 25% lower than the 1991 peak.[3]

The rise in numbers of youth implicated in violent (non-homicide) crimes is likely explained by the implementation of zero-tolerance policies in schools rather than by any actual increase in violent incidents. Thus, it is likely that Canadian youth are not committing more violent crimes, rather that they are now being charged for violent crimes that would have been otherwise dealt with through informal means in the past.

The other exception comes in the areas of domestic violence and sexual violence. While Statistics Canada does not note any substantial rise in these sorts of crimes, social science research, as well as the work of those involved in the anti-violence against women movement, reminds us that most women do not report experiences of violence and assault. Despite this silence, sadly we know from self-report studies that anywhere from 25-to-75% of women and children have been or will be victims of sexual or domestic violence at some point in their lives. This includes molestation, physical assault, rape, emotional abuse, threats, intimidation, humiliation, unwanted sexual touching, harassment, and murder. In the majority of assaults carried out on women and children, the perpetrator is a male who is known to and often related to the victim.

2. Getting tough doesn't deter people from committing crimes

Tough sentencing polices rely on the assumption that a person who is considering committing a crime will pause to take stock of the gravity of the penalty should she or he get caught. This "rational actor" realizes that committing a crime is simply not worth the penalty. Now think for a moment about whatever petty crime you committed in your life. Did you drink under age? Use an illicit substance? Steal a chocolate bar? Trespass? Give a fake name or use a fake ID? Fudge the numbers on your tax return? Get in a bar fight? Purchase something even though you suspected it was stolen?

There are few of us who have lived lives that are totally free of crime. All of these activities carry legally prescribed penalties of varying severity. For whatever the crime committed, when you contemplated doing it, did you give any thought to the penalties? If you did, did you figure you would get away with it, anyway? Most of the time, when people commit crime, they do it without a lot of calculation about how the justice system might respond. Put simply, tough sentences do not deter people from committing crime.[4] When we compare crime rates for jurisdictions that carry harsh sentences with those that are more lenient, almost invariably there is no notable difference in the two crime rates. If there is a difference, it is often in favour of the more lenient jurisdiction.

The lack of what's known in criminal justice as a "deterrent effect" is most obvious with regard to the most serious of crimes. The vast majority of violent crimes — aggravated assault, sexual assault, assault causing bodily harm, manslaughter, and the varying degrees of murder — fall into the category of crimes of passion. This means that most of these crimes are committed by people in heightened emotional states and/or in the heat of the moment. By their very nature, these are not crimes born of rational calculation and as such would not be affected by tougher sentencing provisions.

3. Intense policing does not lower crime rates

One of the strategies advocated and receiving funding through the Harper crime bill is the practice of targeted policing. Here police concentrate surveillance and sting operations in a particular neighbourhood, usually emphasizing the sex and drug trades. Criminal behaviour around the sex and drug trades is quite visible and often very active, which is why it draws the ire of the community in which these activities are taking place. Police respond to community concerns by coming in and "sweeping" the area by conducing mass arrests and crackdowns.[5] While this strategy may well have the effect of cleaning out a community temporarily, it does not lower rates of crime. Most often, in the wake of a sweep, the sex and drug trades simply move on to other communities or return to the same community within a matter of months.

In the end, intensive policing initiatives are extremely expensive, and often serve as the justification for increasing policing budgets, but are largely ineffective at decreasing crime. On the contrary, such initiatives typically increase crime in certain areas. They may also make neighbourhoods in which criminal activity is taking place less safe as the increased police presence works to drive criminal behaviour underground. The chain reaction here is that crime becomes more hidden and has higher stakes. Higher stakes often mean an increase in the violence associated with certain kinds of criminal behaviour as experienced by those involved in crime.

4. The War on Drugs doesn't work

Addiction is a public health issue, not a crime issue. Criminalizing a heroin user is the same as criminalizing a cigarette smoker, and if we follow that logic through we should incarcerate cigarette dealers in the same way we incarcerate heroin dealers. There is no medical or social reason to criminalize one set of substances while we regulate others, such as prescription drugs, alcohol, tobacco, and energy drinks. All of these substances can be harmful, but only a select few are confined to the justice system. Tobacco kills more people than all illicit drugs combined; alcohol is the second most lethal substance and also the one most readily linked to social problems, including violence, unemployment, property crimes, and vandalism.

Canada's history of anti-drug law is rooted in anti-Chinese sentiments born at the start of the last century. The control of the opium trade was first introduced as a means of controlling the Chinese who were no longer needed for labour on the railways and were thus becoming a "problem" in cities like Vancouver. The trouble posed by the Chinese was that they were willing to work for lower wages, edging out their white counterparts in the job market. The application of the criminal law to opium meant that the Chinese could be swept up, charged and deported in the name of protecting good (white) Canadians from the scourge of the Chinese drug.

Criminalization of the Chinese was so effective as a means of controlling and eliminating the population that the government began criminalizing other substances (first cocaine and then marijuana) as they became affixed with problematic behaviours and populations. We see this pattern over and over again as new substances are added to the drug schedule, even up to the present day.[6] Ghat, a mild stimulant used by North Africans, is a case in point. Ghat does not cause any serious addiction, and it is not associated with crime or violence, yet it was added to the drug schedule three years ago, coincidentally at the same time as the North African population in many Canadian cities grew. The criminalization of ghat has proved an effective means by which to control and criminalize this population of people.

The U.S. and Canada have both been fighting a war on drugs for the last 30 years. They are both losing. Greater enforcement has no discernible impact on levels of drug use, which remain more or less constant over time. The point is: people are going to use drugs. Some people are going to get addicted to drugs. If the goal of the government is to protect people's heath and safety, then a public health response makes sense. This is one that offers people health care, treatment, and clean equipment to help stop the spread of diseases. It is one that treats drug users like respectable citizens so that they do not face shame and public stigma and are forced to go underground and engage in criminal activity to support themselves.

If, however, the goal of an anti-drug strategy is to create a burgeoning prison population, to isolate, stigmatize, and ultimately marginalize people to such an extent that crime is their only method of survival, then by all means, a drug war it is. However, we need only to look south of the border to know how very ineffective a drug war is. The U.S. has a crime problem, it has a massive over-incarceration problem, and it is one of the most violent and insecure places to live in the global North. The U.S. also heavily embraces a tough-on-crime stand and has spent hundreds of billions of dollars on the drug war.

5. Guns, gangs and drugs are not the biggest problems facing Canadians

A crime plan comes down to one thing: keeping citizens safe. This mandate demands the question "safe from what?" The answer: safe from the things that threaten their well-being and ability to enjoy life. If a crime plan is meant to keep citizens safe, then it ought to address things that make citizens *un*safe. Consider the following numbers.

- In 2006, 2,889 were killed in motor vehicle fatalities.[7]
- In 2008, 73,800 will die of cancer.[8]
- As of 2006, 4,614,000 live in poverty.[9]

- 90 people a year die from unsafe drinking water.[10]
- In 2004, 74 were killed by abusive spouses.[11]
- In 2006, 786 were killed in workplace accidents.[12]

Some of these things, like cancer and drinking water, do not obviously fall under the purview of the justice system, unless you count the relatively lax enforcement of environmental protection laws and the lack of interest in white collar crime, both of which could easily be implicated in cancer and poverty rates. They are, however, issues that require funding to address. Imagine if the amount of additional funding recently allocated to enforcing drug laws alone ($22 million over two years) was re-directed to clean water initiatives or cancer prevention campaigns. It doesn't take a degree in economics to figure out that, if you pour a lot of money into one area (like law enforcement), it has to come out of another (like community development).

Of the issues which are related to the justice system — motor vehicle deaths, abusive spouses, workplace accidents — the system is woefully ill-equipped to offer meaningful remedies. In fact, despite legislative amendments to "toughen up" judicial responses to all of these crimes, there is little notable change over the last 20 years. The one exception here is with regard to driving under the influence, where we have seen a reduction in incidents. The cause of this reduction is more likely the result of shifts in society attitudes than tougher sanctions for those who commit the crimes. That's because, as noted above, people are rarely deterred by harsh sentences. On the other hand, people are deterred by strong disapproval of their friends and relatives, as well as a generally accepted and widespread social belief that certain behaviours, like drinking and driving, is wrong.

Ultimately, issues like guns, gangs and drugs serve as distractions from more pressing issues like health care, community safety, economic security, and misuse of public funds. Governments routinely use crime as a way of distracting the public from larger areas of concern. Richard Nixon campaigned on a tough-on-crime platform to distract public attention from Viet Nam. Ronald Reagan did the same to shroud a recession, an energy crisis, and his own flagging popularity. Both Bushes did this to distract from hugely problematic foreign relations (especially in the Middle East), as well as tough economic times, and Harper did it in the last election to deflect hard questions about Afghanistan and the environment.

The handy thing about a crime problem is that, if it doesn't exist, it's easy to solve. If the crime rate is already on a decline, it is very simple to claim that it is new legislation, and not changing demographics, that is responsible. Also we are so well trained to fear crime that it makes good sense to the electorate to want to address crime. On this issue, however, perhaps more than any other, citizens are grossly misled. By focusing on crime, we allow ourselves to be totally distracted from the social, economic, and environmental issues that really matter.

Four possible outcomes of Harper's crime plan

1. We become more like the United States

The United States has some of the toughest crime legislation in the world. They have now beat out the former USSR for the dubious distinction of being the world leader in incarceration. Their crime rates also contend for the "world's highest" title. Most social scientists will draw the connection between those facts to postulate that getting tough on crime results in two things: higher rates of incarceration and higher rates of crime.[13] If it didn't, then America would be the safest place to live in the world. It isn't.

American governments have been obsessed with crime since World War II, and that obsession has achieved exactly the inverse of what Americans set out to attain. American cities are notoriously violent and dangerous. American prisons are incredibly overcrowded, becoming veritable breeding grounds for all manner of illness, including tuberculosis and HIV/AIDS. Three times more Americans, per capita, are murdered than Canadians. There are American children who go to school under armed guard and many Americans spend much of their time being watched by Closed Circuit Television (CCTV) cameras and private security agencies, to the detriment of personal liberty and privacy. These are huge costs to society with very little in return.

2. We spend heaps of money

The removal of judicial discretion through the implementation of mandatory minimum sentences means that many of the people who will now be incarcerated would have otherwise received a shorter jail term or have been sentenced to a community sanction like probation. This distinction is important: By putting more people in jail for longer we not only increase our incarceration rates, but we also considerably raise the costs of doing justice. Recidivism rates for those sentenced for the same crime but sanctioned differently (one in prison, one in the community) are comparable; but it costs almost four times as much — $83,000 compared to $23,000 — to incarcerate someone than it does to supervise her or him in the community. Every person in custody costs the government the equivalent of four people on social assistance.[14]

Dawn was once visiting a prison, and a parole officer working at the institution said to her, "You know, for what it costs to keep one guy in this place, I could have him working out in the community, earning money, supporting himself, and pay also to have a team working just with this one guy, watching him 24 hours a day." Food for thought.

In 2006, Canadian governments (both federal and provincial) spent approximately $3 billion on punishing law breakers. Those billions could have built a lot of affordable housing, supported a lot of community building initiatives, funded a lot of children's education, or run a lot of recreation centres.

3. We increase marginalization in our society

The typical profile of someone in conflict with the law in Canada is a young man who comes from a marginal socio-economic status, with little education. Given that we know criminal behaviour is not bound by class or social status, the fact that this profile fits the majority of people in Canadian prisons tells us that the criminal law is applied unevenly. This observation is especially true when we factor in the question of race.

Even though the majority of people in conflict with the law are white, the justice system currently has an exaggerated over-representation of Aboriginal people and people of colour. In 2006, Aboriginal people made up 13% of the population of people in conflict with the law, but only 3% of the total Canadian population.[15]

Since the Ontario Commission on Systemic Racism in 1992, no other statistics on race and the justice system have been kept. That being said, the Commission's own findings, as well as more recent research, underscore the unfortunate observation that it is not just Aboriginal people who are overrepresented in the system. On the contrary, people of colour (largely those of African, Caribbean and Latin American descent) are also notably overrepresented. Likewise, the practice of racial profiling, whereby police deliberately target members of specific racial groups, is practised by both Canadian police and border security guards.[16]

If we continue on the road to toughening up the justice system, the problem is likely to get worse. In the U.S., one in ten young black men is, or has been, in prison. There are communities in which an entire generation of men has been lost to the justice system, and a damaging ripple effect is felt throughout communities. This ripple splits families and communities, causes greater economic disparity, and in many ways contributes to, if not mandates, criminality in the coming generations as children struggle to overcome the tremendous obstacles erected by the loss of one, sometimes both, parents.[17]

4. We devitalize our communities

Many social scientists worry that get-tough strategies create a climate of punitiveness and segregation that fosters a bunker mentality which ultimately weakens the fabric of communities and also disempowers citizens, removing from them the ability to play an active role in creating and maintaining the places where they live, work and play.

> **Dawn:** Here's an example from my own downtown neighbourhood. My partner and I left our house one day to find two police cars blocking our street. Our neighbours had called the police because some kids from the local high school were smoking pot outside their house on their lunch hour. My partner and I, on bikes, rode on the sidewalk to avoid the police cars. I was stopped by the same police and given a ticket for riding my bike on the sidewalk. Kids still smoke pot on the street and I still ride my bike on the sidewalk.

In this example, the law is invited into a community to solve a problem. The problem is not solved, and other members of the community feel like they (me) were placed at a disadvantage by having the police called. There was no community consensus on how to respond to the problem of kids smoking pot on the street, nor was there any chance for any of the other neighbours to have input into whether or not the teens posed a problem at all.

This is a bunker mentality: respond quickly and decisively, ask no questions, and remove yourself from the situation as quickly as possible. This is exactly what we do when we call the police, in the right circumstances, where there is imminent threat to personal safety or property. But does that mean we should see the police as the primary response unit to every problem we face as community members? A get-tough crime policy suggests exactly this, but such a strategy is ultimately ineffective.

Experience in community building and civic engagement reminds us that there are other ways to respond to situations like this one. The neighbours could call a community meeting, phone the school and talk with the principal and parents, approach the kids themselves and explain why smoking pot on our street makes people uncomfortable. None of these initiatives relies on the justice system as a primary response. Some require a little more effort on the part of community members, but all are more effective than simply phoning the police.

Towards a responsible justice strategy

There are alternatives to the "tough for the sake of being tough" stance on crime. Indeed, when we consider new ways to think about and respond to criminal activity, we give ourselves an opportunity to change many of the negative values that have seeped into our society in the past decades. When we start to see justice not for what it is, but for what it can be, we allow for innovative approaches to justice. Below we highlight some of those alternatives taken by communities that have seen positive results.

Decriminalize marijuana

Drug offences comprise close to 15% of the custodial sentences handed down in Canada in any given year. In the majority of cases, marijuana is involved. Decriminalizing marijuana would cut down substantially on the numbers of people involved in the justice system, as well as the overall costs of incarceration.

Jurisdictions in which marijuana has been decriminalized (like the Netherlands and parts of the city of London) have experienced no rise in criminal behaviour associated with its use or in the use of the drug itself.[18]

It is important to note that decriminalization is not the same as legalization. Decriminalization simply means that the criminal justice system is no longer used as a mechanism through which to control the substance. There are many alternative forms of regulation, including ticketing (in the same way one might be ticketed for a bylaw infraction) and controlled access, as with alcohol, tobacco and prescription drugs.

Take money out of justice and put it into communities

The best way to respond to crime is to prevent it in the first place. Crime is not prevented through security systems and police dogs. It is prevented by giving people alternatives to criminality through strengthening the educational and social service systems. This is not to say that an ideal education system in a society where poverty and racism are virtually non-existent would eliminate crime completely. But there is every reason to believe that concrete initiatives aimed at improving people's quality of life would have a notable impact on crime rates.

The Jane and Finch community in Toronto provides an excellent backdrop to see this principle in action. The Jane and Finch neighbourhood has been dubbed one of the most dangerous areas in Canada, with considerable gang violence, criminal activity, unemployment and poverty. It also has a large population of sole-parent-supported families, refugees and new immigrants. In the last decade, dozens of organizations have been created and funded to support the diversity and vibrancy of the community and to establish the social infrastructure that promotes a healthy neighbourhood. Among these groups are the San

Romanoway Revitalization Association, the Black Creek Community Capacity Building Project, and Jane-Finch.com.

Provide the framework for communities to solve their own problems
Governmental initiatives to support community development projects that recruit citizens to become directly involved in local issues and local quality of life are a sensible and cost-effective way to solve local problems. Instead of calling the police when neighbours notice graffiti, they may instead opt to put up a graffiti wall or have a neighbourhood clean-up day where everyone is invited to help take care of the community. Skateboard parks, basketball courts, and lots of communal spaces with multiple purposes are also good examples. This is the Jane Jacobs model of community building, and it works.[19] A healthy community built and sustained by the people who make it up: such a simple concept, but one that has struggled to come to the fore.

There are certainly more ideas in the thousands of communities across Canada. The essence of these alternatives is to think about the people around us not as strangers poised to threaten our personal safety and security, but as just that — people. Whether that's participating in a community initiative, thinking critically about political campaign promises, or becoming more informed about the current status of our communities and Canada at large, we can look past being "tough on crime" and work toward real and positive change.

Privatization Under Harper

Weakening public services and expanding corporate powers

Toby Sanger and Corina Crawley

THE HARPER GOVERNMENT has never made privatization one of its explicit political priorities, but that's because they haven't had to. It's been an implicit part of many of their other priorities and actions.

This direction should come as no surprise. A number of the more powerful members of Harper's team were key members of Mike Harris's Conservative government in Ontario.

The Harris government, which included now federal Finance Minister Jim Flaherty, Environment Minister John Baird, Health Minister Tony Clement, and the Prime Minister's new Chief of Staff, Guy Giorno, was more blatant about its privatization agenda. When he was vying for the leadership of the Ontario Conservatives, Flaherty promised, "If it's in the Yellow Pages, government shouldn't be doing it, and my government won't."[1] Guy Giorno has also been a strong proponent of public-private partnerships (P-3s), while Harper himself ran the National Citizens Coalition, which was a major advocate for privatization and against public health care.[2]

Harper and others in his camp have become considerably more savvy about what they say, but the hostility toward public services still appears ingrained. The Harper government's push to privatize and neuter public services has been both more subtle and politically careful, but also perhaps more pervasive in other ways.

Forms of privatization

There are many different ways of achieving privatization and restrictions on public services and common goods. These include:

- outright privatization and sale of public assets;
- contracting-out delivery of public services;
- deregulation, "self-regulation," commercialization and cutbacks;
- "public-private partnerships," including private financing;
- tax cuts/incentives or individual payments replacing public services;
- legislation and policies to expand corporate powers and restrict the public sphere;
- restricting public discussion, consultations, and dialogue, and making decisions behind closed doors; and
- cutting funding to organizations for advocacy work.

An unstated but fundamental priority

Harper's government has engaged in all of these without explicitly articulating a privatization agenda. For example, four out of his government's five initial priorities have led to increased privatization and restrictions on public services.

1. "Choice in child care"

The Harper government's very first substantive action in power was to cancel the early learning and child care funding agreements that had just been signed with the provinces. These agreements were long-overdue first steps to develop a pan-Canadian child care system, inspired by the Québec program that provides affordable and high-quality child care to all families.

This was replaced with direct payments to families of $100 (taxable) per child per month and a promise to create new child care spaces through tax incentives. This meant a significant loss of funding for provincial child care programs. While parents may have appreciated the extra money, not a single new child care space was created. (See Ballantyne elsewhere in this volume.)

2. *Accountability — for some*

The Conservative party worked hard to make the previous Liberal government's "Adscam" sponsorship kickback scandal into the dominant issue of the 2006 election. Accountability was prominent in the Conservative election platform, and the Harper election victory owes more to this issue than any other factor.[3]

Passage of a sprawling *Federal Accountability Act* was the Harper government's first legislative priority. But in a perverse twist unreported in the media, this legislation actually created major accountability loopholes for government contracts with the private sector, which were at the base of the sponsorship scandal, while creating overly onerous bureaucratic rules for funding to public and non-profit organizations.[4]

The long-term impact will likely be increased contracting-out and privatization, a more cumbersome public service, and reduced overall accountability as federal funds are redirected from public and non-profit organizations to less accountable and secretive private contracts sheltered by commercial confidentiality rules.

3. *Cutting taxes*

Tax cuts, including the cut in the GST, in business taxes, and the wide array of other tax loopholes have been a top and ongoing priority for the Harper government. They have used tax cuts measures with zeal and as a substitute for public programs, in the absence of any evidence that they are effective — and even when they have been shown to be highly ineffective and costly. The tax cuts have been so costly and ineffective that they have forced the federal government to face a deficit for the first time in over a decade.

Harper's government has made it clear that further spending cuts are planned, which will very likely lead to further privatization and restrictions on public services.

4. Fiscal relations and health care wait times

A fourth priority of the Harper government was to negotiate with the provinces to address the fiscal balance and to bring in wait-time guarantees for health care. As part of their negotiations on the fiscal balance, they have repeatedly stated their intention to limit the use of the federal spending power in their election platform, in budgets, and in their Throne speeches. This would make it very difficult to introduce new national programs in areas of social policy such as child care.[5]

The health care wait times guarantee, together with the controversial Chaouilli decision, is being used as a tool to expand private health care in Canada and weaken the public health care system. Harper's government has also provided tacit federal support for health care privatization through its failure to monitor and administer the *Canada Health Act*. This, together with other measures and inadequate funding for health care infrastructure, has allowed commercialization of health care to proceed and private clinics to proliferate, consistent with the Conservatives' election platform support for private health care delivery.[6]

These examples illustrate some of the different ways that privatization can be achieved and how it has been a fundamental element in the Harper government's approach, even when it hasn't been stated as an explicit priority.

The Harper government has also increasingly pushed its privatization agenda in more traditional ways.

The sale of public assets

Asset sales are the most complete form of privatization, and occur when governments sell public programs, infrastructure and land or buildings to the private sector. In mid-2007, the Conservative government sold nine key federal office properties to the Vancouver-based Larco Investments Ltd.[7] A court injunction stopped two of the buildings from being sold because of lack of consultation with the local First Nation. The government will lease back the buildings for the next quarter-century, with an option to further extend the lease.

The Public Service Alliance of Canada calls the sale a "sweet deal" for the private sector and has estimated that the properties were undervalued by $600 million.[8] Further sweetening the deal, public funds will pay for interior upgrades and maintenance in the privately-owned buildings.[9] The Harper government gained a windfall $1.4 billion from the sale, but has saddled future governments with payments of many billions more for the next 25 years.

The properties are the first of 40 tagged "For Sale" by the Conservatives, including the National Library and Public Archives, the Lester B. Pearson Foreign Affairs building, the massive Tunney's Pasture complex, the historic Wellington building, and 20 others in the Ottawa area, many with heritage and ceremonial significance.

Rumours persist that the federal government is preparing to privatize the *Canada Mortgage and Housing Corporation* (CMHC) and the *Atomic Energy of Canada Ltd.* (AECL).[10] There have also been rumours that the Harper government wants to privatize federal prisons. Rob Sampson, the cabinet minister who spearheaded failed private prisons under the Mike Harris government, was appointed to review the operations of the federal prison system.[11]

The Canadian Taxpayers Federation and private insurance companies have strongly urged the Harper government to privatize the CMHC, even though the agency provides the federal government with about $1 billion a year in revenue and is one of the factors credited with helping Canada to avoid the severe housing booms and busts that the U.S. and Australia have experienced. The CMHC also provides a lot of support for affordable housing, efficient and environmentally-friendly construction, and other services/programs that would be endangered with privatization.

Contracting-out

Contracting-out of work by the federal government has increased by about 50% in real dollars since 2000–01, and now amounts to about $10 billion a year, up from $5.8 billion. While the pay for contracted-out workers is often less than public servants, the cost to government is generally higher because private contracting companies can charge twice what they pay their workers. It is estimated that reversing a third of the work currently contracted-out could save the government about half a billion dollars or more per year.[12]

The Conservative government has increased contracting-out and privatization of services at national parks and is now looking to contract out departmental information technology and computer support services. This could become a massive and lucrative contract for the private sector.

Deregulation, self-regulation, commercialization and cutbacks

The Harper government has an extensive deregulation agenda that it is implementing in various ways. A number of these are discussed in other chapters of this book. One area of particular public concern is their approach toward science, research, and federal health and inspection responsibilities.

Despite accumulating more than $10 billion a year in annual surpluses and the pressing need for more research and development in Canada, the Harper government has laid off federal scientists and forced departments and agencies to slash their budgets.[13] Harper eliminated the federal government's national science advisor and has recently appointed his former boss, Preston Manning, to advise the government on science issues. The former Reform party leader has written a number of articles about how religious faith can bear on science, articles which have recently been taken off his website.[14] This approach to science has earned the Canadian government scathing criticism from one of the most respected science publications in the world.[15]

The Harper government is also moving to transfer a number of federal laboratories to universities and/or the private sector, and to eliminate direct federal inspection of food and labelling by delegating this role to the private sector through "self-regulation" (aka: deregulation).[16]

These changes could affect 25,000 federal science and technology workers, and endanger public safety. When a civil servant revealed the government's plans to transfer the duties of the Canadian Food Inspection Agency (CFIA) to his union, he was promptly fired.[17] The Harper government is also pushing to leave the regulation of airline safety to the airline industry. These proposals and the lack of effective protection for whistleblowers have even led to criticism by the Conservative's former star candidate, Allan Cutler, who exposed the sponsorship scandal.[18]

Public scientists play a crucial role in developing standards and policies that protect Canadians, improve their quality of life, and properly manage natural resources.[19] Privatization and elimination of federal science, research, and inspection services are particularly targeted because they are also connected to the Harper government's deregulation agenda.

Not surprisingly, the Harper government has developed a hostile and intimidating relationship with civil servants that still hasn't improved after almost three years. The combination of an overbearingly bureaucratic Accountability Act and distrusting political masters has destroyed morale and stifled innovation, creativity, and leadership in the federal public service, according to a report by a group of highly prominent Canadians.[20]

The tight control over discussion within government, clamping down on whistleblowing and leaks, lack of public consultation, cutting grants for advocacy organizations, and increasing privatization of research and policy have all contributed to a chilling effect that has severely curtailed public discourse in Canada.

Legislation and policies to expand corporate powers and shrink the public sphere

While his minority government status hasn't allowed him to follow through in some areas yet, Harper has also clearly stated his intention to enact legislation that would permanently expand private property rights and reduce the scope for public services and for the common domain. These include:

Property rights

The Conservative 2006 election platform includes a commitment to enshrine property rights in the Canadian Constitution. This would also include enacting legislation to ensure compensation for impacts on private property as a result of any federal government initiative, policy, process, regulation, or legislation. Property rights can be interpreted to cover expectation of profit and thereby form a barrier to expansion of public services or actions to protect the public interest, and could adversely affect municipal zoning rules, native land claims, spousal rights to property, and environmental measures.[21]

Trade agreements

Harper's government has said it will aggressively move to expand bilateral and regional trade deals. It has also pushed provinces to include provisions in internal trade agreements that would allow private corporations to sue governments for actions that would affect their profits and investments. These measures further expand private corporate rights and put a chill on the introduction of regulations and programs in support of the public interest.

Private property on Aboriginal reserves

The Conservative platform also says they would support the development of individual and transferable private property ownership on Aboriginal reserves. This has been strongly promoted by former key Harper advisor Tom Flanagan and by the Fraser Institute and the Canadian Taxpayers Federation. This could lead to the sell-off of land on Aboriginal reserves to outside interests, leaving nothing for future generations.

Copyright laws

The Harper government ignited a storm of protest with its proposed changes to copyright laws. These have been condemned by arts groups, information technology workers, and entrepreneurs, and described as the most repressive in the world, beyond "draconian," catering to the interests of U.S. mass media orporations.

Pushing P-3s

Not content with privatizing, selling assets, contracting-out, and expanding private property and corporate powers within its own legislative domain, the Harper government is also, somewhat hypocritically, using the federal government's spending powers to push other levels of government to privatize their public services through public-private partnerships (P3s).

In the 2007 federal budget, a number of existing federal infrastructure funds were amalgamated into a single Building Canada Fund, and it was announced that recipients would have to demonstrate that they had thoroughly considered the (P-3) option for large projects.[22]

P-3s are very much the Harper government's preferred option.[23] A new P-3 Fund of $1.25 billion has been set up to subsidize these projects across all sectors, and a federal office to promote P-3s has also been established. While senior federal officials have stated that their rules do not "preclude" publicly financed projects, the message is clear.

The Harper government is leaving few stones unturned in its efforts to promote P-3s. Shortly after it came to power, the plug was pulled on the construction of a new National Portrait Gallery in Ottawa, even though about $10 million had already been spent on renovation of a heritage building for that purpose across from the Parliament Buildings. The government subsequently announced that it would only proceed with the gallery, which will house some of the Canadian public's most treasured works of art, as P-3 financed and owned and operated by a private corporation.

Bids have been requested from private sector developers in nine predetermined cities, although leaks suggest that it is destined to go to Calgary, home of the Prime Minister's riding.[24] The bids are being considered by a committee whose membership is being kept a secret.[25] The renowned former director of the National Gallery of Canada, Shirley Thomson, has said the government's plan for a P-3 gallery is "a national embarrassment that makes us look like peasants on the international scene. It's a public cultural asset highlighting a rich public national history, and it should be a public building because it's the responsibility of the state to safeguard our history and culture."[26]

Public-private partnerships: Costly, secret, unaccountable

Under a public-private partnership, a government, public institution or authority contracts with a private corporation to fund, build, operate, and sometimes own a facility that would have normally been in the public domain. The contracts are usually multi-decade agreements, with some as long as 99 years, as seen with Ontario's Highway 407.

Large private corporations, and especially investment banks, have pushed hard for governments to provide more P-3s because they provide high rates of profit over a long period, with very little risk for the private sector. Most large P-3s are structured as separate limited corporations, so, if the project doesn't turn out as profitable as desired, the private backers can walk away, leaving governments to pick up the pieces and the debts.

A growing body of Canadian and international evidence highlights the high costs, low quality, lack of transparency, and loss of public control associated with P-3s.[27]

Creative and opaque accounting by P-3 agencies generally hide the true ongoing costs of these projects, while commercial confidentiality rules make it very difficult for the public to get further information.[28] The Ontario Health Coalition and a number of unions fought for almost four years before winning a court order forcing the disclosure of financial information related to the Brampton P-3 hospital. These documents showed that the P-3 hospital cost the Ontario government at least $300 million more than it would have if it had been publicly financed.[29]

Saint John waterworks: The will of the people vs federal pressure on P3s

The City of Saint John in New Brunswick is being forced to choose between the will of its people and the Harper government in its quest to upgrade its water treatment system.

Stephen Harper's New Brunswick lieutenant, MP Greg Thompson, said the city of Saint John must "fully consider" a P-3 when it applies for the federal share of infrastructure funds to upgrade its water treatment system. In a media interview about Saint John's water needs, Thompson understated the extent of privatization in many P-3s, calling them "future funding arrangements" and an "alternative" way of financing infrastructure.

Thompson made his remarks on the heels of a city council decision not to study privatizing the modernization of Saint John's water system.

The debate over public operation of the city's water system took centre stage in the May, 2008 municipal elections. The winning mayoral candidate, Ivan Court, publicly opposed P-3s and other privatization. In early June, city council voted against exploring a P-3.[30]

The requirement to "fully consider" a P-3 may stand in the way of sound public investment for their community. A P-3 involves such a significant investment of financial, staff, and other resources, at the expense of a properly-prepared public sector alternative, that it may lead many cities and towns down a one-way road to privatization.

Federal support for infrastructure dwindling

The ongoing underfunding of long-term infrastructure needs, particularly for the municipal sector with its very limited means of raising revenues, heightens the pressure to adopt this form of privatization. Federal and provincial transfers to municipalities have only recently recovered to what they were a decade ago in nominal dollars, and are still 40% lower than what they were in 1995, in real dollars per person.[31]

Conservative cabinet ministers have described their Building Canada infrastructure plan as "historic" and "providing more funding over a longer period of time, from 2007 to 2014, than any previous federal infrastructure initiative."

These rhetorical claims are only technically true because the Harper government consolidated the funding for four different existing infrastructure funding programs into one new repackaged program and added up its funding over more years.

In fact, the only increase in funding for infrastructure provided in the 2007 federal budget above previously committed annual amounts was an extra $25 million per year for each province and territory, which was included as part of its fiscal balance deal, and the P-3 Fund, which will go to subsidize private sector projects. Excluding these amounts, funding in some future years actually declines compared to previous commitments.

After 2009–10, when the gas tax funding reaches its maximum, federal funding for infrastructure will only increase by an average of 1.1% a year, below the rate of inflation. Actual dollars provided will even decline in 2013–14. As a share of Canada's economy, federal funding for infrastructure will decline from 0.324% in 2009–10 down to an estimated 0.285% by 2013–14, a decline in commitment of 12%.[32]

This underfunding leaves provinces and municipalities tightening their belts and turning to the private sector for expensive and inflexible financing.

The future of privatization and public services under Harper

The Harper government's approach to privatization has been much more savvy, but also perhaps more pervasive than the more blatant forms of privatization that many Conservative governments have practised in the past.

In many ways, he has adopted the same tactics as George W. Bush and other conservative Republicans in the United States. This approach to eroding the power of government is described by Thomas Frank, author of *The Wrecking Crew: How Conservatives Rule:*

> Rather than cutting down the big government they claim to hate, conservatives have simply sold it off, deregulating some industries, defunding others, but always turning public policy into a private-sector bidding war.
>
> "The best public servant is the worst one," [stated the president of the U.S. Chamber of Commerce in 1928]. And what he meant by that was, you know, you don't want good people in government. You don't want talented folks in government, because then government will work, it will be effective. And if government is effective, then people will start to expect it to solve their problems, you know, and who knows what comes after that, you know?[33]

In the less than three years since the Harper minority government was elected, we have seen the sale of public assets, privatization of public services, restriction in the scope of the public interest, expansion of private and corporate powers, and the stifling of public debate.

Despite this seemingly endless list of privatization initiatives, we have yet to see major concern expressed by the public. This has been possible because this government has been strategic, choosing actions that will continue to sweeten the privatization-pot without causing direct harm to the public.

The Conservatives have also been lucky, benefiting from a strong growth in federal revenues and the Canadian economy as a result of the resource and commodities boom. This has allowed Harper's government to fast-track numerous expensive tax cuts without requiring major cuts to public spending.

But the fortunate economic circumstances are likely to come to an end soon. The federal government's revenues already started to tumble early in the 2008–09 fiscal year as a result of its tax cuts and the slowing economy. If, as expected, the economy worsens and federal revenues decline further, they could easily push the federal government into an ongoing deficit situation. Harper's government has made it clear how it will respond: cut public spending.[34]

If a majority government provides Harper with the opportunity to proceed with his more controversial and drastic privatization plans, he might actually welcome an economic slowdown. The deep tax cuts his government has put in place will have an impact by "starving the beast" and giving his government a ready excuse to more drastically cut government spending, hastening privatization and even further sweetening the pot for the corporate private sector.[35]

SIX

CULTURE AND COMMUNICATIONS

Telecommunication Picks Up Speed On the Free(Market) Way

Marita Moll and Leslie Regan Shade

OVER THE LAST two decades, telecommunications policy has been increasingly driven by an industrial strategy linked to technological innovation and competitiveness rather than national and public interests.

In April 2005, David Emerson, then the Liberal Minister of Industry, launched the most recent challenge, appointing a three-member Telecommunications Policy Review Panel (TPRP) to conduct the first major public review of Canada's telecommunications policy framework since 1993.[1] The Review Panel's final report was submitted in March 2006, conveniently gifting "Canada's New Government" with helpful recommendations that fit right into their policy framework.

In June 2006, then Industry Minister Maxime Bernier put a fence around the CRTC, instructing it to take a "hands-off" approach to regulating the telephone industry.[2] In a response to public concerns, the Minister said that the purpose of this was "not to reduce the role of the CRTC, but rather to act as a signal to the CRTC, the market, and the Canadian public concerning the government's intended course of action for telecommunications policy in Canada."[3] In effect, he said that "from now on, we make the rules here." And indeed, he did.

In November 2006, Bernier overruled a CRTC decision on the regulation of internet phone service (VoIP). In December 2006, he overruled a CRTC decision and gave the major telcos the power to set their own prices as long as there was a telephone company, a cable company, and one unaffiliated wireless provider in the area.[4] In April 2007, despite a specific recommendation to the contrary from the Commons Standing Committee on Science, Industry and Technology, the Minister tabled new regulations deregulating local telephone service.[5]

The delicate issue of foreign ownership restrictions in the telecom sector was handed to a panel of corporate leaders, led by Lynton Wilson, former Bell Canada chief executive and former Chairman of the Board of Nortel Networks, as part of a review of Canada's competition and investment policy. Policy laundering[6] — i.e., using "blue ribbon" panels to "independently" make useful recommendations — has been a favourite Harper tool. In June 2008, this panel recommended that foreign investment rules be eased to allow foreign takeovers of telecommunications companies with less than 10% of national market share.[7] (Currently, foreign investment is restricted to 46.7% in the telecom sector.)

Foreign takeovers of larger companies could be allowed in five years after a broader review of broadcasting and cultural policies. At the moment, Section 7 of the *Telecommunications Act (1993)* says that "telecommunications performs an essential role in the maintenance of Canada's identity and sovereignty." Luckily, the TPRP had already recommended the deletion of that kind of language, deeming it outdated.

The largest corporate takeover in Canadian history, BCE's sale to an investor group led by the Ontario Teachers' Pension Plan and several U.S.-based private equity partners raises more issues of foreign investment and ownership in Canada's telecom sector. While Teachers' put up 51% of the equity in compliance with foreign ownership restrictions and the CRTC attached several conditions about governance before approval, questions remained about how "Canadian" this entity will be. With the recommendations on foreign ownership in hand, we can expect more foreign takeover activity in the near future, despite the fact that many other countries, including the U.S., U.K., France, Germany and Japan, consider telecommunications to be a national security area.

Opening the spectrum to new entrants also raises issues about foreign ownership. The Advanced Wireless Services radio spectrum auction, which ended in early July 2008, surpassed $4 billion. This auction included a set-aside of some spectrum exclusively for new entrants in the wireless market, ostensibly to stimulate greater competition and innovation for Canadian consumers. The $12.7-billion wireless industry, currently dominated by three firms — Bell, Telus and Rogers — will bring two or three new entrants into all provinces except Québec (where Quebecor reigns supreme). The biggest of these is Globalive Communications Corporation (seller of Yak long-distance services, with partners from Egypt and Iceland) which bought 30 licenses distributed across the country for $442 million.[8]

In May 2008, net neutrality became a political issue in Canada as hundreds of protesters demonstrated on Parliament Hill. Net neutrality seeks to ensure that the internet contains no centralized control mechanisms and that those who own the networks do not also control the content that runs over them. Net neutrality is a response to restrictions on free speech and access to information displayed by the actions of some internet service providers to control traffic flow on their services (known as throttling). The CRTC is currently considering a complaint against Bell Canada for slowing down heavy users of internet bandwidth. So far, the Harper government has been mute on the issue.

With respect to telecommunications, there is little to distinguish the Conservatives from their Liberal predecessors. Both have bypassed the public interest and pushed the pro-competitive edge. As a result, Canada has slipped from 5th to 9th place (2006) among OECD countries in per capita subscriber rates to broadband services, well behind Denmark, Sweden, Norway, and Finland,[9] who have pursued a more progressive course on telecom policy.

Industry commentators, members of the opposition, and public interest groups have asked for more money to be put into a national broadband strategy — notably the unexpected profits from the spectrum auction. At publication time, the government had announced that the money from the auction was to be used for debt reduction.

Stay tuned for the next chapter as telecom is a quickly moving target right now.

Harper's Museum and Art Gallery Policy

Cultural devolution and privatization

Howie West

LIBERAL AND CONSERVATIVE governments have historically underfunded Canadian culture. It has been a long-standing problem for Canadians who work in, support, and appreciate the museums and art galleries that enhance our understanding and enjoyment of our culture. Before coming to power, Harper's Tories had promised to address what the Canadian Museums Association says is a 34-year-old funding gap.[1]

Instead, the Harper government is continuing the process of starving museums and galleries of much-needed funding. In addition, they have cut programs and are enthusiastically engaging in a program of privatization and devolution. They appear to be deliberately trying to sabotage any expressions of Canadian culture that don't fit into their ideological assumption that Canada is a collection of market economies that simply co-exist.

Conservative policy around museums and art galleries underscores this ideological crusade. In particular, since coming to power, the Conservatives have initiated a process to privatize and devolve the National Portrait Gallery of Canada. At the same time, they have cut other services like the Museums Assistance Program and the Exhibit Transportation Services that support the regionalization of art and culture. These cuts are only a snapshot of one part of the broader

Conservative attack on Canadian community and identity. (See Rae, Flecker, and the Ad Hoc Coalition on Women`s Equality elsewhere in this volume.) Independent Research organizations like the CLBC and the CPRN, as well as literacy and countless other public community building initiatives, have also been cut. Still, these cuts demonstrate the inconsistency between what the Harper government says and what it truly wants.

In a 1997 CBC interview, while he was still the spokesperson for the National Citizens Coalition, Stephen Harper was asked if there was a Canadian culture. "Yes, in a very loose sense," Harper replied, "It consists of regional cultures within Canada, regional cultures that cross borders with the U.S. We're part of a worldwide Anglo-American culture. And there is a continental culture."

When asked a question by Patrice Roy during the French-language leaders' debate in June 2004, Harper said that many Canadian cultural programs may not benefit the general public but instead only "friends of the Liberal party." Referring to the cancellation of the National Portrait Gallery, author Andrew Cohen noted that the government's agenda was less about allowing Canadians to view Canada's cultural and historical legacy and a lot more about an ideological view of devolution that the Harper government clings to.

The Harper government displays a tendency to peevishly dismiss anything the previous Liberal government initiated. Minister of Canadian Heritage Josée Verner defends Conservative museum policy by comparing it to the policies of a "visionless, centralizing [Liberal] government." All of this has led to a neoliberal cultural policy that Cohen called "cultural devolution."[2]

The auction of the long-awaited National Portrait Gallery is the most revealing example of this devolution. Initially, the National Portrait Gallery was supposed to be housed in a distinctive location on Wellington Street in Ottawa, across from Parliament Hill, while becoming an integral part of the National Museum network. The Portrait Gallery was first conceived under the Chrétien Liberals in 2001. Many observers referred to it as a Jean Chrétien legacy. This perception appears to be at least part of the problem. "Put yourself in Prime Minister Stephen Harper's position," opines *The Ottawa Citizen.* "Across the street from the Parliament Building is a daily reminder of former Prime Minister Jean Chrétien's regime."

The former U.S. embassy that was going to house the Gallery is a stately and historic Ottawa building. By 2006, work had already begun on renovating the building to ensure that it met all of the conservatory and aesthetic requirements suitable for a national monument dedicated to housing national treasures. Writing to *The Ottawa Citizen,* one observer eloquently called it "a gathering of images and stories about famous Canadians and ordinary folk — people who have made Canada the country it is... It is the mirror that reflects who we are. It tells about our aspirations, hardships borne, and difficulties overcome."[3] An internationally famous architect, Edward Jones, who had previously designed the acclaimed Ondaatje Wing at the National Portrait Gallery in London, England, had been retained to design the plans for the new Gallery.

None of this mattered to the Conservatives. Although $11 million had already been spent on the project, the Harper government cut the funding shortly after coming to power. Although the government publicly denied it, the spending estimates that were released in September 2006 showed that no money had been allocated for the Portrait Gallery. Instead, a year later, on November 12, 2007, the government posted a Request for Proposals on the Public Works website, which advised that "developers are responsible for mobilizing community and private sector resources and support" for the project.

Private consortia in nine major Canadian cities were invited to compete. Their proposals are to be judged according to four criteria: a prominent, accessible and suitable location; developer expertise and financial capability; financial support from the private sector and community; and the financial deal or offer. Usually a selection process for a public project includes an architectural competition that helps choose the design skills appropriate for a public monument. The Harper RFP for the Portrait Gallery does not even include design as one of the criteria. The process being used is more similar to one that would be used if the government were leasing office space. Unfortunately, the finalized gallery could also look more like office space, depending on the nature of the bids.

According to the Heritage Minister, the proposal reflects the government's commitment of "open federalism" and the "best value for taxpayers' money." Public Works Minister Michael Fortier said that the government wants to ensure that they obtain "maximum impact from every tax dollar spent by taking advantage of private sector support and expertise."[4]

Comments like this underscore the degree to which Stephen Harper is committed to privatization. His government regularly uses private sector expertise as an excuse for moving forward with priorities that are clearly ideological. This is no exception. Even leaving aside the obvious issue of aesthetics, a good case can be made that devolving the National Portrait Gallery to the private sector in an undetermined Canadian city will be more expensive, but as yet there appears to be no evidence that it would be less expensive.

In a 2006 memo, Susan Peterson, the Associate Deputy Minister of Canadian Heritage, indicated that $11 million (or about ¼ of the price tag for the original cost estimated for the Portrait Gallery) had already been spent. Additionally, Library Archives Canada indicated that an additional $2.5 million in annual costs, or $50 million over 25 years, would be required due to additional travel, relocation, insurance and shipping costs if the gallery were to be moved outside of Ottawa.

The only real indication of savings identified by the government that has been made public, through an Access to Information request, would only be realized by choosing a smaller gallery site.[5] "The only reason to put out a request for proposals is if they don't want the gallery in the nation's capital," said Terry Quinlan, an Algonquin College conservation professor. The $50 million price tag, he noted, "would alone seem to far outweigh any potential capital contribution that might be offered by a developer in another city."[6]

Ironically, the Harper government had previously already flirted with the notion of a P-3 solution, but it backfired on them. EnCana, a large oil company, was prepared to offer space in the company's new Bow Tower. The space offered, however, was so expensive that it was also rejected when offered to the Glenbow Museum in Calgary. A January 18, 2007 government memo shows that the Harper government had responded to a 2006 EnCana request for proposals "seeking cultural organizations to locate in a new complex in Calgary."

The cost for fit-up of a 58,000 square-foot space, the size of the rejected Wellington Street location, was estimated to be $23.8 million, not counting the transportation costs.[7] Fortunately, the Harper government resisted the temptation to make an offer. In February 2007, the Bow Tower was sold to a Toronto-based real estate trust. Although this should have raised warning flags about the problems associated with utilizing a P-3 approach to creating a national monument, the Harper government has continued with its P-3 proposal.[8]

The Minister of Canadian Heritage, Josée Verner, says that, besides the cost savings, "Unlike the previous Liberal regime, which sought to draw public institutions and control to itself, the [present] government of Canada practices open federalism, not just in words but in action." This is a curious statement from a government that early in its term also cut the Museums Assistance Program and the Exhibit Transportation Services.

The Harper government's 2006 federal budget cut the Museums Assistance Program (MAP) by $4.63 million, or half of the $9 million that it has received annually since 1972. This is a far cry from the $75 million that the Canadian Museums Associations have recommended as being required to restore Canada's museums to where they should be.[9] The MAP program provides financial assistance to regional Canadian museums and galleries to help with preservation, protection, and collections management. In 2004–05 before the Harper cuts, 200 projects in all parts of Canada were funded.

Among other objectives, the program funds summer employment for students in the arts and culture sector, Aboriginal museums and cultural development, and touring exhibits of historical artifacts and contemporary art. The lack of funding means that Canadian museums in all regions and communities across Canada have had less money to work with, fewer exhibitions, and diminished ability to share Canadian history and culture with Canadians.

In particular, the cuts will reduce the educational capacity of museums and galleries. As small museums now struggle for funding, it is easy to see how they will be more dependent on the good will of the public and on private sponsorship. It is very unclear how these funding cuts support regional cultural access, which Madame Verner says is her government's goal.

At the same time that the MAP program was cut, another equally important program that encouraged regional and community access to Canadian culture was eliminated: the Exhibit Transportation System (ETS). The ETS was a federal government program that provided exclusive shipping services to museums and art galleries in all regions of Canada. Drivers trained in art handling, operating specialized climate-controlled trucks, criss-crossed the country so that national collections, requiring special handling, could be shared with Canadians anywhere.

Over 54% of all art transportation between museums in Canada was carried out by ETS, compared to 28% of all other specialized art carriers combined. In some isolated areas, ETS was the only carrier available, given the costs of travel to those areas. Over 65% of exhibitions in the Atlantic provinces are delivered by ETS. Gallery and museum directors have estimated that their costs will rise by about 30%, although in areas like Northern Canada the costs could be much higher. Inability to afford the transportation costs for exhibitions will inevitably force their cancellation.

Although a spokesperson for the government claimed that the service had to be discontinued because the drivers weren't easily classified, this argument is outrageously weak. Nothing would have stopped the government from creating a new classification that captured the job requirements carried out by these workers.[10]

The Harper government's museum and arts policy seems to be held together by one core objective — privatization. But privatization will only limit the public's access to heritage and culture. The government's policies do not increase regional access, as they have argued. Instead, the Harper government is leading a "cultural devolution," purposefully putting in place complementary strategies designed to shift more and more of our cultural treasures and fine art under the control of the private sector.

Former director of the National Gallery of Canada Shirley Thomson has indicated that she is embarrassed and appalled by what is being done.[11] All Canadians should be equally appalled and angry as we wait to hear which corporate brand the Harper government will determine is appropriate to stamp on our cultural heritage.

SEVEN

FEDERAL-PROVINCIAL RELATIONS

Harper, Québec and Canadian Federalism

Barbara Cameron

THE MOST SURPRISING initiative of Stephen Harper in office was undoubtedly his sponsorship of the motion in the House of Commons recognizing the Québécois as a nation within a united Canada. This comes from a man who in 1997 denounced successive Canadian Prime Ministers for their "appeasement of ethnic nationalism," citing in particular the attempt to amend the constitution to recognize Québec as a distinct society.[1]

That Harper can shift so dramatically on a central question of Canadian political life raises the question of whether or not he has a consistent view of federalism. Has he matured in office and come to recognize the multinational character of Canadian society with this bold but certainly long-overdue recognition? Does this initiative represent a fundamental break with his past convictions, or is it a tactical move motivated simply by the political necessity of gaining electoral support in Québec?

At one level, Harper's motion was a direct response to the attempt by the Bloc Québécois to undercut Conservative support in Québec by forcing Harper to state where he stands on the fundamental question of the national status of Québec society. The Bloc had given notice of its intention to introduce in the House of Commons on November 23, 2006, a motion "that this House recognize that Québecers form a nation currently within Canada." In a pre-emptive strike, Harper introduced in the House of Commons on November 22 a government motion "that this House recognize that the Québécois form a nation within a united Canada."[2]

Both the Bloc and Harper initiatives took place in the context of a Liberal party convention scheduled to open the following week that was expected to vote on a motion of its Québec wing recognizing Québec as a nation, a motion supported by a leading contender for the party's leadership, Michael Ignatieff.[3] Furthermore, six weeks earlier, the national convention of the New Democratic party had endorsed the Sherbrooke Declaration, which specifically recognizes the national character of Québec and affirms Québec's right of self-determination.[4]

Harper's successful tactical manouvre was undoubtedly part of a larger Conservative electoral strategy grounded in his recognition that an alliance of economic neoliberals and social conservatives in English-speaking Canada is not sufficient to achieve a majority government in the country. He needs the support of Conservative nationalists in Québec and even a smattering of Liberal Québec nationalists to achieve that objective.

Yet, while the recognition of the Québécois as a nation is new, Harper's view of federalism is less of a break with the recent past than one might think. A consistent neoliberal approach to Canadian federalism emerged in the mid-1980s and centres on combining a symbolic recognition of Québec with the so-called "principle" of provincial equality, or the same treatment for all provinces. The formula was first advanced in the Macdonald Commission in 1985, it underpinned the Meech Lake Accord and the Charlottetown Agreement, and was clearly spelled out in the Calgary Declaration endorsed by the Premiers of the English-speaking provinces in September 1997 at the urging of the Business Council on National Issues.[5]

This formula involves recognizing Québec society as "distinct" or "unique" while treating all provinces in the same manner when it comes to the division of powers. Under this approach, whatever responsibilities the Québec National Assembly requires to protect and advance the culture of a predominantly French-speaking society are available to other provincial governments. No further rationale is needed; if Québec requires these powers, the "principle" of provincial equality means that other provinces are entitled to them as well.

The result is an ongoing dynamic of decentralization when it comes to social programs that suits the neoliberal agenda well. Symbolic recognition of Québec costs little, but is worth a lot to neoliberal politicians if the results are electoral support in Québec and a general weakening of the federal social role.

The purely symbolic nature of Harper's "Québécois as a nation" motion was evident within months after it was passed. On May 17, 2007, the House of Commons Standing Committee on Human Resources, Social Development and the Status of Persons with Disabilities conducted a clause-by-clause vote on Bill C-303, an NDP private member's bill directed at establishing conditions for the federal transfer to the provinces for early learning and child care services. Clause 4 of this bill provides an explicit exemption for Québec in the following words:

> Recognizing the unique nature of the jurisdiction of the government of Québec with regard to the education and development of children in Québec society, and notwithstanding any other provision of this Act, the government of Québec may choose to be exempted from the application of this Act and, notwithstanding any such decision, shall receive the full transfer payment that would otherwise be paid under section 5.[6]

The NDP, Liberal, and Bloc Québécois members of the Committee voted in favour of the exemption; all the Conservative members opposed it.[7]

One of the telling features of the debate and vote in Committee is that the Conservative opposition was led by Michael Chong, the former Conservative minister of Intergovernmental Affairs who had resigned six months earlier over the "Québécois as a nation" motion. Given Stephen Harper's well-deserved reputation for micro-management, Chong's role and the unanimous opposition of the Conservative members of the Committee undoubtedly reflected his views.

Nonetheless, even the symbolic recognition of the national status of the Québécois is significant and unquestionably a step forward from the less satisfactory language of "distinct society" or "unique society." One hopes it means that future constitutional discussions in Canada will start from this premise. The difficulty, however, lies in the refusal to acknowledge that this recognition has any implications for the responsibilities of the Québec National Assembly. It is precisely because the Québécois are a national community that there will be ongoing pressures from the Québec government for greater provincial control over social programs.

The effect of trying to contain the national status of the Québécois within a framework of provincial equality is to reinforce a decentralizing dynamic at the centre of Canadian federalism. Despite the often kneejerk reaction in the rest of Canada that "whatever Québec gets, we get," the political reality is that progress on social rights at a Canada-wide level requires ending the link between the recognition of Québec and the notion of provincial equality.

Federal spending power

Dropping the anti-Québec bigotry of the Reform party was part of the strategy to unite the right, first under the Canadian Alliance and then the "new" Conservative party. The Policy Declaration of the Harper Conservatives, adopted in March 2005 in anticipation of an impending federal election, endorsed the notion of "open federalism" which included a restoration of "the constitutional balance between the federal and provincial and territorial governments," "strong provinces," and a limitation on the federal spending power that would authorize the provinces "to use the opting out formula with full compensation if they want to opt out of a new or modified federal program, in areas of shared or exclusive jurisdiction."[8]

Harper used the open federalism slogan to great effect during the 2005/06 federal election campaign in a speech to the Québec City Chamber of Commerce on December 19, 2005, and the press conference following it. He promised his Québec audience that as Prime Minister he would fix the "fiscal imbalance," recognize Québec autonomy, and give Québec a role in international bodies such as UNESCO.[9]

The Conservatives' spending power promise reappeared in the 2007 Speech from the Throne as a commitment to introduce "legislation to place formal limits on the use of the federal spending power for new shared-cost programs in areas of exclusive provincial jurisdiction. This legislation will allow provinces and territories to opt out with reasonable compensation if they offer compatible programs."[10] This is a somewhat scaled-down formulation from the 2005 Declaration, which seemed to offer an unconditional opting-out with compensation of any exercise, cost-shared or direct transfer to individuals, of the federal spending power, past or future, in areas of shared responsibility (e.g., pensions) or exclusive provincial jurisdiction.

In office, the Conservatives have exercised the federal spending power in the form of direct transfers to individuals with the inaccurately named Universal Child Care Benefit and student grants. The 2007 Throne Speech commitment was reaffirmed in the Budget Plan 2008, and a legislative proposal in some form was expected in the fall of 2008 in anticipation of the upcoming election.

An offer by the federal government to limit the exercise of its spending power in areas of provincial jurisdiction is, of course, not new. Louis St. Laurent first suggested it in 1956 in reaction to opposition by Québec's Union Nationale government to federal social welfare initiatives after the Second World War. As passed by Parliament in March 1957, the *Hospital Insurance and Diagnostic Services Act* required the approval of a majority of provinces before Canadians would see any movement toward a Canada-wide system of hospital insurance. This effectively paralyzed the federal initiative until a new Prime Minister, Conservative John Diefenbaker, eliminated the requirement.

A constitutionalized limitation on the federal spending power was one of the five demands put forward in 1986 by Québec Intergovernmental Affairs Minister Gil Remillard for Québec acceptance of the *Constitution Act*, 1982.[11] The Meech Lake Accord contained a proposal to add a new clause as 106A to the Constitution Act of 1867, which would have read as follows:

> The government of Canada shall provide reasonable compensation to the government of a province that chooses not to participate in a national shared-cost program that is established by the Government of Canada after the coming into force of this section in an area of exclusive prov-

> incial jurisdiction, if the province carries on a program or initiative that is compatible with the national objectives.[12]

After the failure of Meech, the Conservative government of Brian Mulroney launched another round of constitutional change, this time proposing that federal cost-shared social program initiatives be subject to the approval of seven provinces representing 50% of the Canadian population, with non-participating provinces being eligible for "reasonable compensation" provided that they "establish their own programs meeting the objectives of the Canada-wide program."[13] In face of public opposition in English Canada, the final text of the Charlottetown Agreement reverted to the language of section 106A in the Meech Lake Accord.

After the defeat of the First Ministers' proposals in the Charlottetown referendum and the near success of the 1995 Québec referendum on sovereignty, the Liberal government of Jean Chrétien pledged in the next Speech from the Throne that:

> The Government will not use its spending power to create new shared-cost programs in areas of exclusive provincial jurisdiction without the consent of a majority of the provinces. Any new program will be designed so that non-participating provinces will be compensated, provided they establish equivalent or comparable initiatives.[14]

This commitment appeared in the 1999 Social Union Framework Agreement (SUFA), extended slightly to include block transfers as well as shared-cost programs. In exchange, all the provincial Premiers except that of Québec acknowledged that "the use of the federal spending power under the Constitution has been essential to the development of Canada's social union," and further, that "conditional social transfers have enabled governments to introduce new and innovative social programs, such as Medicare and to ensure that they are available to all Canadians."[15] SUFA actually picked up on the proposal in section 25 of the rejected Charlottetown Agreement in which the federal and provincial governments committed themselves to develop a framework "to guide the use of the federal spending power in all areas of exclusive provincial jurisdiction."[16]

Constraints on the federal spending power are directed in part at preventing a repeat of the 1960s Medicare experience when the federal government dispensed with the notion that it had to wait until it had a provincial consensus before it could act. Instead, it simply offered to share the costs of any provincially-operated system of publicly administered health insurance that met certain minimum federal conditions, essentially those currently enshrined in the *Canada Health Act*, 1984. One by one, the provinces signed on and Canada today has a country-wide system of health insurance for medically necessary services.[17]

As the federal government has no legal power to force provinces to participate in federally-initiated social programs, the provinces could limit the exercise of the federal spending power simply by refusing to participate in federally-initiated social programs. The problem is that they cannot trust each other not to break ranks. From this perspective, pressuring the federal government to voluntarily limit its spending power is a way to enforce solidarity among the provinces. When combined with the formula requiring that the consenting provinces represent 50% of the population, as initially advanced in the 1991 federal proposals, it would become a means of enforcing the hegemony of the largest provinces. As Québec, on principle, does not recognize the legitimacy of the federal spending power, the population requirement effectively gives Ontario a veto. Under either the majority or the seven-plus-50 formula, Canadians would never have seen Medicare.

Québec's opposition to the federal spending power is long-standing and arises from its understanding that the division of responsibilities among governments in the *Constitution Act*, 1867, was designed to protect the social institutions of Québec. This is historically accurate: Canada would not have been created as a federal rather than unitary system of government had it not been for the existence of a large, French-speaking national minority centred in Québec. Confederation would not have happened if the 1867 constitution had not given jurisdiction over those matters thought at the time essential to the preservation of Québec culture to a legislature elected by a predominantly French, Catholic population. In contrast, the opposition of other provinces has generally been tactical as they temporarily ally with Québec to wring concessions in the form of more money and fewer conditions from the federal government.

Provincial wariness of federally initiated social programs has grown as a result of unilateral federal cuts to social transfers to the provinces, which began as early as 1977 with the re-negotiation of the Established Programs Financing arrangements and extended through the 1995 federal budget. The historic opposition of Québec and the bad faith of successive Liberal and Conservative federal governments have created the conditions for right-wing calls to limit the federal spending power for ideological reasons.

In addition to the constitutional amendment in 1940 making Unemployment Insurance an exclusive federal power and the 1951 amendment making pensions a shared federal-provincial jurisdiction, the federal spending power was the main instrument for the construction of the post-war welfare state in Canada which guaranteed Canadians certain shared rights of social citizenship. Limiting the capacity of future governments to make use of it is entirely consistent with neoliberal objectives of either commercializing social welfare or offloading responsibility for it onto families and charities.

Conservatives and federalist fundamentalism

The answer to the question posed earlier about whether or not the Harper Conservatives have a coherent vision of Canadian federalism is Yes, although their vision is a work in progress. It builds on the neoliberal formula of symbolic recognition of Québec within the framework of provincial equality that was evident in the mega-constitutional proposals of the Mulroney government. The "new" Conservatives have elaborated this formula by recognizing the Québécois as a nation and embracing the language of provincial autonomy. Their vision is far more decentralizing with respect to social welfare than anything contemplated by a federal government since before the 1930s Depression.

In general, the Conservative view of the role of the state and of federalism supports the right-wing goal of rolling back social gains and reorienting the state to more closely serve the interests of capital. This does not preclude acting in a centralizing fashion when it comes to using the power of the central Canadian state to harmonize the regulation of business, as seen in their promotion of a national securities regulator, or coerce those felt to be a danger to public order as they define it.

The starting point for Stephen Harper's vision of federalism is his fundamentalist neoliberal faith in private markets. He starts from the position that the role of the state, whether federal or provincial, should be a market-enabling one providing the legal framework for the operation of markets and eliminating obstacles to the free movement of capital, labour, goods, and services. Beyond that, the state should engage in the limited number of activities that cannot be provided by other institutions, including defence and criminal justice. For the most part, private institutions, whether markets or families, can provide for the well-being of individual members of society.

As outlined in the Conservative party's 2005 Policy Declaration, the role of government generally is to "i) protect the lives and property of its citizens; ii) ensure equality of opportunity; iii) foster an environment where individuals and private initiative can prosper; iv) ensure the security of our nation's borders; and v) provide services to Canadians that cannot be provided more efficiently and effectively by individuals or by the private sector."[18]

The Harper government's approach to the constitutional division of powers involves identifying the "core" responsibilities of the federal government and leaving as much else to the provinces (and through them to the market) as they can politically get away with. The articulation of the Conservative view of "core" federal responsibilities is found in their budgets' documents, with the most complete elaboration appearing in Finance Minister Flaherty's 2008 Budget Speech.[19] While several "core" responsibilities are mentioned, the greatest emphasis is on two main categories: national defence and public security, and the economic union. Public security includes border security, emergency, and pandemic preparedness, and criminal justice. The economic union essentially encompasses measures to facilitate the free movement of capital, goods, services and labour. Specifically, it involves the promotion of a common securities regulator and international trade, although the Conservatives seem prepared to accept a very active international role for the provinces under their "autonomy" approach. One might think that inter-provincial trade would also be a "core" federal responsibility, but at the moment the Conservatives seem to hope that other provinces will sign onto the bilateral Trade, Investment and Labour Mobility Agreement (TILMA) between British Columbia and Alberta.[20]

The 2008 Budget Speech of Finance Minister Jim Flaherty names some other areas as core federal responsibilities, all of which are given an economic twist. Immigration, a shared constitutional responsibility with the provinces, is to be re-focused on the Temporary Foreign Worker Program and attracting skilled immigrants.

The Conservatives cannot avoid acknowledging federal responsibility for First Nations, given that "Indian and Indian Lands" are an exclusive federal responsibility. Flaherty's stated aim is to shift the federal emphasis away from social services and toward skills training. In keeping with this, the 2008 Budget Plan indicates a Conservative desire to offload education and health services to provinces and territories through agreements involving Aboriginal and provincial territorial "partners."[21]

Perhaps surprisingly, aspects of post-secondary education, specifically student aid and support for research, are defined as "core" federal responsibilities.

Starting from the premise of a very restricted role for the state, the Conservatives imagine that it is possible to return to a clear delineation of the responsibilities of each level of government. They espouse a Canadian version of the kind of constitutional originalism prominent in U.S. right-wing political thought. In the words of Lawrence Cannon, Harper's Québec lieutenant, "our autonomy position as a political party is to respect the Constitution as it was written."[22]

From this perspective, nothing has changed since 1867 that should alter the division of responsibilities between the federal and provincial governments. But the *Constitution Act* of 1867 reflected a society in which the well-being of members of society was the responsibility of private institutions, whether the family or religious charities, and, if these couldn't manage, perhaps local governments. The original constitution doesn't mention social welfare programs, but instead talks about "charities, and eleemosynary institutions,"[23] a term that means "of the nature of alms, or almsgiving." Legislative jurisdiction for these activities was assigned to the provinces, along with everything else considered a matter of a "merely private or local nature."[24]

The Harper conservative view of the social role of the state harkens back to this mid-19th century view, and so it is not surprising that his government favours a strict interpretation of the original division of powers.

While most Québec nationalists would reject the Harper Conservatives' conception of the state-family-market relationship, many are not uncomfortable with their view of the limited role for the federal government. The appeal in Québec of an "originalist" interpretation of the Constitution is that the 1867 allocation of responsibilities to provincial legislatures was directed at protecting the social institutions of a French-speaking Catholic society. These cultural protections are linked through the *Constitution Act*, 1867, to mid-19th century notions of the boundaries between the public and the private. At that time, the social institutions closely linked to the cultural survival of French Canada, including the family and the church and its charitable and educational institutions, were located in what was considered the "private sphere." The provincial state in Québec, as in the other provinces, was expected to have a limited role in ensuring the regulatory framework for the activity of private social institutions.

The link between the "private sphere" and cultural protections for Québec allowed the architects of the Canadian state to reach a political accommodation with the French-speaking national community centred in Québec without having to acknowledge officially its existence by enshrining recognition in the constitution.[25] The national status of Québec society was made invisible through the device of assigning to the Québec National Assembly the same responsibilities as the other provincial legislatures.

It is this link between mid-19th century notions of the "private" and provincial powers that is the constitutional basis for the Harper government's alliance with conservative Québec nationalists. At the level of the Québec state, this link is not recognized because the allocation of responsibilities to the provinces provided the Québec National Assembly with many of the powers required to redraw the boundaries between the public and the private. During the Quiet Revolution of the 1960s, the Québec state took over direct responsibilities for education and social welfare activities that previously had been under the control of the Catholic Church. However, at the level of the country as a whole, this link is very real. It was the federal spending power that allowed post-Second World War Canadian governments to finesse the antiquated division of powers in the *Constitution Act*, 1867 and lay the basis for a modern welfare state.

This does not mean, of course, that other provinces have not or cannot use their constitutional powers to redraw the boundary between the public and the private. Certainly Saskatchewan did this with public medical insurance. However, in today's world of heightened international competition, if all provinces opt to go it alone, the likely consequence will be pressures to lower standards to attract capital, with the result that there will be further erosion of the common standards of social citizenship.

Managerial federalism and the Liberals

If Conservatives can be seen as having a "hard" neoliberal approach to Canadian federalism, the Liberals in office during the 1990s typified a "soft" neoliberalism, albeit underpinned by the slashing and burning of the 1995 federal budget. During the Chrétien and Martin eras, the Liberals adopted a managerialist approach to federalism influenced by new public management theories that positioned the central Canadian state as the coordinator of a network of relationships among governments functioning as partners. National objectives for social programs were to be set through intergovernmental negotiations conducted at the executive level among First Ministers or Ministers responsible for social services.

The purposes of federal expenditures appeared in intergovernmental agreements rather than in statutes duly passed by the Parliament of Canada. Accountability was seen as flowing not from Ministers to Parliament, but directly to the public through annual reports that used performance indicators to demonstrate the progress of governments in implementing their commitments to each other. Legislatures at both the federal and provincial levels were effectively bypassed, with the federal Parliament's role being reduced to approving the necessary expenditures of funds to underwrite the intergovernmental agreements.[26] The Québec government, which refused to participate in most agreements, was quietly accommodated through footnotes to agreements noting their lack of participation and affirming that they would nonetheless receive full compensation.

This elitist style of operating excluded legislatures from public debates on social policy and moved discussions entirely behind the closed doors of federal-provincial-territorial meetings. It seriously compromised accessibility and democratic accountability. It succeeded in confusing Canadians even further than they already were about the respective responsibilities of the different levels of government. By deferring to the provinces on the crucial question of Canada-wide objectives for federal social expenditures, the Liberals created the impression of an impotent federal government unable to provide leadership on matters of vital concern to Canadians.

The non-binding nature of the intergovernmental agreements made it easy for the Harper Conservatives to cancel the Kelowna Accord and the child care agreements as their first acts in office. Facing an opposition majority in the House of Commons that supported both agreements, the Conservative government would have been unable to reverse them so easily had the federal commitments been enshrined in legislation.

Solidarity and federalism: An alternative vision

In response to the hard and soft neoliberal approaches, equality-seeking organizations in Canada outside of Québec have begun to develop an alternative vision of Canadian federalism. The starting point for this vision is recognition of the national character of Québec society and the special responsibilities of the Québec National Assembly with respect to this society. The corollary of this is an appreciation that Québec will have a different relationship than the other provinces to the central Canadian state, particularly with respect to social programs.

This vision involves a rejection of the neoliberal formula of confining the recognition of Québec's unique society within the framework of provincial equality (or provincial sameness). It affirms an ongoing responsibility of the central Canadian state for a shared social citizenship, while acknowledging the autonomy of Québec.

This formula presents more difficulties in theory than in practice for, to a great extent, it is how Canadian federalism has operated for the past half century. Since the mid-1960s, the Canada and Québec Pension Plans have co-existed happily, with the provisions of each being similar. Québec now operates its own parental insurance program which parallels and significantly improves upon, the parental benefits available under the federal Employment Insurance Program. Money to fund this program comes through a decrease in Employment Insurance premiums paid by Québec residents and the levying of a Québec premium.

The difference between these arrangements and what is proposed here is that the provisions in the CPP and Employment Insurance inserted to accommodate Québec are actually available to all provinces. The expectation was that only Québec would make use of the provisions, which is what happened. However, the decentralizing pressures of neoliberalism mean that they now provide openings for weakening the social entitlements of all Canadians. (That the right-wing is aware of these openings is seen in the infamous "Firewall" letter signed by Stephen Harper along with other prominent Alberta neoliberals that called, among other things, for Alberta to withdraw from the Canada Pension Plan, resume provincial control for health care policy, and transform federal social transfers to the provinces into tax points. As the letter stated, "If Québec can do it, why not Alberta?")[27]

In contrast, under this alternative vision, the national status of Québec society would be explicitly and publicly recognized and not achieved by stealth through deals concluded at senior bureaucratic and political levels.

This alternate vision has been implicit in the recognition for some time of Québec's right of self-determination by many labour and left organizations. It moved from the realm of abstract and usually quietly expressed principle and entered into public debate in English Canada in the form of the "three nations" position advanced by the National Action Committee on the Status of Women during the debate around the Charlottetown Agreement. It is reflected in the Québec exemption clause in the proposed *Early Learning and Child Care Act* (Bill C-303) put forward by the New Democratic party and which was supported by the Child Care Advocacy Association of Canada, labour unions, and women's organizations.

A vision of Canadian federalism that de-links the recognition of the national character of Québec society from the framework of provincial equality (provincial sameness) creates the conditions for an alliance between organizations supportive of social rights in Québec and the rest of Canada. To some extent, this was evident in the combined support by opposition parties in the House of Commons for Bill C-303, which in effect saw the Bloc Québécois support the exercise of the federal spending power with conditions attached in an area of provincial jurisdiction. Similarly, in response to the 2007 Conservative government's Speech from the Throne, a coalition of Québec women's organizations called on the opposition parties in the House of Commons to push for the introduction of a Canadian system of child care services accompanied by the transfer to Québec of funds for its system.[28]

The solidarity achieved around the child care bill demonstrates that unity on social programs can be achieved between progressive groups in Québec and the rest of Canada, despite the obstacles posed by the current constitutional framework. Such solidarity is a precondition for making progress on social rights at a Canada-wide level. Ultimately, however, the *Constitution Act*, 1867, is too antiquated a framework to meet the aspirations of either the people of Québec or the rest of Canada.

In particular, the links between 19th century notions of the private sphere, the allocation of responsibilities among governments, and the accommodation of Québec are too strong to suit the needs of a 21st century country. At some point, formal amendment to that document will be required to constitutionalize the recognition of the national status of Québec society and the specific responsibilities of the Québec National Assembly related to this. Until then, progressive Canadians will have to mobilize against right-wing initiatives around federalism as part of the overall fight against neoliberalism.

The Harper Government and Federal-Provincial Issues

Turning out the lights in the "fiscal cafeteria"

Hugh Mackenzie

STEPHEN HARPER MAY not have started the book, but he is certainly writing an important chapter in the sad story of the federal government's descent over the past 20 years into irrelevance to the day-to-day lives of Canadians.

Take Harper's belief that the federal government should restrict its activities to its own constitutional responsibilities, add an ideological predisposition against any measure that smacks of social justice (like fixing the broken EI system), and fold in the tried and true right-wing mantra of tax cuts as the solution to every conceivable problem, and you have the perfect recipe for a federal government in decline.

A brief pre-Harper history of fiscal federalism

Historically, Canadian federal governments have had to be both creative and aggressive in carving out a positive role for themselves as leaders on issues of national concern. That is because, in the division of authority between the federal government and the provincial governments in Canada's Constitution, the provinces ended up with exclusive jurisdiction over most of the major social policy issues of importance to Canadians in the 21st century.

As interpreted by the courts over the years, the Constitution confers on the provinces exclusive power over health, social services, education, housing, labour relations, and most economic activities that are not explicitly interprovincial, including transportation and communication.

Federal government powers have been construed much more narrowly in Canada than in other federal systems. For example, there is no constitutional feature in Canada that corresponds to the "interstate commerce" provision of the United States constitution. Provincial governments' taxing powers are limited in that they are prohibited from levying indirect taxes like customs duties, but in practice the scope of provincial revenue-raising power is as broad as that of the federal government.

Significantly, in light of Canada's large and rapidly growing urban population, provincial governments have exclusive control over local governments, to the point where municipalities are characterized as "creatures of the provinces." The federal government acquired two key areas of responsibility as a result of constitutional amendments: old age security and unemployment insurance.

The significance of the constitutional background is that it underlines two key facts about Canadian social and economic policy: 1) the provinces have most of the on-the-ground responsibility and most of the on-the-ground relationship with Canadians when it comes to these issues; and 2) it requires an act of political will to engage the federal government with the key issues that matter most to Canadians.

It also requires a willingness to pursue highly-nuanced strategies that accommodate simultaneously the political imperative for truly national program standards as virtually a right of citizenship and Québec's desire for self-determination and vigorous defence of its constitutional prerogatives. The extent to which federal governments have been able or willing to muster up that political will is perpetually in play.

The constitutional weakness of the federal government was exposed in the 1930s in the face of a national and international economic calamity. The experience was nearly disastrous. As a consequence, the period from the end of World War II until the mid-to-late 1970s was characterized by growing and deepening federal-provincial partnerships in areas of public policy constitutionally under provincial jurisdiction. In this period, the provinces generally performed much of the heavy lifting in the growth of Canadian health, social service and education programs. The federal government, however, played a key role as a catalyst for the development of national social programs, in establishing national standards for those programs, and in ensuring that differences in provincial fiscal capacity would not prevent Canadians from enjoying the benefits of those public services.

The dynamic began to shift in the late 1970s as a growing concern with fiscal issues led the federal government to close off its open-ended fiscal commitments to the provinces. That process continued in the 1980s under the Mulroney government and, as a consequence, the share of the federal government in the funding of what had been cost-shared programs continued to decline. By and large, provincial governments stepped into the gap left by federal funding limits.

The next major change was ushered in by Paul Martin's "come hell or high water" anti-deficit campaign, much of which was funded by cuts in federal transfer payments to the provinces, along with cuts to unemployment insurance benefits. Federal transfers were reduced and de-conditionalized. Federal transfer payments to the provinces dropped dramatically as a share of GDP from the mid-1990s to the early 2000s. While this change had relatively little impact on the fiscal balances of the provinces — in the aggregate, provincial governments simply passed on the pain to local governments by reducing provincial-local transfer payments — it had a significant impact on the federal government's credibility as a fiscal partner of provincial governments in areas of provincial jurisdiction.[1]

The loss of federal credibility was most notable in health care. Federal transfers for health care had been folded into the Canada Health and Social Transfer in the mid-1990s, wiping out the specific link between federal funding and health care spending, and as provincial health care budgets came under increasing economic pressure, the resulting political pressure on the federal government reached a critical level, forcing an about-face in the early 2000s.

Over a four-year period after 2000, federal transfer payments to the provinces recovered, reaching a share of GDP that was actually higher than at the beginning of the period of fiscal constraint in the mid-

1990s. While the amounts recovered, however, the ability of the federal government to use those transfer payments as a policy lever in areas of provincial jurisdiction did not. In part, the gap between funding and influence resulted from the fact that increased federal transfer payments flowed to provincial governments, not under a single national program umbrella (in some cases with an opt-out provision for Québec) as had been the case in the past, but as a series of one-on-one deals with individual provincial governments. In effect, Martin and Chrétien addressed Québec's desire for less federal interference in areas under its jurisdiction by extending the opt-out framework to all provinces, creating an approach to fiscal federalism that has been characterized elsewhere by the author as a "fiscal cafeteria."[2]

Even in the period of transfer payment cuts in the late 1990s, however, the federal government did not abandon its efforts to make policy in areas of provincial jurisdiction. It simply backed away from the previous strategy of using federal provincial agreements on the use of the federal spending power as the vehicle for doing so. In particular, under Finance Minister Paul Martin, the federal government resorted increasingly to the tax system as a social policy delivery vehicle in areas of provincial jurisdiction.

The signature initiative of this type was the Child Tax Benefit/National Child Benefit Supplement system, which delivered income-tested benefits directly to low-and-moderate-income Canadians through the tax system rather than indirectly through the provinces using programs like the Canada Assistance Plan.

Harper's federal government: Going out of business, right down to the fire sale

When the Harper government was elected with its declared intention of getting the federal government out of the business of the provinces and focusing on the federal government's constitutional responsibilities, it inherited a long list of multi-year agreements and political commitments from the outgoing Liberal government. The agreements emanated from a variety of different sources. By far the largest of these flowed from federal-provincial conferences on health care funding in 2001 and 2002, which committed the federal government to a multi-year funding schedule. Other agreements arose from the election platform commitment of the Martin minority government for a national child care program and from the NDP-Liberal budget agreement in 2004 which provided for increased housing, public transit, and post-secondary education funding. In addition, the Martin government had committed the federal government to a program of gradual improvements to child benefits.

The Harper government has proceeded, selectively, to unwind or undermine many of these commitments. While it has avoided the political hot potato of health care, it has been anything but quiet on every other front. It killed the national child care strategy, redirecting the funding to a non-targeted tax break. It ignored the child benefit system as a delivery mechanism for its family-based policies, creating its own program-specific delivery mechanisms instead.

While it has followed through on the housing funding commitments it inherited, it has cancelled all the remaining national housing programs and signaled its intention to wind up the Canada Mortgage and Housing Corporation and sell off its mortgage portfolio, effectively taking the federal government out of the housing business. Pre-existing transit funding commitments survived, but the Harper government flatly rejected the calls from municipal leaders for a share of GST revenue, moving instead to cut the GST and challenge the provinces to move into the tax room thus created if they wanted additional funding.

With respect to post-secondary education, the message from the government has been inconsistent. On one hand, it identified post-secondary education as one of the few areas of provincial jurisdiction in which it sees the federal government as playing a role. At the same time, it is allowing the 2004 Budget's funding for post-secondary to expire without replacement and has announced that the Millennium Scholarship Foundation will be wound up in 2010 with no sign of a replacement.

Child care is a non-starter. Post-secondary education seems to have fallen off the radar screen. The federal government is completing an exit from the housing business that started when Paul Martin canceled the non-profit and cooperative housing program in 1995. The attempt to carve out a role for the federal government in national family income security policy seems to have collapsed as the government has bypassed its own child benefit system as a delivery vehicle for assistance to families. Support for local government is winding down, and infrastructure funding is now little more than a lever to try to force other governments into more P3s (so-called public private partnerships). Even in health care, although the funding is still there, any commitment to use that funding as a lever in support of national program standards has evaporated.

Rather than use its constitutional jurisdiction over unemployment insurance and old age security as leverage for a greater role in employment policy and income security, the Harper government is continuing the devolution of labour market policies that had been delivered through employment insurance back to the provinces and cutting the revenue base of the EI program down to size.

One of the more insidious of the Harper government's strategies has been to cut the revenue base of the federal government down to its (reduced) size on the program side of the ledger. Having recognized that burgeoning federal surpluses amount to an invitation to the federal government to expand its programs, the Harper government has effectively wiped out the surplus by ramping up spending on its priority areas of core federal responsibility and introducing substantial tax cuts.

Not only has the Harper government moved to shrink the role of the federal government in Canadian public policy, but it has done so in a way that puts a huge political barrier — the need to raise taxes — in the way of any future federal government seeking to reverse that policy.

Fiscal equalization — Harper's single new initiative — wrong policy, wrong time

Fiscal equalization is one of the few areas of any significance in which the Harper government has departed from the trend established in the early years of the Chrétien government. As a political response to two decades in which the program was periodically re-designed to limit costs and then turned into a series of one-off deals with provinces to limit the political fallout, the Conservatives made election commitments to reform the system in Québec, Atlantic Canada, and Saskatchewan. Post-election, the Harper government responded to recommendations from a review of equalization — known as the O'Brien Report — that had been commissioned by the Martin Liberals.

In essence, Harper's new deal on equalization restored the ten-province standard for equalization (reduced to six provinces as a money-saving measure in the 1980s and 1990s), mandated the inclusion of 50% of resource revenues in fiscal capacity calculations, and imposed a cap on equalization payments such that a province receiving equalization could not end up with greater total fiscal capacity than the non-recipient province with the lowest fiscal capacity.

While the new policy had the virtue of being rules- and principles-based, overriding the special deals that had cluttered up the program over the previous 20 years, it turns out to have been the right policy only for a context of low resource prices and a currency priced internationally to enable Canadian industries to compete. It may have been the right policy for the first five years of the 21st century, but it does not work now. Higher resource prices both push up measured average fiscal capacity and create significant fiscal capacity gaps among the non-receiving provinces. Although any revenue increase will raise the equalization base, the emergence of resource industries as the revenue growth driver in Canada means that the equalization base has been increasing without any corresponding increase in the revenue base in non-receiving provinces without significant resource revenues, most notably Ontario.

The prospect that Ontario might become a "have-not" province has become popular speech fodder for Conservative critics of the Ontario government. But it is also a huge problem for the federal government. In the current equalization configuration, with Ontario as the non-receiving province with the lowest fiscal capacity, Ontario's fiscal capacity caps the equalization payments of the resource-rich receiving provinces at a relatively low level. If Ontario becomes a receiving province, the non-receiving province with the lowest fiscal capacity becomes British Columbia, at a much higher level of fiscal capacity. That will create a flow of equalization cash into Ontario. It will also markedly increase the flow of cash into resource-rich receiving provinces as the cap level increases.

It is a myth that equalization involves wealth-sharing among provincial governments. Equalization is a federal government program funded from federal general revenues. That highlights the other major problem with running a federal equalization program in an era of high resource revenues. Higher resource revenues drive equalization program costs up. But the federal government does not have access to that resource revenue base. That is a provincial revenue base. The result is that higher resource revenues will put greater pressure on other sources of federal government revenue — more than half of which is raised in Ontario. Ironically, if Ontario achieves "have-not" status, rising resource revenues, the result will be greater fiscal transfers from the federal government's Ontario revenue base to resource-rich have-not provinces.

And what about the federal government's own responsibilities?

The underlying cause of that mess — regionally unbalanced economic growth in Canada — highlights another area in which the Harper government has abandoned a traditional federal government role. Regionally imbalanced growth is not a new phenomenon in Canada. In an economy as resource-price sensitive and as open as Canada's, one of the critical tasks of the federal government has been to establish policies to manage regional economic fluctuations. The equalization program itself is one of those policies. The federal government's responsibility for economic stabilization — a responsibility abandoned in the Martin-Chrétien era's deficit fight and buried under Harper — is another.

In the past, the Bank of Canada's exchange rate policy also played a role. Before it redefined its mandate to focus exclusively on domestic inflation, the Bank of Canada monitored the international exchange rate and intervened to moderate upward pressure on the currency that would damage the competitive position of Canadian exporters. The Bank effectively abandoned exchange rate management as a policy goal in the 1990s and, despite the clear problems for manufacturers and exporters created by an over-valued, resource-inflated currency, the Harper government has done nothing to change that.

The Harper government is presiding over a particularly dark period in Canadian federal-provincial fiscal history. It is in the process of completing the job of getting the federal government out of program areas under provincial jurisdiction. Where it is politically impossible not to pay, it will pay, as is the case with health care; but (no pun intended) it will not prescribe. Where it feels it can extricate itself completely with little political damage, it is getting out entirely, as is the case with housing.

As far as the other side of the Harper government's syllogism is concerned — focusing on the responsibilities of the federal government — ideology trumps all. Canada's international expenditures, on both defence and international development assistance, have been reoriented towards United States' military priorities. The government has essentially washed its hands of the employment insurance program, ignoring the widespread complaints that the sharply-reduced program is out of touch with the realities of today's labour market.

It has fumbled so badly on the greenhouse gas emissions policy that provinces are lining up to implement their own policies, leaving Canada with a hodge-podge of inconsistent policies that exposes this country to justified international criticism. As of the summer of 2008, for example, the main potential driver of policy dealing with emissions from Alberta's tar sands appears to be the Congress of the United States.

Furthermore, the Harper government's new expenditures have worked in concert with its aggressive tax cut policies to limit the fiscal capacity of a future federal government to move in a different direction.

What this means is that, in the areas of public policy with which Canadians are most directly concerned — health care, education, social services, infrastructure, employment and local government — the federal government under Stephen Harper has become largely irrelevant.

The federal government's role in perspective

The absence of the federal government is clearly not a good thing, but it is important to put that absence into perspective. There is no question that federal government programs have served Canadians well in the past in dragging reluctant provincial governments into national social programs and in establishing standards for those programs. The data show clearly, however, that provincial governments were both the main drivers of the relative expansion of the public economy in Canada from the 1960s to the 1990s, and the main drivers of its relative shrinkage after the mid-1990s. The public economy grew not because the federal government transfer payments paid the bills, but because provincial governments were prepared to increase their taxes to pay for public programs that delivered on national objectives. It shrank because provincial fiscal capacity spiraled downwards in the late 1990s in an orgy of competitive tax cutting.[3]

Chart 1 highlights the evolving roles of the federal and provincial governments in Canada's public economy.

In the period 1961 to the mid-1990s, provincial governments' own source revenue increased steadily as a share of GDP as the public economy continued to expand. That trend reversed itself dramatically in the mid-1990s as provincial governments across Canada engaged in competitive tax-cutting. By contrast, the federal government's own source revenue as a share of GDP remained relatively stable, except for the period at the end of the 1970s when it both cut taxes and transferred tax points to the provinces.[4]

The use of the word "national" rather than "federal" is important. The development of national programs in Canada has never been a simple matter of the federal government using its constitutional power or its spending power in areas of provincial jurisdiction to impose those programs nationally. National programs have tended to develop in a dynamic between provinces and the federal government, driven by a national public opinion that is not particularly interested in which government thinks it has jurisdiction, but always respectful of the sometimes nuanced differences in perspective between Québec and the rest of the country.

It is worth remembering:

- that Medicare got its start as a program of the Government of Saskatchewan;
- that the movement towards national Medicare would never have reached critical mass had the Quiet Revolution not taken place in Québec;

CHART 1 *Own-source revenue, % of GDP, 1961–2005*

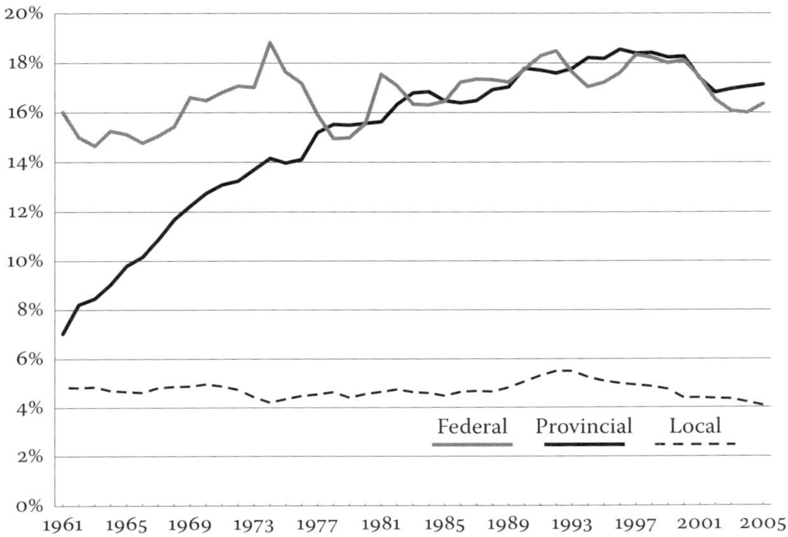

- that Ontario joined Medicare after the then Progressive Conservative government of Bill Davis lost a by-election in a safe seat over that issue; and
- that it was Alberta's public opinion and not the federal government that stopped Ralph Klein's flirtation with two-tier medicine in the early part of this century.

In the uniquely Canadian dynamic that creates our national social policy framework, there have been periods in the past in which the federal government has been largely absent from the debate, and equally periods in the past in which pressure from the federal government has been critical to social policy development.

In the Harper era, Canadians are living through one of those periods of federal absence. That doesn't mean, however, that national social policy projects should grind to a halt. The federal government cannot prevent provincial governments from making progress in their jurisdiction. The federal government cannot even prevent provinces from attempting to fill the policy vacuum it leaves behind, as the output from recent meetings of the provincial/territorial Council of The Federation demonstrates. Federal cuts in taxes and transfer payments to the provinces have not eliminated the revenue base; it is there for provinces to use to support the programs Canadians want.

The $10 Billion Broken Promise

Newfoundland and Labrador and the Harper government

Lana Payne

There is no greater fraud than a promise not kept.
— *Gaelic Proverb*

AS FAR AS broken promises go, this is a hefty one.

Worth about $10 billion to Newfoundland and Labrador, it doesn't take a rocket scientist to figure out why Premier Danny Williams is hopping mad at Prime Minister Stephen Harper for failing to keep his often-repeated commitment on equalization.

That $10 billion broken promise has been the root of a very public spat between Williams and Harper. The Williams government went so far as to spend $250,000 on country-wide newspaper advertisements to tell the province's side of the story to Canadians. The message: Stephen Harper is not to be trusted. He doesn't keep his promises.

"A promise made should be a promise kept, and, as Harper pointed out, there is no greater fraud than a promise not kept," said the Newfoundland and Labrador government-sponsored ad that ran in the spring of 2007.

But the dispute has gone further than newspaper ads. The premier has vowed to campaign against Harper and his Conservatives in the next federal election, encouraging the people of the province and of Canada to vote "ABC," Anyone But Conservative.

For Newfoundland and Labrador, this argument is about more than the money, as important as the $10 billion is.

And the money is important. Labour unions and social groups certainly would not be shy with their demands on how to invest the funds. The province's needs are great after decades of economic struggles and underfunded programs. Imagine the child care facilities or social housing that could be built; the health care that could be delivered; or the roads and infrastructure that could be repaired. Imagine the difference $10 billion could make in the everyday lives of Newfoundlanders and Labradorians.

Resources and The Rock

This dispute, however, has something deeper at its core. It is wrapped up in decades of battles with Ottawa over the province's place in Confederation and its contribution to the nation, economically, culturally, socially, and politically.

The province has always felt that its contribution to Canada has been undervalued, ignored, misunderstood, and often misrepresented. Most people living on "The Rock" believe we have made a difference to Canada, and that difference has been a lot more than our hospitality and wicked sense of humour.

In a speech last fall, Premier Williams pointed out that oil companies and Ottawa have been the biggest winners from the province's petroleum resources. Corporate oil had received $10 billion dollars; the federal government had taken in almost $6 billion, and the province received just $2 billion.

Williams went on to emphasize that the four offshore oil projects — the Upper Churchill (a massive hydroelectric development in Labrador), the Lower Churchill, Voisey's Bay (one of the world's largest nickel mines), and Labrador West (home of two iron ore mines, accounting for more than half of the country's iron ore production) — will contribute $100 billion to the governments of Canada and Québec.

"This staggering reality," said the premier, "is precisely the reason this government has taken such a strong stance when it comes to negotiating greater benefits for this province. Whether it be with Ottawa or the oil companies, we will no longer settle for less."

Exempting the revenue from non-renewable resources

For Newfoundland and Labrador, the equalization fight is a matter of economic justice and fairness. For Danny Williams, it is part of his mission to turn around the economic fortunes of the province. It has also made for some good politics.

He cornered former Prime Minister Paul Martin in 2004 on the Atlantic Accord — resulting in a new deal that allowed the province to keep revenues from its oil and gas sector without having them clawed back under equalization. This was a big boost to the province, both financially and psychologically.

But the province was not finished with the federal government. With another election and with the polls so close, Williams wrested a renewed promise from the federal Conservative leader on resource revenues and equalization. It was not the first time Stephen Harper had committed to exempt non-renewable resources from equalization.

Williams was promised in a 2006 letter that, if he was elected, Harper would "remove non-renewable natural resource revenues from the equalization formula to encourage development of economic growth in the non-renewable resource sectors across Canada."

In 2004, while in Opposition, Harper said in the House of Commons:

> It was an election campaign when the Prime Minister (Paul Martin) was asked to respond to a long-standing Conservative commitment to ensure that the Atlantic provinces would enjoy 100% of their non-renewable resource royalties... This is a commitment made by me in my capacity as leader of the Canadian Alliance... These are long-standing commitments, our commitment to 100% of non-renewable resource royalties. It was our commitment during the election, before the election, and it remains our commitment today.

But that is not what the Harper Conservative 2007 federal budget delivered.

When the premiers couldn't come to an agreement on equalization prior to the 2007 budget, the federal Conservatives laid out a couple of options. Neither of the choices involved excluding non-renewable resources from equalization, as was promised, which meant that, while oil and gas revenues would continue to be protected through the Atlantic Accord until at least 2012, revenues from the giant nickel mine in Voisey's Bay or from iron ore in Labrador West would not receive the same protection.

In addition, the proposals laid out for the provinces could also affect the Atlantic Accord signed by Martin and Williams in 2005, according to the Newfoundland and Labrador government.

The federal Conservatives deny all of this, claiming that they are honouring the Atlantic Accord as promised. The problem is, according to Williams and even the statements made by Harper, that more was promised than the honouring of the Atlantic Accord.

The issue here is not whether or not one agrees with the Newfoundland and Labrador government's position on equalization. The issue is that a promise was made, but not kept — a promise that, if kept, would have made a huge difference to Canada's most easterly province and its people.

The issue here is also one of accountability — something the federal Conservatives would have Canadians believe defines them.

Of course, for Newfoundland and Labrador and many of its citizens, this is also an issue of respect. The cynics might say it is also about politics, but why cloud a perfectly good principled position with something as tawdry as politics?

Notes

Introduction

1. Healy, Teresa. (2007). "Deep Integration in North America: Security and Prosperity for Whom? http://www.canadianlabour.ca/en/Deep_Integration_in_

2. Watkins, Mel. (2008). Round-table on the Hollowing-Out of Canadian Industry", Society for Socialist Studies meetings, Vancouver British Colombia.

3. Healy, Teresa. (2008). "'Evolution by stealth on the big idea': Towards an elite consensus on the future of North America",. Paper prepared for presentation at the international conference, "*Perspectivas criticas sobre la seguridad y prosperidad para America del Norte (ASPAN): Comparaciones entre Canada y Mexico.*" Universidad de las Americas, Puebla.

4. Documents released under Access to Information, Department of Foreign Affairs and International Trade, NAF March 30, 2006 Statement, 00101.

5. Healy, Teresa and Sheila Katz. (Forthcoming 2008). "Big and Little Brother Bilateralism: Security, Prosperity and Canada's Deal with Colombia" *Studies in Political Economy.*

6. Healy. (2007). "Deep Integration in North America."

7. Healy, Teresa. (2007). "North American Competitiveness Council and the SPP: Les Agents Provocateurs at the Montebello Leaders' Summit" Research Paper 44, Social and Economic Policy, Canadian Labour Congress. http://www.canadianlabour.ca/en/North_American_Compe

8. Council on Foreign Relations, Canadian Council of Chief Executives and the Consejo Mexicano de Asuntos Internacionales. (2005). "Building a North American Community: Report of the Independent Task Force on the Future of North America." http://www.cfr.org/publication/8102/

9. Iacobucci Inquiry, "Deadline for Submission of Report of the Iacobucci Internal Inquiry Extended until October 20, 2008" http://www.iacobucciinquiry.ca/en/press-releases/08-11-2008.htm, August 11, 2008.

Governance

Understanding Stephen Harper: The long view

1. O'Neill, Terry, ed. (1991). *Act of Faith.* Vancouver: British Columbia Report Books, pp. 43–48.

2. Johnson, William. (2005). *Stephen Harper and the Future of Canada.* Toronto: McClelland & Stewart Ltd., p. 86.

3. Manning, Preston. (2002). *Think Big: Adventures in Life and Democracy.* Toronto: McClelland & Stewart Ltd., p. 126.

4. Flanagan, Tom. (2007). *Harper's Team: Behind the Scenes in the Conservative Rise to Power.* Montreal & Kingston: McGill-Queen's University Press, p. 14.

5. Martin, Lawrence. (29 May, 2008). "Even a Sun King needs help sometimes," *Globe and Mail,* p. A17.

6. Cited in Flanagan, *Harper's Team,* p. 26.

7. Nicholls, Gerry. "Selling out true conservatism," *National Post,* April 27, 2007, http://www.gerrynicholls.com/index.php?view=article&catid=34%3Agerrys-columns&id=44%3Aselling-out-true-conservatism&option=com_content&Itemid=53 (accessed June 6, 2008).

8. Johnson, *Stephen Harper and the Future of Canada,* p. 35.

9. Plamondon, Bob. (2006). *Full Circle: Death and Resurrection in Canadian Conservative Politics.* Toronto: Key Porter Books, pp. 87–88.

10. Weissenberger, cited in Plamondon, *Full Circle,* pp. 88, 90.

11. Wells, Paul. (2006). *Right Side Up: The Fall of Paul Martin and the Rise of Stephen Harper's New Conservatism.* McClelland & Stewart Ltd., p. 5.

12. Flanagan, Tom. (1995). *Waiting for the Wave: The Reform Party and Preston Manning.* Toronto: Stoddart, p. 54–55.

13. National Citizens Coalition, http://nationalcitizens.ca/ (accessed June 16, 2008).

14. Plamondon, *Full Circle,* p. 222;and Ellis, Faron and Peter Woolstencroft. (2004). "New Conservatives, Old Realities: The 2004 Election Campaign," Jon H. Pammett and Christopher Dornan (ed.) *The General Election of 2004.* Toronto: Dundurn, p. 76.

15. Harper, Stephen and Tom Flanagan. (1998). "Conservative Politics in Canada" Past, Present, and Future," in William Gairdner (ed.) *After Liberalism.* Toronto: Stoddart.

16. Flanagan, *Harper's Team,* p. 19.

17. Johnson, *Stephen Harper and the Future of Canada,* pp. 118–119.

18. Harper, cited in Johnson, *Stephen Harper and the Future of Canada,* p. 120.

19. Flanagan, *Harper's Team,* p. 16.

20. Flanagan, *Harper's Team,* p. 19.

21. Patten, Steve. (2006). "Party Politics and the New Right in Canada," in Joan Grace and Byron Sheldrick, eds., *Canadian Politics: Democracy and Dissent.* Toronto: Prentice Hall.

22. Betz, Hans-Georg, Carol Johnson and Steve Patten. (2005). "Identitarian Politics and Populism in Canada and the Antipodes," in Jens Rydgren, (ed.) *Movements of Exclusion: Radical Right-wing Populism in the Western World.* Hauppauge, N.Y.: Nova Science.

23. Flanagan, *Waiting for the Wave,* p. 60.

24. Johnson, *Stephen Harper and the Future of Canada,* p. 44.

25. Plamondon, *Full Circle,* p. 147.

26. Johnson, *Stephen Harper and the Future of Canada,* p. 68.

27. Wells, *Right Side Up,* p. 314.

28. Mackey, Lloyd. (2005). *The Pilgrimage of Stephen Harper.* Toronto: ECW Press, pp. 65–66.

29. Mackey, *The Pilgrimage of Stephen Harper,* p. 62.

30. Manning, *Think Big,* pp. 48–49.

31. I have explored Canada's conservative populism in a number of other venues: Patten, Steve. (1996). "Preston Manning's Populism: Constructing the Common Sense of the Common People," *Studies in Political Economy,* No. 50; Patten, Steve. (1999). "The Reform Party's Re-imagining of the Canadian Nation," *Journal of Canadian Studies,* 34:1; and Betz, Johnson and Patten, "Identitarian Politics and Populism."

32. Johnson, *Stephen Harper and the Future of Canada,* pp. 51–53.

33. Harper cited in O'Neill, *Act of Faith,* p. 44.

34. Flanagan, *Harper's Team,* p. 13.

35. Harper, Stephen, et al. (2001). "The Alberta Agenda." https://www.albertaresidentsleague.com/letter.htm (accessed June 19, 2008)

36. Cited in Patten, Steve. (2001). "Toryism and the Conservative Party in a Neo-liberal Era," in Hugh Thorburn and Alan Whitehorn, ed. *Party Politics in Canada,* 8th edition. Scarborough: Prentice-Hall, p. 142.

Chill Effect: Stephen Harper's cold war on freedom of speech

1. Lakoff, George. *The Political Mind*. Viking. 2008.

2. http://www.cbc.ca/news/background/parliament39/budgetcuts.html

3. The deficit was over $40 billion and the debt was equivalent to almost 70% of GDP.

4. http://www.ccppcj.ca/e/ccp.shtml

5. http://www.straight.com/article/women-kick-harpers-ass

6. http://www.straight.com/article/women-kick-harpers-ass

7. http://www.thestar.com/News/Canada/article/429903

8. http://www.nationalpost.com/news/story.html?id=242112

9. http://www.nationalpost.com/news/canada/story.html?id=242845

10. http://www.thestar.com/columnists/article/420919

11. http://www.thestar.com/News/Canada/article/419846

12. http://network.nationalpost.com/np/blogs/posted/archive/2008/04/23/harper-discovers-it-s-easy-to-find-enemies-if-you-look-hard-enough.aspx

13. http://www.theglobeandmail.com/servlet/story/RTGAM.20080505.wcomartin05/BNStory/specialComment

14. http://www.ctv.ca/servlet/ArticleNews/story/CTVNews/20080503/ati_registry_080503/20080503

15. CAJ urges Ottawa to reverse decision on information database; Canada News-wire; Monday, May 5, 2008

16. http://www.guardian.co.uk/commentisfree/2008/apr/24/thecanadiannixon

17. http://network.nationalpost.com/np/blogs/posted/archive/2007/10/03/harper-calls-rare-impromptu-news-conference-fall-election-in-offing.aspx

18. http://journalism.ukings.ca/journalism_3673_9591.html

19. http://journalism.ukings.ca/journalism_3673_9591.html

20. http://www.harperindex.ca/ViewArticle.cfm?Ref=003

21. http://www.cbc.ca/story/canada/national/2006/04/25/soldiers-return-media060425.html

22. http://www.theglobeandmail.com/servlet/Page/document/v5/content/subscribe?user_URL=http://www.theglobeandmail.com%2Fservlet%2Fstory%2FRTGAM.20060428.wxmilitary28%2FBNStory%2FNational%2F&ord=135872601&brand=theglobeandmail&force_login=true

23. http://www.ctv.ca/servlet/ArticleNews/story/CTVNews/20060429/afghanistan_media_060430?s_name=&no_ads=

24. Canwest News Service. http://www.canada.com/theprovince/news/story.html?id=969ebcdb-87fb-47fa-9fd4–969657ec6d84&k=81135

25. http://www.torontosun.ca/Comment/Commentary/2006/04/26/1550847.html

26. http://www.embassymag.ca/html/index.php?display=story&full_path=/2006/march/29/durkan/

27. http://www.cbc.ca/news/viewpoint/vp_basen/20061101.html

28. http://www.harperindex.ca/ViewArticle.cfm?Ref=00106

29. Editorial. May 16, 2008. http://www.thestar.com/comment/article/425894.

30. http://communities.canada.com/theprovince/blogs/allthingsconsidered/archive/2008/03/06/tory-blunders-expose-harper.aspx

31. http://www.democraticunderground.com/discuss/duboard.php?az=view_ all&address=190x14645

32. http://www.uofaweb.ualberta.ca/govrel/news.cfm?story=46191

33. http://www.cbc.ca/news/viewpoint/vp_basen/20061101.html

34. http://www.cbc.ca/news/viewpoint/vp_basen/20061101.html

35. http://www.cbc.ca/news/viewpoint/vp_basen/20061101.html

36. http://www.cbc.ca/news/viewpoint/vp_basen/20061101.html

37. At Issue May 15, 2008 http://www.cbc.ca/national/blog/video/at_issue/a_photo_op_too_far.html

38. http://www.guardian.co.uk/commentisfree/2008/apr/24/thecanadiannixon

39. http://www.thestar.com/News/Canada/article/429906

Economy, Trade and Investment

The Conservative Tax Record: More of the same, or a turn for the worse?

1. Lee, Marc. "Eroding Tax Fairness: Tax Incidence in Canada: 1990 to 2005." Canadian Centre for Policy Alternatives. 2007; and Jackson, Andrew. "Why Charity Isn't Enough: The Case for Raising Taxes on Canada's Rich." Canadian Centre for Policy Alternatives. December 2007

2. Murphy, Brian, Paul Roberts and Michael Wolfson. "High Income Canadians." Statistics Canada Cat. 75-001-XIE. *Perspectives on Labour and Income*. September 2007.

3. Heisz, Andrew. *Income Inequality and Redistribution in Canada: 1976 to 2004*. Statistics Canada Cat. 11F00119MIE- No. 298. 2007.

4. Mintz, Jack. "2007 Tax Competitiveness Report: A Call for Comprehensive Tax Reform". C. D. Howe Institute Commentary No. 254, September 2007.

5. Weir, Erin. "Winning the Race to the Bottom: A Critical Appraisal of Corporate Tax Cuts." Canadian Labour Congress. Ottawa. August 2007.

6. KPMG. "Competitive Alternatives 2008—Special Report: Focus on Tax." KPMG International. 2008.

7. Thomas, Allan. "Recent Trends in Corporate Finance: Some Evidence from the Canadian System of National Accounts." Statistics Canada Research Paper -Catalogue no. 13-604-MIE. 2006.

8. Drummond, Don and Ritu Sapra. "Canadian Companies Not Taking Advantage of Investment Opportunities." TD Bank Topic Paper. 2007.

9. Op.cit. Thomas 2006; and Drummond and Sapra 2007.

10. Chen, Duanjie, Jack Mintz, and Andrey Tarasov. "Federal and Provincial Tax Reforms: Let's Get Back on Track." C. D. Howe Institute. July 2007.

11. Mackenzie, Hugh. "Taxation: The Martin Record" in Todd Scarth (Ed.) *Hell and High Water: An Assessment of Paul Martin's Record and Implications for the Future*. Canadian Centre for Policy Alternatives. Ottawa. 2004.

12. Jackson, Andrew. "High Income Earners Will be the Big Winners from Tax Reform in New Brunswick." Canadian Labour Congress. June, 2008.

13. Op. Cit. Murphy et.al.

14. Slemrod, Joel.B. "The Economics of Taxing the Rich" in Joel B. Slerod (Ed.) *Does Atlas Shrug?* Harvard University Press. Cambridge. 2000.

15. Tamagno, Ed and Ken Battle. "Tax Fairness According to Canada's New Government." Caledon Institute. Ottawa. November 2006.

16. Weir, Erin. "Income splitting isn't fair." *Ottawa Citizen*, February 2, 2007: A13.

17. OECD *Employment Outlook* 2006

18. Liberal Party of Canada. "Liberal Leader Stéphane Dion Commits to Lowering Corporate Tax Rates." Press Release. October 2007.

Backsliding: Manufacturing decline and resource dependency under Harper

1. Typically, an "official" recession occurs when real GDP shrinks for at least two consecutive quarters.

2. This effect was called the "Dutch disease" in reference to the experience of the Netherlands in the late 1960s, when discoveries of North Sea gas caused a currency appreciation (much less severe than the rise of the Canadian dollar since 2002) that squeezed out non-resource Dutch exports. This chain of events might today more aptly be renamed the "Canadian condition."

3. For a broader critique of these corporate tax cuts, see "Picking Winners: The Distorting Effects of Federal Corporate Tax Cuts," by Jim Stanford (Ottawa: Canadian Centre for Policy Alternatives, April 2008).

4. Most Asian currencies, in particular, are explicitly or implicitly linked to U.S. dollar exchange rate targets, and hence countries such as Japan, Thailand, and China have not experienced remotely the same pain from currency fluctuations as has Canada. Mexico has also managed to avoid a currency appreciation. It is empirically wrong to assume that the rise of Canada's dollar reflects a global weakness of the U.S. dollar. Canada's unique resource dependence, its unique openness to foreign investment, and the willingness of Canadian authorities to tolerate unrestrained appreciation, have meant that we have borne a vastly disproportionate share of the burden of adjusting to global exchange rate fluctuations.

5. The Bank of Canada also reports to Mr. Flaherty, so the Bank's inaction in the face of the damaging overshoot of the Canadian dollar is also, ultimately, Mr. Flaherty's responsibility—notwithstanding the official fiction that Canada's central bank is "independent."

6., Thomas d'Aquino, head of the Canadian Council of Chief Executives, called the Wilson report "music to our ears." The changes proposed by the Wilson panel, if enacted, would likely have prohibited Prentice's rejection of the MD&A takeover.

7. A detailed critique of the employment and industrial effects on Canadian manufacturing of a free trade agreement with Korea is provided in "Employment Implications of Trade Liberalization with East Asia," by Jim Stanford and Daniel Poon (Toronto: Canadian Auto Workers, September 2006).

8. The 2008 edition of the Alternative Federal Budget proposed several concrete ideas for capturing a larger share of one-time resource super-profits, both provincially and federally. See www.policyalternatives.ca for details.

Continuity and Change: Canadian Trade and Investment Policy, 2006–08

1. This article does not necessarily reflect the views of CCIC or its members.

2. This paper does not review changes in the NAFTA paradigm, which has been another area of significant evolution with the Security Prosperity Partnership Initiative. This is covered elsewhere in this book.

3. These include the Group of 33 countries aiming to carve out specific food security and development provisions in agriculture negotiations, to the Africa group and their proposals for international regulation of commodity prices, to the C4 group of West African cotton-exporting countries, to large constellations like the Group of 120 that emerged in the middle of the 2005 WTO Hong Kong Ministerial in reaction to the intransigence of rich countries on diverse Southern demands.

4. These include analysis by the World Bank and the Carnegie Endowment for International Peace.

5. The offering of "aid for trade" is seen by many Southern governments and civil society analysts as problematic, with descriptions ranging from being ineffective to a distraction to bribery. For a critical review from a Southern perspective see South Centre (2004). *Strengthening Developing Countries' Capacity for Trade Negotiations: Matching Technical Assistance to Negotiating Capacity Constraints* http://www.g77.org/doha/Doha-BP04%20-Strengthening_Southern_trade-related_negotiating_capacity.pdf

6. There have been six WTO Ministerial meetings since 2005 when the WTO was created. They are normally on a two year spacing cycle.

7. See for example the statement of the NAMA 11 Group of developing countries on the Feb 2008 modalities text http://www.iatp.org/tradeobservatory/library.cfm?refID=101799 Also SUNS *South-North Development Monitor*, (Feb 27 2008). "More confusion in NAMA as Chair gives new proposals."

8. For information on the implications to Canadian farmers of the loss of the monopoly powers of the CWB see National Farmers Union website http://thenfu.sasktelwebhosting.com/cwb.html

9. For a review of possibilities for a Canadian approach to agricultural trade rules that builds new North-South alliances on a shared agenda for trade justice see the report of *Sustainable Farm Livelihoods North and South*, May 2005. http://www.ccic.ca/e/docs/003_food_roundtable_report.pdf

10. A Peru investment treaty was concluded in 2007. Others launched include Mongolia, Madagascar, Indonesia and Vietnam.

11. Although now a regular part of trade parlance, this term was first coined by Jagdish Bhagwati in, "U.S. Trade Policy: The Infatuation with Free Trade Agreements", in Jagdish Bhagwati and Anne O. Krueger, *The Dangerous Drift to Preferential Trade Agreements*, AEI Press, 1995.

12. The United Nations Conference on Trade and Development (UNCTAD) warned of the developmental constraints often imposed in bilateral trade deals in its 2007 *Trade and Development Report* http://www.unctad.org/Templates/webflyer.asp?docid=8951&intItemID=2068&lang=1

13. Canada updated its model Foreign Investment Protection Agreement template in 2004 partly in an effort to respond to the major public and political criticisms of NAFTA Chapter 11, but the new model makes few substantive changes. See Peterson (2006) *Evaluating Canada's 2004 Model Foreign Investment Protection Agreement in light of Civil Society's Concerns*. A CCIC Briefing note.

14. See for example the June 2008 testimony before the CIIT of a former analyst with the NAFTA environmental commission (CEC) who was providing advice to parliamentarians for their study on the human rights and environmental issues to be considered in the Colombia Canada trade agreement.

15. See website of NDP trade critic Peter Julian http://www.peterjulian.ca/page/615

16. January 2008, legal analysis undertaken by the Canadian Association of Labour Lawyers (CALL) on the U.S.-Colombia trade deal's labour provisions. Available from the Canadian Labour Congress www.canadianlabour.ca.

17. For an excellent discussion of the Strategy see Arne Ruckert and Laura Macdonald (2008), *Harper Re-Engages the Hemisphere: Canada and Post-Neoliberal Latin America*, Carleton University.

18. See Foreign Affairs and International Trade Canada website for government information on the Americas Strategy http://geo.international.gc.ca/cip-pic/geo/objectives-en.aspx.

19. See the Prime Minister's Speech at http://pm.gc.ca/eng/media.asp?id=1759

20. Healy, Teresa and Sheila Katz, (2008). "Big and Little Brother Bilateralism: Security, Prosperity and Canada's Deal with Colombia", in *Studies in Political Economy*, Fall (forthcoming).

21. See Susan Sell (2008). *The Global IP Upward Ratchet, Anti-Counterfeiting and Piracy Enforcement Efforts: The State of Play.* http://www.ip-watch.org/files/SusanSellfinalversion.pdf

22. Data exclusivity provisions extend the effective monopoly control of pharmaceutical companies over drug patents by preventing generic competitors from using the clinical trial data of the patented medicine to expedite approval of bioequivalent generic medicines.

23. The Canadian Generic Pharmaceutical Association (CGPA) estimated that had the eight-year ban been in place in the previous five years, it would have added approximately $600-million to prescription drug costs in Canada. See CGPA press release November 14, 2006 at http://www.twnside.org.sg/title2/FTAs/info.service/fta.info.service047.htm

24. See the analysis of the Canadian Auto Workers Union on this issue at http://www.caw.ca/campaigns&issues/ongoingcampaigns/korea/index.asp

25. See Department of Foreign Affairs and International Trade, (January 25, 2008). Press Release No. 20 *Backgrounder : Treaty Procedure in the House of Commons* http://news.gc.ca/web/view/en/index.jsp?articleid=374729

Harper and NAFTA-Plus: Deep integration by stealth

1. Canadian Press, June 20, 2008.

2. U.S. Trade Representative, Special 301 Report

3. Cited Geist Blog (www.michaelgeist.ca) March 5, 2007. Michael Geist is Canada Research Chair in internet and e-commerce law.

4. Geist, *Toronto Star*, June 16, 2008.

5. See for example, U.S. Environmental Protection Agency Administrator Stephen Johnson's speech to the Global Chemical Regulations Conference, April 18, 2008

6. Schmidt, Sarah Canwest, July 12, 2008.

7. Sinclair, Scott NAFTA, Chapter 11 *Investor-State disputes*, Canadian Centre for Policy Alternatives, January 2008.

8. The Competition Policy Review Panel Report can be accessed at: www.ic.gc.ca/epic/site/cprp-gepmc.nsf/en/home.

9. Cited Diana Gibson and David Thompson, *Bitumen and plenty of jobs heading south to U.S.: Tories making a huge mistake not upgrading more, and 'scraping off the topsoil, Edmonton Journal*, March 24, 2008.

10. Cited at: http://www.ctv.ca/servlet/ArticleNews/story/CTVNews/20080302/nafta_democrats_080302/2008030

11. Cited IRC Americas Policy Program, Presidential candidates on Trade, March 13, 2008

12. Cited Maude Barlow, *Vancouver Sun*, March 3, 2008.

13. *Globe and Mail* February 28, 2008.

14. See transcript at: http://www.whitehouse.gov/news/releases/2008/04/20080422–5.html

15. Strategic Counsel, A Tale of Two Nations: State of Canadian/American Public Opinion, June 2008. www.thestrategiccounsel.com/our_news/polls/Canada-USA%20Poll%20-%20final2%20-%20posted2.pdf

1. Speech by the Leader of the Official Opposition to the National Caucus of the Conservative Party of Canada in Halifax, September 7, 2005, http://www.gowlings.com/resources/enewsletters/govbrief/Htmfiles/governmentBulletin12092005.en.html, accessed on July 8, 2008.

2. Conservative Party of Canada, Stand Up for Canada: 2006 Federal Election Platform, pp. 19, 44. http://www.conservative.ca/media/20060113-Platform.pdf, accessed on July 8, 2008.

3. Presentation by Guy Chevrette, President Executive Director, Quebec Forest Industry Council, to the House of Commons Standing Committee on International Trade, August 21, 2006, http://cmte.parl.gc.ca/cmte/CommitteePublication.aspx?SourceId=150817, accessed on July 8, 2008.

4. The CBC provides a comprehensive and accessible history of the softwood lumber dispute from 1982 to 2003: At Loggerheads: The Canada-U.S. Softwood Lumber Dispute, CBC News Indepth, http://www.cbc.ca/news/background/softwood_lumber/, accessed July 8, 2008.

5. The Expected U.S. Consumption (EUSC) and Prevailing Monthly Prices are posted on the website of the Department of Foreign Affairs and International Trade at http://www.international.gc.ca/trade/eicb/softwood/reports-en.asp.

6. Prime Minister announces Canada and U.S. reach softwood deal, April 27, 2006, http://pm.gc.ca/eng/media.asp?id=1141, accessed on July 8, 2008

7. CBC News, Canada wins another round in softwood battle with U.S., March 17, 2006, http://www.cbc.ca/money/story/2006/03/17/softwood-nafta060317.html, accessed on July 8, 2006.

8. CBC News, Canada wins softwood case at WTO, August 15, 2006, http://www.cbc.ca/money/story/2006/03/17/softwood-nafta060317.html, accessed on July 8, 2006.

9. Hamilton, Gordon, Court orders U.S. to repay all $5.3 billion in softwood duties, *Vancouver Sun*, October 14, 2006, http://www.canada.com/vancouversun/news/business/story.html?id=7a3d8697-fa6a-4efd-b1de-3ecb2fc5485d&p=1, accessed July 8, 2008.

10. Presentation by Carl Grenier, Vice-President, Free Trade Lumber Council, to the House of Commons Standing Committee on International Trade, May 29, 2006, http://cmte.parl.gc.ca/cmte/CommitteePublication.aspx?SourceId=145451, accessed on July 8, 2008.

11. Presentation by Jamie Lim, President and Director General, Ontario Forest Industries Association, to the House of Commons Standing Committee on International Trade, May 29, 2006, http://cmte.parl.gc.ca/cmte/CommitteePublication.aspx?SourceId=145451, accessed on July 8, 2008.

12. Presentation by John Brodrick, Project Manager, Buchanan Lumber, to the House of Commons Standing Committee on International Trade, August 21, 2006, http://cmte.parl.gc.ca/cmte/CommitteePublication.aspx?SourceId=150817, accessed on July 8, 2008.

13. Presentation by Mr. Simon Potter, Partner, McCarthy Tétrault LLP, As an Individual, to the House of Commons Standing Committee on International Trade, July 31, 2006, http://cmte.parl.gc.ca/cmte/CommitteePublication.aspx?SourceId=150608, accessed on July 8, 2008.

14. Gibson, Gordon, The 'Softwood Sellout Agreement' is not the final word, *Globe and Mail*, October 17, 2006, p. A21.

15. O'Neill, Peter, Emerson plays down leaked U.S. letter on softwood, CanWest News Service, June 21, 2006, http://www.canada.com/topics/news/national/story.html?id=794d2d04-a5dd-4eed-927c-fae6b40f613c&k=73817, accessed on July 8, 2008.

16. Statement by the Prime Minister on the softwood lumber agreement, August 22, 2006, http://pm.gc.ca/eng/media.asp?id=1289, accessed on July 8, 2008.

17. B.C. Government Supports Softwood Lumber Agreement, August 16, 2006, http://www2.news.gov.bc.ca/news_releases_2005–2009/2006OTP0135–001044.htm, accessed on July 8, 2008.

18. Toronto Star (The), U.S. Triggers Softwood Test, from Canadian Press, August 7, 2007, http://www.thestar.com/News/World/article/243952, accessed July 8, 2008.

19. Todgham Cherniak, Cyndee, London Court of Arbitration Issues Ruling in First Softwood Lumber Agreement Arbitration, Trade Lawyers Blog, March 8, 2008, http://www.tradelawyersblog.com/blog/article/london-court-of-arbitration-issues-ruling-in-first-softwood-lumber-agreement-arbitration/, accessed on July 8, 2008.

20. U.S. Custom HouseGuide, Additional Softwood Lumber Agreement Arbitration Planned, January 22, 2008, http://blogs.customhouseguide.com/news/?p=360, accessed July 8, 2008.

21. Hamilton, Gordon, U.S. ties Canadian lumber exporters in red tape, *Vancouver Sun*, May 14, 2008, http://www.canada.com/vancouversun/news/story.html?id=056a4c3d8f0e-46cf-b23d-b21009601067, accessed July 8, 2008.

22. Feldman, Elliot J., Replacing Law with Negotiation in International Trade, Baker Hostetler LLP, 2007.

23. *National Post*, Gone Soft on Softwood, April 28, 2006, http://www.nationalpost.com/news/story.html?id=e16c5646-ea96–4afc-9ec6-b9e42e4b3e61, accessed July 8, 2008.

24. Hamilton, Gordon, Court orders U.S. to repay all $5.3 billion in softwood duties, *Vancouver Sun*, October 14, 2006, http://www.canada.com/vancouversun/news/business/story.html?id=7a3d8697-fa6a-4efd-b1de-3ecb2fc5485d&p=1, accessed July 8, 2008.

1. Dugan, Kathleen and Kevin Easdale. "Colombian Free Trade Pact Shot Down: One Step Forward for the U.S., One Back for Canada." Council on Hemispheric Affairs, July 19, 2007. www.coha.org (Retrieved January 20, 2008).

2. Gordon, Todd. "Disaster in the Making:Canada Concludes Its Free Trade Agreement With Colombia." *The Bullet* (Socialist Project e-bulletin, 112, June 11, 2008).

3. Whittington, Wes. "PM sees payoff in adding Americas to foreign agenda." *The Toronto Star*, June 22, 2007. http://www.thestar.com/article/228271 (Retrieved July 24, 2008)

4. Berthiaume, Lee. "Emerson sees Americas as Extension of Continental Commercial Platform." *Embassy Magazine*, May 30, 2007.

5. Government of Canada, Office of the Prime Minister. "Prime Minister Addresses the Council on Foreign Relations." 25 September, 2007. www.pm.gc.ca

6. Harper, Tim. "Bush cites Harper on Free Trade...sort of." *Toronto Star*, December 5, 2007.

7. Government of the United States, White House. "President Discusses Free Trade Agreements." 12 October, 2007. www.whitehouse.gov

8. Government of the United States, Office of the White House "President Bush Visits Jacksonville, Florida, Discusses Trade Policy." March 18, 2008. www.whitehouse.gov

9. Government of the United States, Office of the White House "President Bush Discusses Colombia Free Trade Agreement", April 7, 2008. http://www.whitehouse.gov/news/releases/2008/04/20080407-1.html

10. Government of Canada, Comité permanent du commerce international (CIIT)/ Standing Committee on International Trade "Human Rights, the Environment and Free Trade with Colombia: 5th Report of the Standing Committee on International Trade." June, 2008. http://cmte.parl.gc.ca/cmte/CommitteeList.aspx?Lang=1&PARLSES=392&JNT=0&SELID=e22_.4&COM=13181&STAC=2393871

11. Ljunggren, David. "Canadian opposition slams Colombia free trade deal" *Reuters*, June 9, 2008

12. 39th Parliament, 2nd Session, Edited Hansard. Number 108, Monday, June 9, 2008. http://www2.parl.gc.ca/HousePublications/Publication.aspx?Language=E&Mode=1&Parl=39&Ses=2&DocId=3560493#Int-2518306%23Int-2518306

13. *El Tiempo*, "Ministro de Comercio inició gira en Washington para intentar 'descongelar' trámite del TLC", 9 de Junio, 2008. http://beta.eltiempo.com/archivo/documento/CMS-4243322 (Translation by Katz).

14. Goverment of Canada, Comité permanent du commerce international (CIIT)/Standing Committee on International Trade, "Human Rights, the Environment and Free Trade with Colombia." 5th Report of the Standing Committee on International Trade, June, 2008. http://cmte.parl.gc.ca/cmte/CommitteeList.aspx?Lang=1&PARLSES=392&JNT=0&SELID=e22_.4&COM=13181&STAC=2393871

15. Government of Canada, Comité permanent du commerce international (CIIT)/Standing Committee on International Trade Mission to Colombia, May 2008, Human Rights, the Environment and Free Trade with Colombia." 5th Report of the Standing Committee on International Trade, June, 2008. http://cmte.parl.gc.ca/cmte/CommitteeList.aspx?Lang=1&PARLSES=392&JNT=0&SELID=e22_.4&COM=13181&STAC=2393871

16. Collins, Michelle. "Wrangling Over Colombia Trade Deal Continues," *Embassy Magazine*, June 25, 2008. http://www.embassymag.ca/html/index.php?display=story&full_path=/2008/june/25/columbia/

17. Government of Canada, Foreign Affairs and International Trade, "Canada-Colombia Free Trade Negtiations," June 7, 2008. http://www.international.gc.ca/trade-agreements-accords-commerciaux/agr-acc/andean-andin/can-colombia-colombie.aspx (Retrieved June 26, 2008)

Racialization and (In)Security

Conservative Colours: The Harper Conservatives and the colour-coding of Canada

1. See video of Conservative member Tom Lukiwski and his anti-gay statements at http://www.cbc.ca/canada/saskatchewan/story/2008/04/03/lukiwski-video.html and "race card" comments by Jason Kenney at http://www.canada.com/ottawacitizen/news/story.html?id=61e93c71-44d8-4f73-96b4-f68a75dbfcc3

2. The Heritage Front Affair Report to the Solicitor General of Canada Security Intelligence Review Committee December 9, 1994 http://ftp.nizkor.org/hweb/orgs/canadian/sirc/heritage-front/

3. Ibid, Chapter 7 http://www1.ca.nizkor.org/hweb/orgs/canadian/sirc/heritage-front/75.html

4. Peter McKay, Minister of Foreign Affairs wrongly referred to the loss of only 8 family members of the El-Akhras, when he appeared in front of the Standing Committee on Foreign Affairs and International Development on August 1, 2006. Surviving family member, Hassan El-Kharas noted that in fact he lost 12 family members in the Israel attack. See http://tadamon.resist.ca/index.php/?p=213 where Hassan wrote a letter to the *National Post* dated August 23, 2006, which they refused to publish.

5. Standing Committee on Foreign Affairs and International Development, Tuesday, August 1, 2006 Edited evidence transcript Number 015 (Official Version) p. 22.

6. *Globe and Mail,* "The PM and his photographer" & "Evacuation begins in earnest" July 21, 2006 pp. 1, 10.

7. C.D. Howe Institute, The Passport Package: Rethinking the Citizenship benefits of non-resident Canadians John Chant, Dec. 2006 http://www.cdhowe.org/pdf/backgrounder_99.pdf

8. Op Cit.

9. Canwest News Service, "Dual citizenship review worries some MPS" December 22.

10. CBC News, "Ottawa reviewing rules of dual citizenship" Nov 7, 2006.

11. Ibid.

12. Numbers sourced from Standing Committee on Foreign Affairs and International Development, Tuesday, August 1, 2006 Edited evidence transcript Number 015 (Official Version) p. 22.

13. Conservatives to target urban, ethnic ridings in next *Election, The Hill* Times January 22, 2007 http://www.thehilltimes.ca/html/index.php?display=story&full_path=/2007/january/22/conservatives/&c=1

14. CBC News "Conservatives would reduce immigration barriers" January 4, 2006.

15. Press release, Conservative Party of Canada, 4 January 2006, http://www.conservative.ca/EN/1738/37785

16. Professor Micheal Keefer's essay, "The Harper Government and Canada's 'War-on-Terror' Immigration Policy" points out Harper counts among his formative influences the writings of the American right-wing intellectual Peter Brimelow, whose books include *Alien Nation: Common Sense About America's Immigration Disaster* (1995). In 2001 Harper gave voice to opinions that seem recognizably connected to Brimelow's alarmist vision of a country losing its cultural (read racial) identity in a swamp of ethnic otherness.

17. *Now Magazine,* "The Devil in Stephen Harper" June 3–9, 2004.

18. Report Canada's Independent Newsmagazine, "Stephen Harper: The Report Interview" January 6, 2002.

19. Citizenship and Immigration Canada (CIC), Immigration overview, Fact and Figures 2006; See also CIC data for stock of adult refugees by top source countries from 1997–2006.

20. Action, Access Diversity: A guide to multicultural/anti-racist organizational change December 1991 Section 1A.

21. *Globe and Mail,* "All immigration by 2030" March 14, 2007.

22. CLC Immigration briefing notes for Ambassadorial delegations Norway & Sweden, November 2006 (see also CIC Facts and Figures Immigration Overview documents). While economic hothouse cities in Canada are attracting newcomers the percentage is small by comparison. The next largest locales hosting newcomers—Calgary, Ottawa, Winnipeg—are far behind attracting less than 5% vs. 40%.

23. http://www.theglobeandmail.com/v5/content/pdf/ethnicOutreach.pdf

24. *The Hill Times*, "Conservatives to target urban, ethnic ridings in next election" July 228, 2008.

25. In May 2007, under Harper's leadership, the federal government finally announced an inquiry into the investigation of the Air India bombing. Supreme Court Justice John Major leads the inquiry and is free to hold public or in camera hearings. The Air India Flight 182 bombing took place in June 1985 and killed 329 people aboard the flight. The calls for this inquiry grew louder after two men charged in the bombings were set free after a lengthy trial found them not guilty. The judge ruled that the Crown's case against the charged men was too weak.

26. In the case of the Chinese head tax, in June 07, Harper offered a full apology to Chinese Canadians on behalf of the Government of Canada for charging the head tax from Chinese immigrants between 1885 and 1947. The federal government also offered "symbolic individual payments of $20,000 to living Chinese head tax payers and living spouses of deceased payers". In addition, the government announced the establishment of a "$24-million community historical recognition program to provide grant and contribution funding for community projects linked to wartime measures and immigration restrictions and a $10-million national historical recognition program to fund federal initiatives, developed in partnership with other stakeholders".

27. Library of Parliament: "Canadian Multiculturalism": March 2006 Excerpt: In the February 2005 budget, the Liberal government announced that $56 million would be invested over five years to implement Canada's Action Plan Against Racism. The budget also allocated $25 million over the next three years for an Acknowledgement, Commemoration, and Education Program that would undertake commemorative and educational initiatives to highlight the contributions of groups that have troubling memories as a result of historical events during times of war, or as a result of immigration policies of the day. In August and November 2005, as part of that program, the government announced agreements-inprinciple with the Ukrainian-Canadian, Italian-Canadian, and Chinese-Canadian communities. The Program would fund proposals that acknowledge the historical experience of these ethnocultural communities.

Meanwhile, in March 2005, the Liberal government released *A Canada for All: Canada's Action Plan Against Racism*. The Action Plan's objectives were to strengthen social cohesion, further Canada's human rights framework, and demonstrate federal leadership in the fight against racism and hate-motivated crime.

28. CLC report from the "National Task Force on Anti-Racism Durban follow-up report", October 2001.

29. CLC Letter to The Honourable Monte Solberg, Minister of Citizenship and Immigration Canada, September 12, 2006.

30. Minister Diane Finley, "Speaking Notes for the Honourable Diane Finley", Minister of Human Resources and Social Development public policy forum conference, "Integrating Immigrants: Building Partnerships That Work" Toronto March 19, 2006.

31. Ibid.

32. CLC Anti-Racism and Human Rights (AR&HR) Department. Changing Demographics Power Point July 2008.

33. Progressive Conservative Party, "Building Bridges with Ethnic Communities" March 2008. See slide 8.

34. See CLC AR&HR Department: Changing Demographics, July 2008; CLC Research Paper #34, Racial Status and Employment Outcomes, See also M. Ornstein studies on racial inequality.

35. *Canadian H*uman Resources *Reporter*, , "The Canadian Immigrant Labour Market in 2006", March 10, 2008.

36. Drummond, Don "If immigrants fall behind, all of Canada will join them".*Globe and Mail* May 2, 2008.

37. Op cit.

38. Department of Finance Canada Budget 2007, "Chapter 5: A stronger Canada through a stronger Economy: Knowledge Advantage." In addition to the $50.5 million over two years for the TWFP a $33.6 million allocation was made via CIC to improve the security side of the TFW program for a grand total of over $84.1M. Budget 2007 by comparison allocated $6.4 million to annual operation of the FCRO.

39. *Canadian Issues: Immigration and Families*, "Interview with Honourable Monte Solberg" pp. 7–9, Spring 2006.

40. Flecker, Karl. "Building 'The World's Most Flexible Workforce' The Harper government's double-doubling of the Foreign Worker Program", *Briarpatch Magazine* November 2007. Under the Conservatives, many changes have been made to the Foreign Worker Program and virtually all are focused on serving employers' demand for migrant workers as quickly as possible. For example, the Conservatives have established lists of occupations and sectors that qualify for fast tracking permits to import migrant labour, created a step-by-step guide in "employer-friendly language" on how to hire a foreign worker, and assigned government staff "to assist employers seeking to hire foreign workers in cases where a labour market opinion is not required."

41. Department of Finance Canada Budget 2007, "Chapter 5: A stronger Canada through a stronger Economy: Knowledge Advantage."

42. Alberta Federation of Labour, Temporary Foreign Workers-Alberta's Disposable Workforce, November, 2007. NB: In 2006, Alberta became the first province in Canada to bring more workers into the country under the TFW program than under the mainline immigration program. In 2007, that troubling trend accelerated with the number of TFWs growing to nearly double the number of new immigrants coming to the province.

43. Ibid. See also Flecker, Building 'The World's Most Flexible Workforce' " *Briarpatch Magazine* November 2007; http://www.canadianlabour.ca/en/Migrant_workers; www.migrants.ca; http://www.kairoscanada.org/e/refugees/migrants/index.asp;

44. CIC News Release: "Canada to accept up to 265,000 new immigrants in 2008 Ottawa", October 31, 2007

45. CLC AR&HR Department Briefing Note on the CEC initiative. January 2008

46. Report Canada's Independent Newsmagazine, "Stephen Harper: The Report Interview" January 6, 2002

47. See note 28.

48. Department. of Finance Canada News release, "Canada's New Government cuts wasteful programs, refocuses spending on priorities, achieves major debt reduction as promised", September 25, 2006.

49. *Toronto Star*, "Finley's bill side swipes Kenney", July 31, 2008.

50. See "OCASI comments on CIC's consultation on the new process for the selection of immigrants" October 2008; Scrap Bill C-50: joint statement, April 16, 08; 10 Reasons to be concerned about bill C-50; and CLC AR&HR Bill C-50 briefing note, May 2008.

51. See CLC Briefing Notes on Bill C-50 for a detailed critique of the bill's flaws.

52., "Contentious immigration ads to be extended: Another 2 million spending planned to sell reforms not yet passed by Parliament" *Globe and Mail* May 15, 2008 and "$1.1. ad campaign sells reforms not yet passed" *Globe and Mail* May 8, 2008.

53. Hansard, #102, 39th Parliament 2nd session, May 30, 2008 http://www2.parl.gc.ca/HousePublications/Publication.aspx?DocId=3532310&Language=E&Mode=1&Parl=39&Ses=2

54. CIC News release, "Government of Canada announces consultations on immigration priorities", July 3, 2008.

55., "New law would put skilled immigrants before families, opposition MP's say", *Globe and Mail* April 29. 2008 p. 4.

56. CIC backgrounder for consultations, http://www.cic.gc.ca/english/department/media/backgrounders/2008/2008–07–03a.asp

57. Ibid.

58. Correspondence with Tom Dufresne, President of ILWU Union, Sept 2007.

59. *The Dispatcher,* Tom Price, "Repressive new screening rules invade privacy, take jobs." Feb. 3. 2005.

60. Ibid.

Canada's Secret-Trial Detentions: The country's "intelligence" agencies set the agenda

1. Flecker, Karl,"Presentation to OSSTF Human Rights Conference, Ours to Defend", January 6, 2007

2. http://www.macleans.ca/article.jsp?content=20070209_104208_10076

3. Supreme Court of Canada, Charkaoui, February 23, 2007

4. Canadian Security Intelligence Service, "Summary of the Security Intelligence Report concerning Mohamed Zeki Mahjoub", February 22, 2008

5. Colin Freeze (Nov. 15, 2004) "CSIS has easy time getting warrants, documents reveal". *Globe and Mail* http://www.theglobeandmail.com/servlet/story/RTGAM.20041115.wxc-sis14/tional/

6. http://decisions.fct-cf.gc.ca/en/2007/2007fc1025/2007fc1025.html

7. Ibid

8. http://www.thestar.com/Unassigned/article/217952

9. http://groups.yahoo.com/group/NC4P/message/7523

10. Inspector General, CSIS, 2006, http://www.publicsafety.gc.ca/abt/wwa/igcsis/cert2006-eng.aspx

11. Colin Freeze. "CSIS has easy time getting warrants, documents reveal". *Globe and Mail* (November 15, 2004).

12. Kutty, Faisal. Passenger Protect Program: Too Guilty to Fly, Too Innocent to Charge. Social Science Research Network http://ssrn.com/abstract=962797 (January 31, 2007).

13. Christoff, Stefan. "Spies at work: CSIS questioning of Canadian Muslims threatens their jobs, *The Dominion*, http://www.dominionpaper.ca/articles/1119 (April 20, 2007).

14. Akkad, El, Omar. "Muslims Say CSIS Has Spies in Many Mosques", *Globe and Mail* (July 28, 2006).

15. CAIR-CAN, (2003) "Presumption of Guilt", 2004, http://www.caircan.ca/ps_more.php?id=2010_0_6_0_M) , also "In The Shadow of The Law", a report by the International Civil Liberties Monitoring Group (ICLMG), , www.devp.org/devpme/documents/ eng/pdf/InTheShadowOfTheLaw_ENG.pdf

16. Canadian Council of Refugees, submission on C-3, http://www.ccrweb.ca/documents/ C-3submission.pdf), also "Disclosure to the Defence after September 11", Peter Rosenthal.

17, Svalingam, Harini. "And Then They Came for the Tamilas," *Toronto Star*, (June 25, 2008); also "Rights, Limits, Security: A Comprehensive Review of the Anti-terrorism Act and Related Issues", (March, 2007) Report of the Standing Committee, Public Safety and National Security, http://cmte.parl.gc.ca/cmte/CommitteePublication.aspx?COM=10804&L ang=1&SourceId=199086

18. See Canadian Islamic Congress Annual Studies of Anti-Islam in Canadian Media http://www.canadianislamiccongress.com/rr/rr_index.php

19. Report of the Auditor General of Canada to the House of Commons(May 2008), Chapter 7, Detention and Removal of Individuals, Canadian Border Services Agency, p. 15 http://www.oag-bvg.gc.ca/internet/English/aud_ch_oag_200805_07_e_30703.html

20. http://decisions.fct-cf.gc.ca/en/2007/2007fc379/2007fc379.html

21. www.thestar.com/comment/columnists/article/281760

22. Gillespie, Bill, "The 9/11 effect: Has $24 billion made Canada safer? CBC http://www.cbc.ca/news/viewpoint/vp_gillespie/2008/03/the_real_cost_of_911_has_24_bi.html

Migrant Workers Under Harper: "Guests," servants and criminals

1. Sharma, N. (2006). "Home Economics: Nationalism and the Making of "Migrant Workers" in Canada." Toronto, University of Toronto Press, p. 67.

2. Justicia for Migrant Workers is now working with Alicia in a pilot project by selling her handmade Justicia tote bags as a way to supplement her income in order for her to stay with her son and in her community. Most women in her situation seek ways to migrate north as the only way to ensure survival.

Canada and International Human Rights: Opportunity abandoned

1. Creskey, Jim "New UN Rights Chief Moves Into Battered Office" *Embassy Magazine*. July 23, 2008

2. Akin, David, Canwest News Service. "Toews attacks Arbour in House: Calls human rights campaigner "a disgrace" on floor of Commons". June 17, 2008. www.canada.com/components/print.aspx?id=df4bc8-d901–495d-a5fl-d5423f6a53... Accessed 7/16/2008

3. L"Heureux-Dube, Clair "A disgraceful attack", *The Ottawa Citizen*, June 21, 2008.

4. Kinsman, Jeremy, CBC News, Diplomatically Speaking. "What brought down Louise Arbour", March 11, 2008. http://www.cbc.ca/news/viewpoint/vp_kinsman/20080311.html. accessed 7/17/2008

5. "Harper officials freeze out UN rights chief" *The Washington Times*, March 17, 2008

6. CBC News Online. "In depth: Louise Arbour", Updated March 11, 2008

7. Kay, Jonathan "Jonathan Kay on Louise Arbour: So long. You won't be missed" Posted: July 01, 2008, 1:59 PM http://network.nationalpost.com/np/blogs/fullcomment/archive/2008/07/01/jonathan-kay-on-louise-arbour-so-long-you-won-t-be-missed.aspx

8. United Nations High Commissioner for Human Rights. Presentation of the Office of the United Nations High Commissioner for Human Rights Ms. Louise Arbour to the International Conference on LGBT (Lesbian, Gays, Bisexual and Trasgender [sic] Human Rights. Montreal, 26 July 2006 http://www.unhchr.ch/huricane/huricane.nsf/view01/B91AE52651D33F0DC12571BE002F172C?opendocument

9. Richter, Paul and Holley, David, "Rice Fails To Clarify U.S. Vies on Torture" *The Los Angeles Times*. December 8, 2005

10. Edwards, Steven. Canwest News Service. "Israel to boycott UN anti-racism conference" February 24, 2008

11. Arbour's successor has not been named at time of writing. *The Washington Times* reported (June 27, 2008) that President Jose Ramos-Horta of East Timor had stated he had been invited to take up the post and had accepted, but UN Secretary-General Ban Kimoon denied that he had made a final decision on the appointment. Pisik, Betsy. "Ban denies he has filled human rights post", *The Washington Times*. June 27, 2008.

12. "Harper officials freeze out UN rights chief", *The Washington Times*. March 17, 2008.

13. Associated Press. "UN Human Rights Chief Louise Arbour Announces Resignation", March 07, 2008. www.foxnews.com/world/index.html

14. "Louise Arbour Steps Down". Danish Institute for Human Rights. Denmark's National Human Rights Institution. March, 2008. See also the "Welcome home" salute to Arbour in the Osgood Hall Law School (York University) blog *The Court*, for April 10, 2008. http://www.thecourt.ca/2008/04/10/louise-arbour-welcome-home/

15. Kinsman, Jeremy, CBC News, Diplomatically Speaking. "What brought down Louise Arbour", March 11, 2008. http://www.cbc.ca/news/viewpoint/vp_kinsman/20080311.html. accessed 7/17/2008

16. Canadian Hertitage. Multilateral human rights treaties to which Canada is a party. http://www.pch.gc.ca/progs/pdp-hrp/docs/treat-trait/index_e.cfm

17. Security analyst Maureen Webb, notes that many of the recommendations of Commission of Inquiry into the Arar case remain without implemented more than a year after being issued. See Webb, Maureen. "Security Integration and Rights Disintegration In the Post 9–11 World." Lawyers' Rights Watch Canada. March 15, 2008.

18. Austen, Ian, "Canada to rewrite torture manual linking U.S. and torture" *The New York Times*. January 20, 2008. http://www.alertnet.org/thenews/newsdesk/N17388465.htm The Times description includes reference to one slide" titled "Definition of Torture," lists six "U.S. interrogation techniques" that it describes as nonphysical, including blindfolding, covering heads in hoods, forced nudity and sleep deprivation."

19. "Canada puts U.S., Guantanamo and Israel on torture 'watch list'" On Deadline. *USAToday.* 17/01/08 blogs.usatoday.com/ondeadline/2008/01/canada-puts-us.html See also "Canada puts U.S. on torture watch list: CTV", January 16, 2008 www.ctv.ca and David Ljunggren. "Canada Places U.S., Israel on Torture Watch List" Reuters. Friday, January 18, 2008

20. Turley, Jonathan. "Canada Lists the United States as a Torture Nation", January 19, 2008 http://jonathanturley.org/2008/01/19/canada-lists-the-united-states-as-a-torture-nation/

21. Lljunggren, David, "Canada takes U.S., Israel off torture watchlist", Reuters Alert Net, January 19, 2008 http://www.alertnet.org/thenews/newsdesk/N17388465.htm

22. Foreign Affairs and International Trade Canada. "Minister Bernier Requests Review of Training Manual" News Release. January 19, 2008. No. 15 www.international.gc.ca/index.aspx

23. Morris, Helen, *Canwest News Service.* "Shame on Bernier to remove U.S. and Israel from torture list." January 20, 2008.

24. Boychuk, Regan. "A History of Hypocrisy: Canadian complicity links U.S. Cold War torture with cases like Maher Arar's." An Essay. Literary Review of Canada. Vol.16, No. 4. May 2008. Boychuk reviews the Canadian participation in the CIA's extensive development of psychological torture techniques in the 2950, with "sensory deprivation" including "sleep deprivation" at its core. Included in the scheme was research undertaken by two McGill University professors, Donald Hebb, chair of the Psychology Department and Ewen Cameron, director of the Allan Memorial Institute, which received "lavish" funding from the Canadian government.

25. Cooper, Barry, "Re: A History of Hypocrisy" *LRC* May 2008.

26. Wark, Wesley, "Re: A History of Hypocrisy" *LRC* May 2008.

27. Paris, Erna, "Re: A Ceaseless Search for Justice" *LRC* May 2008.

28. See for example CTV News staff. "Interrogation video to show wounded, tearful Khadr", Monday, July 14, 2008. www.ctv.ca

29. Curry, Bill "Ottawa defends role in renditions." *The Globe and Mail,* January 8, 2008

30. Canadian Arab Federation & International Civil Liberties Monitoring Group. "Canada, Under Harper, Supports Use of Torture". *News Release.* Toronto. July 10, 2008. www. caf. ca

31. Broadbent, Ed and Neve, Alex. "Prime Minister Harper is complicit in this injustice: Omar Khadr's rights are being trampled at Guantanamo", Toronto. *The Globe and Mail,* July 15, 2008

32. Lakritz, Naomi. "Ottawa should do the right thing and bring Khadr home". *The Calgary Herald*, July 18, 2008. Kapoustin is the Canadian businessman imprisoned for 12 years in Bulgaria on charges of fraud and embezzlement, returned to Canada in mid-2008, due to what Secretary of State Jason Kenny referred to as "extraordinary lengths" undertaken by the government on his behalf.

33. Open letter from over 100 legal experts and scholars. UN Declaration on the Rights of Indigenous Peoples: Canada Needs to Implement This New Human Rights Instrument, May 1, 2008 Legal scholars and experts urge Canadian government to abandon "erroneous" and "misleading" opposition to *UN Declaration on the Rights of Indigenous Peoples* http://www.itk.ca/Media-Release-Archive/2008/press-archive-20080501.html

34. CBC News. "PM cites 'sad chapter' in apology for residential schools", Wednesday, June 11, 2008 http://www.cbc.ca/canada/story/2008/06/11/aboriginal-apology.html

35. The Declaration builds on the other primary international instrument recognizing indigenous peoples, the ILO Convention 169 (1989) Concerning Indigenous and Tribal Peoples in Independent Countries. The fact that it has only been ratified to date by 19 countries (13 of them in South America) testifies to the difficulties facing such initiatives. The vote in the General Assembly would appear to indicate some forward movement.

36. Indian and Northern Affairs Canada. "Statement by Canada's New Government Regarding the United Nations Declaration on The Rights of Indigenous Peoples." Ottawa, September 12, 2007/ 2–2036. http://www.ainc-inac.gc.ca/nr/prs/s-d2007/2–2936-eng.asp

37. Ibid.

38. "Indigenous rights, indigenous wrongs: risks for the resource sector" Briefing. Ethical Investment Research Services and Centre for Australian Ethical Research. October 2007.

39. Cevallos, Diego. "Latin America: Native Leaders Half-Heartedly Embrace 'Historic' Declaration", Mexico. Inter-Press Service (IPS) September 14, 2007.

40. Ibid.

41. Joint Statement by International Non-Government Organizations. Rights and Democracy and KAIROS were among the organizations making the statement. 14 September, 2007

42. Fontaine, Simon and Chartier Congratulate Canadian Parliament for their support of the United Nations Declaration on Rights of Indigenous Peoples. Release. AFN. April 9, 2008. http://www.afn.ca/article.asp?id=4067

43. White, Marianne, "AFN urge premiers to back UN rights declaration" *The Leader Post*. Regina. July 15, 2008. http://www.canada.com/reginaleaderpost/news/story.html?id=0f64cdc6–7181–40ab-81a1–326d64ec7675

44. Amnesty International (Canada) Canada and the International Protection of Human Rights: An Erosion of Leadership?. Ottawa, Amnesty International (Canada). December, 2007.

45. AFN National Chief Phil Fontaine, Former Conservative Minister, Urge Support for passage of the UN Declaration on the Rights of Indigenous Peoples. *NationTalk*. August 9, 2007. http://www.nationtalk.ca/modules/news/article.php?storyid=2572

46. Legal scholars and experts urge Canadian government to abandon "erroneous" and "misleading" opposition to *UN Declaration on the Rights of Indigenous Peoples* http://www.itk.ca/Media-Release-Archive/2008/press-archive-20080501.html

47. Indian and Northern Affairs Canada. Statement by Ambassador John McNee Permanent Representative of Canada to the United Nations to the 61st Session of the General Assembly on the Declaration on the Rights of Indigenous Peoples. New York, September 13, 2007. www.ainc-inac.gc.ca/ird/2007/undir_e.html

48. Letter to Hon. Kevin Rudd, M.P., Prime Minister from Kevin Lynch and Megan Davis. 16 May, 2008. www.ilc.unsw.edu.au.news&events/documents

49. Gale Courey Toensing, "Endorsing their rights", Indian Country Today, April 21, 2008

50. Indian and Northern Affairs Canada. Speaking Notes for the Honourable Chuck Strahl, PC, MP Minister of Indian Affairs and Northern Development and Federal Interlocutor for Metis and Non-Status Indians to the Luncheon hosted by Canada's Permanent Mission to the United Nations. New York, N.Y. May 1, 2008. www.ainc-inac.gc.ca/nr/spch/ma2008/may0108-eng.asp

51. Office of the High Commissioner for Human Rights. Special Rapporteur on the situation of human rights and fundamental freedoms of indigenous people. http://www2.ohchr.org/english/issues/indigenous/rapporteur/

52. Amnesty International (Canada) Canada and the International Protection of Human Rights: An Erosion of Leadership? Ottawa, Amnesty International (Canada). December, 2007.

53. White, Marianne, "AFN urge premiers to back UN rights declaration" *The Leader Post.* Regina. July 15, 2008. http://www.canada.com/reginaleaderpost/news/story.html?id=0f64cdc6–7181–40ab-81a1–326d64ec7675

54. White, Marianne, "Council addressing First Nations issues", *The Leader Post.* Regina. July 17, 2008

55. Legal scholars and experts urge Canadian government to abandon "erroneous" and "misleading" opposition to *UN Declaration on the Rights of Indigenous Peoples* http://www.itk.ca/Media-Release-Archive/2008/press-archive-20080501.html

56. Webb, Maureen, Security Integration and Rights Disintegration in the Post 9–11 World. *Lawyers Rights Watch Canada.* March 15, 2008.

57. Amnesty International (Canada). Canada and the International Protection of Human Rights: An Erosion of Leadership? Ottawa, Amnesty International (Canada). December, 2007.

Energy and Environment

Stuck in the Muck: The Harper tar sands legacy

1. Flint, Len. "*Oil Sands Experts Group Workshop Houston Texas, January 24–25, 2006*" Leneff Consulting (1994) http://www.rqic.alternatives.ca/psp/os_ spp_wwr.pdf (January 31, 2006).

2. Asbreuk, Lisa M. "*Proposed Major Oils Sands Project GHG Emissions Subject of Litigation* " Toronto: McCarthy Tetrault LLP http://www.mccarthy.ca/article_ detail.aspx?id=4001 and Ecojustice news releases (May 23, 2008).

3. For a chronology of the Kearl litigation see: "*Backgrounder: Kearl Tar Sands Litigation Ecojustice,*" (June 2008). http://www.ecojustice.ca/media-centre/media-backgrounder/backgrounder-kearl-tar-sands-litigation

4. Herbert, Yuill. "Smoking in the Greenhouse". *The Dominion*. October 29, 2007.

5. Clarke, Tony; Campbell, Bruce; & Laxer, Gordon.(2006) "*Fuelling Fortress America*", Ottawa: Canadian Centre for Policy Alternatives.

6. Ibid.

7. Environment Canada news release on CNW Telbec. "*Economic Analysis shows implementing Bill C-288 would plunge Canada into a recession*". (April 19, 2007).

8. Wakefield, Benjamin J. and Price, Matt. (June 2008) "*Tar Sands: Feeding U.S. Refinery Expansions with Dirty Fuel*" Washington D.C.: The Environmental Integrity Project and Environmental Defence. http://www.environmentalintegrity.org

9. Environment Canada (March, 2008) "*Turning the Corner: Regulatory Framework for Industrial Greenhouse Gas Emissions*" Ottawa. http://www.ec-oc.ca/doc/virage-corner/2008–03/541_eng.htm

10. De Souza, Mike "Oil Sands Emissions Could Triple Under Conservative Plan" *Vancouver Sun*, March 14, 2008.

11. Penikett, Tony (2006) "*Reconciliation: First Nations Treaty Making in British Columbia*" Vancouver: Douglas and McIntyre, pages 68 and 69.

12. Woodfor, Peter "Health Canada Muzzles Oil Sands Whistleblower" *National Review of Medicine*, March 30, 2007, Volume 4, No. 6. http://www.nationalreviewofmedicine.com/issue/2007/03_30/4_policy_politics1_6.html

13. Lanktree, Graham "Oil Sands Whistleblower MD Cleared", *National Review of Medicine* January 15, 2008, Volume 5, No. 1. http://www.nationalreviewofmedicine.com/issue/2008/01_15/5_patients_practice02_1.html

14. For more on the health issues facing Fort Chipewyan, see: Hatch, Christopher and Price, Matt. (February 2008) "*Canada's Toxic Tar Sands: The Most Destructive Project on Earth*", Toronto: Environmental Defence. http://www.environmentaldefence.ca/reports/tarsands.htm and Brethour, Patrick "Why is Cancer Sweeping Tiny Fort Chipewyan?" *Globe and Mail* ,May 22, 2006. http://www.commondreams.org/headlines06/0522-05.htm

15. Murphy, Tim. "Temporary Labour or Disposable Workers?" *The Dominion,* November 24, 2007.

16. "Canada's guest workers; not such a warm welcome". *The Economist*. November 22, 2007.

17. For much more background on the SPP, see the "Integrate This" website of the Council of Canadians. http://www.canadians.org/integratethis/

18. Flint, Len. (January 31, 2006) "*Oil Sands Experts Group Workshop, Houston, January 24–25, 2006*" Lenef Consulting (1994). http://www.rqic.alternatives.ca/psp/os_spp_wwr.pdf

19. Acuna, Richard. "Time for us to say 'No More Oil for U.S. War", *Vue Weekly* January 17, 2008. http://www.tarsandswatch.org/time-us-say-no-more-oil-war-us

20. Shrybman, Steven. "*Petition to the Governor in Council regarding applications to the National Energy Board by Enbridge for the Southern Lights and Alberta Clipper Expansion Projects* " Sack, Goldblatt and Mitchell on behalf of the Communications, Energy and Paperworkers Union of Canada. http://blogs.cep.ca (March 14, 2008).

21. Shrybman, Steven. *"Petition to the Governor in Council regarding an application to the National Energy Board by Trans Canada Corporation for the Keystone Pipeline"* Sack, Goldblatt and Mitchell on behalf of the Communications, Energy and Paperworkers Union of Canada. http://blogs.cep.ca (October 17, 2007).

22. Hatch, Christopher and Price, Matt. (2008). *"Canada's Toxic Tar Sands: The Most Destructive Project on Earth"* Toronto: Environmental Defence. http://www.environmentaldefence.ca/reports/tarsands.htm

23. Campbell, Charles. "The Tar Sands come to Kitimat," *Lands and People,* March 22, 2007. Dogwood Initiative. http://www.dogwoodinitiative.org/

24. Pollen, Christopher. "B.C.'s Big Pipeline Plans Draw Fire from First Nations", *The Tyee,* August 23, 2006. http://thetyee.ca/News/2006/08/23/Enbridge/

25. Harding, Jon. "Kinder Morgan ramping up pipeline plans," *Vancouver Sun*, July 2, 2008.

26. Foster, Jason. (2008). "Manufacturing Gone Missing: Canada's Economic Disappearing Act," *Our Times,* http://ourtimes.ca/Featured_Story/article_59.php

27. Dillon, John and Ian Thomson. (2008) *"Pumped Up: How Canada subsidizes fossil fuels at the expense of green alternatives,"* Toronto: Kairos Canadian Ecumenical Justice Initiatives. http://www.kairoscanada.org/ and Taylor, Amy. (February 2007) "*Submission to Standing Committee on Finance*". Calgary: Pembina Institute. http://www.pembina.org/pub/1378

28. Ibid. Dillon and Thomson quoting Hydrocarbon Depletion Study Group of Uppsala University in Sweden.

29. Government of Alberta. (December 29, 2006). "*Investing in our Future: Responding to the Rapid Growth of Oil Sands Development — Final Report Oil Sands Ministerial Strategy Committee*". Edmonton. http://www.alberta.ca/home/395.cfm

30. Standing Committee on Natural Resources of the House of Commons of Canada (March 2007) *"The Oil Sands: Toward Sustainable Development"*. Ottawa. http://cmte.parl.gc.ca/Content/hOC/committee/391/rnnr/reports/rp2614277/rnrrp04/04_TOC_Feds_Eng.htm

31. Environment Canada (2004). "*Western Boreal Conservation Initiative — Backgrounder*" Ottawa.

32. Woynillowicz, Dan. "The Harm the Tar Sands Will Do," *The Tyee*, September 20, 2007. http://thetyee.ca/Views/2007/09/20/TarSands/print.html

33. There are many campaigns on the tar sands to connect to. Just a few include:

Indigenous Environmental Network http://www.ienearth.org/CITSC/Sand_Tar_Campaign.html

Polaris Institute—Tar Sands Watch http://www.tarsandswatch.org

Oil Sands Truth http://www.oilsandstruth.org

Greenpeace Canada http://www.greenpeace.org/Canada/en/campaigns/tarsands

Dogwood Initiative—No Tankers http://www.dogwoodinitiative.org

Communications, Energy and Paperworkers Union of Canadahttp://blogs.cep.ca

Tar Sands Free B.C. http://www.tarsandsfreebc.org

Environmental Defence http://www.environmentaldefence.ca

Downstream From the Tar Sands, People are Dying

1. Timoney, Kevin P. *A Study of Water and Sediment Quality as Related to Public Health Issues, Fort Chipewyan, Alberta.* Fort Chipewyan, Alberta: Nunee Health Board Society, http://www.connectingthedrops.ca/docs/fc-final-report-revised-dec2007.pdf, p. 62.

2. Hatch, Christopher, and Matt Price. (2008). *Canada's Toxic Tar Sands: The Most Destructive Project on Earth.* Toronto: Environmental Defence, p. 3.

3. Montgomery, Shannon. "Those Touched by Cancer on Alberta Reserve tell Their Stories at Legislature," *The Canadian Press*, March 1, 2008, http://www.tarsandswatch.org/those-touched-cancer-alberta-reserve-tell-their-stories-legislature.

4. Ibid.

5. Harden, Andrea and Holly Levalliant. (May 2008). "4. Fort Chipewyan". *Boiling Point: Six community profiles of the water crisis facing First Nations within Canada,* Polaris Institute p. 17

6. Knudson, Tom. "The Oilsands Downstream Worries; Along the Athabasca River North of the Oilsands, Euphoria over the boom is met with fear over Habitat loss, Rising Emissions and Growing Concerns about Cancer," *Calgary Business*, January 6, 2008.

7. Timoney, Kevin P. *A Study of Water and Sediment Quality as Related to Public Health Issues, Fort Chipewyan, Alberta.* Fort Chipewyan, Alberta: Nunee Health Board Society, http://www.connectingthedrops.ca/docs/fc-final-report-revised-dec2007.pdf

8. Harden, Andrea and Holly Levalliant. (2008). *Boiling Point! Six community profiles of the water crisis facing First Nations within Canada.* Ottawa: Polaris Institute, Assembly of First Nations and Canadian Labour Congress, p. 16–19.

9. http://www.keepersofthewater.ca

10. Keepers of the Water III Conference Program 2008 http://www.keepersofthewater.ca/keepers3/program2008.pdf

11. Hatch, Christopher and Matt Price. (2008). *Canada's Toxic Tar Sands: The Most Destructive Project on Earth.* Toronto: Environmental Defence, p. 6.

12. Harden, Andrea and Holly Levalliant. (2008). *Boiling Point! Six community profiles of the water crisis facing First Nations within Canada.* Ottawa: Polaris Institute, Assembly of First Nations and Canadian Labour Congress.

13. http://mikisew.org/ ; http://www.atc97.org/acfn.html.

The Harper Government and Climate Change: Lost at sea?

1. The authors would like to thank Clare Demerse (Pembina Institute) and Dale Marshall (David Suzuki Foundation) for their comments on an earlier draft of this chapter, but the authors are solely responsible for any errors or omissions.

2. Available on-line at Climate Action Network website: *Harper Talks Kyoto.* http://www.climateactionnetwork.ca/e/issues/harper-talks-kyoto.html

3. Conservative Party of Canada (2006). *Stand up for Canada: Conservative Party of Canada Federal Election Platform 2006.* p. 37.

4. Bhattacharya, Shaoni (2003). "European heatwave caused 35,000 deaths". *New Scientist.* 10 October 2003. http://www.newscientist.com/article.ns?id=dn4259

5. Stern, Nicholas (2006). The Stern Review on the Economics of Climate Change. London, U.K. Treasury www.sternreview.org.uk/

6. Intergovernmental Panel on Climate Change (2007). *IPCC Fourth Assessment Report.* Geneva, IPCC http://www.ipcc.ch/

7. Environment Canada (2006). *Canada's 2004 greenhouse gas inventory.* http://www.ec.gc.ca/pdb/ghg/inventory_report/2004/2004summary_e.cfm

8. NRTEE (2005). *Economic Instruments for Long term Reductions in Energy based Carbon Emissions.* Ottawa, NRTEE, 2005; http://www.nrtee-trnee.ca/eng/publications/energy-based-carbon-emissions/index-energy-based-carbon-emissions-eng.htm ; Marc Jaccard et al (2006). *Burning our Money to Warm the Planet.* Toronto, C.D. Howe Institute, May 2006. http://www.cdhowe.org/pdf/Commentary_234.pdf

9. Marshall, Dale (2004). "The Gap Between Rhetoric and Action: Paul Martin's Environmental Record" in *Hell and High Water.* Ottawa, Canadian Centre for Policy Alternatives.

10. http://www.oag-bvg.gc.ca/internet/English/aud_ch_cesd_200609_0_e_14982.html

11. Sallot, Jeff "Kyoto plan no good, minister argues". *Globe and Mail,* Saturday April 8, 2006. p. A5

12. Government of Canada (2006). *The Budget Plan 2006.* Ottawa pp. 124, 161. http://www.fin.gc.ca/budget06/pdf/bp2006e.pdf

13. Sierra Club of Canada (2007). *Kyoto Report Card 2007.* Ottawa, Sierra Club of Canada.

p. 16. http://www.sierraclub.ca/national/kyoto/kyoto-report-card-2007.pdf

14. Sierra Club of Canada (2007). *Kyoto Report Card 2007.* Ottawa, Sierra Club of Canada. pp. 2, 16. http://www.sierraclub.ca/national/kyoto/kyoto-report-card-2007.pdf

15. Pembina Institute (2007). *A Preliminary Analysis of Bill C-30 — The Clean Air Act.* Ottawa, Pembina Institute. http://pubs.pembina.org/reports/CAA-analysis_oct2006_MW.pdf

16. Forge, Frederic 2007. *Biofuels—An Energy, Environmental or Agricultural Policy?,* Library of Parliament, 8 February 2007. http://www.parl.gc.ca/information/library/PRBpubs/prb0637-e.pdf;

17. Parliament of Canada, LEGISinfo. Bill C-288. *An Act to ensure Canada meets its global climate change obligations under the Kyoto Protocol* http://www.parl.gc.ca/legisinfo/index.asp?Language=E&query=4741&List=toc&Session=14

18. Government of Canada (2007a). *The Cost of Bill C-288 to Canadian Families and Business.* Ottawa, Environment Canada. http://www.ec.gc.ca/doc/media/m_123/report_eng.pdf

19. Government of Canada (2007b). *Regulatory Framework for Air Emissions.* Ottawa, Environment Canada. http://www.ec.gc.ca/doc/media/m_124/toc_eng.htm

20. Bramley, Matthew (2007). *Analysis of the Government of Canada's April 2007 Greenhouse Gas Policy Anouncement.* Ottawa, Pembina Institute. http://pubs.pembina.org/reports/Reg_framework_comments.pdf

21. Prime Minister Stephen Harper calls for international consensus on climate change. http://pm.gc.ca/eng/media.asp?category=2&id=1681

22. CBC News in depth. *Kyoto Alternative*, September 27, 2007. http://www.cbc.ca/news/background/kyoto/asia-pacific-partnership.html

23. Demerse, Clare, Matthew Bramley and Dale Marshall (2007). *Canada in Bali: A Backgrounder on the 2007 UN Climate Negotiations.* Ottawa, Pembina Institute. November 22, 2007. p. 8 http://pubs.pembina.org/reports/Bali-backgrounder.pdf

24. UNFCC. The United Nations Climate Change Conference in Bali. http://unfccc.int/meetings/cop_13/items/4049.php

25. Sierra Club of Canada (2008). Kyoto Report Card 2008 *Lead, follow, or get out of the way.* Ottawa, February 13, 2008. http://www.sierraclub.ca/national/kyoto/kyoto-report-card-2008.pdf

26. NRTEE (2007). *Getting to 2050: Canada's Transition to a Low-emission Future.* Ottawa, NRTEE, January 2008.http://www.nrtee-trnee.ca/eng/publications/getting-to-2050/Getting-to-2050-low-res-eng.pdf

27. http://www.bcbudget.gov.bc.ca/2008/default.htm

28. Fong, Petti (2008). B.C. unveils carbon tax plan. *Toronto Star*, February 20, 2008. http://www.thestar.com/News/Canada/article/305170

29. Government of Canada (2008). *Government Delivers Details of Greenhouse Gas Regulatory Framework.* http://www.ecoaction.gc.ca/news-nouvelles/20080310-eng.cfm; Demerse, Clare and Matthew Bramley (2008). *The March 2008 Federal Regulatory Framework for Industrial Greenhouse Gas Emissions.* Ottawa, Pembina Institute, March 2008.http://www.climateactionnetwork.ca/e/resources/publications/member/reg-framework-update-03–2008.pdf

30. McCarthy, Shawn (2008). "A lobby machine that runs on ethanol". *Globe and Mail,* May 30, 2008. http://www.tficb.com/News.aspx?id=23908

31. Harris/Decima (2008a). *Understanding Modern Environmentalism.* April 8, 2008.p. 31. http://www.slideshare.net/adk338/understanding-modern-environmentalism-byharris-decima-april-08/

32. Baird's initial reaction to Dion's announcement was quoted as: "I think Canadians, you know, this tax will be revenue neutral it's like the cheque is in the mail, it's like I'll respect you in the morning."

33. O'Neill, Julliet and Akin, David (2008). "Harper calls it a crazy plan". *National Post*, June 20, 2008. http://www.nationalpost.com/related/links/story.html?id=599795

34. Harris/Decima (2008b). *Pricy Oil Fules More, not Less, Environmentalism.* July 8, 2008. http://www.decima.com/en/pdf/news_releases/080708E.pdf

Policy Drought: The Harper government's mismanagement of Canada's water

1. Bakker, Karen (2006) *Eau Canada; The Future of Canada's Water*, UBC Press

2. "Clean, Safe and Secure Water: The Need for Federal Leadership," 2005, leaked Environment Canada internal document

3. Budget 2008: http://www.budget.gc.ca/2008/home-accueil-eng.asp

4. Centre for Strategic and International Studies, (2007) "North American Future 2025 Project": http://www.canadians.org/DI/index.html

5. Environment Canada news release, April 2007: http://www.ec.gc.ca/default.asp?lang=En&n=714D9AAE-1&news=B362E955–305B-49FB-BA8B-AD6292238387

6. Heinmiller, Timothy (2003) "Emulation: Federalism and Water Export Policy in Canada," Candian Public Administration Journal,.

7. Barlow, Maude (2007). *Blue Covenant: The Global Water Crisis and the Coming Battle for the Right to Water.* Toronto: *Mclelland and Stuart*, p. 190

8. Centre on Housing Rights and Eviction, meeting notes, March 2008.

9. "Mining Projects in Canada for Which Companies have Proposed the Use of Healthy Natural Water Bodies for Mine Waste Disposal",adapted from Environment Canada (2007) by *Mining Watch Canada*

10. "Lakes across Canada face Being Turned into Mine Dump Sites": http://www.cbc.ca/canada/story/2008/06/16/condemned-lakes.html

Putting Commerce Before Safety in the Nuclear Industry

1. Ferguson, Rob. "Safety concerns raised about Pickering B plant; Utility plays down watchdog's letter warning of 'erosion of safety margins'" *The Toronto Star.* Wednesday, May 14, 2008.

2. Wikipedia. Precautionary principle. http://en.wikipedia.org/wiki/Precautionary_principle

Pat Mooney's Testimony On Biofuels to the Canadian Senate

1. Testimony of Pat Mooney before the Standing Committee on Energy, the Environment and Natural Resources-regarding Bill C-33 (the "Biofuels Bill") Senate of Canada, Wednesday, June 25, 2008 http://etcblog.org/2008/06/27/pat-mooneys-biofuels-testimony-in-the-canadian-senate/

2. Government of Canada, (2008) *The Budget Plan 2008* , p. 164 ; Curry, Bill and Kevin Carmichael, "Harper's biofuels policy sputters out on the Hill" *Globe and Mail* April 30, 2008 http://www.theglobeandmail.com/servlet/story/RTGAM.20080430.wethanol30/BNStory/specialComment

3. Government of Canada, "The Government of Canada Biofuels Bill receives Royal Assent" Newsrelease, June 26, 2008 http://ecoaction.gc.ca/news-nouvelles/20080626-eng.cfm?rss

(In)equality and Public Services

Women's Equality and Human Rights

1. Quoted in Beattie, 2006: A12

2. Quoted in *O'Neill, 2006: A17*

3. Quoted in *Beattie, 2006: A12*

4. Brodie, Janine "We are all equal now: Contemporary gender politics in Canada" *Feminist Theory* 9(2) 2008 pp. 145–164

5. Gidengil, Elizabeth et al., "Women to the Left/Men to the Right", 2006, http://www.ces-eec.umontreal.ca/documents/CES2006gendergap.pdf

6. Gidengil, Elizabeth et al., "Women to the Left/Men to the Right", 2006, http://www.ces-eec.umontreal.ca/documents/CES2006gendergap.pdf

7. Gidengil, Elizabeth et al., "Women to the Left/Men to the Right", 2006, http://www.ces-eec.umontreal.ca/documents/CES2006gendergap.pdf

8. Lang-Dion, Raylene & Wicks, Anne, "Women in Politics: Still Looking for an Equal Voice" Spring 2008, http://www.parl.gc.ca/Infoparl/31/1/31n1_08e_Wicks-Lang-Dion.pdf

9. Lang-Dion, Raylene & Wicks, Anne, "Equal Voice: Electing More Women in Canada", Canada Parliamentary Review, Vol 30 no 1, 2007 , http://www.parl.gc.ca/Infoparl/english/issue.htm?param=180&art=1231

10. Harper, Stephen, National Citizens' Coalition *Overview*, Fall 1998 (Cookbook for Women's Equality, p. 19)

11. Jackson, Andrew "Women in the Workforce : Still a long way from equality", Canadian Labour Congress, 2008, p7, Table 1.

12. Jackson, "Women in the Workforce", p. 7

13. Pay Equity Task Force, *Pay Equity:A Fundamental Human Right*, Ottawa, 2004, p. 36 and 41.

14. National Association for Women and the Law, *Jurisfemme*, Spring 2007.)

15. Yalnizyan, Armine, Canadian Centre for Policy Alternatives, "Budget 2008: What's in it for Women?" March 2008 p. 17, http://www.growinggap.ca/files/Budget_2008_Whats_in_it_for_women.pdf

Harper and Child Care

1. Battle, Ken. (2006). *The Choice in Child Care Allowance: What You See Is Not What You Get.* Ottawa: Caledon Institute of Social Policy, p. 2.

2. Urquhart, Ian. "Premiers Rebuff Child Care Advocates," *Toronto Star*, August 2, 2006.

3. Environics Research Group. (2006). *Canadians' Attitudes Toward National Child Care Policy.* Ottawa: Environics Research Group, p. 2.

4. Code Blue for Child Care. (2006). *What's Wrong with the Federal Child Care Spaces Initiative?* Ottawa: www.buildchildcare.ca.

5. Childcare Resource and Research Unit. (2007). *Trends & Analysis 2007: Early childhood education and care in Canada 2006."* Toronto: Childcare Resource and Research Unit, p. 5.

6. Department of Finance Canada. (2007). *The Budget Plan 2007.* Ottawa: Government of Canada, p. 126.

7. Friendly, Beach, Ferns and Turiano. (2007). *Early childhood education and care in Canada 2006, 7th Edition.* Toronto: Childcare Resource and Research Unit, p. 205.

8. Childcare Resource and Research Unit. (2007). *Child Care Space Statistics 2007.* Toronto: Childcare Resource and Research Unit, p. 1.

9. Savoie, Denise. (2006). *Bill 303: An Act to establish criteria and conditions in respect of funding for early learning and child care programs in order to ensure the quality, accessibility, universality and accountability of those programs, and to appoint a council to advise the Minister of Human Resources and Skills Development on matters relating to early learning and child care.* Ottawa: Parliament of Canada.

Retro-Social Policy: Child benefits under the Harper government

1. For an overview of the history of child benefits, a detailed critique of the current system and a costed proposal for reform, see Battle, Ken (2008). *A Bigger and Better Child Benefit: A $5,000 Canada Child Tax Benefit.* Ottawa: Caledon Institute of Social Policy. For a summary version, see Battle, Ken (2008). *A $5,000 Canada Child Tax Benefit: Questions and Answers.* Ottawa: Caledon Institute of Social Policy.

Prescription for Trouble: The Conservative government and big pharma

1. Canadian Institute for Health Information, *Drug Expenditure in Canada: 1985–2007*, Ottawa 2008, p. 12.

2. Calculated from Patent Medicines Prices Review Board, "Annual Report", Ottawa, 2000, p. 28, and "Annual Report", 2001, 2002, 2003, 2004, 2005, Annex 2.

3. Lexchin, J. "Are Drugs too expensive in Canada?" *Canadian Family Physician*, May 2006. Vol. 52: p. 573.

4. Kassirer, J.P. On the Take: How Medicine's Complicity With Big Business Can Endanger Your Health. Oxford University Press, 2004.

5. Cassels A. and Lexchin J. "Potential savings from therapeutic substitution of 10 of Canada's most dispensed prescription drugs", in Temple N., *Excessive Medical Spending: facing the challenge*, Radcliffe, 2004, pp. 80–92.

6. Steward, Gillian, *Life Before Pharmacare*, Report on the Canadian Health Coalition's Hearings into a National Drug Plan, Canadian Centre for Policy Alternatives, Ottawa, forthcoming Fall 2008.

7. Morgan S.G., "Influencing Drug Prices through Formulary-Based Policies: Lessons from New Zealand", *Healthcare Policy*, 2007, 3(1) 1–20

8. "Clement should know better", *Montreal Gazette*, June 12, 2006.

9. Wilson, Jennifer, "Clement transfers shares in Toronto drug company", The Huntsville Forester, October 18, 2006.

10. Lippman, Abby, Melnychuk, Ryan Carolyn Shimmin and Madeline Boscoe, "Human papillomavirus vaccines and women's health: questions and cautions", *Canadian Medical Association Journal*, 2007, 177: 484–487.

11. Talaga, Tanya ,"Lobbyists boosted vaccine program. Ex-government advisers worked on drug firm's campaign to push immunization program", *The Toronto Star*, August 16, 2007.

12. "Boessenkool re-emerges as a Taser lobbyist. Long-time friend and advisor to PM also lobbied for cancer drug plan in budget", *Ottawa Citizen*, June 22, 2007.

13. Federal/Provincial/Territorial Ministerial Task Force on the National Pharmaceutical Strategy, "National Pharmaceutical Strategy: Progress Report", Health Canada, Ottawa, June 2006.

14. Health Council of Canada, "Rekindling Reform: Health Care Renewal in Canada, 2003–2008", June 2008, p. 19

15. Canadian Generic Pharmaceutical Association, "Consumers, Taxpayers to Pay More for Drugs Under Proposed Changes to Patent Rules", News Release, Toronto, May 6, 2008.

16. Galloway, Gloria "Provinces angry over drug rules", *Globe and Mai*l, May 27, 2008.

17. Kondro, Wayne "Health Canada proposes new regulatory regime for drugs", *Canadian Medical Association Journal*, April 24, 2007, 176(9), 1262–1262.

18. Graham, David J., "Risk of acute myocardial infarction and sudden cardiac death in patients treated with cyclo-oxygenase 2", *The Lancet*, 2005; 365:9456

19. Carpenter D., Zucker E.J., Avorn J. "Drug-review deadlines and safety problems", *New England Journal of Medicine*, 2008; 358:1354–62.

20. Morgan S.G., 2007. "Direct-to-consumer advertising and expenditures on prescription drugs: A comparison of experiences in the United States and Canada." *Open Medicine*, 20071(1): 37–45.

21. Bill C-51, Definitions, p. 5.

22. Steward, Gillian, *Life Before Pharmacare, Report on the Canadian Health Coalition's Hearings into a National Drug Plan*, Canadian Centre for Policy Alternatives, Ottawa, forthcoming Fall 2008.

Two Steps Forward and Two Steps Backward: The legacy of disability rights in Canada

1. Government of Canada, 2008 Budget, Ottawa (2008) http://www.budget.gc.ca/2008/plan/chap3a-eng.asp

2. For background on Canada's Court Challenges Program see www.ccppcj.ca

3. Council of Canadians with Disabilities, "Groups in Court to Seek Restoration of Funding to the Court Challenges Program" Joint Media Release, February 25 2008 www.ccdonline.ca/

4. Council of Canadians with Disabilities, "Groups in Court to Seek Restoration of Funding to the Court Challenges Program" Joint Media Release, February 25, 2008 www.ccdonline.ca/

5. For a text of the UN Convention on the Rights of Persons With Disabilities and Optional Protocol, visit: http://www.un.org/disabilities/default.asp?navid=12&pid=150

6. Government of Canada, Conservative Party of Canada, 2005 Policy Declaration, K-71. *National Disability Act* http://www.conservative.ca/EN/2692/41647

7. Government of the United States (1990) "*Americans With Disabilities Act*, 1990" Washington, July 26, 1990 104 Stat. 327, Second Session, One Hundred First Congress of the United States of America www.ada.gov/statute.html

8. Gordon, Phyllis (2006) "A Federal Disability Act: Opportunities and Challenges," Toronto, October 2006

9. Government of Canada, 1981, "Obstacles Report-Report of the Special Parliamentary Committee on the Disabled and the Handicapped", Ottawa, 1981

10. For more information on the End Exclusion process, visit www.endexclusion.ca

11. End Exclusion process, visit www.endexclusion.ca

12. Rae, John (2007) Statement at Centennial Flame during End Exclusion event on Parliament Hill, Ottawa, November 22, 2007

Harper and Crime: The great distraction

1. Wood, Evan et al., "Methodology for evaluating Insite: Canada's first medically supervised safe injection facility for injection drug users" (2004) 1 Harm Reduction Journal pp. 9–14; and Evan Wood et al., "Summary of findings from the evaluation of a pilot medically supervised safe injection facility" (2006) 175(11) Canadian Medical Association Journal pp. 1399–1404; and Dan Small, "Fools rush in where angels fear to tread: Playing God with Vancouver's Supervised Injection Facility in the political borderland" (2007) 18 International Journal of Drug Policy pp. 18–26.

2. Dauvergne, Mia "Crime statistics in Canada, 2007" (2008) 28 Juristat: Canadian Centre for Justice Statistics 7.

3. Thomas, Jennifer "Youth court statistics, 2006/2007" (2008) 28 Juristat: Canadian Centre for Justice Statistics 4.

4. A.H. Sitren and B.K. Applegate, "Intentions to offend: Examining the effects of personal and vicarious experiences with punishment and punishment avoidance" (2006) 29(2) Journal of Crime & Justice pp. 25–50.

5. Chambliss, William J. "Policing the ghetto underclass: The politics of law and law enforcement" (1994) 41(2) Social Problems pp. 177–194.

6. Moore, Dawn *Criminal artefats: Governing drugs and users* (Vancouver: UBC Press, 2007); and Catherine Carstairs, *Jailed for possession: Illegal drug use, regulation and power in Canada, 1920–1961.* (Toronto: University of Toronto Press, 2005).

7. Transport Canada, *Canadian motor vehicle traffic collision statistics: 2006* (Ottawa: Her Majesty the Queen Right of Canada, 2007).

8. Canadian Cancer Society/ National Cancer Institute of Canada, *Canadian cancer statistics 2008* (Toronto: Public Health Agency of Canada, 2008) at p. 12.

9. Statistics Canada, "Persons in low income before tax, by number" 2002–2006.

10. Boyd, David *The water we drink: An international comparison of drinking water standards and guidelines* (Vancouver: David Suzuki Foundation, 2006).

11. Statistics Canada, "The Daily: Homicides" (6 October 2005).

12. Canadian Centre for Occupational Health and Safety, online: http://www.ccohs.ca/events/mourning.

13. Austin, James Marino A. Bruce, Leo Carroll, Patricia L. McCall, and Stephen C. Richards, "The use of incarceration in the United States" (2001) 10 Critical Criminology pp. 17–41.

14. Marron, K *Slammer: The crisis in Canada's prison system* (Toronto: Doubleday, 1996).

15. Vago, Steven and Nelson, Adie *Law and society: Second Canadian edition* (Toronto: Pearson Prentice Hall, 2008) at p. 83.

16. Wortley, Scot and Tanner, Julian "Data, denials, and confusion: The racial profiling debate in Toronto" (2003) 45 Canadian Journal of Criminology and Criminal Justice pp. 367–390.

17. Mauer, Marc"Thinking about prison and its impact in the twenty-first century" (2005) 2 Ohio State Journal of Criminal Law pp. 607–618; and David Cayley, *The crisis in crime and punishment and the search for alternatives* (Toronto: Anansi Press, 1998).

18. Slaughter, James B "Marijuana prohibition in the United States: History and analysis of a failed policy" (1988) 21(4) Columbia Journal of Law and Social Problems pp. 417–474; and Robert MacCoun and Peter Reuter, "Interpreting Dutch cannabis policy: Reasoning by analogy in the legalization debate" (1997) 278(3) Science pp. 47–52.

19. Jacobs, Jane *Dark age ahead* (New York: Random House, 2004); and Jane Jacobs, *The death and life of great American cities* (New York: Random House, 1992).

Privatization Under Harper: Weakening public services and expanding corporate powers

1. Canadian Broadcasting Corporation. (2004). "Tory new leader of the Ontario PC party," Canadian Broadcasting Corporation, September 19, 2004. http://www.cbc.ca/canada/story/2004/09/18/tories_ontario040918.html

2. Harper Index. "*National Citizens Coalition* (NCC) — *Harper's presidency was a critical period.*" http://www.harperindex.ca/ViewArticle.cfm?Ref=0010; Giorno, Guy. (2005). *Public perception and Political Will: Overcoming Obstacles to Public-private Partnerships in Canada.* http://www.fasken.com/files/Publication/dc2ecabd-7e56-4725-8987-169f6738ee38/Presentation/PublicationAttachment/1ab9ee67-11c3-42be-b5e5-4227616dbd22/PUBLICPERCEPTIONANDPOLITICALWILL.PDF;

3. Conservative Party of Canada. (2006). *Stand up for Canada: Conservative Party of Canada Federal Election Platform 2006.* Ottawa: Conservative Party of Canada, 2006. http://www.conservative.ca/media/20060113-Platform.pdf

4. Crawley, Corina and Sanger, Toby. (2006). *Presentation to the Legislative Committee on Bill C-2* Ottawa: Canadian Union of Public Employees, May 2006; Sanger, Toby. (2006). *Submission to the Senate Standing Committee on Legal and Consitutional Affairs.* Ottawa: Canadian Union of Public Employees, September 2006. http://cupe.ca/updir/Presentation_ to_the_Legislative_Committee_on_Bill_C-2.pdf http://cupe.ca/updir/Proposed-changesto-Bill-C2-Senate-revised.pdf

5. Canada, Department of Finance. (2006). *Restoring Fiscal Balance in Canada.* Budget 2006, Ottawa: Department of Finance, p. 22. http://www.fin.gc.ca/budget06/pdf/fp2006e.pdf

6. Moist, Paul. (2008). *Submission to the House of Commons Standing Committee on Health (Canada) in relation to its review of the 10-Year Plan to Strengthen Health Care.* Ottawa: Canadian Union of Public Employees, May 13, 2008. http://cupe.ca/healthcare/Moist_to_committee_hhttp://cupe.ca/updir/Eval-Ten-Year-Healthcare-Plan.pdf

7. Harper Index. (2007). *Privatizing federal buildings a "sweet deal" for new owners,* September 6, 2007. http://www.harperindex.ca/ViewArticle.cfm?Ref=0088

8. Public Service Alliance of Canada. (2007). *Feds give away more than $600 million in building sale,* August 20, 2007. http://psac.com/news/2007/releases/26–0807-e.shtml

9. Ibid.

10. Scoffield, Heather. (2006). "Ottawa eyes privatization of CMhC", *Globe and Mail,* October 16, 2006. http://www.theglobeandmail.com/servlet/story/LAC.20061016.RCMhC16/TPStory; Ivison, John. (2008) "Tories mulling private AECL?", *National Post,* January 14, 2008. http://www.nationalpost.com/story.html?id=237451; CBC Political Bytes. (2008) "Privatize if necessary , but not necessarily privatization". Canadian Broadcasting Corporation, May 6, 2008. http://www.cbc.ca/news/canada/politicalbytes/2008/05/privatize_if_necessary_but_not.html

11. Harper Index (2007). "Privatization—Harper Conservatives quietly eye options," December 17, 2007. http://www.harperindex.ca/ViewArticle.cfm?Ref=0067

12. Sanger, Toby and West, Howie. (2007). "Privatization, Contracting-Out and P3s". *Alternative Federal Budget 2007.* Ottawa: Canadian Centre for Policy Alternatives, p. 97.

13. The Professional Institute of the Public Service of Canada (PIPSC). (2007). "Cuts "disheartening" as public policy research shifts quietly into private hands," PIPSC September 13, 2007. http://www3.pipsc.ca/portal/page/portal/website/issues/science/science/3F11B6EF46F20733E0440003BA0B1A4B

14. Preston Manning website. http://www.prestonmanning.ca/html/reprotechbill/pm_comments.html

15. Nature Magazine. (2008). "Science in Retreat: Canada has been scientifically healthy. Not so its government," *Nature*, 28 February 2008. http://www.nature.com/nature/journal/v451/n7181/full/451866a.html

16. Treasury Board of Canada (2007). *Inter-Sectoral Partnerships for Non-Regulatory Federal Laboratories*. Ottawa: Treasury Board of Canada, June 5, 2008. p. 1 http://www.tbs-sct.gc.ca/fedlab-labfed/docs/2008/tnfl-tglfvn/tnfl-tglfvn01-eng.asp#Toc192039956

17. Demers, Michelle. (2008). "Delegating food inspection to provate industry a huge cost to taxpayers," and Kilgour, David et al. (2208). "Bureaucrats attach food safety system, and truth-tellers who would defend public interest," *The Hill Times*, July 28, 2008.

18. Cutler, Allan. (2008). " Whistling in the dark; without proper whistleblower protection in the airline industry, serious safety issues could simply be ignored," *Ottawa Citizen*. January 28, 2008.

19. PIPSC. (2007b). *Submission to the Independent Panel of Experts on The Transfer of Federal Non-Regulatory Laboratories*. Ottawa: PIPSC, November 2007. http://www3.pipsc.ca/portal/page/portal/website/issues/science/science/ipe_submission_nov07.en.pdf

20. May, Kathryn. (2007). "Accountability act creates PS 'Dilberts'; Bureacrats afraid to take action for fear of breaking rules, think-tank says," *Ottawa Citizen*, October 5, 2007.

21. Conservative Party of Canada. (2006). *Stand up for Canada: Conservative Party of Canada Federal Election Platform 2006*. Ottawa: Conservative Party of Canada, 2006. http://www.conservative.ca/media/20060113-Platform.pdf p. 43

22. Canada, Finance Canada. (2007). *The Budget Plan 2007*. Ottawa: Department of Finance, p. 165–169. http://www.budget.gc.ca/2007/pdf/bp2007e.pdf

23. Forster, John. (2008). "Presentation by John Forster, Senior Assistant Deputy Minister of Infrastructure Canada at the Federation of Canadian Municipalities Annual Conference," *Session on Municipal Finance and Intergovernmental Arrangements*. May 31, 2008. Québec City.

24. Ross, Val. (2006) "National Portrait Gallery: 'It's pork barrel politics,'" *The Globe and Mail*, December 6, 2006.

25. Czekaj, Laura. (2008). "Portrait of a scandal in the making," *Ottawa Sun*, July 8, 2008. http://www.pauldewar.ca/en/node/304

26. Rupert, Jake. (2008). "Portrait Gallery of Canada an embarrassment", *Ottawa Citizen*, January 18, 2008. http://www.canada.com/ottawacitizen/news/story.html?k=10613&id=81c8dc06–57a8–4813-b80d-76d7011c118f

27. Infrastructure Canada. (2007). *Building Canada Backgrounder: Funding the Plan*. http://www.buildingcanada-chantierscanada.gc.ca/plandocs/bg-di/bg-di-info4-eng.html

28. This is often accomplished by exaggerating the value of the risk transfer involved, by manipulating the discount rate to underestimate the present value of future payments, and by overestimating the public sector comparator costs.

29. Ontario Health Coalition. (2007). *Secret Documents Released Through Court Challenge Reveal Extraordinary Costs in Privatized P3 Hospital.* Ontario Health Coalition, May 9, 2007. http://www.web.net/ohc/P3s/MediaReleaseQueensParkFinalMay92007.pdf; Backgrounder http://www.web.net/ohc/P3s/MediaBackgrounderFinalMay92007.pdf

30. Canadian Broadcasting Corporation. (2008). "Saint John council rejects public-private partnership for water, CBC, June 10, 2008. http://www.cbc.ca/canada/new-brunswick/story/2008/06/10/nb-saint-john-water.html, accessed July 29, 2008.

31. Sanger, Toby. (2007). "Transfers to Municipalities Fell Billions Short in 2006," *CUPE Economic Brief.* Ottawa: Canadian Union of Public Employees, November 2007. http://cupe.ca/updir/Municipal_Transfer_Shortfall.pdf

32. Sanger, Toby. (2007). "Building Canada, but not by much…," *CUPE Economic Brief.* Ottawa: Canadian Union of Public Employees, November 2007. http://cupe.ca/updir/Building_Canada_-_but_not_by_much.pdf

33. Frank, Thomas. (2008). The Wrecking Crew: How Conservatives Rule. New York: Metropolitan Books, insleave.; "The Wrecking Crew: Thomas Frank on How Conservatives Rule". Interview with Amy Goodman, *Democracy Now*, August 8, 2008. http://www.democracynow.org/2008/8/8/the_wrecking_crew_thomas_frank_on

34. Whittington, Les. (2008). "Flaherty says he'd cut to avoid a deficit; 'We're not raising taxes,' finance minister adds," *The Toronto Star*, April 10, 2008, p. A19.

35. Bartlett, Bruce. (2007). "Starve the Beast: Origins and Development of a Budgetary Metaphor," The Independent Review, Summer 2007. http://www.independent.org/pdf/tir/tir_12_01_01_bartlett.pdf

Culture and Communications

Telecommunication Picks Up Speed On the Free(Market) Way

1. The 3 panel members were Dr. Gerri Sinclair (former academic and now internet technology consultant to industry and government), Hank Intven (partner in the Toronto office of McCarthy Tétrault LLP, a Canadian law firm and former CRTC commissioner) and André Tremblay (President and Chief Executive Officer of Microcell Telecommunications Inc.). See Final Report at: http://www.telecomreview.ca/epic/site/tprp-gecrt.nsf/en/h_rx00054e.html

2. CBC News. (2006). "Ottawa directs CRTC to rely on market forces." June 13. http://www.cbc.ca/money/story/2006/06/13/crtc.html

3. Letter from Maxime Bernier, Minister of Industry. Mar. 14, 2007. http://www3.fis.utoronto.ca/research/iprp/cracin/alttelecomcontent/Bernier%20Letter%20p.%202.pdf

4. Industry Canada. (2007). "Canada's New Government accelerates deregulation of local telephone service to benefit Canadian consumers" Newsrelease: April 4. http://www.ic.gc.ca/cmb/welcomeic.nsf/ddb0aecf65375eb685256a870050319e/85256a5d006b9720852572b400524ba5!OpenDocument

5. Canadian Press. Feds to push on with phone service deregulation. http://www.ctv.ca/servlet/ArticleNews/story/CTVNews/20070404/phone_dereg_070404?s_name=&no_ads

6. The Policy Laundering Project. "The problem of policy laundering." http://www. policylaundering.org/PolicyLaunderingIntro.html>http://www.policylaundering.org/PolicyLaunderingIntro.html; Jacqui McNish. "This Law Is Brought To You By..." *The Globe and Mail*. September 19, 2007. B8. http://osgoode.yorku.ca/media2.nsf/83303ffe5af03ed585256ae6005379c9/51390dd22007ea3d8525735b0061f207!OpenDocument

7. Competition Policy Review Panel. (June 2008). *Compete to Win: Final Report*. URL:www.competitionreview.ca

8. Nowak, Peter. (2008, July 21). Cellphone market poised for shakeup as spectrum auction ends. CBC News.ca http://www.cbc.ca/technology/story/2008/07/21/tech-spectrum.html

9. OECD. OECD Broadband Statistics to June 2006. http://www.oecd.org/document/9/0,3343,en_2649_34225_37529673_1_1_1_1,00.html.

Harper's Museum and Art Gallery Policy: Cultural devolution and privatization

1. McAvity, John Director Canadian Museums Association, as cited in *Ottawa Sun*, 16 July 2006.

2. Cohen, Andrew *Ottawa Citizen*, November 15 2007.

3. Smith, Doris, M. Letter to the editor *Ottawa Citizen*. Nov 14 2007.

4. Government of Canada, Department of Canadian Heritage, *News Release*, November 9, 2007.

5. Aubrey, Jack. "Portrait Gallery to cost $2.5 M/ year," *Ottawa Citizen*. Dec 12 2007.

6. Cook, Maria. "Gallery backers turn to Facebook for support," *Ottawa Citizen*, March 16 2008.

7. Aubrey, Jack. "Portrait Gallery to cost $2.5 M/ year," *Ottawa Citizen* Dec 12 2007.

8. Ross, Val. "Art transport service killed," *Globe and Mail* 27 March 2007.

9. Ibid. *Ottawa Sun* July 16 2007.

Ibid. Ross, Val. "Art Transport Service Killed," *Globe and Mail*, March 27, 2007.

Rupert, Jake. "Portrait plan a national 'embarrassment'". *Ottawa Citizen*, Jan 19, 2008.

Federal-Provincial Relations

Harper, Québec and Canadian Federalism

1. Canadian Press, "Full Text of Harper's 1997 Speech", Updated December 14, 2005. Available: http://www.ctv.ca/servlet/ArticleNews/story/CTVNews/20051213/elxn_harper_speech_text_051214/20051214/ (August 8, 2008.) The speech also contained this description of the *Charlottetown Agreement*: "The package included distinct society status for Quebec and some other changes, including some that would just horrify you, putting universal Medicare in our constitution, and feminist rights, and a whole bunch of other things". This is the same speech in which Harper described Canada as "a Northern European welfare state in the worst sense of the term".

2. Government of Canada. House of Commons. Debates, 39th Parliament., 1st Session, vol. 141, issue 084. Wednesday, November 22, 2006. Available: http://www2.parl.gc.ca/HousePublications/Publication.aspx?Language=E&Mode=1&Parl=39&Ses=1&DocId=2528725

3. CBC News. "Liberal Party. The Issues: Quebec and National Unity", November 28, 2006. Available: http://www.cbc.ca/news/background/liberals/quebec-nationalunity.html. Ignatieff had announced his position on Quebec the previous June. On this, see Herbert Bauch, "Quebec is a nation within Canada Ignatieff: Federal Liberal leadership contender says he's open to new constitutional talks", *The Gazette*, June 28, 2006.

4. The *Sherbrooke Declaration* is found in a *Quebec's Voice and a Choice for a Different Canada. Federalism, Social Democracy and the Quebec Question. A* Statement Adopted by the General Council of the NDP Quebec Section, May 7, 2005. The Statement was adopted on September 9, 2006, by the NDP convention. Available: http://www.npd.qc.ca/sites/default/files/Declaration_Sherbrooke_ENG.pdf It is available on the website of the Quebec section of the NDP but not on the federal site. A press release on the convention adoption appears on the NDP federal website under the title, "NDP overwhelmingly adopts Sherbrooke Declaration: For a Strong Quebec in a United Canada". Available: http://www.ndp.ca/page/4264

5. Business Council on National Issues, Memorandum for the Honourable Frank McKenna, Premier of New Brunswick and Chairman-Designate, Council of Premiers, July 15, 1997. Available: http://www.uni.ca/library/bcni.html. A proposed Draft Declaration for the Premiers was attached to the letter.

6. Government of Canada, Bill C-303: *An Act to establish criteria and conditions in respect of funding for early learning and child care programs in order to ensure the quality, accessibility, universality and accountability of those programs, and to appoint a council to advise the Minister of Human Resource and Skills Development on matters related to early learning and child care.* [Early Learning and Child Care Act]. Report Stage, House of Commons, November 21, 2007. 39th Parliament, 2nd Session, 2008. Ottawa: Public Works and Government Services Canada, 2008. Available: http://www.parl.gc.ca/legisinfo/index.asp?Language=E&Session=15&query=5101&List=toc [August 8, 2007].

7. Canada. Parliament. House of Commons. Standing Committee on Human Resources, Social Development and the Status of People with Disabilities. Minutes of Proceedings. (Meeting No. 75, May 17, 2007), 39th Parliament 1st session. Available: http://cmte.parl.gc.ca/cmte/CommitteePublication.aspx?SourceId=207639&Lang=1&PARLSES=391&JNT=0&COM=10478 [August 7, 2008].

8. Conservative Party of Canada. *Policy Declaration.* March 19, 2005. Available: http://www.conservative.ca/EN/2692/.

9. CTV, "Harper Promises More Autonomy for Quebec", December 19, 2005. Available: http://www.ctv.ca/servlet/ArticleNews/story/CTVNews/20051218/elxn_update_051219/20051219?s_name=election2006

10. Government of Canada, "Strong Leadership. A Better Canada. Speech from the Throne". September 16, 2007. Available: http://www.sft-ddt.gc.ca/grfx/docs/sftddt-e.pdf.

11. Remillard, Gil Speech to the Symposium on 'Rebuilding the Relationship: Quebec and its Confederation Partners', Mont-Gabriel, May 9, 1986. Available: http://www.saic.gouv.qc.ca/publications/Positions/Part2/GilRemillard1986_en.pdf

12. *1987 Constitutional Accord*, June 3, 1997. Available: http://www.solon.org/Constitutions/Canada/English/Proposals/MeechLake.html

13. Canada. *Shaping Canada's Future Together. Proposals.* Ottawa: Government of Canada, 1991. \ [Available on the website: http://www.uni.ca/library/future.html#intro

14. Government of Canada. Parliament. House of Commons. Debates. 35th Parliament, 2nd Session, vol. 133, issue 001, February 27, 1996. Available: http://www2.parl.gc.ca/HousePublications/Publication.aspx?Language=E&Mode=1&Parl=35&Ses=2&DocId=2332540http://www2.parl.gc.ca/HousePublications/Publication.aspx?Language=E&Mode=1&Parl=35&Ses=2&DocId=2332540.

15. *A Framework to Improve the Social Union for Canadians. An Agreement between the Government of Canada and the Governments of the Provinces and Territories* , February 4, 1999. Available: http://www.unionsociale.gc.ca/news/020499_e.html.

16. *Consensus Report on the Constitution*, August 28, 1992. Available: http://www.thecanadianencyclopedia.com/index.cfm?PgNm=TCE&Params=A1SEC831504.

17. Johnson, A. W. *Social policy in Canada : the past as it conditions the present.* Ottawa : Institute for Research on Public Policy, 1987.

18. Government, Conservative Party of Canada. *Policy Declaration.* March 19, 2005. Available: http://www.conservative.ca/EN/2692/.

19. Government of Canada, Honourable James M. Flaherty, *Responsible Leadership. Budget Speech 2008.* February 26, 2008. Ottawa: Department of Finance, 2008. Available: http://www.budget.gc.ca/2008/speech-discours/speech-discours-eng.asp.

20. See for example the speech by the Honourable Jim Flaherty, Minister of Finance, to the Canada West Foundation, Calgary, Alberta, August 30, 2007. Available: http://www.fin.gc.ca/news07/07–069_1.html.

21. *Responsible Leadership: The Budget Plan 2008,* February 26, 2008, pp. 18–19. [Thanks to Teresa Healy for this reference].

22. As quoted in the *Globe and Mail,* July 31, 2008. A4.

23. *Constitution Act, 1867.* 30 & 31 Victoria, c. 3. (U.K.). Section 92(7).

24. *Constitution Act, 1867.* 30 & 31 Victoria, c. 3. (U.K.). Section 92(16).

25. The argument about the link between nineteenth century conceptions of the "private sphere" and protections for Quebec social institutions is developed more fully in my article "Federalism and Social Reproduction", in Bezanson, Kate and Meg Luxton, (eds.), *Social Reproduction: Feminist Political Economy Challenges Neo-Liberalism.* (Montreal/Kingston: McGill-Queen's University Press, 2006).

26. I have explored the problems with the Liberal approach further in "The Social Union, Executive Power and Social Rights", *Canadian Woman Studies,* 13(3/4), Spring/Summer 2004 and in "Accounting for Rights and Money in Canada's Social Union", in Boyd, Susan et al. (eds.), *Poverty: Rights, Social Citizenship and Legal Activism* (Vancouver: University of British Columbia Press, 2007).

27. « An Open Letter to Ralph Klein », *National Post,* January 24, 2001. Available: http://www.cbc.ca/canadavotes/leadersparties/leaders/pdf/firewall.pdf

28. The precise language called for « l'instauration d'un programme canadien de services de garde et le transfert au Québec des sommes qui lui reviennent ». Press Release, *Discours du Trône : Des groupes de femmes déçus !,* October 16, 2007. The release was issued on behalf of Afeas; Conseil d'intervention pour l'accès des femmes au travail; Fédération des associations de familles monoparentales et recomposées du Québec; Fédération des femmes du Québec; Fédération de ressources d'hébergement pour femmes violentées et en difficulté du Québec; Fédération du Québec pour le planning des naissances; L'Regroupement des centres de femmes du Québec; Regroupement Naissance-Renaissance; Regroupement provincial des maisons d'hébergement et de transition pour femmes victimes de violence conjugale; Regroupement québécois des centres d'aide et de lutte contre les agressions à caractère sexuel; Relais-femmes; Réseau des lesbiennes du Québec.

The Harper Government and Federal-Provincial Issues: Turning out the lights in the "fiscal cafeteria"

1. The "pay for say" argument linking federal leadership with federal funding has been a recurring theme in debates over health care funding and policy in Canada ever since federal health transfers were folded into a (reduced) Canada Health and Social Transfer in the 1995 federal Budget. The sense of this issue is captured in the following excerpt from the *Report of the Commission on the Future of Health Care in Canada* (2002), otherwise known as the *Romanow Report.* From page 70 of the report:

This increased investment by the federal government is not only consistent with the original medicare commitment, it is essential to protect, promote, and enhance the national dimensions of public health care in Canada. The final recommendation is also consistent with a recent proposal by Tom Kent (2002), one of the architects of medicare in the 1960s, who argued that such a reinvestment would be a prerequisite to the federal government resuming a leadership role with the provinces in shaping the future of medicare.

2. Hugh Mackenzie, quoted in "The uncertain leadership of Canada's Paul Martin" *The Economist*, Feb 17th 2005

3. For a detailed review of the history of fiscal federalism in Canada and the dynamics of the development of the Canadian public economy, see Hugh Mackenzie, "The Art of the Impossible: Fiscal Federalism and Fiscal Balance in Canada", Canadian Centre for Policy Alternatives, July 2006

4. Mackenzie, "The Art of the Impossible", p. 23

About the Authors

The **Ad-Hoc Coalition for Women's Equality and Human Rights** represents more than 25 women's equality-seeking organizations. It was established in 2007 to oppose the action against women's rights taken by the Government of Canada.

Morna Ballantyne, Mother of two child care graduates, served as the volunteer coordinator for Code Blue for Child Care until September 2007, and is Managing Director of Union Development for the Canadian Union of Public Employees.

Maude Barlow is the National Chairperson of the Council of Canadians and author of 16 bestselling books, including *Blue Covenant: The Global Water Crisis and the Coming Battle for the Right to Water.*

Ken Battle is President of the Caledon Institute of Social Policy and one of Canada's most influential thinkers on social policy reform.

Matthew Behrens is a Writer and Coordinator of the non-violent direct action network Homes not Bombs.

Barbara Cameron is an Associate Professor of Political Science at the School of Social Sciences at York University.

Bruce Campbell is the Executive Director of the Canadian Centre for Policy Alternatives.

Guy Caron is a Researcher with the Communications, Energy and Paperworkers Union of Canada.

Eileen Corbet is a former Journalist, a diehard Socialist, and, above all, a hard-core Mother.

Corina Crawley is a National Research Representative with the Canadian Union of Public Employees.

Erika Del Carmen Fuchs is a Member and Organizer with Justicia for Migrant Workers in Ontario and British Columbia.

Erin Donohue is a PhD candidate at the University of Ottawa.

John Hugh Edwards worked for 20 years in the Extension Department of St. Francis Xavier University and is currently a Staff Member in the Social and Economic Policy Department of the Canadian Labour Congress.

Evelyn Encalada is a Member and Organizer with Justicia for Migrant Workers in Ontario and British Columbia.

Karl Flecker is a Board Member of the Polaris Institute and National Director of the Anti-Racism and Human Rights Department of the Canadian Labour Congress.

Helen Forsey is a Writer and Activist based in Eastern Ontario.

John W. Foster is a Lecturer in globalization and human rights at the Department of Justice Studies at Carleton University, Ottawa. He is former Ariel F. Sallows Professor of International Human Rights at the College of Law at the University of Saskatchewan.

Caelie Frampton was part of a group of British Columbians brought together by the Council of Canadians to visit the tar sands in March 2008. The group included representatives from Check Your Head, the Institute for Citizen Journalism, the Canadian Union of Public Employees, Greenpeace Canada, the Stop TILMA Working Group, and the Canadian Centre for Policy Alternatives.

Joel Davidson Harden is with the War Resisters Support Campaign.

Teresa Healy is a Senior Researcher in the Social and Economic Policy Department of the Canadian Labour Congress.

Trish Hennessy is the Director of the Canadian Centre for Policy Alternatives' Inequality Project.

Andrew Jackson is National Director of Social and Economic Policy for the Canadian Labour Congress.

Jessica Kalman is originally from Calgary, Alberta, and is currently the Tar Sands Watch Campaigner for the Polaris Institute, an Ottawa-based non-governmental organization working for democratic social change.

Meera Karunananthan is the National Water Campaigner at the Council of Canadians.

Sheila Katz is with the International Affairs Department of the Canadian Labour Congress.

Hugh Mackenzie is an Economist and a Research Associate with the Canadian Centre for Policy Alternatives.

Michael McBane is Executive Director of the Canadian Health Coalition.

Marita Moll is a Researcher, free-lance Writer, and a CCPA Research Associate.

Pat Mooney is Executive Director of the ETC Group, which for the past 25 years has been an advocate on global issues such as the conservation of agricultural biodiversity and food security, and on the impact of new technologies on the rural poor.

Dawn Moore is an Assistant Professor in the Department of Law at Carleton University, Ottawa. She is currently researching Canadian drug treatment costs. Her book *Criminal Artefacts: Governing Drugs and Users* is available through UBC Press.

Steve Patten is an Associate Professor of Political Science at the University of Alberta.

Lana Payne works in research and communications for FFAW/CAW and is First Vice-President of the Newfoundland and Labrador Federation of Labour.

Adriana Paz is a member and organizer with Justicia for Migrant Workers in Ontario and British Columbia.

John Rae is a long-time human rights and disability rights advocate.

Blair Redlin was part of a group of British Columbians brought together by the Council of Canadians to visit the tar sands in March 2008. The group included representatives from Check Your Head, the Institute for Citizen Journalism, the Canadian Union of Public Employees, Greenpeace Canada, the Stop TILMA Working Group, and the Canadian Centre for Policy Alternatives.

Leslie Regan Shade is an Associate Professor at Concordia University.

Toby Sanger is an Economist with the Canadian Union of Public Employees.

Graham Saul is the Executive Director of Climate Action Network Canada.

Gauri Sreenivasan is a Senior Policy Analyst at the Canadian Council for International Cooperation, where she heads the Global Economic Justice System.

Jim Stanford is an Economist with the Canadian Auto Workers and the author of *Economics for Everyone: A Short Guide to the Economics of Capitalism.*

Steven Staples is President of the Rideau Institute and a Research Associate of the Canadian Centre for Policy Alternatives.

John W. Warnock has retired from teaching political economy and sociology at the University of Regina. He is author of *Creating a Failed State: The U.S. and Canada in Afghanistan*, Fernwood Publishing, 2008, Halifax and Winnipeg.

Mel Watkins is Professor Emeritus of Economics and Political Science at the University of Toronto and is Visiting Professor of Canadian Studies at Simon Fraser University, Spring 2009.

Erin Weir is an Economist with the United Steelworkers.

Howie West is the Work Reorganization Officer for the Public Service Alliance of Canada.

Julie White is Director of Research for the Communications, Energy and Paperworkers Union of Canada.